Mark Corner
A Tale of Two Unions

This open access publication was enabled by the support of POLLUX – Informationsdienst Politikwissenschaft

POLLUX Informationsdienst Politikwissenschaft

and a network of academic libraries for the promotion of the open-access-transformation in the Social Sciences and Humanities (transcript Open Library Community Politik 2023).

Hauptsponsor: Fachinformationsdienst Politikwissenschaft – POLLUX

Vollsponsoren: Technische Universität Braunschweig | Carl von Ossietzky-Universität Oldenburg | Universiätsbibliothek der FernUniversität Hagen | Freie Universität Berlin – Universitätsbibliothek | Niedersächsische Staats- und Universitätsbibliothek Göttingen | Goethe-Universität Frankfurt am Main | Gottfried Wilhelm Leibniz Bibliothek – Niedersächsische Landesbibliothek | TIB – Leibniz-Informationszentrum Technik und Naturwissenschaften und Universitätsbibliothek | Humboldt-Universität zu Berlin | Justus-Liebig-Universität Gießen | Universitätsbibliothek Eichstätt-Ingolstadt | Ludwig-Maximilians-Universität München | Max Planck Digital Library (MPDL) | Rheinische Friedrich-Wilhelms-Universität Bonn | Ruhr-Universität Bochum | Staats- und Universitätsbibliothek Carl von Ossietzky, Hamburg | SLUB Dresden | Staatsbibliothek zu Berlin | Universitätsbibliothek Chemnitz | Universitäts- und Landesbibliothek Darmstadt | Universitätsbibliothek „Georgius Agricola" der TU Bergakademie Freiberg | Universitätsbibliothek Kiel (CAU) | Universitätsbibliothek Leipzig | Universität Wien | Universitäts- und Landesbibliothek Düsseldorf | Universitätsund Landesbibliothek Münster | Universitäts- und Stadtbibliothek Köln | Universitätsbibliothek Bielefeld | Universitätsbibliothek der Bauhaus-Universität Weimar | Universitätsbibliothek Kassel | Universitätsbibliothek Osnabrück | Universitätsbibliothek St. Gallen | Universitätsbibliothek Vechta | Vorarlberger Landesbibliothek | Zentral- und Hochschulbibliothek Luzern | Zentralbibliothek Zürich | ZHAW Zürcher Hochschule für Angewandte Wissenschaften, Hochschulbibliothek

Sponsoring Light: Bundesministerium der Verteidigung | Bibliothek der Hochschule für Technik und Wirtschaft Dresden | Bibliothek der Hochschule für Technik, Wirtschaft und Kultur Leipzig | Bibliothek der Westsächsischen Hochschule Zwickau | Bibliothek der Hochschule Zittau/Görlitz | Hochschulbibliothek der Hochschule Mittweida | Institut für Auslandsbeziehungen (IfA) | LandesbibliothekOldenburg | Österreichische Parlamentsbibliothek

Mikrosponsoring: Bibliothek der Berufsakademie Sachsen | Bibliothek der Evangelische Hochschule Dresden | Bibliothek der Hochschule für Musik und Theater „Felix Mendelssohn Bartholdy" Leipzig | Bibliothek der Hochschule für Bildende Künste Dresden | Bibliothek der Hochschule für Musik „Carl Maria von Weber" Dresden | Bibliothek der Hochschule für Grafik und Buchkunst Leipzig | Bibliothek der Palucca-Hochschule für Tanz Dresden | Leibniz-Institut für Europäische Geschichte | Stiftung Wissenschaft und Politik (SWP) – Deutsches Institut für Internationale Politik und Sicherheit

Mark Corner

A Tale of Two Unions

The British Union and the European Union After Brexit

$$[\text{transcript}]$$

Bibliographic information published by the Deutsche Nationalbibliothek

The Deutsche Nationalbibliothek lists this publication in the Deutsche Nationalbibliografie; detailed bibliographic data are available in the Internet at http://dnb.d-nb.de

First published in 2023 by transcript Verlag, Bielefeld
© **Mark Corner**

Cover layout: Maria Arndt, Bielefeld

https://doi.org/10.14361/9783839464823
Print-ISBN: 978-3-8376-6482-9
PDF-ISBN: 978-3-8394-6482-3
EPUB-ISBN: 978-3-7328-6482-9
ISSN of series: 2702-9050
eISSN of series: 2702-9069

Epigraph
Would it be Britain alone or England alone?
Philip Stephens. Britain alone: The Path from Suez to Brexit.

Contents

Chapter One: Introduction

In his autobiography *Interesting Times*, the economic historian Eric Hobsbawm used an unforgettable image when he spoke of writing books. He referred to 'the desert island on which we usually sat, writing messages for unknown recipients in unknown destinations to be launched across the oceans in bottles shaped like books.'[1] It has been so hard to get *A Tale of Two Unions* published, that I feel like someone whose bottle is launched only to be washed back to the shore by a perpetually incoming tide, however hard I try to throw it. Perhaps it would have been easier if I had been prepared to see Brexit as a tale of one union, the European Union, but as the more insightful commentators have recognised, it is not. It is as much a tale of the British Union as of the European Union.

Some seven years ago I published a book entitled *The EU: An Introduction*. It was written just before the referendum on whether Scotland would stay inside the UK and two years before the referendum in which the UK voted to leave the EU. If I can be forgiven for quoting myself, I wrote as follows in 2014.

> Like the proverbial Pushmi-pullyu of Hugh Lofting's Doctor Dolittle stories, Westminster feels itself pulled in two directions at once by two different 'heads'. One minute it worries about losing powers to Brussels. The next minute it worries about losing powers to Edinburgh. One minute it talks about a referendum on whether the UK stays in the EU. The next minute it agrees to a referendum on whether Scotland should stay in the UK. Caught between the two centres of power it sometimes seems to be paralysed. When the Scots claim that they can stay in the EU after leaving the UK, the Prime Minister is the first to warn them that this may not be so. But when they hear his stern lectures to the EU and about a possible 'Brexit' (British exit), they may well feel that leaving the UK is actually the only way of

---

1   Hobsbawm, *Interesting Times*, p. 300.

ensuring that they stay in the EU. Paradoxically, the more UKIP (the United Kingdom Independence Party) calls for the UK to leave the EU, the more Scots may feel that their safest bet is to leave the UK, leaving UKIP presumably to campaign as the Former United Kingdom Independence Party, a situation which at the very least will give it an unfortunate acronym.[2]

It seemed to me then, and seems even clearer now, that the story of the UK and the European Union is the story of two unions, not one, and that both are put at some risk by the events of the last decade. In the immediate aftermath of the vote to leave the EU in 2016, the emphasis was largely upon whether the EU would survive. Would 'Brexit' have a domino effect? Would the Netherlands be the next to go (Nexit?) Or perhaps, for very different reasons, Hungary (Hexit?). It was hardly a surprise when 2016 saw the respected writer on European Integration John Gillingham produce a book entitled *The EU: An Obituary*.

Six years on, Gillingham's work seems rather out-of-date. For one thing, his hostility towards the EU was always underpinned by a free-market ideology which is much less persuasive than it once was. *In the EU: An Obituary* he wrote:

> The US and China, followed by others, have adapted successfully to the new conditions of a neo-liberal global economy. Europe has not: command and control methods have remained a constant in a world of dynamic change.[3]

In 2023, that 'neo-liberal global economy' seems less like a world of 'dynamic change' than one lurching from pillar to post. The 'command and control' (not quite so absent as Gillingham appears to think from the Chinese economy) mechanisms in Europe seem more like sane management. For Gillingham, Brexit was a chance for the UK to become more like the United States, and there has always been a substantial body of opinion in the UK wanting to do that. But much has changed in the last six years, not least the Trump presidency, the challenge of Covid and Russian expansionism. Institutional arrangements that might have seemed cumbersome and bureaucratic in 2016 seem defensible in the more uncertain and dangerous environment of the 2020s.

Partly because of the political developments just mentioned, the emphasis in the post-Brexit world has been shifting towards the future of that other union, the UK, and the prospect that this might be the union whose obituary

---

2   Corner, *The EU: An Introduction*, p. 91.

3   Gillingham *The EU: An Obituary*, p. 240.

comes to be written. It is a perspective reflected in the title of a recent book by Gavin Esler, *How Britain Ends: English Nationalism and the rebirth of four nations.*

As the title of Esler's book implies, there has been increasing emphasis upon these so-called 'four nations' in recent political discourse, not least when it comes to dealing in different ways with the problems of COVID-19. But 'four nations' talk hardly deals with the problems that arise when all four are meant to co-inhere within a single nation-state. As will be examined in more detail below, it is difficult to see how such language could apply to Northern Ireland. Sinn Fein would certainly not want to think of the 'six counties' as being a nation separate from the Republic, while the DUP would hardly welcome the idea that Northern Ireland was a nation separate from Britain – in the context of present debates about the so-called Northern Ireland Protocol, they would see that as accentuating the danger of a border in the Irish Sea cutting them off from the mainland. It would be salutary to recall the so-called 'doomsday plan'[4] for Northern Ireland entertained by Harold Wilson after the collapse of the Sunningdale Agreement in 1973. He considered the possibility of Northern Ireland becoming an independent state like the other former 'dominions', though without being part of the Commonwealth. The plan was abandoned when a shocked reaction on both sides of the border warned him that the consequence would be a catastrophic civil war. The 'four in one' scenario, almost casually adopted in the last couple of years, perhaps with the confidence that too much theory about constitutions was unnecessary and even alien to a British spirit of compromise and muddling through, looks highly problematic on closer scrutiny.

End of the unions?

Both unions, British and European, have had their critics, and many people would like to see the end of one or both of them. This has long been clear in the case of the European Union, which if one includes its predecessor the European Economic Community (EEC) has been a subject of debate for at least three generations (or one lifetime). In 1975, now nearly half a century ago, there was a referendum on whether the UK should remain inside the EEC (European Economic Community), which though carried by a clear 2:1 majority did

---

4   See the BBC News report on September 11th 2008 http://news.bbc.co.uk/2/hi/uk_news /politics/7610750.stm

nothing to end the debate about Britain's role in Europe. But the 'Europe issue' goes back further than that. UK resistance to any form of cooperation between nation states that involved the pooling or sharing of sovereignty was evident during the previous twenty-five years, following the Schuman Declaration of 9th May 1950 and the creation of the first sovereignty-sharing body, the Coal and Steel Community. It was even apparent in the immediate post-war period when the UK alongside other European nations was discussing how they might receive assistance from the American Marshall Plan. This is discussed in a later chapter, though in a way that recognises it is ground that has been well covered already.

Where that other union, the UK, is concerned, the desire to end (or at least modify) it goes back even further. Where the intricacies of devolution are concerned, it is worth bearing in mind that in 1886 the Liberal Unionist Joseph Chamberlainproposed the idea of 'Home Rule All Round' and the notion was subsequently backed by the Earl of Rosebery, Liberal Prime Minister, in 1895 (as it was at the time by the Welsh MP and future Prime Minister David Lloyd George). It was Joseph Chamberlain who as Colonial Secretary struggled to find a way of bringing together a disparate Empire under the banner of 'Empire Free Trade'. He sought to unite an Empire (and particularly the so-called 'dominions' which were controlled by white settlers) initially around a common defence policy and then, when that failed, around a common economic policy, anticipating the route which the founders of the European Economic Community took in the 1950s when the plan for a European Defence Community collapsed in the face of French opposition. This was a British Union that was at the same time a global union built around a huge empire. Yet it failed to take off and Chamberlain's ideas were never carried to fruition.

Home Rule All Round was therefore a spin-off from a much more ambitious design, and it too proved unsuccessful. To some extent, it represented the Westminster government trying to offer more autonomy than it would have liked to the Scots and Welsh in order to offer less autonomy to the Irish than it feared they would demand. When most of Ireland ended up with more autonomy than even Westminster had feared, the result was to encourage the view that devolution was a half measure that was bound to lead to something more and that it was best not to whet the appetite of the parts of the UK outside England. The 'thin end of the wedge' argument that was often heard during discussions of devolution in the 1970s was simply repeating arguments that had been heard fifty years earlier in the aftermath of the creation of the Irish Free State.

Unsurprisingly, then, many took – and take – the view that the history of devolution will always be a process of trying and failing to create a halfway house short of independence. They therefore conclude that creating new independent nation-states is the only way forward towards resolving the difficulties inside the British Union. Whether or not the European Union comes apart, they argue, the British Union certainly should.

A Tale of Two Unions has two concerns about this viewpoint. In the first place, it presumes that the existence of several hundred nation-states vying for position in the world represents the workings of an inherently stable system. It does not. It simply leaves in place an anarchic system of unrestrained competition – and conflict- between nation-states whose actions are subject to no effective constraints at an international level. In an earlier book, *The Binding of Nations: From European Union to World Union*, I suggested that the pooling of sovereignty, that is to say the willingness of nation-states jointly to be bound by the decisions of bodies that they themselves create, is the only effective way of bringing some order to the chaos of international relations, which continues to cost so many lives. It is worth quoting the words of the current President of the Commission, Ursula von der Leyen, when she announced the EU-UK Trade and Cooperation Agreement to the media at a press conference in Brussels on Christmas Eve, 2020. The agreement was designed to establish a way of working together after Brexit, and the issue of sovereignty intruded time and time again into the discussions. Van der Leyen remarked:

> Of course, this whole debate has always been about sovereignty. But we should cut through the soundbites and ask ourselves what sovereignty actually means in the twenty-first century. For me, it is about being able to seamlessly work, travel, study and do business in twenty-seven countries. It is about pooling our strength and speaking together in a world full of great powers. And in a time of crisis it is about pulling each other up – instead of trying to get back on your feet alone. [5]

The words cut little ice with the UK delegation. Within a month the Prime Minister, Boris Johnson, would be crowing about being first in the race to get everyone vaccinated. His 'political sherpa', David Frost, tweeted that the agreement 'restores Britain's sovereignty in full...our country begins a new journey

---

5   Quoted in Duff, *Britain and the Puzzle of European Union*, pp. 102–3. These remarks were made on Christmas Eve 2020 by President of the Commission Ursula van der Leyen at a press conference on the outcome of the EU-UK negotiations concerning Brexit.

as a fully independent country once again...'[6] Nevertheless, the two years that have followed, with the ongoing pandemic, the Russian invasion of Ukraine and its continuing fall-out in Europe, make van der Leyen's comments even more pertinent. Frost thought that it was all about finding your feet again as an independent nation. But the last two years have demonstrated the urgent need for cooperation between nations that cannot hope to deal effectively with crises by acting alone. Frost's buoyant 'with one bound we are free' mentality, like Gillingham's enthusiasm for the dynamic change powered by a neo-liberal global order, appears painfully out of place in these troubled times.

This remains the perspective from which I regard the European Union as a pioneer of what may eventually be an effective means of managing the 200 or so nations that currently relate to one another without any effective constraints on what they do. It should be noted that this Union is a body which all the countries who may eventually leave the United Kingdom will probably want to join. The Republic of Ireland is already a member, so a re-united Ireland will simply continue to be part of the European Union in the way that a reunited Germany was accepted overnight as part of the EEC in 1990. The Scottish National Party, which in the earlier referendum on the EEC in 1975 was the only party to campaign for a 'leave' vote, has come down firmly on the side of remaining in or re-joining the EU. Wales, though it narrowly voted to leave the EU in 2016, might well wish to join were it to become an independent nation-state. Only England itself, whether or not it will feel quite as self-assured on its own as supporters of English independence claim, may choose to go down a different route.

My second concern with the view that the problems of the British Union can be resolved by creating four new independent nation-states is that it doesn't examine the potential of maintaining the UK with a far greater degree of devolution than has been shown so far. The central argument of this book is that ironically it is precisely the sort of mechanisms that the UK resisted when it was a member of the EU that can prevent it from imploding now as the UK. Even more ironically, the mechanisms which might upset the English as part of a British Union are precisely those which inside the EU protect the rights of individual member-states. They prevent the sort of loss of freedom that the UK so consistently complained about when it was part of the European Union.

Hence the book tries to suggest what a British Union might look like if it was to have a chance of survival after Brexit. It will suggest that as in the EU

---

6   Ibid.

itself, there should be policy areas inside a British Union where any member state has an effective veto. Inside the EU, for instance, no new treaty can be passed without the unanimous consent of existing members. If the UK had been managed on such lines, it would have been unthinkable that Scotland could have voted to stay in the EU and yet the UK be able to insist on Scotland being dragged out of it on the basis of votes in England and Wales. Later chapters will examine what form a British Union might take in more detail. The general point is that, as Chesterton said of Christianity, it is not that devolution has been tried and found wanting; it has been found difficult and therefore not tried.

In trying to look carefully at what a more extensive commitment to devolution would look like, this book is indebted to the writings of Vernon Bogdanor, and in particular to *Beyond Brexit: Towards a British Constitution*, where he suggests that some of the constitutional reforms that were at best *implicit* while the UK was a member of the European Union, might have to become *explicit* in a reformed British Union. It may well be that in the 2020s such an approach increasingly has the look of trying to close the stable door after the horse has bolted. Many in Wales, Scotland and Northern Ireland may feel that the UK is beyond repair, however much the process of devolution was to be extended in ways that have hardly been explored so far. Nevertheless, it is a worthwhile exercise, if only to try to see why these nations, even if they have despaired of the future of the UK, are not unwilling to become part of the EU.

As I began writing the book in 2021, I expected that in the light of Brexit there would be serious consideration in the UK of how a constitution might be developed in a manner that could help to strengthen the nature of the British Union. There were some books that made an attempt to do so, and some serious consideration has been given to the subject by politicians (for instance the Labour leader Mark Drakeford's interesting proposals as leader of the Welsh *Senedd*, published in 2019 and then revised in 2021). All the same, I soon realised that I should not under-estimate the influence of those for whom leaving the EU is only the first part of a process whereby England leaves the UK and even finally emerges in all its glory as a fully independent nation-state. Moreover, this seems to be a view evidenced on both sides of the political spectrum. On the Right it is seen as England asserting its virile nationhood. On the Left it is seen as England waking up from imperial delusions (including imperialism at home in its treatment of the other nations inside the UK). Norman Davies, author of highly influential tomes on Europe and 'The Isles' (the UK and the Republic of Ireland), insisted in his later book *Vanished Kingdoms* that the collapse of the United Kingdom 'is a foregone conclusion.'[7] Davies recalls that one of the more moderate leaders of Sinn Fein, Arthur Griffith, had called for a 'dual Kingdom' solution to Ireland's search for independence on the model of Austria-Hungary. Yet such an outcome never materialised in either case. The Austro-Hungarian Empire imploded after the First World War, and the United Kingdom had to come to terms with the Irish Free State coming into being four years later, removing proportionately more territory from the UK than Germany had lost at the end of the war. Davies suggests a similar implosion for what might be regarded as an internal British Empire, namely what has remained of the United Kingdom for the last century.

Another more recent example is Anthony Barnett's introduction (written in 2021) to the third edition of Tom Nairn's *The Break-Up of Britain* (originally written in 1977). Barnett writes that 'by making British sovereignty the measure of the country's freedom, the English who backed Brexit have turned the UK into a prison for its smaller nations' His reaction is to call for what he calls 'the only exit' from the breakdown of the UK, which he describes as 'a course of action that shatters the spell of the Brexiteers', namely for 'the English to insist on the break-up of Britain.'[8] These are not the words of an English nationalist but of an anti-imperialist who has come to the conclusion that the smaller nations are 'imprisoned' inside the United Kingdom.

However, there is another way of looking at it. If the English were to put together a proposal for a new constitution such as the later chapters of this book try to describe in more detail, then they would shatter the spell of the Brexiteers far more effectively by showing how the sovereignty-sharing that was at the heart of the EU project can be at the heart of the UK project too. Barnett does not seem to recognise that a sizeable slice of the Brexiteers would love to move on from trying to break up the European Union to trying to break up the British Union. Having rejected supranationalism without, supporters of an English nation-state would see it as only logical to reject supranationalism within. The David Frost language about 'a new journey as a fully independent country' would apply to the 'four nations', disentangled at last and able to make their own way in the world. The trouble is that Right and Left combine in thinking that the unregulated nation-state is the only kid on the block. The Right thinks that this is a matter of national pride. The Left thinks it is a matter of becoming free from control by other, larger nations or empires. But

---

7   Davies, *Vanished Kingdoms*, p. 679.

8   Nairn, *Break-up of Britain*, p. xxiii.

the result is to have an even higher number of nation-states in an essentially anarchic environment where nation-states are bound by no effective control mechanism. There is only one exception to this rule – the European Union in which nation-states have voluntarily agreed to be bound by a legal system that they have jointly created. It is a unique system to whose merits many on both Right and Left of the political spectrum appear to be oblivious.

The book concludes that the pooling of sovereignty remains the vital ingredient of an international order that is not going to end up in chaos. The last century has seen huge loss of life following the descent of nations into open warfare with one another. Encouraging them to consent to the formation of institutions by whose decisions they jointly agree to be bound remains a crucial part of the process of making warfare a thing of the past, something that has happened in parts of Europe but not, as the tragic events of 2022–3 have shown only too well, the whole of it. It may not be a familiar approach to international relations, and it may express itself through the formation of institutions that are unlike those which apply at the national level, but this does not make such a system unworkable. Nor does it automatically make it elitist, as if it was more susceptible to the formation of undemocratic bodies.

Outline of the book

The first part of the book outlines the process by which the United Kingdom joined the European Economic Community and then left the European Union forty years later. It is very aware of the fact that this is a story that has been told many times before, so it focuses on the key concept of sovereignty-sharing and why it was both fundamental to the so-called 'European Project' and anathema to successive British governments. This then paves the way, in the second half of the book, for a suggestion of how it is precisely this principle, which was consistently rejected by the UK, that is essential to its capacity to maintain itself as a United Kingdom. At the same time, it gives consideration to those who are pressing for a less elitist form of government both at the EU and at the UK level. In conclusion, it examines what prospects there are for a real reform of the constitutional status of the United Kingdom. It is notable that in a recent book Michael Keating[9] argues that the EU and the UK are both highly compat-

---

9   Keating, Michael. *The Fractured Union.*

ible plurinational unions. This book seeks to explore further the nature of that claimed compatibility.

Whether what is proposed here will prove helpful I have no idea. The one thing that seems clear to me is that leaving the European Union and then breaking up the British Union will not solve the UK's problems but make them even worse. The undoing that began with Brexit is in danger of being only half-complete. The question now is whether it can be stopped from going any further. It is perfectly possible that the candle could burn once again at both ends of the political spectrum in order to facilitate a breaking-up of the British Union, just as it facilitated the withdrawal of the UK from the European Union. English nationalism on the Right could be joined by a desire on the Left to unravel the Empire 'at home' and give independence to what would be seen as the colonised parts of the United Kingdom, just as independence was given to the British Empire abroad. In a recent Podcast Professor Edgerton declared that an independent England was an 'unfortunate necessity', the 'only way out of this mess' (he meant Brexit) and even a way of 're-enabling' democracy in the UK.[10] Thus, the same combination threatens as that which led to Brexit – English nationalism on the right and on the Left a sense that there is unfinished business to be done which means getting rid of the 'Empire within', much as in the last century the UK got rid of the 'Empire without'. For both ends of the political spectrum, Brexit has become a halfway house towards the final dismantling of the United Kingdom into its constituent parts. This book is intended to show why that is not a desirable outcome and that it can be avoided by recognising the value of what has been and is being done to hold together the European Union. In that case the centre may be able to reassert itself against the destructive forces which, having tried and failed to pull the European Union apart, now seek to do the same with the British Union.

When Elizabeth II died in 2022, many commentators at once brought up the prospect of former 'dominions' following Barbados in the direction of declaring themselves republics. They were less willing to address the question of how far Charles III would be a less effective head of the British Union than his predecessor. They reminded us that an earlier Charles, Charles I, lost his head, but were less aware of the fact that he fought what is now often called

---

10   Edgerton, Podcast entitled 'Disunited Kingdom', 28/1/2020, https://shows.acast.com/o
pinionhasit/episodes/60dc5b861f5e91001249f664.

a 'War of Three Kingdoms' rather than an 'English Civil War'.[11] The future of the British Union, not to mention its long-lasting fragility, was still far away at the back of their minds. It may not be able to stay there for long. Justifying the sub-title of his recent book, *The Fractured Union*, Professor Michael Keating wrote that: 'The United Kingdom has not, at the time of writing (July 2020) suffered a complete break, but the Union is subject to increasing stress.'[12] That is still a reasonable assessment of a union that remains strained, but not quite yet to breaking-point.

This chapter began with Hobsbawm's imagery of launching a message in a bottle and the difficulties of getting *A Tale of Two Unions* published. I would like to thank transcript publishing for launching this particular message in a bottle, and in particular Dr Mirjam Galley for her painstaking editorial assistance in the preparation of the book.

---

11   See, for example, Trevor Royle's *Civil War: The Wars of the Three Kingdoms 1638–1660*, originally published by Little, Brown in 2004 and then re-published in 2014 by Palgrave Macmillan under the slightly different title *The British Civil War: The Wars of the Three Kingdoms 1638–1660*.

12   Keating, *The Fractured Union*, p. viii.

Chapter Two: Very well, alone!
Denying the narrative arc

The first chapter insisted that Brexit was a tale of two unions, not one, and that it was at least as likely to upset the British Union as the European Union. It is unsurprising that Philip Stephens' recent book *Britain alone* ends with the question: Would it be Britain alone or England alone?[1] Later this book will attempt to outline both how the British Union might hope to survive Brexit and how the European Union might reform itself after the withdrawal of the UK. But the book begins by considering what it is that so easily encourages a large number of people inside the UK in general, and England in particular, to relish the thought of being on their own in a world that is clearly becoming not only ever more inter-connected but also more dangerous.

In April 2010 the historian Niall Ferguson wrote an article in the *Financial Times* arguing that an excessive focus on the Third Reich and the Tudors was harming the teaching of history in British schools.[2] He pointed to a disturbing paradox. On the one hand, the general level of interest in history appeared to be high. Historians on television attracted large audiences and a large following for the books that followed their broadcasts (one million copies of Simon Schama's *History of Britain* were sold), while journalists like Jeremy Paxman and Andrew Marr reached mass audiences with historical material. But despite this high level of general interest, history was unpopular in British schools. It was not a compulsory part of the secondary school curriculum after the age of 14, which it continued to be in most other European countries. In 2009 only 4% of GCSEs taken were in history – fewer than sat the Design and Technology GCSE. Only 6% of 'A' levels taken were in history – more pupils sat 'A' level Psychology.

---

1 Stephens, *Britain Alone*, p. 418.
2 Ferguson, Niall. 'Too much Hitler and the Henrys', *Financial Times*, 9th April 2010.

The immediate presumption is that this must be because the teaching of history is littered with dates – it's a case of *1066 and all that*, the title of W.C. Sellar and R.J. Yeatman's famous satire written nearly a century ago. But Ferguson's take is different. What has gone from the teaching is what he calls a 'narrative arc', essentially the sort of historical overview that existed in Henrietta Elizabeth Marshall's *Our Island Story, A Child's History of England* published in 1905 (modern editions feel free to make the title a history of 'Britain') and is outlined in Brendan Simms' 'update' of that story, *Britain's Europe: A Thousand Years of Conflict and Cooperation*. Instead, students picked from a smorgasbord of unrelated topics – and when they did, a huge number of them chose to concentrate (for both GCSE and 'A' Level) on Hitler (studied by over half of GCSE candidates and four-fifths of 'A' Level students) and the Tudors. As Ferguson put it in his *Financial Times* article: 'Knowing the names of Henry VIII's six wives or the date of the Reichstag fire is no substitute for having a real historical education.'

Ferguson's article was a snapshot from a decade ago, and one must be careful about 'narrative arcs.' Some of those who, like the well-known British politician Michael Gove, criticise what they see as the 'unpatriotic' approach of history professionals, have done so in terms of claiming that their approach is essentially fragmentary, ignoring the single, unifying narrative of 'our island story.' But even if Gove is correct to call for the 'narrative arc' to be maintained, there is every reason not to make it describe a linear chronology of national progress.[3] Such a reading of the past is particularly associated with the idea of an 'ancient constitution' handed down through the ages. It is closely associated with the sovereignty of a parliament which, having thrown off the constraints of monarchy, gradually came to represent the will of the people and was always associated with the preservation of liberty. Such a narrative not only misrepresents the past but frustrates the attempt to develop a constitution which might keep the United Kingdom from fragmenting today. However, a false narrative is no reason for commending silence.

Nor does the recent concern to stress women's history or black history, for instance, undermine the concern for a narrative arc. No one can suppose that 'black history month' means abstracting people of colour from the flow of history and studying them in the abstract. A focus on Hypatia, mathematician, astronomer and philosopher, as an example of the importance of women in the

---

3   See Professor Matthew Watson's contribution to the LSE blog: 'Michael Gove's war on historians: extreme Whig history and Conservative curriculum reform', https://blogs.lse.ac.uk/politicsandpolicy/michael-goves-war-on-historians/

history of philosophy, is going to place her in historical context and talk about Neoplatonist ideas in Alexandria, as well as the society in which she lived and (probably) died at the hands of a Christian mob. This is a case of strengthening the narrative arc, not abandoning it.

Ferguson is therefore right to have criticised a fixation on specific periods rather than placing them in the context of a long process of historical development. It could be argued that concentrating on the highlights is a natural part of studying history. But the highlights may be misleading when studied without their broader setting. Shorn of context – but only when shorn of context – these two periods of history can easily be seen in 'island fortress' terms. Taken in isolation, they bolster a belief that we do better on our own, tied to no one else. And it is precisely that belief which has helped to detach the United Kingdom from the European Union and now threatens to unravel the United Kingdom itself. For the 'Very well, alone!' attitude, the phrase in the famous David Low cartoon after the fall of France in 1940, with the shaking fist held high on the cliffs of Dover behind the protective moat of an angry sea, could easily transpose itself into an angry fist shaken across the border between (for instance) England and Scotland. That is why this book is a tale of two unions rather than one.

The Tudors

Take the first of the two periods mentioned by Ferguson. The Tudor period begins with England as a member of Christendom (or at least the Western half of it), a supranational organisation based on the Roman Catholic Church. Membership arguably began with the adoption of the Roman liturgy and Roman calendar at the Synod of Whitby in 664. For nearly 900 years after this, the English church was the church not 'of' but 'in' England. There was one English Pope during all this time, Adrian IV in the 12th Century.[4] There were also protest movements against the ecclesiastical establishment such as the Lollards, gathering pace as the Reformation approached, arguing for the equivalent of more

---

4   Norman Davies argues that 'the tradition in England until well into the twentieth century was to minimise if not deny completely the country's long association with the Papacy.' Of Adrian IV he comments wryly: 'He ascended the throne of St Peter in the same year as Henri Plantagenet ascended the throne of England. As things stand, this is not considered a particularly memorable achievement.' See *The Isles*, p. 339.

national autonomy where the form of Church services was concerned. The relevant issues concerned matters such as the chance to read the Bible in English translation (rather than in the Vulgate, the official Latin translation of the original Greek and Hebrew texts) and to celebrate communion in both kinds (receiving both the bread and the wine). The theological details are not essential: the point is that there should be a degree of what would today be termed subsidiarity, having the Bible available in the language spoken by the common people in one of the distant parts of Western Christendom, and tailoring the ritual practices of different areas to the needs of their inhabitants. Receiving communion in both kinds might seem irrelevant and abstruse; yet in its way it was the equivalent of any protest against an elite trying to reserve to itself the privileges of enhanced status. The priest who alone is entitled to receive the blood of Christ in an age of faith later became the male property-owner who alone was entitled to have a say in his nation's affairs during a time when democracy was beginning to establish itself.

In the reign of Henry VIII, these protest movements exploded into a decision to withdraw from the Western Christian establishment. How did this come about? Despite the influence of Lollardy and the writings of John Wycliffe among others, the divide was hardly ideological, in the sense of reflecting the deep theological issues like 'justification by faith' and 'predestination' that concerned the famous Protestant Reformers on the continent, Luther and Calvin. Indeed, Henry VIII seems to have been theologically conservative throughout his reign. He received the title *Fidei Defensor* (Defender of the Faith) from Leo X for an early work in support of the seven sacraments and defending papal supremacy. F.D. remains on British coins beside the sovereign's head to this day, the present monarch content to inherit the title awarded to his ancestor for defending the Catholic Church against the heretical ideas of Martin Luther. Indeed, Henry was steadfast in his opposition to Luther and spent several vacillating years trying to find a way of remarrying within the Church. In theological terms he wanted Catholicism without the Pope, just as some people in the UK would like the single market without the European Court of Justice. He didn't want the Protestant faith. In a famous speech to Parliament in 1545, towards the end of his life and ten years after the Acts cementing the break with Rome had been passed, Henry conceded that the Bible was now available to people in their mother-tongue but complained in his final speech to Parliament in 1545 about the way 'that most precious jewel, the Word of God, is disputed, rhymed, sung and jangled in every ale-house and tavern.' It was hardly the words of a Protestant Reformer celebrating the power of Scripture. From Henry's point of view, he did not want anarchy breaking out in his realm.

He might have been bought off. Emphasis is always placed upon the issue of Henry's divorce, but there were other matters too, like his desire for a more prominent place inside Western Christendom, perhaps as Holy Roman Emperor, or through receiving a share in the new lands being opened up in South America (which ended up being divided between Spain and Portugal).[5] Naturally enough, the Pope's own room for manoeuvre was limited and there were plenty of other powerful monarchs insisting that such prizes should go to them. But it provides important perspective to recognise that Henry was interested in playing the power game from within the ecclesiastical establishment for as long as he could and had no ideological convictions motivating him to leave it.

Although these debates from nearly half a millennium ago are centred upon theological divisions that for most people would not be nearly so important today, a parallel with Brexit is not hard to discern. Whatever the influence of sheer passion (or lust) upon a King who is fated to be remembered above all for having had six wives, one can perfectly well see a purely political motivation for the break with Rome. It could even be described (to borrow the language of Nigel Farage) as an attempt to 'take back control' – or perhaps to take control for the first time. The Church of England that emerged had (and arguably has) no distinct theology. Despite Thomas Cromwell's attempt to portray the English Reformation in terms of a return to an older, purer state of affairs before papal corruption, (an argument repeated to more effect by Cardinal Newman as part of the nineteenth century Oxford Movement before his conversion to Rome) it was closer to the Caesaropapism of the Orthodox Church. In the best Byzantine tradition, Henry VIII was ensuring that he had a religion tailored to supporting his dynasty, the 'defender of the faith' managing to turn himself into the Ivan the Terrible of the Western church. Anglican theology would be bound by the interests of the English state rather than by external controls. It was for this reason that Henry VIII banned the study of canon law

---

5   Simms says that Henry saw himself as 'Europe's arbiter, no less.' See Simms, *Britain's Europe*, p.23. This was a view originally made clear by J.J.Scarisbrick's *Henry VIII*, in the chapter on 'The Renewal of the Hundred Years War', pp. 21–40. First published in 1968, Scarisbrick's book remains magisterial – a new edition by Yale University Press was published as recently as 2011.

and made it treasonable to contact Roman jurists. For canon law was something that applied throughout Christendom. It was an example of supranational law, a higher legal order than that which exists at the national level. For this reason, canon law has sometimes been seen as anticipating the supranational law which Robert Schuman introduced through the Treaty of Paris establishing the Coal and Steel Community.[6] Some critics of the Schuman Plan, noting the fact that five of the six original members of the European Community were overwhelmingly Catholic and the sixth, West Germany, was evenly divided between Protestants and Catholics, even managed to see in the formation of the EEC a Catholic plot to restore mediaeval Christendom.

When Henry's divorce from Catherine became unavoidable, the popular mind was steered towards certain perceptions of Rome, just as it has more recently been steered towards certain perceptions of Brussels. Rome was presented as a centre of indulgence and corruption, full of pampered prelates, just as Brussels is seen as full of over-paid bureaucrats. As John Wycliffe had attested more than a century earlier, the criticism was not without foundation. Similarly, the financial arrangements of the time were interpreted to mean that a lot of money streamed out of England to the hotbed of corruption in Rome, while nothing was ever seen as coming in the other direction. An act concerning 'Peter's Pence' (1534) ended financial contributions to Rome, the equivalent of ending the UK's contribution of 1% of GDP to the EU budget. In fact, in Henry's case it was much clearer than it is today in the context of Brexit that there were financial advantages to be had from leaving. The dissolution of the monasteries (1536) brought considerable benefits to the Crown, which acquired a great deal of land that could be redistributed to Henry's supporters.

In the end, the son that Henry VIII had so desperately sought to have turned into the traditional 'sickly boy' who doesn't survive, and ironically it was his two daughters, both strong women in different ways, who survived and (at least in the case of Elizabeth) showed that the country could prosper in a Hexit environment. An attempted Spanish invasion was foiled by Francis Drake (but with crucial help from the Dutch that is often under-stated), while the nation's wealth increased through the buccaneering equivalents of modern venture capitalists. A cultural Renaissance through Marvell, Shakespeare and others completed the picture. England (plus Wales, which was effectively

---

6   See A.C. Fimister's *Neo Scholastic Humanism and the Reunification of Europe*. Fimister's book is one of the few to give serious attention to the influence of conceptions of mediaeval Christendom upon the 'fathers' of the European Union.

.nnexed in 1536) went on to become a successful trading nation open to the whole world, as the Brexiteers have convinced themselves that it will now. Nothing could better respond to their hopes than a connection between the end of the second Elizabethan age and the glories of the first Elizabethan age, when a generation after the break with Rome England began to 'connect' with the rest of the world through the development of ships that were able to cross oceans. All the trade deals 'waiting to be had' after throwing off the shackles of EU legislation provide the equivalent of the exploits of those Elizabethan adventurers.

Reconfiguration through the narrative arc

This is, of course, a far from complete account of the century in question, but what would immediately render its incompleteness clear is the recovery of Ferguson's 'narrative arc' that was mentioned earlier. It needs an examination of the century that followed when England was plunged into what used to be called the 'English Civil War' but is now more often referred to as the 'War of the Three Kingdoms'. It also needs an examination of the century before, when England came to terms with the loss of territories in France at the end of the Hundred Years War. It is the picking and choosing that by focusing on a particular period obscures the complexities of England's (and later Britain's) real past.

If, for instance, we take the narrative arc backwards and follow the account given by Brendan Simms, we can return to the moment when the Normans were victorious at the Battle of Hastings. At this point the ruling class of clergy and nobles in conquered *Angleterre* spoke French and wrote in Latin, while a carefully planned inventory of the spoils of war (the Domesday Book) was used to allocate them to the victors. Victorious though they had been, the Norman conquerors remained culturally and socially attached to French-speaking Normandy. They thought in what some people today call 'continental' terms because this is where they had their legal obligations and their cultural roots, besides being the land where they spent much of their time and perhaps even where their hearts lay. They, and the Plantagenet Kings who succeeded them, never distanced themselves from their French origins.[7]

The extent to which mediaeval England remained essentially part of a French-run feudal network has been understated because of the focus on the period of the English Reformation described above. The 'break with Rome' appears differently when it is remembered that for many centuries England remained a significant part of Catholic Europe, and indeed the sort of dispute over marriage and divorce that finally led to the English Reformation had been a regular feature of disputes between the mediaeval papacy and various heads of state. It is worth recalling that a similar conflict between monarch and pontiff took place three centuries before Henry VIII, when Pope Innocent III made Cardinal Stephen Langton Archbishop of Canterbury, investing him in Rome without the King's knowledge. The King reacted by expelling the clergy at Canterbury and confiscating their property. As a result, King John was excommunicated. England was placed 'under interdict', its places of worship closed, and its sacraments suspended. In theory anyone who died was now denied salvation. In an age of faith, it was the equivalent of a trade war. In the end, King John backed down, Archbishop Langton was received in England and there was restitution for the exiled clergy. This is important background for the events taking place at Runnymede. The signing of Magna Carta in 1215, often seen as a crucial moment in the evolution of some kind of homegrown parliamentary democracy, was partly an expedient to deal with England's problems in Europe. Duly conciliated, the Pope went on to excommunicate all the barons who had forced John to sign the Great Charter.[8]

These events illustrated that 'the Kingdom of England was not a modern sovereign state, but an integral part of that great inchoate feudal commonwealth of Latin Christendom, of which, in theory at least, the Pope was head.'[9] After all, it was hardly as if Innocent III was exclusively concerned with King John of England. He was also busy managing the rivalry between the Guelphs

---

7   The point about how much of English culture post the Norman invasion was imported from France is brought out in David Carpenter's contribution to the Penguin History of Britain, *The Struggle for Mastery. Britain 1066–1284*.

8   Keen, Maurice *English society in the Later Middle Ages 1348–1500*, p. 301. He concludes that 'the Parliaments that answered the summonses of Yorkist and early Tudor kings are recognisable as the ancestral form of the institution that we know; the gathering that met King John at Runnymede is not...'

9   Davies, Norman *The Isles*, pp. 302–303.

and the Ghibellines in order to ensure the success of his candidate for emperor, Frederick II. He applied another interdict, this time to France, forbidding the rites of the church until Philip Augustus, searching for an heir and wanting to give up his Danish wife Ingeborg in order to marry the daughter of a Bavarian duke, agreed to remain with Ingeborg. One of Philip Augustus' arguments was that King John of England had received a papal dispensation to leave his wife Isabella, Countess of Gloucester. Mediaeval history is full of instances where monarchs demand a divorce, often with precisely the sort of concerns about securing a line of male descendants and thereby (they imagined) a stable dynasty which applied to Henry VIII. Often the arguments surrounded the issue of whether the King had married someone to whom he was related by blood (and the definition of how close a blood relation had to be was revised during the period). Thus, Innocent III chose to annul the marriage of Alfonso IX and Berengaria of Castile on grounds of consanguinity (Berengaria eventually retired to a convent). The same pope deposed the King of Navarre for making a treaty with the Moors and in 1212 approved a crusade against the Moors which began the 'reconquest' of Spain. In 1215, the year of Magna Carta, he summoned the Fourth Lateran Council, which the King of England (alongside those of France, Aragon, Hungary and Jerusalem) rushed to attend.[10]

There was therefore a lot more happening in early thirteenth-century 'Christendom' than troubles with the English king, and where royal marriages were concerned there was already ample precedent for the sort of difficulty in which Henry VIII was to find himself three hundred years later and the sort of arguments which he used in order to seek papal sanction for his divorce (such as the fact that his wife Catherine of Aragon was his late brother's widow).

Following the narrative arc backwards from the Tudors provides one with a rather different impression to that of an independent country finally throwing off the shackles of continental involvement. It is more as if the country was used to defining itself in terms of its continental role and presence. It expected to have an important part to play in the affairs of Christendom. The problem where Henry VIII was concerned was that the usual levers which could be pulled in order to ensure that he was a powerful player on the continental scene didn't work for him in the way they should have – and in different circumstances might have. Was he not a 'Renaissance prince' who could take his

---

10   See the summary in Roland Bainton's *Penguin History of Christianity*, Volume Two, pp. 37–40.

place at the heart of Europe and even in due course have a claim to the imperial throne?

Part of the reason why this was such a sensitive issue in the sixteenth century lay in the events of the previous century when England had to come to terms with losing the Hundred Years War with France. England had to accept the loss of territories on the mainland, of Europe and acceptance came only after a traumatic period of civil conflict in the late fifteenth century with the Wars of the Roses. It was the Tudor dynasty that finally put an end to that civil war when Henry VIII's father ascended the throne in 1485 after the Battle of Bosworth, but the Tudors were uniting a nation against the background of its exclusion from the mainland so far as the possession of territory was concerned.

Therefore, the broader narrative arc suggests that when the Tudors came to power England had been thrown onto the defensive, losing much of its presence on the continent and some of its ability to be at the centre of European affairs. Henry's failure to secure papal support for his divorce from Catherine (not least because her nephew was the emperor Charles V) reflected this loss of influence. When England (and Wales, which was annexed in 1536) broke with Rome, it was more a reaction to loss of influence in mainland Europe than a desire to be free of European control. Moreover, the English Reformation itself threw the country even further onto the defensive against Catholic reprisals and for precisely that reason increased rather than decreased its involvement in European affairs.

In the late sixteenth century England had to face the might of the Spanish Armada. In this context it was careful to maintain links with the Dutch, partly because of a shared Protestant faith but also because this was another coastline from which attacks could be launched against England. It was vital to ensure that the Dutch ports were not taken over by Spanish forces. The ability of ships from Dutch ports to blockade the Spanish Duke of Parma's forces was crucial to the success of English resistance to the Spanish Armada. This reinforced the significance of the North European coastline to English security. Having lost control of parts of France, England remained concerned about what was happening in the Netherlands and the German principalities, but this continental interest was primarily defensive, a means of deterring invasion when it was impossible to have complete control of the seaways.[11]

---

11   Simms remarks that 'the defence of Protestantism and liberty in England, it was generally believed, demanded the defence of Protestantism in the Dutch Republic and,

These essentially defensive concerns kept England constantly involved in the affairs of mainland Europe throughout the period after the Anglican Reformation, an interest to which the break with Rome made absolutely no difference. England showed itself prepared to be involved in later military actions on the continent, such as the siege of the Habsburgs in Cleves, and in dynastic affairs which were always part of building alliances, such as the marriage of James I's daughter to Frederick, the Elector Palatine, later deposed as King of Bohemia. In the early seventeenth century, the Czechs were certainly not living in a 'faraway land of which know nothing', as Neville Chamberlain famously said about them during the Munich crisis of 1938. In the seventeenth century, though regrettably not in the twentieth, their interests were recognised to be part of the defence of the English realm.

The narrative arc thus reminds us that the break with Rome fell within a context in which England sought to retain its influence and to maintain its security through an enduring involvement in European affairs after it had lost territories on the mainland. Since mainland Europe was vital to England's own security, the country was quite prepared to become involved in military operations to increase that security. Viewed from the wider perspective provided by the narrative arc, it is clear that the break with Rome could never possibly have amounted to a break with Europe. This might provide contemporary Brexiteers with some insight into why, while their hearts may be set in the 2020s on trade deals with faraway places like India and Australia, their heads must focus among other things on finding enough truck drivers from mainland Europe and how to secure sufficient energy supplies from across the Channel.

The Second World War

As the narrative arc moves in the other direction after the Tudors, we observe how in later centuries what becomes Britain and later the United Kingdom acquires a worldwide Empire. The loss of the American colonies in the late eighteenth century was as traumatic as the expulsion of England from France three centuries earlier. Yet Britain recognised that it happened partly because she had made enemies of other European powers (who intervened to considerable

---

ultimately, of the European balance everywhere.' (*Britain's Europe*, p. 30) Even in the sixteenth century one can recognise an intense concern with maintaining a balance of power in Europe.

effect to ensure a victory for the settlers). Just as Britain maintained its Empire partly in order to strengthen its hand in Europe, so it needed to strengthen its hand in Europe in order to avoid the sort of imperial disaster (from a British perspective) that came with the loss of the American colonies. By the end of the eighteenth century, it had become clear again that Britain must focus its attention on Europe, a lesson that it learned from the American Revolution just in time to deal with the revolution brewing in France.

Simms admits that in nineteenth-century Britain there was now a clear school of thought advocating an 'imperial' rather than 'continental' approach.[12] But he insists that Britain always kept a watchful eye on Europe throughout the nineteenth century, pleased with the limitations put upon French power through the creation of an independent Belgium in 1830 and later keen on a united Italy and on a strong Germany to deter Russia and France. Hence there is every indication that Britain's 'balance of power' concerns were as strong as ever. Even the role of its navy was not only to build up and police a world empire. It was instrumental in ensuring that the balance of power was maintained in Europe, for instance by enabling Britain to mobilise and transport (by ship) forces to fight in the Crimean War. Thirdly, even that world empire secured primarily through naval expansion was inextricably linked to European interests. This became clear at the end of the century when Britain reacted to its unexpectedly long Boer War (1899–1902) by summoning an imperial conference whose real purpose was to enable what Joseph Chamberlain described as 'the weary Titan', one that 'staggers under the too vast orb of its fate,' to deal with a growing threat from within Europe. Chamberlain's words were hardly the bluster of someone proud of an empire on which the sun never set. It was an address designed to deal with his growing awareness of a menace near to home.

New technology also increased the concern with Europe, as the spread of railways across the Eurasian land mass made the Western expansion of Russia more plausible, while the development of aeroplanes only reinforced the traditional concern for the Low Countries and Northern France, once feared for being able to despatch hostile invasion fleets but now also for being places from which air attacks could be launched. Britain spent the first decade of the twentieth century with its focus on Europe, looking for allies, worrying about

---

12   Simms, B. *Britain's Europe: A Thousand Years of Conflict and Cooperation*, Chapter 6, pp. 116–142.

new threats to its survival and seeking to draw its Empire into the European fight when necessary.

That war should come over the invasion of the Belgium in 1914 was entirely consistent with traditional British and earlier English concerns about the lands opposite, following the same pattern as the declaration of war against Napoleon over his actions in Flanders in 1793. The mobilisation of forces from the colonies was enormous. Something like a million fought in the trenches in the First World War. The huge number of Indians who fought there has often gone unacknowledged.[13] And not only in the trenches. The fate of Australians and New Zealanders at Gallipoli is well-known. They also provided material help – a quarter of Britain's munitions needs were supplied by Canada. Of course, they were often compelled to fight – but the key point is that once again Britain's Empire was put to the service of its European commitments rather than being a means of escaping those commitments. Between the wars Britain managed to get support from the dominions by granting them equality and the right of secession, so that once again, in the Second World War, support from Canada, Australia and New Zealand (whose casualties in proportion to population were the highest of any country bar Russia) was vital to the success of Britain in another continental conflict, albeit a conflict that soon became a global one. The conclusion is that Britain never sought isolation from the European mainland, even when it acquired an empire. It was determined to be involved and it knew that involvement meant building alliances. It meant bringing the Empire in moments of crisis to fight with the 'motherland' in Europe.[14]

However, this perspective does not emerge so clearly when the focus is simply upon the Second World War and when the wider context provided by the narrative arc is forgotten. Instead, the focus becomes Low's cartoon of the lone soldier with the caption: 'Very well, alone!' This caption, produced shortly after the fall of France, becomes the image of go-it-alone Britain resisting the Nazis single-handedly. It is significant that Philip Stephens' recent tome on what it calls 'the path from Suez to Brexit' is entitled *Britain Alone*, and at the beginning of the book he remarks of Britain: 'How many times we were reminded that it

---

13   For a very revealing four-volume account of that war from the perspective of those who fought in it, see David Hargreaves and Margaret-Louise O'Keeffe, *As We Were*.

14   See David Edgerton's *Britain's War Machine. Weapons, Resources and Experts in the Second World War*, especially Chapter Three: 'Never Alone'.

had stood alone against the Nazis in 1940.'[15] It was in June 1940 that the King, George VI, declared himself pleased at having no allies to 'pamper and be polite to'. Perhaps he'd forgotten that he was still the head of a vast empire that had once again to be pressed into the service of liberating Europe, not to mention exiles from occupied Europe such as the many Polish pilots who were to fight in the Battle of Britain.

The idea of Britain standing alone against the Nazis, the only country to stay fighting from beginning to end, is still dominant three generations on and is in danger of obscuring the point about its traditional need for alliances in Europe. A generation or more ago it used to be said half-jokingly that it was time to move on from war films, from *Dam Busters* and even *The Battle of Britain*, to the challenges of another time. But the problem was never the interest in history as such; the problem was context. Two films made in the last decade focusing upon 1940, *Dunkirk* and *Darkest Hour*, reflect a continuing interest in that year of surviving alone before Hitler launched his invasion of the Soviet Union. Both films are largely accurate historically, though *Dunkirk* underplays the French role in the evacuation and *Darkest Hour*, in which Churchill is effectively rebuffed by Roosevelt in a 'phone call he makes from the loo, underplays the extent to which ways were sought and found to get round restrictions on American aid (something Jean Monnet, the most important of the 'founding fathers' of the European Union, was deeply involved in).

In fact, the screenplay seems to have made use of the account given by John Lukacs in *Five Days in London; May 1940*, which showed the enormous pressure Churchill was under to reach a deal with Hitler and his determination to accommodate the concerns of his inner cabinet colleagues while resisting at all costs the deal they were pushing him towards.[16] But once again this represents a narrowing of focus to the year of hanging on and refusing to be drawn into some kind of 'compromise peace' between the fall of France, through the Battle of Britain and the Blitz, to the launch of Operation Barbarossa when the Germans put the UK to one side and turned East. It is a focus which gives rise to the sort of view which says: 'we do best when we're alone', something that the narrative arc, even when it takes in the time when the Empire was at its height, shows to be completely unrealistic.

Churchill was a great leader because he refused to do the deal with Hitler that Halifax might have done and the country managed to survive, making it

---

15   Stephens, *Britain Alone*, p. xv.

16   Lukacs, John *Five Days in London: May 1940*.

as far as possible too much of a distraction for Hitler to divert all his resources to invading Britain. The strategy was perilous, but it worked. What Britain managed to do was to hang on until help arrived, a strategy it arguably shared with the occupied countries of mainland Europe. Everyone, whether occupied or unoccupied, was waiting for the fateful moment when Hitler overreached himself by moving against the Soviet Union. Just six months later the Japanese bombed Pearl Harbour, bringing the Americans into the war. Once again Hitler, who might have done better to have condemned the Japanese attack, overreached himself by declaring war on America. By the end of 1941 Churchill had been vindicated for his strategy of survival rather than surrender, but it was others who would play the biggest role in winning the war and in the case of the Soviet Union at far greater cost in terms of human life.

When the war was over, the UK did not come down to earth in the way that the occupied or defeated countries had to. This was perhaps understandable. It had emerged victorious from six years of conflict. But the point about the country's dependence upon others throughout its history, made clear by the narrative arc, remained just as pertinent after the war was over. Western Europe was now trapped between the Big Two (the USA and the USSR) and forced into the sort of cooperative venture that eventually produced the European Union. The UK's place was obviously to be part of that cooperation, but as we shall see later in the book it never accepted this (until too late, when the edifice was already half built). The narrative arc might have shown that the proposal for a European Economic Community was simply an extension of traditional alliance-making in Europe. But the undoubted courage of its plucky single-handed resistance to German might between 1940 and 1941 tended to override the UK's traditional search for alliances (which had been all too evident a generation before in the run-up to the First World War). Instead, it tried to cling to Great Power status and this made it a late arrival at the EEC, which was already up and running before it even tried to join. By the time it did join (after de Gaulle's two vetoes had delayed entry further) the EEC had been fashioned in a way that made British participation difficult. By not being one of the first in, it became more rather than less likely that it would be first out.

The 'Inner Empire' and the 'Outer Empire': the other narrative arc

This chapter started by talking about England and ended talking about Britain or the United Kingdom. This illustrates the point that within the narrative arc of what Norman Davies' massive tome chose to call 'the Isles' in their relation to Europe, (a shorter attempt at neutrality than the historian J.G.A. Pocock's suggestion in 1975 of 'Atlantic archipelago') there is another narrative concerning the way the different parts of the Isles developed in their relation to one another. It also raises the question of whether the sort of analysis offered in Michael Hechter's revealingly titled *Internal Colonialism. The Celtic Fringe in British National Development 1536–1966*, published half a century ago, is a fair one.[17]

In *Britain's Europe: A Thousand Years of Conflict and Cooperation*, Brendan Simms argues that Wales, Scotland and Ireland were looked upon by the English partly as potential sources of supplies for continental campaigns, and partly as potential threats in the event of a pincer movement attacking from North and South at the same time. After all, that is what had happened to devastating effect in 1066, when Harold had to overcome the King of Norway at the Battle of Stamford Bridge before heading South to be defeated by the Norman King William at the Battle of Hastings. This is often presented as the last successful invasion of England, and it produced a determination not to have to fight on two fronts again.

The argument is that England was therefore driven by its engagement with mainland Europe to seek what Simms calls 'some sort of constitutional order' in both islands taken as a whole.[18] He links the Act of Union between England and Scotland in 1707 to the threat from France at the time of Louis XIV. He suggests that the same concern for French exploitation of the 'back door' at the time of Napoleon led to a further Act of Union in 1800, drawing Ireland into Britain by merging the Parliaments. Thus, Napoleon forced Britain and Ireland together, just as a century earlier Louis XIV had forced England and Scotland together.

Simms believes it is possible to interpret English expansion into the rest of the Isles in essentially defensive terms as a means of deterring attacks from mainland Europe. It is a similar point to the one made earlier in relation to England and later Britain's involvement in Europe, where England's occupation of some of the coastal ports, like Calais, on the other side of the Channel could be presented as an essentially defensive manoeuvre. The problem is that

---

17   Hechter, Michael *Internal Colonialism. The Celtic Fringe in British National Development 1536–1966*. See especially chapter 3, 'The Expansion of the English State' and chapter 8, 'Servitor Imperialism and National Development in an Age of Empire.'

18   Simms, *Britain's Europe*, p. 47. He notes the 'back door' idea came from Daniel Defoe.

both Europe and (for England) the rest of the Isles are presented as a shield behind which England can make itself secure rather than as part of what fashions the identity of England to be what it is. It is not just that the idea of the other nations in what became the UK as 'back door' and 'supply store' (presumably the back door was a kind of tradesmen's entrance for deliveries from the wilder parts of the Isles) hardly attests to a very respectful view of what lay outside England. It is that England is set apart from both its European and British neighbours whose role is simply to be part of the fortifications around which England protects itself from its enemies. They cease to be influences that have made it what it is. Europe ceases to flow through England's veins and instead becomes what exists on the other side of the Channel, the mainland 'over there'. And what came to be called disparagingly 'the Celtic fringe' becomes the Other which must be under constant surveillance lest it be the launchpad for an assault coming from a different direction. It is this perception that is so damaging to the attempt to defend both the European and the British character of every part of the Isles, including England.

The sort of approach which sees the rest of the Isles as nothing more than a shield behind which England can simply hide itself from its enemies easily develops into the view than in more secure times the rest of the Isles can simply be shrugged off. England can now 'do without' the outer wall protecting the fortress. What is lacking is a sense of the intermingling and mutual growth of the four nations so that each would be poorer without the others. It is this sense that needs to be at the basis of attempts to make a British Union effective. On the other hand, treating the rest of the Isles as an umbrella to be thrown away when the sun comes out will only encourage the view that in better times England can 'go its own way' without the encumbrances it had to put up with in the past.

One clear influence upon the relationship between the various parts of the Isles was religion. The break with Rome threw them into a religious ferment whose consequences have continued to this day. It not only led to a fear of invasion by foreign powers like Spain and France who considered how they might restore the Catholic faith. It also intensified concerns about rebellion within England (Henry VIII faced major rebellions in Yorkshire and Cornwall) and within the Isles as a whole, which became the location of several different and competing forms of Christianity. There was a religious dimension to conflict between the different parts of Britain and Ireland which even in a 'secular' age has never entirely gone away. The religious differences which emerged as a result of the break with Rome proved crucial to the history of the Isles in the seventeenth century, when the extraordinary developments that led to what was traditionally called 'The English Civil War,' but might better be seen as the War of Three Kingdoms, led to the execution of a monarch and then the enthronement eleven years later of his son.[19] These differences also provided important background for developments in later centuries through industrialisation and imperial expansion. They remain significant in the present day as the Isles struggle to determine their identity in a post-Brexit environment. The book will return to aspects of this other narrative arc, since its central theme is that the UK's relation to the European Union is always linked to its own perception of itself as a British Union.

Conclusion

The argument of this chapter is that although the sort of chronological tale which tells 'our island story' as a narrative of continuous progress is clearly inappropriate, without a 'narrative arc' which sets key moments in the nation's history in context it is all too easy to misunderstand their significance.

In the sixteenth century, during the reign of Henry VIII, the country ended its participation in a supranational order in a way that throws up obvious parallels with the modern day. However, neither before nor after the break with Rome did England (at that time) intend to detach itself from the European mainland or lose its interest in European affairs. If there is, as we have suggested, a certain parallel between the break with Rome and the modern-day 'break with Brussels', the narrative arc reminds us that this never entailed a belief that England could go it alone. It was out of the civil wars provoked by its forced retreat from the continent in the fifteenth century that the Tudor dynasty asserted the need for a strong ruler at home. That was the background to Henry VIII's famous divorce, but what is not often emphasised is the fact that this divorce followed strenuous efforts on Henry's part to assert his position at the heart of Europe.

In later years, with the rise of Empire, the British continued to treat their Empire as a support for their continental interests in Europe. The brief moment of isolation 1940–1 was in fact an aberration, something forced

---

19   See 'Two Isles: Three Kingdoms', Chapter 8 of Norman Davies' *The Isles*. The nomenclature has been picked up by others. See, for instance, Trevor Royle's *Civil War: The Wars of the Three Kingdoms 1638–1660*.

upon Britain by the unexpected Nazi-Soviet pact and the later fall of France. Survival in such conditions was certainly an extraordinary achievement, but it cannot be treated as an advantageous strategy to be exploited in normal circumstances.

The trouble with the 'fortress England' (later Britain) idea is that it forgets how vital an involvement across the Channel has been to the security of the fortress itself over the last millennium. It encourages the thought that what is now the UK can go it alone in a way that it could never have thought itself able to do even at the height of Empire, when the 'weary Titan' found itself entering into a desperate search for allies and friends.

A stronger sense of the narrative arc might have made Britain more willing to participate in attempts made after 1945 to find a way of ensuring that the mistakes made after the end of the First World War were not repeated after the Second. The country might even have been more willing to support the development of an effective supranational structure in the Western part of what had become a divided continent.

In the event, a few years after its successful efforts to survive the Nazi onslaught, the UK saw the proposal to share sovereignty as an intrusion upon its national identity rather than an invitation to share in the rebuilding of Europe. In this there were echoes of an earlier insistence that whatever the theological implications of doing so, the country must sever its ties with the Church of Rome and reap the immediate economic and political benefits. England's Reformation was in effect a letting loose of the chains that held its rulers under some sort of control. In a famous quote of St Thomas More, the Chancellor executed by Henry VIII, 'If the lion knew his own strength, hard were it for any man to rule him.' The sovereignty-sharing proposals of the late 1940s represented those controls seeking to reassert themselves in a more secular age. But as we shall see, they were no more acceptable then than they were in the sixteenth century.

Finally, we should never forget that other narrative arc, that which saw the development of Britain and eventually the United Kingdom as a single nation-state. This was a more complex development than a simple expression of England trying to shore up its base. It was deeply influenced by the religious turmoil unleashed by the Henrician Reformation. And it is of crucial significance today, as the 'four nations' seek to understand their future in a post-Brexit environment. While the book can in no way claim to give an adequate account of the history of the Isles, we shall certainly look in closer detail at the history of these nations in the chapters to come. For just as 'Hitler and the Henrys' has a tendency to focus on the 'highlights' and in doing so distort their significance by taking them out of their European context, so there is a tendency to see the development of Wales, Scotland and Ireland as if they can simply be seen as appendages to the history of England. In both cases England's neighbourhood, whether across the Channel or to the West and North, is seen more as a barrier behind which she can be kept secure than as part of what has made her what she is, a part of Europe and a part of Britain.

There is one other important narrative arc which must be mentioned before we can look more closely at developments in post-war Europe and Britain. Europe too has a narrative arc, and although we cannot possibly claim to be able to trace it in the way Norman Davies has attempted in another of his monumental tomes,[20] it is necessary to highlight some of the features of Europe's development too in order to provide a suitable context for what is to come. The next chapter will attempt to do that.

---

20   Davies, Norman *Europe: A History.*

Chapter Three: Europe's narrative arc

The second chapter emphasised how important it was to have a 'narrative arc' through which to put the history of a country into perspective. It suggested that when this was done in the case of what became the UK, it was clear that it never perceived itself as able to survive in isolation from the rest of Europe, even when it had a global empire. But what did it think that it was part of? What was always drawing it towards the mainland across the Channel? Was it simply a case of military necessity and the need to protect itself from enemies? Or was there something else drawing it to belong to a wider community? The first chapter mentioned the controversial break with Rome in the sixteenth century, whose effects within the Isles themselves were felt throughout the succeeding centuries. Was that religious separation part of a wider cultural disengagement that meant a loss of something more difficult to define that is sometimes discussed in terms of 'European values?'

Here we must be careful. Like the Isles, Europe also has a 'narrative arc', and though the lessons are in certain respects different, it is useful to consider this arc too. For if there are deficiencies in the way the history of the Isles has been presented, the same can be said of the history of Europe.

At the end of the last century Cris Shore published a book entitled *Building Europe: The Cultural Politics of European Integration*. It highlighted ways in which that integration had proceeded more as a coming together of elites than a meeting of peoples – a theme taken up elsewhere in this book. It also contained interesting observations on Europe, whose development, Shore believed, was often seen in a way that didn't do justice to the complexity of its roots and development – an observation that might just as easily be made about the UK.

Shore takes issue with an approach to European Studies which, while by no means unique, is common enough to be more than an aunt sally. He cites Jean-Baptiste Duroselle's *Europe: A History of its Peoples* (1990), suggesting that the chapter entitled 'Greek Wisdom, Roman Grandeur' puts a very positive spin on the ancient world, the gateway through which Christianity becomes the dominant force in Europe before Charlemagne cements its identity and the Roman Empire turns into the Holy Roman Empire. As with the Roman Empire itself there are 'barbarians at the gates' of the Holy Roman Empire, and the 'new Rome' may fall to them. Chapter 8 is entitled 'Europe under Siege', opening with banner-waving Saracens on horseback being held at bay by the forces of Christendom. Shore points out that Europe becomes equated with Christian civilisation defending itself against Islamic 'barbarians', a view that submerges all the important ways in which Islam has contributed to European civilisation. It is an approach that parallels the imperial histories of the nineteenth century in which the 'Christian' powers of Europe brought civilisation to other parts of the world which supposedly had none.

Such an account of European history is highly questionable. For one thing, it presents Europe as a united whole facing external threats, whether it is Greek 'civilisation' against the 'oriental despotism' of the Persians or Christian 'civilisation' fighting Islam. It was understandable that Paschalis Kitromilides, in reviewing Duroselle's book, wrote that 'although this is the creation of a distinguished historian, it is not a work of critical scholarship but the product of faith in an idea, the idea of European unity.'[1] The reality is that there were always significant divisions within Europe itself. Mediaeval Christendom, as confirmed by the Great Schism of 1054, was divided between the Latin-speaking West and the Greek-speaking East (a division which arguably began during the Roman Empire itself, when Diocletian divided the Empire into western and eastern halves in the late 3rd Century). There were theological differences between the two parts of Christendom, for instance over the doctrine of the Trinity. Yet however significant the theological differences were, underlying them was powerplay.

Thus, when the Western Patriarch (the Pope) backed the Normans in driving the Saracens out of Southern Italy in the 11th Century, the Eastern Christians based in Constantinople saw this as an attempt to increase the power of the West and believed that the Normans themselves were 'barbarians' no less than the Saracens. From a Western perspective the crowning of Charlemagne in 800 in Rome is commonly regarded as the beginnings of a Holy Roman Empire which is to supplant its unholy pagan forebear, and even as the beginnings of what might eventually become a united Europe. Did not Alcuin

---

[1]   See *European History Quarterly*, Volume 24, Issue 1 (1994), pp. 123–127, here p. 123.

hail the new emperor as presiding over *regnum Europae*, the kingdom of Europe? And yet the crowning was viewed by the imperial court in Constantinople as an upstart Frankish King challenging European unity, not creating it. It is noteworthy that the Byzantines disliked the crusades, since they saw them as part of efforts by Western Christians to dominate the rest of Christendom rather than as part of a campaign against Islam. And well they might, given that the first warriors to sack Constantinople itself were Christian crusaders who in 1204 took the city over, spoke of establishing a 'Latin' empire there and told the Byzantine emperor that he would be in exile for fifty years. The crusades indicate something far more complex than Christians uniting against the forces of Islam.[2] They were often more a question of Christians fighting one another or (as in the case of the Albigensian crusade in the early thirteenth century) fighting against supposed heretics. Taking on the 'forces of Islam without' also led to persecution and expulsions of Jews, who were always liable to be viewed as 'the enemy within'.

A connected reason for challenging the understanding of Europe as a cohesive whole definable against the other is that such an approach presents those against whom Europe was supposedly united as if they were 'barbarians' rather than the bearers of a civilisation of their own, one that had a considerable influence on Europe itself. Large regions of modern-day Italy and Spain were once part of the Islamic world, and that world helped to bring civilisation to the West. The Caliphate of Cordoba was a conduit for Greek, Persian and Indian science reaching Europe. Nor is this simply a matter of intellectual and cultural progress. There was arguably more tolerance and respect for diversity within Islam than within Christianity during crucial periods of European history. In the fifteenth century Constantinople fell (in 1453) to the Ottoman Empire and in the same century the Spanish *Reconquista* succeeded in 'rechristianising' Spain. But the fate of Jews and Christians under Moslem rule in the East

---

2   'The Franks did not see Byzantium as part of their civilisation and some of their churchmen hardly even saw it as a part of Christendom, given a century and a half of schism between the churches.' Roberts, J.M. *A History of Europe*, p. 183. See also Davies, Norman. *Europe: A History*, p. 360. '...the city of Constantinople was comprehensively ransacked, the churches pillaged, the citizens butchered, the icons smashed. Baldwin, count of Flanders, was crowned "Basileus" in St. Sophia by a Venetian patriarch' From the Byzantine point of view, what happened in 1453 was no worse than this, and the turning of St Sophia into a mosque was no worse than the crowning of the 'infidel' Count of Flanders by Christians two centuries earlier.

was much less harsh than that of Jews and Moslems in Christian Spain after the *Reconquista*.[3]

The millennium during which much of the European mainland was united under the 'Holy Roman Empire' was not, therefore, one in which 'fortress Europe' battled to resist the 'Saracens at the gate.' It was one in which Christian leaders persecuted their enemies within as well as those 'at the gates'. They vied for power and fought against one another, using the ideal of 'Christendom' to serve their purposes when necessary. Europe's history can never be adequately addressed as a prolonged campaign to defend itself against its enemies, since conflicts against external enemies have been inextricably linked to its own internal conflicts – as the history of the crusades shows.

This was made even clearer by the bitter European conflicts which turned into global warfare at the beginning of the twentieth century, particularly the Second World War which produced the circumstances in which a sovereignty-sharing body could emerge. If earlier crusades had led to the sacking of Constantinople by fellow Christians, a new crusade in the twentieth century would lead to the destruction of much of Eastern Europe by fellow Europeans. Hitler's attack on Russia in June 1941 not only took the name 'Operation Barbarossa', adopting the name of the emperor who drowned during the 3rd Crusade in the late twelfth century, but claimed to be defending Europe itself. In a radio broadcast on 30th January 1945, marking his twelve years as Chancellor, Adolf Hitler declared (at a time when he was three months from final defeat):

> However grave the crisis may be at the moment...we shall all overcome this calamity, too, and this fight too will not be won by Central Asia but by Europe; and at its head will be the nation that has represented Europe against the East for 1,500 years and shall represent it for all times: our Greater German Reich.[4]

Defending Europe became a cover for national aggression. Even during the last months of the Hitler regime, he was still appealing to Europe's historic role against its enemies, presumably Slavs at the gate rather than Saracens at the gate.

---

3   The Turkish record with Jew and Christian was to prove better than that of Christian Spain towards Jew and Moslem' Roberts, J.M. *A History of Europe*, p. 188.

4   You can read the whole speech on https://www.jewishvirtuallibrary.org/adolf-hitler-b roadcast-on-the-12th-anniversary-of-the-national-socialist-regime-january-1945

s to counter this that after the Second World War European countries
ed, through the sharing of sovereignty, to make the reconstruction and
pment of Europe something realisable only through their jointly build-
the individual member states. In a famous image the nation-states were
_ed into an embrace not because they were lovers but because if they were
nolding on to each other in that way they would be unable to achieve the distance from which they could lash out and strike. And though this is often un-
der-played inside Europe, they did so under considerable pressure from the
USA, which wanted to ensure a united front against what it perceived to be
the threat from the East. However great the threat was from the new 'barbarians' at the gates, by now communists as opposed to Slavs and Saracens, it was
primarily to deal with conflicts between European nations themselves that the
European Coal and Steel Community and its successors emerged.

Hence, we have to be careful about thinking of Europe as a united continent determined to preserve its values and traditions against the enemy without. Fortress Europe, like Fortress Britain, hardly makes sense of what has happened in European history. External threats were often mere cover for jostlings
for power between various groups inside the continent who officially shared
the same outlook. Moreover, the values they claimed to have were often values
taken from those they now presented as their foes, supposedly storming the
gates of the fortress from beyond.

Where is Europe?

The European narrative arc reveals something else apart from a continent
regularly at war with itself. There is an inherent fluidity about Europe and
its boundaries which makes the attempt to see it as a coherent whole very
difficult. This is partly because of expulsions and wars within the continent
but is also a product of the constant churn produced by migration, which
is certainly not a new phenomenon. It is arguably implicit in the story of
Europe's origin, when Europa the Phoenician princess is abducted by Zeus,
the head of the gods on Mount Olympus, who transforms himself into a bull
and takes her away to Crete. Europe (it is not alone in this, of course) has
always faced movements of people that have both been enriching and at times
overwhelming. The nature of the sack of Rome in 410 is not recognised if it is
thought that this was a defeat by a foreign enemy. Alaric sacked Rome because
they refused to make him a Roman citizen. Thousands of so-called barbarians

were used for work in the Roman Empire, many of them as slaves but son of whom acquired Roman citizenship and learned to read, write and speak in Latin. It did not spoil Theodosius' chances of becoming emperor that he was descended from Visigoths. Many so-called barbarians were absorbed into the imperial armies and settled inside imperial provinces – just as many of the Welsh were absorbed into the English armies that fought at Crécy and elsewhere.[5] It was a form of managed migration that became too much when large numbers of people driven by economic necessity moved westwards in the fourth and fifth centuries. This is just as true in a British context when it comes to constructions like Hadrian's Wall. The wall was less a defence against the enemies of Rome than a control point for managing the number of 'barbarians' who came in. It was more sentry post and customs barrier than fortress protecting a line that could never be crossed.

In the present day that fluidity is evident in the continuing migration flows that are as much a feature of the present as the past. It is also evident in the sense that the boundaries of Europe remain undefined. It is not an island (or near-island) continent like Oceania, Africa or North and South America. It might be seen as the Western peninsula of Asia, a subcontinent like India. But even India has a natural barrier in the form of the Himalayas which is not exactly replicated in Europe's case, despite the Urals. As a consequence, people talk of 'Eurasia' as if one part of the world shades into another or, as J.G.A. Pocock put it, 'a continental heartland in which all frontiers are indeterminate.'[6]

The geographical indeterminacy of Europe is reflected in the European Union's attitude towards who might be a member. In principle, a candidate country must be from Europe, but the EU has been careful to produce no list of the countries it believes to be in Europe and therefore potential candidates for membership. Geographical indeterminacy is matched by a similar indeterminacy over values. Talk of 'European values' needs to be treated with circumspection. It is not as if such values become immediately evident upon

---

5   See the discussion in J.M. Roberts' *A History of Europe*, pp. 72–73. Roberts points out that from 406 the Empire was employing barbarian tribes as 'confederates' (foederati). As late as 451 the Huns were defeated at Troyes but, writes Roberts, 'the victorious 'Roman' army was made up of Visigoths, Franks, Celts and Burgundians – all barbarians – commanded by a Visigothic king' (p. 73).

6   J. G. A. Pocock was a New Zealander, able to view Europe from a distance as well as from close-up through his connections to the U.K. See his 'What do we mean by Europe?' published in *The Wilson Quarterly*, Volume 21 No. 1 (Winter 1997), pp. 12–29.

crossing some kind of border – Europe has no clear border. Nor are they somehow created by geographical location.

Geography has occasionally been pressed into the service of explaining cultural and social difference at the continental level – or the lack of it. Those 'oriental' Persian despots facing Greek civilisation were rationalised by the French writer Montesquieu in terms of the idea that the geography of Asia favours empires because those immense plains, uninterrupted by mountains or rivers, were somehow susceptible to the despotic rule appropriate to large spaces. One wonders how this might apply to the rulers of Australia or a future Emperor of the Antarctic, but the view has sometimes had resonance with those who see the complex groupings of small nations in Europe as a mark of respect for diversity or what the Czech writer (now living in France) Milan Kundera called 'the greatest variety in the smallest space'.[7] An earlier Czech writer, Karel Čapek, had suggested that 'the creator of Europe made her small and even split her up into little parts so that our hearts could find joy not in size but in plurality.'[8] Such sentiments are not perhaps surprising given the way in which their own country emerged from the collapse of the Austro-Hungarian Empire in 1918 and then the 'velvet divorce' that produced two separate nation-states, The Czech Republic and Slovakia, out of Czechoslovakia as recently as 1993.

The suggestion seems to be that these small European countries emerged out of respect for diversity, a sort of LGBT+ of nations where those despots in the East simply thought everyone was the same. But it is a mistake to identify such variety with toleration and mutual acceptance. Hobsbawm had a point in his criticism of what he called the 'Wilsonian system', named after American President Woodrow Wilson, who after World War One sought to create a number of smaller states out of the collapsing Ottoman and Austro-Hungarian empires, not least as buffer states to resist the 'infection' of bolshevism from Russia:

---

7   Kundera's 'The Tragedy of Central Europe' was an essay published in the *New York Review of Books* in 1984, some five years before the collapse of communism in Central Europe.

8   Čapek wrote this in a letter to the *New York Times* in 1926. It has been quoted many times since. It is used as an epigraph at the start of 'Varieties of Europe', chapter 23 of Tony Judt's classic *Postwar: A History of Europe since 1945*.

...it demonstrated to no great surprise that the nationalism of small nations was just as impatient of minorities as what Lenin called 'great-nation chauvinism.'[9]

In reality, the 'little' nations of Europe have often been the source of bitter wars, pitting them against each other with many casualties. The former Yugoslavia, for instance, created in 1918 as a country of 'Southern Slavs' as opposed to the 'Western Slavs' in Czechoslovakia, imploded in the 1990s and the result was a series of five wars in which hundreds of thousands died and many more went into exile. Such conflicts have to be set against the idea that Europe has somehow been at peace since 1945, a view which is hardly heard any more following the long-drawn-out invasion of Ukraine by Russia. They also serve as a warning for those who think that nothing but good can come from breaking up the UK into its constituent parts.

The conclusion is that the difficulty of defining *where* Europe is reflects the difficulties in defining *what* it is. It is hardly credible to see it as fifty or so small nations who have managed to trim their size down to a point where they can manifest a huge variety of different cultural and social perspectives. 'European values', whether or not laced with religious language about a 'Christian' culture, have too often been a cover for national aggression. It would be better to think in terms of such values emerging from what bodies like the European Union have tried to do in order to deal with problems between nation-states, than to see them as somehow pre-existing the efforts to create a community of nations on what has proved itself time and time again to be a warlike continent. In his autobiography *Interesting Times*, published in 2002, Hobsbawm referred to '...the almost total failure, largely for institutional and linguistic reasons, of history to emancipate itself from the framework of the nation-state.'[10] But it was not just an institutional and linguistic failure but a failure of imagination on the part of historians, not least Hobsbawm himself whose writings paid little attention to the European Union.

---

9   Hobsbawm, Eric *Nations and Nationalism since 1780*, p. 134.
10   Hobsbawm, Eric. *Interesting Times*, p. 293.

Creating European Values

At the time of the formation of Italy only 2% of the population actually spoke Italian and D'Azeglio remarked that having created Italy (following Italian Unification in 1860) it would now be necessary to make Italians.[11] Perhaps the same remark could be made of Europe. In other words, rather than trying to claim that the European Union arose out of the inspiration provided by European values, would it not be better to say that European values can be created out of the European Union? What nation-states can do now is develop the values that correspond to the sovereignty-sharing system that they have adopted. Europeans in the twenty-first century, like Italians in the nineteenth, have yet to be created.

There were profound social changes in nineteenth-century Europe, when people's lives ceased to be largely determined by their local communities and the trappings of a modern state began to emerge, with mass involvement in national education and a national bureaucracy, in some cases with national conscription. Cohesive nation-states emerged, whose citizens realised that their lives were profoundly affected by the country they lived in. This was to make the often intense and uncontrolled rivalry between nation-states a potent force, one into which the overwhelming majority of citizens in these states were drawn. The world wars of the early twentieth century drew whole peoples into conflicts which produced millions of deaths and injuries among both soldiers and civilians. At the end of a half-century of slaughter the planet remained divided into two hundred or so nation-states returning to their old rivalries or devising new ones. New conflicts and outbreaks of warfare were bound to break out – and have done so. Though there are international bodies like the United Nations which try to prevent or mitigate the effects of such conflicts, their success has been limited. What has been done in part of Europe through the sharing of sovereignty is an attempt to create a structural mechanism whereby the intense attachment to the nation-state created in the nineteenth century can be managed in such a way that outbreaks of violent conflict are made much less likely. This mechanism involves nation-states

---

11   See Hobsbawm, Eric *The Age of Capital*, p. 111. It is worth reading the whole chapter, entitled 'Building Nations,' pp. 103–122 of the book. See also 'The Nation as Novelty', chapter 1 of Hobsbawm's *Nations and Nationalism since 1780: Programme, Myth, Reality*, pp. 14–45. d'Azeglio's remark about making Italians comes from the first meeting of the parliament of the newly united Italian kingdom.

agreeing to be bound by decisions that they jointly reach but which may be against the wishes of some individual members – in effect they give up the veto they have at the national level. They therefore create rules and an enforcement mechanism (European Law) which is binding upon them. This mechanism has facilitated the creation of many programmes that are now organised through the European Union, such as the regional funds which are made possible by the existence of an EU budget, the Erasmus and Solidarity programmes, scientific and research projects and the infamous (but defensible) Common Agricultural Policy. From this perspective, it is through the effective management of social, educational and technological developments at the European level that European 'values' will emerge, just as it was through the development of national administrations, (such as postal systems, taxation systems and conscription), news outlets and educational systems (based on the national language) that a heightened national consciousness emerged in the nineteenth century.[12] It is not European values which has made it possible for the European Union to be created; it is the European Union that has the chance to create European values – if, that is, it is able to survive.

Conclusion

Where the UK was concerned, the narrative arc stressed its continuous involvement with the rest of Europe and the dangers of seeing English and, later, British history in terms of 'Britain alone.' There is also a narrative arc where the development of the different nations making up the UK is concerned. Here the danger was seeing the nations outside England as no more than a shield, a northern and western equivalent to the Channel as (in Shakespeare's famous image) a moat to protect England from its enemies. Where Europe is concerned, some of the lessons are similar. Europe's history has sometimes been presented as if it is a case of a Christian fortress defending itself against its foes, whereas closer inspection showed that these so-called 'foes', and Islam in particular, contributed through their culture and scholarship to making Europe what it is, as they still do. The Islamic influence on Europe is as clear as

---

12   See 'Building Nations', chapter 5 of Eric Hobsbawm's *The Age of Capital*, pp. 103–121. Benedict Anderson's *Imagined communities: Reflections on the Origin and Spread of Nationalism* is particularly helpful on the impact of language and the development of the written word through books and later newspapers upon the growth of national feeling.

the Celtic influence on England. External threats were often used as cover for power bids by rival Christian groups in Europe, just as the threat from outside England was used to advance the power of various groups within it.

However, there are some differences too in the case of Europe's arc. Unlike the Isles, Europe (the Western peninsula of Asia?) remains an ill-defined land mass, whose borders have been drawn in various ways over the centuries. Partly because of its lack of clear borders, it has been subject to constant churn as people have migrated in and out.

Europe's history presents a continent riven by divisions, divisions that have often led to conflict. Small countries have shown themselves to be just as capable of fragmentation and civil war as larger ones. The collapse of the former Yugoslavia in the 1990s led to over 100,000 deaths. The Russian invasion of Ukraine will lead to even more. The conclusion is that there is little in Europe's political history to suggest the sort of preparedness to tolerate diversity that is so emphasised today. The respect for diversity is deeply welcome, but it has hardly been a characteristic trait of European history. To Davies' *Vanished Kingdoms* could be added a vanished social mix as countries have pursued so-called 'ethnic cleansing'. Tony Judt made the point is his magisterial *Postwar: A History of Europe since 1945*:

> The continent of Europe was once an intricate, interwoven tapestry of overlapping languages, religions, communities and nations. Many of its cities-particularly the smaller ones at the intersection of old and new imperial boundaries, such as Trieste, Sarajevo, Salonika, Cernovitz, Odessa or Vilna-were truly multicultural societies avant le mot, where Catholics, Orthodox, Muslims, Jews and others lived in familiar juxtaposition. We should not idealise this old Europe. What the Polish writer Tadeusz Borowski called 'the incredible, almost comical melting-pot of people and nationalities sizzling dangerously in the very heart of Europe' was periodically rent with riots, massacres and programs-but it was real, and it survived into living memory.
>
> Between 1914 and 1945, however, that Europe was smashed into the dust.[13]

This is the context within which we should judge Čapek's idea that 'the creator of Europe made her small and even split her up into little parts so that

---

13   Judt, Tony *Postwar*, pp. 8–9.

our hearts could find joy not in size but in plurality.'[14] Čapek's words may have some romantic appeal, but they hardly reflect the violent history of Europe. European values are less likely to be a reflection of Europe's past than of its determination to have a different future after two world wars that nearly destroyed a continent. This arguably strengthens the case for the structures which have been put in place with the European Economic Community and later the European Union. It is why the sharing of sovereignty must be the vital ingredient in the European values which have to be developed now rather than imagined from a largely mythical reading of the past. Indeed, they may be developed and even created precisely through the institutions that are sometimes portrayed as merely being their consequence. This is what Habermas, among others, suggests.[15] Rather than the institutions springing out of the values, it may be that the institutions themselves can help to embed those values in a democratic European landscape.

---

14   Čapek wrote this in a letter to the New York Times from 1926. It is discussed in Wilson, Kevin and van der Dussen, Jan *The History of the Idea of Europe*, p. 124.

15   See Habermas, Jürgen 'The Postnational Constellation and the Future of Democracy'.

Chapter Four: Early attempts at supranationalism

Chapter Two sought to suggest how the national psyche is still primed to going it alone. Chapter Three suggested that given Europe's past, it would be more appropriate to see a new form of cooperation between nation-states as a way of building European values than as a way of reflecting them. But what exactly does 'going it alone' mean, and what exactly is meant by the sharing of sovereignty? The first chapter, for instance, talked of England breaking away from a 'supranational body' in the sixteenth century. But what exactly is a supranational body and why, for that matter, is it so important to have one?

The first point to make is that this obvious question has rarely been asked and even less rarely discussed outside (or even inside) academic circles. Precisely because political and social changes don't simply reflect values but also create them, it is unfortunate that, as we shall see, there was little attempt to popularise Monnet's programme for a sovereignty-sharing body. He proceeded in the manner he'd adopted when he first went to French Prime Minister Rene Viviani to persuade him that there should be coordination of wheat supplies during World War One. His method was to select someone in authority and target them. His subsequent target was Robert Schuman, whose grandiose words supporting the principle of sovereignty-sharing during his speech at the Salon d'Horloge of the French Foreign Ministry on 20th June 1950 were essentially a triumph of the Monnet approach:

> Never before has such a system that we advocate been tried out as a practical experiment. Never before have states delegated a fraction of their sovereignty jointly to an independent, supranational body. They have never even envisaged doing so...

Yet despite all the rhetoric about such a system 'never before' being tried out, Schuman smuggled the idea through his cabinet and made little attempt to impress the French people with the significance of what he was doing.[1] You'd think that if you were advocating something that had never been tried before, there would be an attempt to elicit mass support for it. But this is not what happened.

It is therefore no surprise that a generation later so-called 'revisionists' like Alan Milward[2] suggested that the whole sovereignty-sharing mechanism was nothing more than an attempt to bolster the interests of nation-states. The 're-visionists' were doing no more than reiterate how the system had been presented by most of those who introduced and supported it. Rarely can an approach, declared at its inauguration to be so revolutionising, have been introduced with such little effort to proclaim the revolution. Instead of providing the basis for developing a different set of values, what was done by Schuman was simply seen as suiting French interests, another move in the endless chess game (if that is the right analogy for what has often been more like gang warfare) between nation-states advancing as best they could their national concerns.

Given the reluctance of its advocates to trumpet its merits, sovereignty-sharing was in danger of being seen as less revolutionary than it was or even dismissed as a label for something that had already been tried before. Alan Milward and those he influenced, like Andrew Moravscik, were reluctant to see anything revolutionary in the sovereignty-sharing system of the European Union partly because the advocates of the new system were themselves reluctant to explain its revolutionary credentials. The way was open for 'revisionists' to claim that the whole system was essentially the same old system of competing nation-states in new clothes. They would not accept that an effective system might be put in place that is neither nation-states acting without restraint on the one hand nor a federal superstate with semi-autonomous regions on the other. Moreover, since a federal superstate is essentially nothing more than another big nation-state to add to all the others, their real position was that nothing can exist in international politics besides nation-states acting in whatever

---

1   The German chancellor Konrad Adenauer described the Schuman Plan as 'a victory of the minister over his officials.' It was also a victory over the many French cabinet ministers for whom any agreement with Germany was anathema. See Duchêne, *Jean Monnet: The First Statesman of Interdependence*, p. 206. See the chapter The Citizen Among States (pp. 345–368) for a discussion of Monnet's approach to politics, with its advantages and drawbacks. 'His approach was based on gaining and maintaining direct access to the source of power' (p. 354).

2   See Milward, Alan *European Rescue of the Nation-State*.

way will satisfy their national interests. The only other option they could imagine was one of creating (or recreating) an empire, the position of Jan Zielonka.[3]

Moravscik described his position as one of 'liberal intergovernmentalism,' given the acronym LI. LI means that 'states are actors,' and he went on to say that 'the EU is best studied by treating states as the critical actors in a context of anarchy.' This is a fair description of the situation which the EU was designed to ameliorate – to remove some of the consequences of that anarchy. But that is not how Moravscik sees it. He believes 'states achieve their goals through international negotiation and bargaining, rather than through a centralised authority making and enforcing policy decisions.' He suggests that in the EU 'member states are masters of the treaty and continue to enjoy preeminent decision-making power and political legitimacy.'[4] The discussions of 'liberal intergovernmentalism' are hard to pin down and the succession of concepts swapped around by the political theorists never seem to emerge for very long into the daylight before being plunged back into the darkness of abstruse definition.

Milward, Moravscik and others are certainly right when they stress the central role of the member-states within the EU and how far that body is from becoming a single 'superstate'. To that extent one cannot quarrel with the idea that 'member states are masters of the treaty' – after all, it has already been pointed out that any member state can veto a new treaty, as Denmark did with the Treaty of Maastricht or Ireland with the Treaty of Lisbon. But they seem to completely exclude the possibility that the EU nevertheless represents something new, that a degree of sovereignty-sharing represents a revolutionary move that as Schuman pointed out in the *Salon d'Horloge*, had never been tried before. This has been recognised by some of those for whom living in a 'post-sovereign age' could be understood in terms of a shared or pooled sovereignty.[5]

We can best defend the idea that what became the European Union represented something new and transformative in the relations between nation-states by going back to the questions asked at the beginning of this chapter. What exactly is meant by the sharing of sovereignty? What exactly is a supranational body? And why do we need to have one?

---

3   See Zielonka, Jan *Europe as Empire: The Nature of the Enlarged European Union.*

4   Both quotes come from Andrew Moravcsik and Frank Schimmelfennig's chapter 'Liberal Intergovernmentalism' in *European Integration Theory* edited by Antje Wiener, Tanja A. Börzel and Thomas Risse, 3rd Edition, pp. 64–87, here p. 65.

5   See MacCormick, Neil. *Questioning Sovereignty: Law, State and Nation in the European Commonwealth.*

The nature of supranationalism

A supranational body is one that makes binding laws above the level of the nation-state. The example considered in Chapter Two was the Church of Rome. Mediaeval Christendom was a haphazard organisation, but in its own way it represented a genuine attempt to bring different groupings under a common framework defined in terms of their obedience to God. It was a jumble of competing interests formed and reformed during the millennium after the collapse of the Roman Empire. Religious authority could often seem weak as well as ill-defined. Powerful rulers managed to ensure that they had their way and overrode the wishes of Popes. It is also important to point out that just as the imposition of ecclesiastical law upon the members of Christendom was sporadic and often politically motivated, so also these members of Christendom were not the developed nation-states of the modern era, but groups of people who lacked the sense of national identity that mass education and communications provided in later centuries.

Nevertheless, it was clear that in a nascent way the binding nature of supranational authority was at stake when Henry VIII's Chancellor, Thomas More, went to his death in 1535 saying that he served the King, but God first. It wasn't simply that the King had defied his Maker: it was that he had chosen to defy the principle that a law higher than national law could be binding upon nations and even upon their monarchs. It was not just a matter of Henry's passion for Anne Boleyn set against the wagging finger of God up above. It was the whether the monarch accepted any legal obligations beyond those established by the laws of England and Wales.

In John Osborne's play *Luther*, the young monk Martin Luther confronts Cardinal Cajetan, who tries to convince him of the damage his opinions might do:

> You know, a time will come when a man will no longer be able to say, 'I speak Latin and am a Christian' and go his way in peace. There will come frontiers, frontiers of all kinds – between men – And there will be no end to them.[6]

Did Cajetan not anticipate future trends accurately when he warned the reformer of the consequences of his opposition to Rome? Did the frontiers spoken of not solidify into separate national blocs which were to spend much of the next five centuries at war, whilst the common language of Christendom

---

6   A new edition of the play was published by Andesite Press in New York in 2017.

dissolved into a Babel of different tongues? Cajetan has no very effective *theological* answer in the play to Luther's complaints. He can offer no resistance to the barbs of the great reformer when Luther points out how odd it is that whereas there were only twelve apostles the remains of eighteen of them have apparently been buried in Germany. The corruption of the Church and the irrationality of many of its beliefs, which reformers like John Wycliffe had brought out so well, is bypassed rather than defended. Cajetan's point is *political*. The irrationality and the corruption are part of a system, he claims, which nevertheless keeps the lid on some of the most undesirable human tendencies, including the tribalism that seeks enemies in order to reinforce confidence in its own identity. Catholicism, as its name implies (and as is retained in a notion like having catholic tastes), is universal. A universal church can never be a national church; it can never be hijacked, in the way that Russian orthodoxy or Anglicanism have been, to represent the supposed soul of a nation. Without it, Cajetan suggests, a patchwork Europe in which hostile nations rub up against one another in a constant state of friction might prove a worse arrangement. It would be difficult to argue, given the events of the centuries that followed, that he (or John Osborne) didn't have a point. Once the constraints of supranational authority are lifted, monarchs and later more representative governments can effectively follow their own whims. That point is as relevant today when Russia and Ukraine are at war as it was a century ago in the aftermath of the Great War and as people began to develop the unsuccessful League of Nations.

The attempt at pooling sovereignty, though it is often complicated and involves a difficult process of institution-building, is arguably a vital step towards healing divisions between nations. If one accepts that, then many of the failures that have underlain the 'European project' appear in a different light. If, on the other hand, one takes the pooling of sovereignty out of the equation, then the 'European project' can easily dissolve into a mass of quangos and jobs for overpaid eurocrats. Any discussion of the value of the EU and, I would argue, any discussion of the value of the UK, has to understand the reasoning behind the demand for a binding authority above the level of the nation-state.

There is a well-known memorial in Central London to Edith Cavell, the English nurse who was working in Brussels when the First World War broke out. In violation of military law, she helped wounded allied soldiers to escape from German-occupied Belgium to the neutral Netherlands. The Germans arrested her and on October 12th, 1915, she was executed by firing squad. Her statue stands in St. Martin's Place near Trafalgar Square in the heart of the English capital. The inscription on the plinth beneath repeats her famous words to the

Anglican Chaplain who was allowed to give her Holy Communion on the night before she was killed: *Patriotism Is Not Enough*.

The dangers of unbridled nationalism were only too clear to Edith Cavell at the time of the First World War. She was working a few miles from the trenches, the thin dividing–line between hundreds of thousands of young men who were daily engaged in killing each other. In other circumstances they might have been drinking or playing football together. For a period of weeks around Christmas 1914 they actually did so, in a No Man's Land between the trenches which hardly had room for a makeshift pitch. Then they returned to the mutual slaughter.

Note that the inscription beneath the statue does not say that patriotism is wrong or undesirable. It knows that love of country is almost as much of a basic instinct as love of family. But it adds the 'not enough.' Patriotism needs management. It needs a context. Otherwise, it can lead to outbreaks of nationalist fervour that produce violence and even mass killing.

Are nations manageable?

I would like to recall some points I made in *The Binding of Nations* ten years ago, points which have arguably not lost their validity over the last decade.[7] Four centuries ago, (in 1625) Hugo Grotius' *De jure belli ac pacis* (*On the Law of War and Peace*) was published. Writing in the middle of the Thirty Years War (and at the same time the so-called Eighty Years' War between Spain and the Netherlands), Grotius had every opportunity to observe the problem of war between nations. The words from the Prologomenon to his *Law of War and Peace* have not lost their power:

> Throughout the Christian world I observed a lack of restraint in relation to war, such as even barbarous races should be ashamed of; I observed that men rush to arms for slight causes, or no cause at all, and that when arms have once been taken up there is no longer any respect for law, divine or human; it is as if, in accordance with a general decree, frenzy had openly been let loose for the committing of all crimes.[8]

---

7   Corner, Mark *The Binding of Nations: From European Union to World Union* was published by Palgrave Macmillan in 2010, particularly chapter 2, 'The Rise of the Nation-State', pp. 17–34.

8   See the student edition of Grotius' classic edited by Stephen C Neff, p. 8.

Grotius is a very important figure for emphasising the place of law at an international as well as national level. No single figure did more to establish the law of nations as a distinct body of doctrine. Moreover, he knew enough of war to recognise its vital significance. He wanted to devise rules for managing the conflicts that he recognised all too well and made a significant contribution to a 'law of the seas' and to the 'just war' debate. But he did not explain how a law enforceable by sheriffs, magistrates and (later) policemen at home, with the authority to impose fines and imprison offenders, could be enforced in international relations.

At the time Grotius wrote the nations of Europe were becoming free from the shackles of what were ultimately religious control mechanisms (to some extent Henry's break with Rome anticipated that). But what was going to manage their relations with one another in this new world? In the sixteenth century the different countries of Western Europe gave up their common religious bond and agreed to a policy of non-interference in each other's affairs, at least so far as religious belief (narrowly defined in terms of options, of course) was concerned. This is the principle of *cuius regio, eius religio* (let the ruler determine the religion) enshrined in the Peace of Augsburg of 1555. It initially applied only to Catholics and Lutherans.[9] A century later, at the end of the Thirty Years War that ravaged much of Europe between 1618 and 1648, the Treaty of Westphalia agreed to extend the *cuius regio, eius religio* principle of Augsburg to Calvinists. Grotius' work was written in the middle of that destructive thirty-year war, which anticipated an even more destructive thirty-year war in Europe three hundred years later.

By now hopes of a united Christendom had been dashed forever, a realisation that lay behind Pope Innocent X's outburst against the 1648 Treaty of Westphalia as 'null, void, invalid, iniquitous, unjust, damnable, reprobate, inane and devoid of meaning for all time.'[10] This was language that made the remarks of a British eurosceptic commenting on the latest treaty proposed in Brussels (or nowadays on post-BREXIT relations with the UK) seem positively benign. But did the Pope have a point, at least in the sense that the nation-state had fi-

---

9   The phrase was first coined by the Protestant canon lawyer Joachim Stephani. See Cross, Leslie and Livingstone, Elizabeth A. *Oxford Dictionary of the Christian Church*, 3rd Edition, p. 566.

10   The quotation comes from his encyclical Zelus domus Dei (1650). See Robert Jackson's *Sovereignty: Evolution of an Idea*, p. 51.

nally been released from any participation, however notional, in a higher order which might have checked its activities?

In contemporary writing there is a tendency to use the term 'Westphalian' of any approach which rules out interference in the domestic affairs of another country, thus extending what was originally applied to religious interference to all kinds of interference. Hence Robert Cooper talks of 'the old Westphalian concept of state sovereignty in which others do not interfere.'[11] No one tells you what to do within your own borders, and when it comes to other nations you do what you can to get the better of them in a constant diplomatic and, where necessary, military game. There is nothing above the nation-state, nothing at the 'supranational' level, empowered to make binding laws with which nation-states must comply.

Hobbes and the nation

Most people agree with the idea of a voluntary limitation of individual rights to receive some sort of protection and security inside a national community – the 'social contract' that attracted many of the readers of Hobbes' *Leviathan* in 1651, one of the great textbooks of political thought. To some extent his book was a rationalisation of the decision to execute King Charles I, itself a challenge to the so-called Divine Right of Kings, the belief that monarchs were effectively put in place by God. Hobbes wrote his book during that remarkable decade (the 1650s) when England was distinctive by being a republic. Monarchy was the established form of government willed by God. Across the Channel, a century and a half before the French Revolution put to work the tumbrils and the guillotine, Louis XIV was beginning a long reign as the Sun King. Hobbes had to find a way of convincing people that removing the head of a King was not an act of defiance against the Almighty. He suggested that states were constructed through a 'social contract,' according to which we voluntarily invest certain authorities with the power to act on our behalf. The hierarchy we chose to live under was the result of a human decision, not a simple act of obedience to God's will. It was based on the understandable wish to live secure lives rather than face the law of the jungle, an existence in a 'state of nature' where lives are lived in a state of constant insecurity and occasional suffering, because there are no checks

---

11   Robert Cooper, *The Breaking of Nations*, p. 58.

on human behaviour.[12] The social order was not a simple response to the command of a God who required kings as God had once required patriarchs; it was a product of human need.

The interesting thing about Hobbes' argument is that in order to suggest the practical necessity of a social contract, he presents human beings as jointly willing to accept a limitation of their own powers in order to receive the benefits of social order. In practice, though we certainly dislike it when others tell us what to do, we accept that there must be binding rules governing our lives in a community. They may be trivial, such as agreeing what side of the road we will drive on (not that this is trivial if not observed). They may be crucially important, like rules about how we should treat our children. To enforce these rules, we jointly agree to invest authorities like magistrates and police with considerable authority. Even when it comes to the things that we hold most dear, we accept certain rules and give certain authorities the right to intervene in our lives – to break into our homes if necessary – in order to enforce those rules.

Looking back on *Leviathan* over three and a half centuries later, we might well be struck by an obvious limitation in Hobbes' approach. His suggestion of recourse to a social contract to resolve conflicts between individuals in a 'state of nature' might seem persuasive. But what if the nations that result from such an arrangement, receiving as they do the unswerving loyalty of their citizens, were *themselves* to become part of an anarchic tribal conflict between hundreds of states, a conflict that precisely mirrored that between individuals in a state of nature? What if all that Hobbes achieves is to transpose the state of nature to another level? Surely he needs something similar where it comes to relations between nation states. We need the equivalent of the magistrates and police and security services to break into our countries rather than our homes in order to enforce rules of conduct we jointly agree upon.

Hobbes did not take this further step. Whereas he had a strong sense of the destructive anarchy prevailing in a country without strong central government, he did not extend this to the relations between states. Quite the opposite. In chapter XXX of *Leviathan* he declares that 'the people are to be taught not to love any form of government they see in neighbouring nations.'[13] Such a de-

---

12   See especially Part One Chapters 13 'Of the Naturall condition of Mankind as concerning their Misery and Felicity' and 14 'Of the First and Second Naturall Lawes and of Contract', pp. 72–89 of the edition of *Leviathan* published by Dover Publications, New York 2018, which retains Hobbes' original spelling.

13   Thomas Hobbes, *Leviathan*, p. 289.

sire, he claims, is like a breach of God's Commandment: 'Thou shalt not have the Gods of other nations.' A prohibition of idolatry is thus secularised into a prohibition against any form of attachment to other states. 'Thou shalt not have any other Gods but me' is secularised into 'Thou shalt not have any other states but the one you live in.' Monotheism becomes 'monostatism'. Heresy becomes treason. The believer in Christendom becomes the secular equivalent of the polytheist, and attachment to the one true god becomes loyalty to a single state.

Thus, Hobbes not only provided a justification for the authority of national rulers: he also provided a justification for rejecting any supranational authority which might attempt to regulate the anarchic relationship between states themselves. He was not a friend of the so-called 'domestic analogy', which tries to lift the conflicts between individuals that a social order must resolve, by force if necessary, to a higher level. Hobbes felt that whereas a 'state of nature' among individuals was absolutely intolerable, a state of nature among states could be bearable, since nations could do all that was needed to ensure the maintenance of internal peace and prevent conflict between states from spilling over into the lives of their inhabitants. He under-estimated the extent to which that internal peace might be eradicated by warfare between states. If he had lived in mainland Europe, where a devastating thirty-year war had just ended, he might have had a greater awareness of the disruption that plundering armies (or even billeted soldiers) could do to ordinary life. But he was coming from a country in which all the disruption had come from what he looked upon as a civil war, not from fighting others. His focus was simply on the security that a powerful national government could impose and protect.

Time was to make the 'domestic analogy' more pressing rather than less. It might have seemed unimportant to the Britain that faced Napoleon a century and a half later, when the 'internal peace' was largely maintained away from the battlefront and people could immerse themselves in the latest Jane Austen and enjoy the romantic entanglements of late Georgian society. It was much more significant for those observing millions slaughtered in the trenches during Edith Cavell's day a century after that. It remained significant for those who were bombed a generation later, and it is a vital question for our survival in the present day when faced by the perils of nuclear annihilation between countries keeping their weapons systems on hair-trigger alert, not to mention the slow burn of irreversible climate change.

International anarchy

Despite the continued and growing importance of the 'domestic analogy', the three centuries after Hobbes produced few attempts to control the 'international anarchy' which at national level had been restrained by increasingly professional police forces. Occasionally, when one country threatened to dominate the others, there were calls for some kind of control over the perpetual rivalry and conflict which the Westphalian 'system' (or lack of system) had produced. The Napoleonic wars gave rise to the short-lived 'Congress' system in 1815, but barely a decade had gone by before the British Foreign Secretary George Canning was falling out with the other powers over intervention to suppress the revolution in Spain and made his famous remark: 'things are getting back into a wholesome state. Every nation for itself, and God for us all'.[14] It was an expression of support for international anarchy that would be music to the ears of a contemporary Brexiteer. In any case, Britain scuppered the system. In Thomson's words: 'First among the important victorious Powers, she broke with the system and thereby made it crumble'.[15] Arguably, it would have collapsed in any case. At all events, the Congress system proved ineffective, and the nineteenth century progressed with increasingly dangerous rivalries between European nations threatening an even greater conflagration.

Compared with its successor, the nineteenth century was certainly a time of peace in Europe (though not outside Europe, where imperial ambitions and rivalries led to a series of wars and occasional massacres). The only 'serious' conflict between states was the Crimean War of 1854–6, and that was restricted to a relatively small theatre of war in South-East Europe. But the 'century of peace' was also a century of preparation for war, culminating in a massive arms race and an explosion of colonial expansion. Lack of general conflict or all-out war between European states proceeded alongside a state of perpetual friction and tension which expressed itself in many ways, of which the most notable was the scramble for Africa at the end of the century as each state sought to outflank the others. It was a struggle which in the light of Darwin's *The Origin of Species* was sometimes compared to struggles for dominance in the animal kingdom, an analogy that reinforced the idea such conflicts were natural and

---

14   Canning made the remark as a sign of his breaking with the Concert of Europe. See Robert Jervis' chapter 'Security Regimes,' pp. 173–193 of Krasner, Stephen D. (ed.) *International Regimes*, p. 183.

15   David Thomson *England in the Nineteenth Century*, p. 27.

therefore inevitable. The 'great game' was akin to the struggle for survival in the evolution of species.

The vacuum in terms of enforceable international law remained right up to the time of Edith Cavell, but it was even more of a problem by the time she began her work. One might suppose that this was a simple product of technological advance. The 'moat' around Britain that had served it so well in the past could be overcome by aircraft and their bombing raids. Later technological development meant that whole populations of men, women and children could be slaughtered in an instant and that in certain extreme circumstances nation-states were prepared to use such weapons, as the USA did twice in August 1945 against Japan. It was a process that made the failure to control relations between nations even more serious and threatened to produce precisely the sort of war which was to cost tens of millions of lives in the next century and would be even more destructive in our own century.

Nations become nation-states

The important developments during the centuries after Hobbes did not simply concern technology. The also concerned key social and political changes that occurred. Because in the twenty-first century the particular nation people belong to is almost universally a major determinant of their lives, we easily forget the fact that before 1800 this was not the case. Because nations have been in existence for centuries, we think that they have played a major part in people's lives for centuries. But this is not so. 'National feeling' could be stirred up easily enough by John of Gaunt's famous speech in *Richard II* about a 'precious stone set in a silver sea', in Shakespeare's day as in our own. But national feeling has a very different effect on a nation which has been organised into a nation-state, one which has started to manage people's lives through 'state service', including in many cases military service, 'state administration' and 'state education', while providing them with various 'state benefits.'

Where Europe is concerned, the key changes took place in the nineteenth century. Nationalism was something that initially appealed to the middle classes, to teachers, clergy, administrators, and some better-off artisans, rather than to the masses. This wasn't because the masses were all devotees of international socialism or some other trans-national ideal. It was because they weren't yet sufficiently drawn into the nation to feel nationalistic. In contemporary jargon, they didn't have enough of a stake in it.[16]

The liberal state of the nineteenth century felt itself in a bind as it embarked upon the process of 'democratisation'. If it refused the vote to increasing numbers of articulate people, it would surely provoke revolution; yet if it granted these people voting rights, it was surely doomed to feed its own destruction by making it inevitable that its leaders would be voted out of office.

It didn't happen that way. As the franchise was extended it didn't bring revolutionary governments to power. At least part of the reason for this was the ability of governments, conceding that they were forced to absorb the masses into the developing structure of the nation state, to turn this process into a means of encouraging nationalism. Once people felt able to identify with their country they could be drawn into an uncritical support of its aims and interests (and possibly be made to serve in its army through conscription). To the governments themselves nationalism was not a measure to keep people from communism, of which very few of them had much idea, but rather a way of managing their entry into mass politics and the life of the nation.

The masses made their entry in other ways too. Though secondary and tertiary education remained largely the preserve of an élite before 1900, primary education did not. By the end of the century, it was almost universal. This provided another opportunity to manage the growing significance of the masses in the state. Mass education, in an age before the existence of 'mass media' such as newspapers, (mass circulation newspapers were just beginning at the end of the nineteenth century), radio, television and today's explosion of social media, was the best means of instilling a sense of belonging to a state. Twenty-first century talk of a 'national curriculum' and 'citizenship classes' is simply the further refinement of a process which began in the nineteenth century with the first attempts at a national education system.

Education also raised the question of language. At the time of the formation of Italy only 2% of the population actually spoke Italian and D'Azeglio made his remark quoted earlier that having created Italy (following Italian Unifica-

---

16   See Hobsbawm, Eric *Nations and Nationalism since 1780: Programme, Myth, Reality*, esp. chapter 2 'Popular proto-nationalism', pp. 46–79 and chapter 3, 'The Government Perspective' pp. 80–100. But the whole of this classic work, which had its fifteenth printing in 2008, is worth absorbing.

tion in 1860) it would now be necessary to make Italians.[17] Eugen Weber made a similar remark about the need to turn peasants into Frenchmen.[18] It is interesting to reflect on whether the same remark could be made today when saying that having created a European Union, we now need to create Europeans. When people's lives were largely determined by their local communities and business was conducted through oral transactions, there was little need for an 'official' language spoken in the same way throughout the country. Different dialects, in some cases as different from one another as separate languages, could happily coexist when there was no need to talk to people from other parts of the country or to exchange correspondence with them. But once the trappings of a modern state began to emerge, with mass involvement in national education and a national bureaucracy, things had to change. That 98% who did not speak Italian could no longer be tolerated in a 'modern Italy'.

Earlier in this chapter it was suggested that while Hobbes had a sense of the need for a state to manage relations between individuals and prevent the conflict that arose in a 'state of nature', he didn't see any reason for an international authority to govern the relation between 'Leviathans.' Part of the reason for this was that the Leviathans had hardly developed into the closely-knit organisations that make up the modern nation-state. Hobbes refers to the nation as an 'artificial man', with law as the mind or reason, rewards and punishments as the nerves, officials as the joints and so on.[19] But in the seventeenth century these joints had hardly been knit together in the way that they were by 1900. Individual monarchs squabbled and went to war, using professional armies and mercenaries to gain more territory or repel an attack. In the process they certainly caused many deaths, not least as the indirect consequence of armies crossing a continent and living off the land, effectively spreading disease and famine wherever they went. But they could not produce the consequences that the nation-state could in the time of Edith Cavell, when huge populations could be mobilised for war and indeed willingly threw themselves into a conflict (Britain had no conscription before 1916) which the generals confidently told them would be over by Christmas. Few people anticipated the daily ritual of slaughter which was to follow the outbreak of war and continue for four long years, before repeating itself a generation later.

---

17   See 'Mass-Producing Traditions: Europe 1870–1914', chapter 7 of Ranger and Hobsbawm, eds, *The Invention of Tradition*, pp. 263–307.

18   See Weber, Eugen *Peasants into Frenchmen: The Modernisation of Rural France 1870–1914*.

19   He introduces this image in the Introduction to Leviathan. See Hobbes, *Leviathan*, p. 5.

Hence two key developments had taken place by the early twentieth century that made the 'domestic analogy' relevant. One was the technological development that meant that weapons could easily cross borders, though this had always been true to some extent, even at the time when Hobbes wrote *Leviathan*. The other was the development of cohesive nation-states, all of whose citizens realised that their lives were profoundly affected by the particular country they lived in.

The fear of world rulers

Since nations have been around for hundreds of years, it is easy to conclude that forming oneself into a national group is somehow part of the human condition. The nation acquires some of the natural authenticity accorded to the family. Patriotism becomes as natural as the love of daughter for mother or son for father (hence we talk of a 'motherland' or 'fatherland'). Our country is our 'national home' or 'homeland', and other countries are 'neighbours'.

If this is so, then it is important to stress, as we tried to illustrate earlier, where the analogy breaks down. In countries subject to the rule of law families in a street are bound to abide by various rules or face penalties. Even if they only behave badly inside their own homes (for instance if children are abused), the families can be split up and their children taken away. If necessary, the police can break into their homes and arrest their occupants. We may be familiar with sayings (coined at a time when language was not inclusive) such as 'An Englishman's home in his castle' to stress the importance of being able to close the front door and have some privacy. We may often find ourselves saying 'what you do in your own home is your business.' On the other hand, we accept that there are circumstances where it is right that the magistrate issues a warrant and the police arrive in the early morning to break into the home and, if necessary, arrest some of the occupants. If there is abuse of some kind, we stop short of saying: 'Don't interfere: it's domestic.'

There is no such effective sanction for a breakdown that occurs within a nation state. Although the UN has talked about something called a 'responsibility to protect' (R2P) developed at the end of the last century when Kofi Annan was General Secretary, it has no authority to intervene unless sanctioned at the very least by a majority in the Security Council, including all five of the veto-wield-ing powers.[20] This is often impossible to secure. As a result, intervention from outside is often not forthcoming, and any 'responsibility to protect' rarely leads to anything in the way of effective action. The case for regulating national behaviour is hardly weakened by pointing out how natural it is to love one's country, since even the love of mother or father for child is not seen as a reason for complete non-interference in the affairs of individual families.

But applying such restraint to nations has always been considered too difficult to try, as the seventeenth century thinkers who originated much of what we now call 'international law' realised. 200 Leviathans (of varying size and power, of course) are hard to manage. Moreover, as the nation evolved into the nation-state during the nineteenth century, it became a much more powerful and integrated unit which could unleash (quite apart from technological developments) terrible atrocities against others.

Any progress of 'civilisation' in the nineteenth and twentieth centuries is therefore easier to recognise in terms of behaviour *within* states rather than relations *between* them. What use were the improvements noted by sociologists like Norbert Elias when states still went to war with one another and when technology took their violent behaviour, when they were at war, to new limits of destructiveness?

Norbert Elias made a point of stressing that things we used to tolerate within states, like public torture and hangings (and later all hangings) or cruelty to animals through bear-baiting and cock-fighting, were in the process of dying out or had died out already.[21] We were becoming more 'civilised'. But this was only true if you considered what happened within states when they were at peace. Elias' book was first published in 1936, so it preceded the outbreak of the Second World War. By then it had become clear that in wartime the children who might no longer be exposed on hillsides or sold into slavery would face cluster or phosphorus bombs that would tear off their limbs or skin instead, or mines that would explode under them and disable them permanently. Meanwhile the people who were no longer being executed in large numbers at home could and can be slaughtered in their thousands by their 'enemies' abroad. One only has to read the extraordinary account of the First World War mentioned in Chapter Two, *As We Were* (which in fact was a

---

20   See https://www.un.org/en/genocideprevention/about-responsibility-to-protect.sh tml for the official UN understanding of Responsibility to Protect. In practice it has been very difficult to enforce.

21   See Elias, Norbert *The Civilising Process*, especially pp. 47–72.

slaughter on many fronts, the more mobile ones to the East and South also producing thousands of casualties). 'As we were', and yet in many parts of the world, such as Ukraine in 2023, it is as we are. We return precisely to the point made by Grotius four hundred years ago:

> when arms have once been taken up there is no longer any respect for law, divine or human; it is as if, in accordance with a general decree, frenzy had openly been let loose for the committing of all crimes.[22]

As nations coalesced into nation-states in the nineteenth century, the potential for organised aggression against other states grew. The 'nasty, brutish and short' lives from which people managed to move away in their domestic affairs, failed to become any less nasty, brutish and short where external relations were concerned. The sort of social contract which had brought people out of a state of nature into a social contract could not, it seemed, be applied to the state of nature that existed between states themselves. It was a heavy price to pay for being unable to prevent the slaughter and killing, which seemed to have been largely eliminated *within* countries, from returning when relations *between* countries broke down. Of course, there are various rules of engagement in warfare and there are certain things that have been outlawed as war crimes, but the mechanism for enforcement just isn't there in the way that it usually is at the domestic level.

Why hasn't the domestic analogy been accepted so that people have recognised the need for the sort of binding and enforceable legislation at the global level that they are willing to accept at the national level? It may seem that I am presuming the inadequacy of bodies like the United Nations or legal institutions like the International Criminal Court, the limitations of which I tried to outline in *The Binding of Nations*. But it hardly seems to be an exaggeration to say that while at the national level there are crimes that go unpunished, there are bodies which have the powers to enforce certain rules, even though they may be too corrupt or incompetent to do so. At the international level, no such body exists with a comparable power of enforcement. At the international level, we resist Leviathans of any kind.

There have been a number of studies as to why the domestic analogy has never been convincing to many people. What might seem at first sight to be a curious reluctance to apply measures, which are readily accepted where individual nation-states are concerned, to a wider international setting, has been

---

22   See the student edition of Grotius' classic edited by Stephen C Neff, p. 8.

examined by writers like Hidemi Suganami.[23] The reasons for the failure of the domestic analogy to be convincing are many, but Suganami highlights one in particular.

He shows that whenever – for instance in the aftermath of World War One – there was general consensus that some form of control at the international level was needed, the presumption that it would entail the creation of an all-powerful superstate stopped progress towards binding international arrangements in its tracks. One can see the logic of this. If one finds living in one of the 200 countries in the world intolerable, it is possible in principle (of course there may be many difficulties in practice) to go and live in another one. But if you found living under some global Leviathan intolerable, where would you go? Space travel is expensive, a plaything for billionaires and even then they only get to escape for a few minutes. The moon or other planets hardly seem to be hospitable environments. Suganami sees that the idea of world rulers (like masters of the universe) conjures up the sense of overwhelming and irresistible powers imposing their will on everyone, a scenario which can easily be turned into quasi-science fiction horror stories. It is the inescapability of world rule, as opposed to national rule, that drives people back before long to the unsatisfactory system of treaties (and entreaties). It's not just better the devil you know. It's more a case of better the evil you can get away from (although getting away may prove difficult if not impossible, as the refugee trails all too painfully illustrate).

The danger therefore remains that unless we manage to create an effective form of international supervision, our lives in one of 200 nations that exist in their own form of a 'state of nature' may turn out to be as 'nasty, brutish and short' as the lives of those forced to live in a country where all control at the national level has broken down. The understandable fear of inescapable control at the global level by a 'world ruler' or 'world council' appears to make us prepared to accept anarchy between states when we would not be prepared to accept it within them. There is an urgent need to apply the sort of controls to the way in which nations behave that most of us accept as essential when it comes to the way individuals behave. But could such controls ever be introduced without threatening the creation of a totalitarian order through an inescapable 'world state'?

Against this background we can understand better the claim that the creation of what became (from 1993) the European Union provided a way of squar-

---

23   Suganami, Hidemi. *The Domestic Analogy and World Order.*

ing the circle, a means of having effective international supervision without an inescapable global superstate. For one thing the EU is escapable – after all, the UK has just escaped it. On the other hand, it is a collection of nation-states who have agreed jointly to share sovereignty, who have freely put themselves under the yoke of European law. This is not, as we shall see in the next chapter, to deny that the European Union came into being for other reasons altogether. It was not an answer to the philosophical dilemma of how to control the actions of nation-states without subjecting them to some kind of totalitarian global overlord. But whatever the intentions behind its formation, it has had an influence far beyond the practical issues that encouraged its formation. As we shall see, it came about through the ideas of a man who did little to campaign publicly for his proposals (Jean Monnet) and through the political effectiveness of another man (Robert Schuman) who was secretive and embarrassed (at times) about what he was doing. As a result, it was open from the beginning to the criticism that it was an elitist invention smuggled into being for dark political purposes. That criticism is still deserved, though a later chapter will attempt to propose a way round it. But it does not undermine the significance of what was achieved in creating perhaps the only effective method of managing relations between nation-states that has ever been devised.

Conclusion

This chapter has argued that it makes sense to have binding and enforceable rules at the supranational level, just as it makes sense at the national level, where we are prepared to give power to bodies that can even break into our own homes if necessary. Hobbes' *Leviathan* provides a compelling rationale for a social contract at the national level but rejects the idea that nations should also agree to limit their power in the interests of international security. In the centuries after Hobbes, during which the nation-state became much more cohesive and bound the lives of its citizens much more than in the past, these powerful units adrift in an anarchic world of unenforceable agreements and treaties showed the need to move beyond what came to be called 'Westphalian' arrangements. The last century shows how that need has become even greater as catastrophic wars have claimed millions of lives and climate change makes the only planet we can live on increasingly uninhabitable.

It is because of this urgent need to find an effective way of managing the relations between states, that the ideas of Monnet and Schuman are so important. Early attempts at supranationalism failed, however desirable they may have been in principle, because they seemed to require the imposition of a global authority that was effectively inescapable. But with the development of the European Union an effective form of supranationalism became evident, one which was certainly not inescapable, as recent British history shows.

By looking at the post war arrangements into which much of Europe was pushed (and partially embraced), this book will show how difficult it was to introduce such a system of binding law which member states had to abide by – and how difficult it remains. But the point of this chapter is to argue that it was as important as it was difficult. It therefore becomes possible to view the attempts at sovereignty-sharing which appeared in the twentieth century as attempts to find a solution to a growing problem, rather than as a form of self-indulgent tinkering with a system of international relations that the world could perfectly well manage without, despite two world wars and the ever-present threat of a third one.

Chapter Five: Monnet and his limitations

By looking at the historical background to some of today's arguments we can get a much better idea of why a form of supranationalism is essential in a European context. At the same time this book is called *A Tale of Two Unions* because I believe that the attractions of supranationalism may finally resonate with an island nation that likes to think of itself as going alone. The claim is that this will happen because of its own growing concern about an internal fracture that nothing but a form of supranationalism will be able to prevent. That is the interconnection that makes this a tale of two unions rather than one.

To begin with, however, it is useful to examine the way in which Monnet came to the conclusions he did and how he sought to implement his ideas. It is a story that has often been told, so the chapter will limit itself to points that bear upon the main thesis of this book.

The little man from Cognac

Few disagree that Jean Monnet was the founding father of the EU system, but they often criticise his methods. Yet in his defence it could be argued that he operated in the best way he could, given the circumstances he found himself in.

Monnet was born in the small French town of Cognac, but it was a town whose provincial nature was offset by its role as the world capital of brandy. Cognac salesmen travelled the world to hawk their wares and Monnet's family belonged to that Cognac world. Even as a child he found himself part of the welcoming party for visitors from many different countries who stayed with his father, a brandy salesman, for want of hotel rooms in town. Hence despite being brought up in a provincial French town, Monnet was thrust into a cosmopolitan environment. His first experience of networking was with Cognac salesmen who'd be invited to the family house and primed for information – not only strictly commercial information but also insights into the social and economic conditions of countries that represented actual or potential markets for the brandy business. This was where Monnet first discovered his talent for eliciting information and being persuasive in small groups.[1]

He enjoyed these meetings with travelling salesmen rather more than he enjoyed school, so it was unsurprising that he left school at 16. In this sense Monnet was the very opposite of a member of the élite. Instead of studying at university or seeking access to power through one of the *grandes écoles*, he decided to go to London in order to help his father's firm by learning English – an essential prerequisite for any brandy merchant – and the ways of business. At the still tender age of 18 he was sent to Canada with a trunk full of samples of the family brandy and instructions to spread the Monnet brand around the world. He seems to have been successful, securing a deal with the Hudson Bay Company in 1911 which made J G Monnet & Co. the sole supplier of brandy to its Canadian market.

Selling cognac for the family firm involved a lot of travelling, not only to English-speaking countries like the USA, UK and Canada but also to Scandinavia, Russia and Egypt. As the elder son, Jean Monnet would have been expected to take the firm over eventually. In any case, the Hudson Bay Company deal shows that he was entrusted with negotiating large contracts before he was out of his teens. Better a life of travel, responsibility and real decision-making than being trapped behind a desk in a school, however prestigious.

The prospects of a business career were altered significantly in 1914 when the First World War broke out. Monnet was exempted from military service because of nephritis but wanted to find another way of helping the allied cause. He believed that he could best do this by applying the skills he had already shown in negotiating business contracts to the task of promoting cooperation between nations in the war effort.

How would he get a chance to influence the war effort? His father pointed out that the government in Paris was not going to listen to someone like Jean. His son disagreed. The overall philosophy he lived by is made clear in his *Memoirs*:

---

1   See the biography of Monnet by Duchêne, François *Jean Monnet: First Statesman of Interdependence*, p. 29. See the chapter 'A Talent at Large' (pp. 27–63) for many of the points outlined in the next few paragraphs.

First have an idea, then look for the man who can put it to work.[2]

It is a revealing description (couched in language which shows how a century ago the presumption was that only men could put an idea to work). It is precisely the opposite of the populist approach. The populist studies the ideas that are already in play and then presents himself or herself as the champion of the idea likely to do best. In effect it is demagoguery masquerading as democracy. But there was nothing of the demagogue in Monnet. He was not one of those who find out what the people want and then ride into power on their backs, promising to back 'their' cause against the establishment.

However, in another sense Monnet's approach is not so laudable. He does not talk about spreading his ideas through campaigning or forming a political movement. He simply talks about finding the right person to influence in the right way. He wasn't a populist, but less laudably there was nothing of the populariser in him. He would not try to mobilise popular discontent with the way the war was being fought or hold public meetings to encourage allied cooperation. Such an approach might not have been possible in wartime anyway, but in peacetime its absence became a disadvantage. Monnet's approach was to single out the people in authority whom he needed to persuade and then move in on them indirectly:

> ...having identified the target for persuasion, he sought the acquaintance of the individual of lesser rank in his target's chain of command who actually prepared the initial drafts of documents that provided his boss with advice and new initiatives. He sometimes spent day after day with that lowly but tactically placed minion.[3]

His first 'tactically placed minion' was a family friend who enabled him to meet the French Prime Minister, René Viviani. This gave him a contact, but there was also the matter of timing. He had to make his pitch at the right moment. Timing was, after all, recognised as crucial by anyone in the business he came from. 'In Cognac they are good at waiting. It is the only way to make good brandy.'[4] He waited before seeing Viviani until shortly after the Battle of the Marne. The

---

2   Quoted in Sherrill Brown Wells, *Jean Monnet: Unconventional Statesman*, p. 10.

3   Bill, James A. *George Ball: Behind the Scenes of U.S. Foreign Policy*, p.107. It is also quoted in George Ball's foreword to Duchêne, François *Jean Monnet: First Statesman of Interdependence*, p.11.

4   See Duchêne, François *Jean Monnet: First Statesman of Interdependence*, p. 347.

conflict had 'settled into' trench warfare and was a moment when those optimistic 'it will all be over by Christmas' assumptions about a short war were giving way to a more realistic assessment. The war was more likely to be a long haul which would require proper organisation. Monnet was one of the few that recognised this and could present himself as someone who knew how to manage the long haul.

By the end of 1914 Monnet was back in London working for the French Civil Supplies Service with a key position in helping to co-ordinate allied supplies. Britain and France were supposed to be on the same side, but they were unused to working together. They competed for access to supplies, which soon became scarce and then the scarcity caused prices to rise. The result was that both countries ended up paying more for supplies than they needed to. As German submarine attacks mounted, co-ordination became not only essential to managing the long haul but to survival itself.

Yet even in such a desperate situation as this the British and the French in 1915 were still competing against each other to buy wheat on the Australian and Argentine markets.

Monnet's solution was to propose a Wheat Executive. It was hardly a mass organisation – just three officials who assessed what each country needed and what supplies were available, before allotting a share to each country and then ordering the supplies jointly. It had no power to act on its own – its recommendations required acceptance by the national governments. But the governments usually agreed with the Wheat Executive's proposals.[5] They recognised that such a system not only kept the wheat flowing but made it less expensive and saved shipping space at a time of severe shortages for the merchant marine. When wheat proved a success, the system was extended to other cereals and other countries joined the scheme.

The Wheat Executive influenced Monnet's later approach in creating the European Coal and Steel Community and the European Economic Community. There was the urgent need for nations to work together and yet it had clearly been difficult to make it happen. Even during wartime, and even when it was clearly in their economic interest to do so, the British and the French had shown themselves reluctant to cooperate.

After the First World War, Monnet attended the Paris Peace Conference and later became a top official (deputy secretary general) at the League of Nations, forerunner of the United Nations. His role in organising inter-allied in-

---

5   Duchêne, François *Jean Monnet: First Statesman of Interdependence*, p. 36.

stitutions during World War One made him seem naturally suited to an organisation trying to develop global cooperation. But Monnet did not stay with the League beyond 1922. He considered that it had a fatal weakness, generally recognised now but not so clear to many at the time.[6] It had no means of enforcing a decision over a national veto. If a single member state was opposed to doing something, it didn't happen. Monnet could already see that an intergovernmental organisation, essentially one that requires everyone to be willing to do something before anything is done, would be unable to deal with an increasingly unstable international situation. National vetoes were incompatible with effectiveness. This was vital to the later development of his thinking.

As the Second World War approached Monnet was one of the few who recognised the danger posed by Hitler and the need to organise resistance. Once again, as he had done during the earlier war, he threw himself into the organisation of supplies. He travelled to the United States in 1938 seeking to purchase military aircraft and meeting, among others, President Roosevelt. Once more the arts of persuasion were essential. America was in a more isolationist mood than its president and was unwilling to be 'tricked into' another war in Europe. The Neutrality Act of 1935 forbade sales of completed weapons to belligerents. Monnet argued that the act could be circumvented by moving aircraft parts across the American frontier to assemble planes in Canada (Montreal), where they would be fitted together by US engineers.[7] In the end, he only acquired a few hundred planes in this roundabout way, (it was a remarkable achievement to have acquired any), but at least it meant that US aircraft production was already developed when the country finally entered World War Two.

By the end of 1939, Britain and France were once again allies in war and once again Monnet was involved in trying to coordinate their war effort, continuing his previous work through promoting a joint approach by both countries to the US for aircraft. Back in the USA Monnet did not secure many supplies

---

6   Sherrill Brown Wells describes Monnet as 'especially frustrated by the League's fatal flaw: its inability to enforce a decision over a national veto'. See Wells, Sherrill Brown *Jean Monnet: Unconventional Statesman*, p. 19.

7   Duchêne, François *Jean Monnet: First Statesman of Interdependence*, p. 67. Monnet had written about the need to build up an aeronautical industry abroad out of the reach of enemy attack in early 1938, at a time when many others thought that peace with Germany was possible. See Duchêne, op. cit., p. 65.

for the UK, but what he did manage to do was stimulate American war production and prepare it for moving onto a war footing before the Japanese attack on Pearl Harbour suddenly propelled the country into the conflict. The famous economist John Maynard Keynes suggested that Monnet may have shortened the war by a year,[8] a claim that receives remarkably little attention now when Monnet is generally dismissed as the patron saint of eurocrats. Given that an extra year might have given the Nazis the chance to manufacture nuclear weapons, such an achievement is hardly slight.

Monnet made a huge contribution during these years. Yet the fundamental conviction which he maintained throughout this period was straightforward. Nation-states needed to cooperate during wartime against a common enemy; they also needed to cooperate in maintaining peace and resolving disputes after conflict was over. The question was how to ensure that they continued the cooperation forced on them during wartime into the time of rebuilding when they might be more likely to revert to their old antagonisms. The failure of the League of Nations between the two world wars had shown how wartime collaboration tended to melt away in a fog of good intentions once the conflict was over.

Towards the end of the Second World War Monnet was once again in the sort of position he had virtually made his own – as a manager of supplies – and was once again in place at just the right moment. France (now with a Provisional Government) had to find a way either of living without American help or of qualifying to receive it by having an economic programme in hand. Monnet had just such a programme. It was the right moment for the Monnet Plan.

Formally appointed the Planning Commissioner (*commissaire général au plan*) and granted a small staff directly responsible to the head of government but unattached to any ministry, Monnet had the freedom of manoeuvre he desired.[9] His Commission was another group of policy entrepreneurs – effectively a small group of dedicated people with an intense sense of loyalty to Monnet himself. It was the same way of working that he had always adopted and in many ways similar to the structure he was to advocate when building what was to become eventually the European Commission. He was not a member of the government, and he did not wish to seek parliamentary approval for the plan. He wanted to get on with the job. He was part of another group

---

8   Duchêne, François *Jean Monnet: First Statesman of Interdependence*, p. 93.

9   See 'Rebirth of France: The Monnet Plan 1945–1952', Chapter 5 of Duchêne, François *Jean Monnet: First Statesman of Interdependence*, pp. 147–180.

dedicated to maintaining the flow of supplies in an organised way – in this instance, not supplies to fuel a war effort but supplies to fuel post war recovery.

The strategy advanced by the Planning Commission was to prioritise investment over consumption. France must use foreign credit to buy equipment, not in order to fill the shops with consumer goods or even build more homes. This was a political decision, precisely the sort of issue that one might expect to be controversial. Yet the *Commissariat du Plan* believed that it was not a body resisting (or supporting) the prevailing political ideology. It was a body trying to push forward what it saw as an essential programme of modernisation while politicians of different persuasions rose to glory and then evaporated like soap bubbles.

In the circumstances, the politicians were happy to let it do its work while they pursued their internal wrangles. Monnet's experience of politics in the Fourth Republic encouraged him to see politicians as people who needed to be persuaded of the vital work he had to do and would then stand aside in order to let him get on with it.[10] That had been his approach from the very beginning, when he went to Viviani with a plan for improving wheat supplies. But that was when wartime governments were desperate for solutions to problems about which there was no disagreement – they were, after all, governments of national unity fighting a common enemy. After the war it might have been different, but the governments of the Fourth Republic lacked the stability to give any particular policy steer. However, in a more stable political environment politicians might reasonably argue that they were elected as representatives of the popular will, and officials must do their bidding as servants of the people. After all, a decision to prioritise investment in infrastructure rather than consumer spending (the gist of the Monnet Plan) was, as we have said, a profoundly political one. Monnet had dealt with wartime governments where everyone was united against a common enemy, or peacetime governments which were too weak and fragile to govern effectively at all. What he had not anticipated was the arrival of a strong peacetime government. De Gaulle, the most powerful European leader of the late twentieth century apart from Margaret Thatcher,

---

10   Wells, Sherrill Brown *Jean Monnet: Unconventional Statesman*, p. 107. She points out that 'as Head of the Planning Commission, Monnet was not a member of the government and, at his insistence, this first plan was never submitted to parliament for approval.' Monnet's staff of 'apolitical planners' were under his control and answerable to the Head of Government alone.

was to fill the gap in his knowledge. Duchêne comments as follows in his biography of Monnet in relation to the Fourth Republic in France (1946–58):

> The most famous of its (the Fourth Republic's) twenty-four premiers in twelve years was arguably Pierre Mendès-France, and the most powerful perhaps Guy Mollet. They held power for eight and sixteen months, respectively. Monnet the planner had the ear of government for at least seven years.[11]

De Gaulle, on the other hand, was to hold the presidency for more than a decade. During the period in which the European Coal and Steel Community was formed and the Treaties of Rome signed, France was going through leaders at the rate of two per year. To advance a particular cause, it seemed better to have nothing to do with the game of musical premiers and to exercise influence instead from the outside. De Gaulle, it has to be remembered, did not come to power in France until 1958, seven years after the Coal and Steel Community came into being and one year after the Treaties of Rome were signed.

In circumstances such as this, the policy entrepreneurs could achieve more than the political insider, though there would be a price to be paid after the successful implementation of their ideas. For though the policy entrepreneur might be able to persuade the political insider to adopt an idea, he or she has to give up the power to determine how the idea is presented and how it is defended against its critics. Will it be changed in the presentation? Will it be paraded in triumph before the electorate or smuggled in as an electoral hot potato? Will it be something to help put the world to rights or will it be a way out of a tricky situation for France? That was not something Monnet could have had any influence over.

The influencer and the campaigner

Monnet's experience of helping allied governments in wartime, supporting the work of the League of Nations and trying to influence France's recovery after the war brought home to him one essential point. If there was to be effective cooperation between nation-states, they would have to show a common willingness to be bound by decisions that they jointly reached. This was a radical

---

11   Duchêne, François *Jean Monnet: First Statesman of Interdependence*, p. 148.

– even a revolutionary – idea. But how would it ever be realised in practice? Nationalism might be a besetting sin, but national sovereignty was a sacred right.

The battle lines might have been clearer if Monnet had been an effective orator. He was not. His talents lay in persuading people in positions of power what they should do. Though totally uncharismatic as a public speaker, he apparently exercised an almost charismatic influence not only upon the members of his Planning Commission but upon those outside the Commission with whom he had to deal. Ball talked about their 'collective spiral cognition' and how in working with Monnet he was 'helping a wise man shape ideas like a sculptor with a knife'.[12] He then continued:

> My role was essential for Monnet himself was no writer...he evolved letters, papers, plans, proposals, memoranda of all kinds by bouncing ideas against another individual.

It is an intriguing description, as if Monnet won people over and then extracted every ounce of assistance they could supply, draining them of ideas like an intellectual Dracula driving his fangs into willing victims in the search for inspiration.

But there was a problem with this. As Ball points out later in his foreword to Duchêne's biography, 'he (Monnet) accomplished a profound redrawing of the economic map of Europe without ever holding elective office.'[13] In fact, he never even joined a political party. Duchêne writes as follows:

> His few platform appearances were models of histrionic incompetence. His voice failed to carry. His delivery stumbled. He had no instinct for projecting an aura in public.[14]

Nor was Monnet a writer. He wrote no textbook or even pamphlet in order to explain his ideas. Even where writing letters to people of influence was concerned, his preferred method was to talk things through with supporters and ask them to write a summary of the discussion.[15] They would then refine it together (often several times) before the letter finally went off.

---

12   Quoted in Sherrill Brown Wells, *Jean Monnet: Unconventional Statesman* p. 118.
13   Duchêne, op. cit., p. 11.
14   Duchêne, op. cit., p. 21.
15   Duchêne, op. cit., p. 13.

Not everyone who brings about change in society – academics, civil servants, diplomats, not to mention fashionable professionals like consultants – has to be elected in order to do so. In some ways Jean Monnet would have been perfect in the twenty-first century. He was a born networker or influencer. Nevertheless, Monnet's preferred way of working was essentially a top-down approach, where officials and political leaders were persuaded to improve their cooperation across different policy areas.

The crux of the matter was not that Monnet was undemocratic or an uncontrolled bureaucrat. The crux was that the lessons he learned from thirty years of very effective public service could not simply be imposed on strong governments with a clear electoral mandate. In this sense there was a democratic deficit in Monnet's approach, even if it was one that could be justified by the exigencies of wartime or the weaknesses of governments overseeing post war reconstruction. By 1958 that era was over in France. But it had been over in the UK for much longer, for more than a decade, ever since the Labour government was elected with a landslide majority in 1945.

The supranational option is adopted

The UK was not alone in its reluctance to give up inter-governmental arrangements. What has happened over the last 75 years in terms of relations between European states is misunderstood if it is simply seen as the UK *contra mundum*. If the UK, enthused by its going-it-alone wartime resistance, had a tendency towards nationalism, Monnet knew that in France there was a nationalistic spirit as strong as in the UK, one that sought to reassert the identity of a nation that had suffered (at least over much of its territory) occupation.

But he also knew that pressure was coming from the USA for European integration after World War Two, at least in the sense that there had to be a united front against the threat from the Soviet Union, just as there had to be a common policy for receiving Marshall Aid. That united front meant that West Germany would have to be brought into the equation – and for many in France bringing West Germany in was much more of a problem than operating independently of the UK.

This was the moment when the famous Schuman Plan was put forward by the French foreign minister. We can understand how it arose out of life experiences that would hardly have been matched across the Channel. Robert Schuman grew up in Lorraine, which was annexed by Bismarck after the Franco-

Prussian War in 1870. That meant he was a German citizen, conscripted into the German army in 1914 although declared unfit to serve. Then, after the redrawing of boundaries following the First World War, he became a French citizen. Such experiences were not unusual in a mainland of Europe where boundaries had proved fluid.[16] The sharing of sovereignty did not seem so revolutionary to someone who had grown used to sharing both territory and nationality.

Schuman grasped the importance of Monnet's idea. He made it clear that it was necessary to envisage something entirely new in international relations – something that hadn't been attempted between nation-states before. He explained this in the famous speech at the Salon d'Horloge of the French Foreign Ministry on 20th June 1950 quoted earlier:

> Never before has such a system that we advocate been tried out as a practical experiment. Never before have states delegated a fraction of their sovereignty jointly to an independent, supranational body. They have never even envisaged doing so.[17]

The Treaty of Westphalia was now three centuries old, and it had essentially established the principle of national sovereignty as the bedrock of international relations. The Treaty began as a way of ending the conflicts started by religious wars. But a principle which was intended to let states choose their own religion (effectively their own version of Christianity) could be expanded to let them have absolute control over anything that went on within their own borders. Treaties between states were desirable and indeed continued to be signed, but always on the understanding that they would never threaten this principle of national sovereignty.

Now Schuman was proposing to do something entirely different. He was going to break down the barriers to any binding legal arrangement above the level of the nation-state. The problem was that for all the emphasis in his speech at the Salon d'Horloge upon an experiment of historic dimensions in the way nations lived together, Schuman wasn't acting out of idealist zeal. He was acting because he saw Monnet's system as the only way out for France. It was the

---

16   Wells, Sherrill Brown *Jean Monnet: Unconventional Statesman*, p. 132.

17   Jean Monnet, *Memoirs*, translated from the French by Richard Mayne, p. 322. Note that this was said some six weeks after the famous declaration on May 9th (which led to May 9th being designated Europe Day). Schuman was spelling out the implications of his declaration at a conference of the six founders of the first supranational organisation, the European Coal and Steel Community.

only way in which to permit German economic recovery without losing a degree of control over German resurgence.[18] And German economic recovery was inevitable – why would America pour aid into West Germany with one hand and then limit its industrial development with the other? Necessity made Europeans of the French, just as necessity had made them accept the Monnet Plan for the modernisation of France. Managing German recovery was worth a dose of sovereignty-sharing to Schuman, as Paris had once been worth a mass to Henry IV. But those who do something because it is necessary are not always those best suited to defending its intrinsic merits or remaining passionately committed to it.

The fact that they were acting under constraint rather than from commitment was reflected in the hasty way in which the proposal was rushed through the French Cabinet. It was the day before a tripartite meeting of the British, French and U.S. foreign ministers, and when the three ministers met the UK foreign minister, Ernest Bevin, was not pleased that he hadn't been consulted on the decisions taken the day before. He accused the other two of plotting behind his back. The British ambassador of the time commented with some justice that the plan succeeded by 'shock tactics' which had prevented the plan being 'strangled at birth'.[19] Not only had Schuman avoided any public campaign to popularise his approach, he hadn't even tried to convince his own cabinet of its value!

Thus, the moment of triumph for Monnet came by having his plan adopted by a man who didn't even bother to argue its case with his cabinet colleagues, let alone the wider population. It was introduced to solve the intractable problem of constraining a Germany that the United States was determined to strengthen against Communist aggression. It was not introduced as a way of countering the curse of nationalism which had laid waste a continent over half a century, if not for half a millennium. Those sentiments were perhaps there, in Schuman as well as Monnet, but they never came to the fore. The revolution (which it certainly was) was a silent one, and they are always vulnerable to a backlash.

---

18   'By 1950 it was clear to many that West Germany had to be allowed to rebuild if it was to play a useful role in the western alliance, but this would best be done under the auspices of a supranational organisation that would tie West Germany into the wider process of European reconstruction.' McCormick, John *Understanding the European Union*, 5th Edition, p. 53.

19   Duchêne, op. cit., p. 201.

The flaws in the Monnet system

In its final form, the Coal and Steel Community contained (at Dutch insistence) a Council of Ministers, which would vote (without unanimity being required) on policies proposed by the High Authority. The High Authority thus had the right of initiative which has now become the prerogative of the European Commission in most policy areas. One can therefore see how even when the first sovereignty-sharing arrangements were put into place back in the 1950s, Monnet's traditional way of working was reflected in them. The High Authority, of which he was the first President, was like the *Commissariat du Plan*, a body of people who had ideas and then took them to those with influence – in this case the politicians who formed the Council of Ministers.[20] As President of the High Authority, Monnet was operating as he had when he managed to get his first appointment with René Viviani soon after the outbreak of the First World War. It was no different from the way he had taken ideas about the Monnet Plan and presented them on the shifting sands of political authority in the French Fourth Republic.

A Court of Justice was established in Luxembourg, since the enforcement of decisions made by the High Authority would require them to have the force of law in the individual member-states. There was one other institution that formed part of the make-up of the European Coal and Steel Community, a common assembly (made up of delegates from national parliaments) but it only met once a year – Duchêne compared it to the annual shareholders meeting of a firm.[21] This was the forerunner of the European Parliament in the present day, and arguably an essential feature ensuring that the Community had popular support. But characteristically, Monnet didn't recognise its importance. If one assumes a simple continuity between the assembly of the Coal and Steel Community, the later assembly of the European Economic Community and the eventual creation of a European Parliament, one can say that this body had no direct elections for the first thirty years of its existence (until 1979), since when it has steadily acquired more authority, initially as a body that had to be consulted and later one that had the power of 'co-decision' with the Council of Ministers in most policy areas, effectively granting it the power of veto over what

---

20   See Duchêne, François *Jean Monnet: First Statesman of Interdependence*, chapter 6: 'Europe's breakthrough', pp 181–225.

21   Duchêne, François *Jean Monnet: First Statesman of Interdependence*, p. 210.

was passed into European law. But that development took half a century, and there are still important ways in which it could be strengthened.

This provides some indication of the 'democratic deficit' in the EU inherited from Monnet. The European Parliament is clearly not the policy leader that many think it should be. It is still imbued with the spirit of the French Fourth Republic, where Jean Monnet sought the blessing of one prime minister after another for getting on with the business of implementing the right plan for rebuilding France. The result is that the EU loses out twice over. On the one hand, the right of initiative means that the Commission is attacked for the way that the unelected 'bureaucrats in Brussels' decide everything. On the other hand, since nothing proposed based on that right of initiative gets anywhere without the consent of both the Council and the Parliament, the Commission in reality decides nothing and frequently fails to get its way. The EU has developed a system in which it looks as if the 'eurocrats' decide everything when in fact they decide only one thing, namely what will be passed on for decision by others. But that alone is enough to undermine the whole idea of 450 million people sending 700 representatives to Strasbourg to implement their wishes.

If Monnet himself had recognised the importance of embedding a complicated institutional structure in the popular mind, what was to develop over the next fifty years might not have been so readily seen as an elitist invention. The sharing of sovereignty needed to be understood and recognised as a popular cause, a way of cementing the end of conflict and making peace among nations something viable in a way it had not proved to be over the last few centuries. An effective parliament would have helped to provide that support. But appealing to popular sentiment was not Monnet's way of working, while Robert Schuman, as we have seen, despite recognising the significance of Monnet's idea, had no desire to popularise it. So a nod was made to popular representation in the form of an assembly filled with delegates seconded from national parliaments, a provision likely to fill it with those whom national leaders wanted out of the way or who could be bought off with the prospect of savouring the delights (such as they were) of Brussels.

Conclusion

The European Coal and Steel Community was something new, creating institutions to which nation-states voluntarily ceded the power to make decisions that were binding upon them. Monnet's experience throughout the early part of his life, from the time of his management of wheat supplies during the First World War and through a lifetime of successes and failures, had convinced him of one thing which is clearly expressed by his friend George Ball:

> Monnet had seen the failure of many well-intentioned efforts to achieve co-operation among governments, and those examples had convinced him that unless national governments were to transfer substantive power to some supranational institution, the result would be mere organized impotence. That had been the case with other international institutions formed.[22]

This willingness to be bound by the decisions of an institution which a group of nation-states voluntarily agreed to create is the key to supranationalism. It should have been launched with great fanfare to proclaim that this was the way to cement peace in a continent which had been devastated by war. In practice, it was the only way of getting France out of a hole, just as for Germany it was a way of helping to ensure, despite the steady disclosure of the awful things that had happened during the holocaust, that the country survived with even a limited control of its own affairs. No popular movement had grown up demanding that national governments share sovereignty as a way of curing their centuries-old antagonisms. Governments were pushed into the system as a way of dealing with the problems of the moment.

Monnet forced the Community into being by the brilliance of his network-ing and his persuasive skills with the movers and shakers. Yet it had flaws in its design which reflected the insufficient value he gave to gleaning popular support. At a time of weak political management, he succeeded in persuad-ing enough politicians to bring the Coal and Steel Community into being. Its structure reflected the way of bringing about change he had always been used to. Create a High Authority of the great and the good taken from the differ-ent member states and let these 'little Monnets' persuade the politicians (in the Council of Ministers) to adopt their ideas. If they did, make sure you have put in place a legal body to enforce their decisions. If a 'national assembly' is thrown into the mix, let it be hand-chosen from national parliaments and play a role more of overseeing than initiating. Arguably that is the role of the Eu-ropean Parliament even today, despite its being elected by all EU voters and despite the fact that it has the power of co-decision, meaning that it can veto proposals for new legislation. It does not have the power to initiate legislation and therefore there is no sense of a Parliament being elected on a manifesto

---

22   Duchêne, op. cit., p. 10.

placed before the people and then drawing up legislation to implement what the electorate have voted for. This is perhaps the main reason why turn-out for European elections remains very low.

What was left out of the equation was a role for *the popular will as the agent of change*. The limited role of the Assembly, which struggled for a generation to become a directly elected Parliament and even then lacked and lacks significant powers, followed directly from this. The European Parliament plays a role more of keeping what is frequently referred to as the 'executive' (the Commission) in check rather than driving forward policies of its own, or rather the policies demanded by the voters in elections. As a later chapter tries to show, it is inconceivable that the present institutional structure of the European Union can continue like this, irrespective of UK withdrawal.[23] Even if one is deeply opposed to the decision by the UK to leave the European Union, one should not ignore the structural faults within that Union itself. Though this book will argue that in order to survive the British Union will have to adopt some of the institutional arrangements of its European counterpart, not least the sharing of sovereignty, one should not suppose that those European institutions can or should remain in their present form.

Monnet became something of a prophet without honour in his own country after de Gaulle rose to the presidency and even for a while afterwards. It was François Mitterand who as President of France moved Monnet's remains to the Pantheon in Paris. It has been suggested that this was partly because Monnet supported his bid to defeat de Gaulle in the presidential elections of 1965, but his admiration for Monnet surely goes beyond that. He genuinely saw the man from Cognac as providing a means to reign in the destructive consequences of unbridled nationalism. In a speech to the European Parliament in 1995, the year in which his fourteen years in the French presidency came to an end, he remarked that *Nationalisme? C'est la guerre.* (Nationalism means war). It was an appropriate remark for a decade when five wars in South-East Europe, not to mention the present conflict in Ukraine, caused tens of thousands of deaths and hundreds of thousands of exiles, showing that much of Europe was and is still capable of exploding into violent conflict. It is with Mitterrand's remark that Vernon Bogdanor concludes his recent work *Britain and Europe in a Troubled World*.[24]

---

23   See chapter 16, 'On embedding the Upward Cascade'.

24   Bogdanor, Vernon *Britain and Europe in a Troubled World*, p. 145.

None of this, however, alters the fact that Monnet paid far too little attention to the need for his ideas to win popular support. The same is true of those he persuaded to implement them. Just as Monnet underplayed the importance of the popular will as agent of change, so the politicians he influenced did little to explain to their electorates why it was such an important idea. The consequences of this were to haunt the Community for decades to come, just as they haunt it now. In particular, they were to affect the way in which the UK understood its membership of the European Economic Community and later the European Union. To this we now turn.

Chapter Six: The long road towards British entry

The last chapter looked in some detail at Jean Monnet's early life and work up to the end of the 1940s. It emphasised his firm embrace of what came to be called the supranational option rather than the inter-governmental, but it also tried to explain why he did little to popularise his idea and why in certain crucial respects it was flawed. This chapter looks at a development that was doubtless affected by that omission – the long, tortuous process by which the UK finally secured entry to what was called at the time the European Economic Community.

There have been plenty of books covering the developments leading to Britain's entry to the EEC and the country's later departure from the EU.[1] This book retraces the steps of the country's accession and later departure solely in terms of Britain's reluctance to embrace the supranational option, something that is frequently misinterpreted or underplayed in the literature. It is the contention of this book that a refusal to share sovereignty has always been fundamental to the UK position but has not been sufficiently recognised. It is in the context of trying to defend this position that the book explores the history of the UK's relations with the EEC and later the EU. It will then seek to show that the sharing of sovereignty will be crucial to the establishment of a viable British Union post-Brexit.

---

1 Philip Stephens' *Britain Alone: The Path from Suez to Brexit* provides an excellent narrative of the main events. Britain's struggles with Europe should always be read with an eye to the wider European context. See Ian Kershaw's *Rollercoaster: Europe 1950–2017* and (still a masterpiece, despite its age), Tony Judt's *Postwar: A History of Europe since 1945*. Alasdair Blair's most recent edition of *The European Union since 1945* is an excellent summary of events up to and including the Treaty of Lisbon, and contains useful excerpts from key documents as part of the Seminar studies in history series. I try to summarise the history of the EU's development from a UK perspective in *The European Union: An Introduction* Chapter 2: History, pp. 9–50.

The Labour government and supranationalism

The first serious engagement of the UK with supranationalism after World War Two came over the Marshall Plan. The allocation of aid was organised through the Organisation for European Economic Cooperation (OEEC) and the US was resistant to any system where there was a unanimity rule – in effect where one country could exercise a national veto over the details of the aid programme. The foreign secretary in the Labour government formed after World War II, Ernest Bevin, helped to co-ordinate the recovery plans of 16 European states and turn them into a single programme. Despite US opposition, he insisted that that the OEEC must not become the sort of supranational body with real powers that Monnet was keen on. That would simply mean what he called a 'bunch of intrusive middlemen' inserting themselves into the decision process, which should be left to national governments.[2]

The UK had come out of a six-year war which it was more likely to see as a war between one nation-state and another than as a common act of resistance across national boundaries against the menace of fascism. Unlike countries that had been occupied, it saw its institutions as exonerated by a common act of resistance rather than compromised by the dilemma of occupation. Moreover, this was the first ever Labour government with a working majority. Any suggestion of sharing power with others, whether at home or abroad, was anathema.

Many on the British Left in the 1940s were intensely patriotic, believing that patriotism could be a vehicle for social reform. It is important to bear in mind a point made by Eric Hobsbawm, namely that the original meaning of patriots was not right-wing flag-wavers but what Hobsbawm called 'disturbers of government,' people who wanted to show their love of country by reforming it or even by revolution. That sense of people creating a nation by asserting their rights as citizens must be set against the way in which patriotism was later hijacked by the Right in the late nineteenth century. It was turned into a means of converting the beneficiaries of a broader franchise, which included many

---

2   See Bogdanor, Vernon *Beyond Brexit: Towards a British Constitution*, pp. 24–25. Bogdanor describes Bevin's famous remark on the Council of Europe 'If you open that Pandora's box, you never know what Trojan horses will jump out' as 'perhaps the most prescient remark ever made about Britain's involvement with the European movement' (p. 25).

poorer voting citizens, to reactionary governments that offered to defend them against external enemies.[3]

Furthermore, post-war decolonisation took the form of national movements demanding and winning independence from colonial régimes. Patriotic feeling, Hobsbawm points out, could prove an effective agent of social change, as it had done both in colonies resisting their imperial controllers and in nations resisting Hitler and fascism.[4] Patriotism was an integral part of rebuilding the UK after the war, with the first ever Labour government to enjoy a working majority elected in 1945 under the slogan 'Now, let's win the peace!' The Labour leader, Clement Attlee, had fought in the First World War (he was at Gallipoli) and was determined that a country 'fit for heroes' would be built after the Second World War in the way it had not been after the First. Socialism was to be implemented by a victorious nation after a huge national effort.

In this context, proposals to get together with other countries came to be seen as impediments to realising this aim of national renewal. Hence the widespread resistance to an agreement like that proposed by Robert Schuman in 1949. Sovereignty-sharing was seen less as a way of embedding peace in Europe than as a way of frustrating British plans for social reform. To many on the Left the supranational projects associated with Monnet looked more like a vehicle for right-wing ideas. The Coal and Steel Community was viewed as an industrial cartel, the later European Economic Community as a capitalist club of rich nations.[5]

It was perfectly clear by 1949, as the post war European order began to take shape, that the UK wanted to avoid any arrangements that were not inter-gov-

---

3   Hobsbawm, Eric *Nations and Nationalism since 1780*. See especially Chapter Two, 'Popular proto-nationalism'.

4   See the chapter 'Nationalism in the late twentieth century' in Hobsbawm, Eric *Nations and Nationalism since 1780*, pp. 163–192.

5   Alex May in his useful book as part of the *Seminar Studies in History* series, *Britain and Europe since 1945* (although being published in 1999 it covers only the years up to the Blair government elected in 1997) points out that 'the Labour government had nationalised coal and was committed to the nationalisation of steel, whereas the Schuman Plan appeared to involve the formation of an effective cartel, run in the interests of industrialists.' He then quotes Herbert Morrison's famous remark about the Schuman Plan, 'the Durham miners won't wear it!' May, Alex *Britain and Europe since 1945*, p.18. Note also that the association of the Coal and Steel Community with a 'cartel' is still held by some on the Left, such as Yanis Varoufakis. See his *And the Weak suffer What They Must?*, p. 58, where he talks of building the new Europe on 'a cartel of big business'.

ernmental. It believed government representatives should meet their counterparts from other nations and seek to reach unanimous agreement on joint action. If a single member state found a proposal unacceptable, then the proposal should be withdrawn. The only unclear thing about the UK's attitude was whether it was happy for everyone else to adopt a sovereignty-sharing programme, even if it refused to do so itself.

Rejection of the Coal and Steel Community

Once Schuman's announcement from the Salon d'Horloge made clear that the UK could not prevent the Coal and Steel Community from happening, it attempted to change it (despite refusing to be a member) into something intergovernmental. That, essentially, was the Eden Plan, for by the time it was attempted the Labour government had fallen (in 1951) and the new foreign secretary was the Conservative Anthony Eden. The Eden Plan was an attempt to subordinate the European Coal and Steel Community (ECSC) to another recently formed body, the Council of Europe. However, the Council of Europe was a very different animal to the Coal and Steel Community. It was not – and is not – a sovereignty-sharing body. Set up by ten states, including the UK, in London in May 1949, it had a Consultative Assembly as well as a Council of Ministers, but the UK insisted on a national veto in the Council of Ministers.[6] This meant that the consultative assembly could not decide anything without unanimity, a condition that often led to it deciding nothing of importance. It simply gravitated towards those policy areas where it could manage to get everyone to agree. The body soon became little more than a talking shop, an organisation (now of about fifty states) which offends no one precisely because it cannot make rules binding upon anyone.[7] The Eden Plan was designed to en-

---

6   Duchêne writes that 'the British insistence on the national veto in the Council of Ministers left the limp hand to the Consultative Assembly, not the governments' Duchêne, François *Jean Monnet: First Statesman of Interdependence*, p. 187. Duchêne concludes that 'Though the assembly attracted glittering names. it soon became a byword as a talking-shop' (p. 187).

7   This is perhaps a little unfair. Russia has recently left the Council of Europe in anticipation of being expelled after its invasion of Ukraine, Belarus has never been accepted as a member owing to its retaining the death penalty and the UK has recently found its attempt to deport refugees to Rwanda thwarted (or at least delayed) by the Council. Broadly speaking, however, it remains little more than a talking shop.

sure that institutions which worked on the basis of sharing sovereignty would be dissolved in (the image used at the time was sugar being dissolved in tea) institutions that did not.

However, the Eden plan was rejected by the Six who had signed the Treaty of Paris bringing the Coal and Steel Community into being and the ECSC kept its supranational form. Then 1951 saw a new problem emerging. Shortly after the Schuman plan was launched, North Korea attacked the South and the Korean War began. Immediately alarm bells rang in Europe. If communists were going to exploit a divided Korea, what might they do to exploit a divided Germany? Could Soviet troops take the opportunity to move westwards and what might stop them? The result was both additional support for a European army and increasing demands from the USA for higher levels of European commitment to the defence of Western Europe. For the French, there was a similar dilemma to that which had led to the Schuman Plan – either refuse to allow German revival (in this case military rather than economic) or find a way of managing it at the European level. Such a way emerged through the so-called Pleven Plan (named after the French Minister of Defence René Pleven), a proposal for a European army with a European Minister of Defence, a joint commander, common budget and common arms procurement. But this time the plan fell through. In 1954, when the European Defence Community (EDC) proposal came up for ratification, the Communist Left and the Gaullist Right in the French assembly combined to prevent the plan from being ratified. The political candle was burning at both ends.

Once the demise of the EDC was clear, the UK moved in with its familiar inter-governmental alternative. A conference was held in London in the early autumn of 1954, where it was agreed to incorporate Germany into NATO's integrated command structure under American leadership. The UK re-committed itself to the Western European Union set up by the Treaty of Brussels in 1947, assuring other members that it would not withdraw its troops from the continent without agreement from the other members of the Union. It had never given such a commitment to the proposed European Defence Community. The familiar world of intergovernmentalism had returned and to many inside the UK it seemed as if it was the Coal and Steel Community that had been out of place, a supranational hiccup on the way to establishing a sound post war order.

The Treaties of Rome

The setback over the European Defence Community produced two very different reactions. In Monnet's case, it led to a redoubling of his commitment to supranationalism. He resigned as President of the High Authority and formed a so-called Action Committee for a United States of Europe. The choice of terms was unfortunate. Monnet did not see his Action Committee as pushing for a single federal nation-state on the east of the Atlantic to match the single federal nation-state to the West of the Atlantic. That would have done no more than make Europe another large nation-state among the 200 or so unregulated nation-states, some of them minnows and some of them sharks, swimming around in the world aquarium and occasionally gobbling each other up. It would have been like creating another Italy or Germany or even another Britain. Monnet did not want to build a superstate. He wanted to build a new relationship among nation-states that went on being nation-states.[8]

The Action Committee he founded was in no way a mass movement and didn't try to be one. It was a pressure group of 100 influential people, mostly union leaders and leaders of political parties from the Six (later on representatives of three UK parties joined). In Monnet's own words from his *Memoirs*, it was made up of people who'd 'move the political and union machinery led by them'.[9] In the twenty years of its existence, it certainly exercised an important influence. But it made no attempt to turn European integration into a mass movement.[10]

The area that now appealed most to Monnet for extending supranationalism was that of atomic energy. A civil nuclear power community would be in the same field as coal and steel, the energy field, rather than taking on a new field like defence. It had the glamour of the 'atomic age' and could be presented as nations pooling their resources to achieve together a 'new industrial revolution' which they could hardly manage on their own. If a coal and steel community had been sold to people as a means of taking the industries used to fuel the war effort and making them instead instruments to promote peace, an atomic energy community could be sold as a way of entering the future rather than of

---

8   See 'Introducing the Quagga', pp. 1–3 of my *The European Union: An Introduction*.

9   Monnet, *Memoirs*, p. 609.

10   See Szele, Bálint 'The European Lobby: The Action Committee for a United States of Europe' *European Integration Studies* Vol. 4 No. 2 (2005), pp. 109–119, here p. 110.

simply avoiding the mistakes of the past. It had all the attractions of modernity. And more controversially, it could provide a means of restraining states from using atomic power to develop nuclear weapons. This would require a system of mandatory controls and the sort of oversight of the whole atomic energy programme that the High Authority had attempted in coal and steel. Indeed, it was an area where everyone accepted the need for regulation, not least the free-market Americans. Nuclear power, Duchêne concludes, was 'God's gift to integrators'.[11]

There were difficulties. In the atomic energy field, there was the problem of France's determination to be a nuclear power, not least because the UK had just done the same. It was becoming clear by the autumn of 1956 that France would insist on developing its nuclear deterrent. But as so many times before, Monnet found a way out of the difficulty through the support of the United States.[12] There is no doubt that the USA was once again willing to exercise political pressure on the Western Europeans to restart the integration programme that had begun with the Coal and Steel Community. In the event work on what was to become EURATOM, the European Atomic Energy Community, proceeded alongside proposals for a European Economic Community (EEC) or Common Market.

The USA was coming to the rescue of supranationalism once again. It was a system that was anathema to the United States itself, but many American leaders felt that it was an ideal arrangement for creating some order among those small countries on the other side of the Atlantic who seemed to be forever falling out. Churchill's famous words about the US and the UK as 'friends and sponsors' of a new Europe applied far more to the USA, that wanted a stable neighbour overseas but felt no need to join their system, than it did to the UK, which was unable to remain detached from whatever system emerged. Indeed, U.S. enthusiasm for European integration could annoy the British. Former Prime Minister Anthony Eden in his *Memoirs* declared that the Americans were pushing Western Europe into something that the UK regarded as dangerous.[13]

---

11   Duchêne, François. *Jean Monnet: First Statesman of Interdependence*, p. 265.

12   Duchêne, François *Jean Monnet: First Statesman of Interdependence*, pp. 292–299. Note the comment on p. 298: 'The Americans, through Adenauer, had again proved the ultimate weapon in Monnet's armoury.'

13   See Eden, Anthony. *Memoirs: Full Circle*, pp. 265–312.

But what of the UK's reaction in those fateful months leading up to the Treaties of Rome? It was invited to participate in the negotiations but seems to have done so rather half-heartedly. An official from the Board of Trade (no one high-ranking) turned up at the first meeting of foreign ministers in Messina and rarely spoke except to express a preference for a free trade area, the devil he knew, over whatever the others had in mind. Negotiations continued at the chateau of Val-Duchesse, outside Brussels, where the French diplomat and politician Jean-François Deniau reported that the British official present 'never opened his mouth unless it was to insert his pipe.' Andrew Duff quotes Deniau's account of what the official said when he finally opened his mouth for the purpose of speaking:

> Mr. Chairman, Gentlemen. I would like to thank you sincerely for your hospitality and to let you know that it is going to cease from today. Indeed, I am going back to London. As a responsible official, it bothers me if I am wasting my time and failing to justify the modest expense I am costing my government. I have followed your works sympathetically and with interest. I must tell you that (a) the future treaty you are talking about and are tasked with drafting here has no chance of being concluded; (b) if it is concluded it has no chance of being ratified; (c) if it is ratified it has no chance of being applied. Moreover, please note, that if it were, it would be totally unacceptable to Great Britain. You are talking of agriculture which we don't like, of customs dues on which we have nothing to say, and of institutions which horrify us.[14]

He then left the room wishing them all '*bonne chance*' (Good luck). Deniau possibly put words into the official's mouth in his report.[15] Nevertheless, the mix of incomprehension, indifference and hostility is not inappropriate as a description of the British position in these years. Philip Stephens records that when a French official had asked his British counterpart whether London would be represented in Messina, the reply had been that it was 'a devilish awkward place to expect a minister to get to.'[16]

The Spaak Committee, named after the Belgian foreign minister Paul-Henri Spaak, submitted its report in April 1956 on the creation of a common European market. By now it was clear that supranationalism was not a unique venture in the area of coal and steel which had effectively been put back in its

---

14   Quoted in Andrew Duff. *Britain and the Puzzle of European Union*, p. 16.
15   See J-F. Deniau *L'Europe Interdite*, p. 59 for the original French.
16   Stephens, Philip. *Britain alone: The Path from Suez to Brexit*, p. 89.

box by the failure of the European Defence Community and was now destined to go no further.

The UK continued to expostulate as the EEC (European Economic Community) came into being. Sir David Eccles, the President of the Board of Trade, attacked EEC institutions in July 1957 as 'irresponsible aggregates' of European civil servants. It echoed Ernest Bevin's complaint about 'intrusive middlemen' when it was suggested that the OEEC, the organisation coordinating Marshall Aid, might become a supranational body with real powers, able to override national governments in applying the Marshall Plan. When asked why he thought EEC institutions irresponsible, Eccles explained that it was because 'they were not answerable to the House of Commons'.[17] It was a classic expression of the view that nothing could have authority above that of national parliaments.

Harold MacMillan, who became Prime Minister in 1957, the year the Treaties of Rome were signed, was no more understanding. He had a less accommodating view of what was proposed than anyone would imagine from Winston Churchill's language ten years earlier at a Congress in the Hague. Gone was the enthusiasm for an integrated Europe, with the US and UK as 'friends and sponsors.' This was neither friend nor sponsor, but an adversary responsible for dangerous developments across the Channel. If the Common Market reminded MacMillan of anything, it was a continental blockade.[18]

British governments could understand the need for Europeans to talk to one another. But they could not understand the language about a European level of decision-making and control. They could make no sense of what is at the heart of a supranational approach, namely that one must go above the level of the nation-state in order to solve the problems of the nation-state. They could only see another attempt by a single power (or maybe more than one) to dominate the continent. If you genuinely believe a sovereignty-sharing body is less a close relationship between states than an artifice to create a new and more powerful state out of several smaller ones, then you are bound to perceive it as another behemoth upsetting the balance of power on the continent, another Philip II, Louis XIV, Napoleon or even Hitler (an analogy the UK Prime

---

17   James Ellison, 'Britain and the Treaties of Rome 1955–59' in Roger Broad and Virginia Preston, eds., *Moored to the Continent? Britain and European Integration* p. 42.

18   May, Alex *Britain and Europe since 1945*, p. 30. In the documents at the end May quotes Macmillan writing shortly after he became Prime Minister that the UK needed to counteract 'what Little Europe was doing to us. We should fight back with every weapon in our armoury' (see p. 104).

Minister Boris Johnson was not above making sixty years later). You insist that there is no halfway house between the system of nation-states acting independently and the creation of a superstate in which existing countries are turned into little more than regions. There is simply no room for a Third Way. That is still the perspective of many in the UK, whether from the Left or the Right of the political spectrum.

The UK tries to join

When the European Economic Community had come into being, the UK went on trying to influence proceedings from without, once again trying to throw an intergovernmental spoke into the supranational wheel. In the case of the ECSC the spoke in the wheel had taken the form of the Eden Plan. This time the spoke was the European Free Trade Area (EFTA) proposed by Harold Macmillan, which came into being on 1st January 1960. Despite the difference between a common market (which has a common external tariff) and a free trade area, the UK hoped that it could somehow smother the former with the latter – or that the market could melt in EFTA like that proverbial lump of sugar in a cup of tea.[19]

The threat of a free trade area dominated by the British encouraged de Gaulle to soften his attitude towards the Common Market. it might have been expected that the EEC would flounder once General de Gaulle returned to power in France in the year after the Treaties of Rome were signed (he became President in 1958). Certainly, he sought to move towards the intergovernmental form of cooperation that he (like the British) preferred. But he was also forced to recognise, as the British were not, that the 'Monnet system' brought many advantages to his country. He therefore chided the Community, declared his undying hostility to any supranationalist ideas, and then let them continue to work in favour of France.

---

19   See Duchêne, François *Jean Monnet: First Statesman of Interdependence*, pp. 236–7. Monnet called the Eden Plan 'a most dangerous suggestion' and Duchêne comments that 'it seemed to him another British gambit to influence the community without paying the membership fee' (p. 237). In fact, it was more like an attempt to change the rules of the club. For a reference to the Common Market melting in the Free Trade Area 'like a lump of sugar in a cup of tea,' see p. 320.

Hence, to angry denunciations of 'France the Wrecker' in the *Times* news-paper, de Gaulle made sure that the sugar was kept out of the tea – all discussions of relations between the Common Market and the Free Trade Area must cease.[20] The EEC would pursue its own independent trade policy with the rest of the world – and it would pursue it in a collective manner, with the Commission negotiating on behalf of the member states on trade. De Gaulle could not change the Common Market into a purely inter-governmental body without making it ineffective. To defend it against Britain's EFTA alternative, he had no alternative but to support the supranationalism he disliked so much in principle.

Given Whitehall insouciance and hostility towards supranationalism, it might appear remarkable that within four years the UK reacted to the successful establishment of the European Economic Community – and the failure to replace it with something along the lines of EFTA – by pressing for entry itself to the organisation it had tried to smother at birth or dilute out of existence. Macmillan was often chided for being 'last in and first out' where the Suez Crisis was concerned; his U-turn over the EEC was just as marked. Duchêne recalls how Monnet and Macmillan walked side by side to the Senate House in the University of Cambridge to collect honorary degrees.[21] A month later Macmillan, now Prime Minister, applied to join the EEC. The first formal application was made in 1961. The Conservatives were still in power. Harold Macmillan was now Prime Minister. It was just five years since he had said to de Gaulle: *The Common Market is the Continental system all over again, Britain cannot accept it. I beg you to give it up.*[22]

How did it happen? How on earth could the UK join a system which enshrined the principle which all along they had bitterly opposed, that of sharing sovereignty? One reason is that many who favoured entry believed that once in they could lead the new Community in a different direction. They'd failed to

---

20   The story of the UK's first application and the veto from de Gaulle is nicely told in the chapter entitled 'A Thousand Years of History' in Philip Stephens' *Britain Alone*, pp. 71–103. For a reference to France the Wrecker, see Duchêne, François *Jean Monnet: First Statesman of Interdependence*, p. 321.

21   Duchêne, François. *Jean Monnet: First Statesman of Interdependence*, p. 326.

22   As recorded by de Gaulle in his *Memoirs of Hope*, p.188. For an excellent discussion of Macmillan's attitudes to the EEC, see Bogdanor, Vernon *Britain and Europe in a Troubled World*, chapter 2: 'The Pandora's Box and the Trojan Horses', pp. 43–79. Macmillan's words to de Gaulle are discussed on p. 50.

change it from without; now they'd have a chance to change it from within.[23] This suggests that by applying to join the UK was not giving up its delusions; it would be more apt to say that it was taking its delusions with it as it sought to enter the Community.

A second application followed in 1966, under Harold Wilson as Labour Prime Minister. By now the Commonwealth was even more clearly a dwindling source of trade as compared to the EEC than it had been at the beginning of the decade. The economic case for joining the EEC, which had already been clear in the early 1960s was becoming overwhelming, now that the Six had developed into what an official report to ministers in 1966 called a 'group of advanced industrial countries forming a tariff-free area comparable in size with the United States and the USSR.'[24] By the late sixties the UK was beginning to lose some of its illusions. Alex May records that 'a story went the rounds in London at this time, that Macmillan had left a black box in Downing Street, to be opened by a future prime minister in a moment of despair. Inside was a simple message: "Join the Common Market".[25]

Yet despite the fact that the EEC had been up and running for nearly a decade, the UK government (now with a Labour Prime Minister) still seemed to imagine that it would transform the Community once the UK had been allowed in. In his memoirs *In My Way*, the Labour Foreign Secretary, George Brown, describes how once inside the Community Britain was 'destined to become *the* leader of Europe' (his italics).[26] This was a delusion. The longer the Community remained up and running without Britain, the more difficult it would be to bend the Community to British interests – far more difficult than it had been for France, as a founder member, to bend it to French interests.

---

23   Wolfram Kaiser in 'Party Games: The British EEC Application of 1961 and 1967' points out that the man who became foreign secretary in 1966, George Brown, was convinced that Britain was 'destined to be *the* leader of Europe,' controlling 'a new European bloc which would have the same power and influence in the world as the old British Commonwealth had in days gone by.' See Broad, Roger and Preston, Virginia (eds.), *Moored to the Continent? Britain and European Integration*, p. 64.

24   The report, entitled 'Future Relations with Europe', was published on 5th April 1966, one year before the UK's second unsuccessful application to join the EEC, this time under a Labour government. See Broad, Roger and Preston, Virginia, (eds), *Moored to the Continent? Britain and European Integration*, pp. 64–65.

25   Alex May, *Britain and Europe since 1945*, p. 42.

26   Brown, George *In My Way. the Political Memoirs of Lord George-Brown*, pp. 209–211.

In any case, the second application was vetoed by de Gaulle just like the first one. It was clear that British entry would be postponed until after de Gaulle was out of office, and the prospect of assuming the leadership mantle of the Community once it had become a member would then be even more remote.

It was only after de Gaulle's resignation in February 1969 that the way was clear for a third British application which had a real chance of success. Moreover, the EEC of 1971 had moved significantly in the direction of a more intergovernmental organisation than it had been ten years earlier. The Labour government produced a White Paper recommending entry in February 1970, shortly before it unexpectedly fell from office. It described the EEC as follows:

> The practical working of the Community accordingly reflects the reality that sovereign governments are represented round the table. On a question where a government considers that vital national interests are involved, it is established that the decision should be unanimous.[27]

This was strictly speaking correct. Ever since the Luxembourg Compromise of 1967, it had been agreed that if a member state considered an issue to be of vital national interest, it could veto any decision surrounding that issue which it disliked. The Labour government was therefore suggesting that the EEC was not a sovereignty-sharing body. This was not correct. We need to bear in mind that the institutions of the Community were not just determined by what could be proposed and passed into law in the future. There was also the matter of accepting at the national level any laws that had already been passed at the European level, transposing them into national legislation and complying with them. That part of the system remained in place. Through the so-called 'Empty Chair Crisis' of 1966–7, when de Gaulle withdrew French representatives from EEC meetings and effectively business ground to a halt until the Luxembourg Compromise ended the crisis, the French president had managed to limit the number of laws that could be passed in the future, but he had not tampered with the way in which whatever had already been passed into law (and in prin-

---

27   See the White Paper on Britain and the European Communities (Command Paper No. 4289). It was discussed in the House of Commons and the Hansard record shows that many of the arguments about what became the European Union have not changed, though one may feel that the standard of debate has fallen. See https://hansard.parliament.uk/commons/1970-02-24/debates/e0025b00-cb04-4 60c-b2d7-7a5fc6dc457f/BritainAndTheEuropeanCommunities(WhitePaper)

ciple might be passed into law in the future) was binding upon the member states.

The real point of the Luxembourg Compromise, from the French point of view, was that arrangements made in the 1960s could be set in stone and could not be reversed.[28] De Gaulle was effectively ensuring that if Britain did eventually join it couldn't remove the aspects of the EEC which it didn't like. The Luxembourg Compromise was a way of freezing the EEC in its present form in order to ensure that the UK could neither alter established arrangements that benefited France, like the Common Agricultural Policy, nor introduce any new arrangements once it had joined that didn't suit French interests.

This was the apparent paradox of the UK's relations with de Gaulle. De Gaulle's vetoes presented the UK as essentially different from the other members of the Six, including France, whether because it was too tied to the United States or too 'maritime' in its outlook, looking to the wider seas rather than to the continent it belonged to. And yet, whatever the validity of these observations, in one respect de Gaulle and the UK were on precisely the same wavelength. They favoured inter-governmentalism, opposed supranational structures and were highly suspicious (in de Gaulle's case contemptuous) of the ideas of Jean Monnet. De Gaulle's advocacy of a 'L'Europe des Patries' was essentially in accord with the UK's belief that it was national governments that must ultimately call the shots in any grouping of nations. Harold Macmillan, the Prime Minister who led the UK's first application to join the EEC, recognised this only too well:

> The strange feature of the present situation is the paradox that de Gaulle wants the kind of Europe we would be able readily to join, but he doesn't want us in it (L'Europe à l'anglais sans les anglais). As so often before I found it difficult to fathom the character of this strange and enigmatic man.[29]

It is not, perhaps, so very difficult to fathom what de Gaulle was up to. He wanted a European bloc that was large enough to dominate Europe, but small enough to be dominated by France. But the upshot was that in the light of the

---

28   Bogdanor, Vernon *Britain and Europe in a Troubled World*, chapter 2: 'The Pandora's Box and the Trojan Horses', pp. 43–79. Bogdanor sums up the precise reasons for the Luxembourg Compromise and why the UK was in two minds about it on p. 69.

29   Macmillan, Harold. *At the End of the Day*. Quoted in Duff, *Britain and the Puzzle of European Union* p. 19.

Luxembourg compromise the UK could persuade itself that it was not joining a supranational organisation at all.

A White Paper issued in February 1971 under the new Conservative government of Edward Heath referred to the Luxembourg Compromise and emphasised the implication that sovereign governments would be sitting around a table and deciding whether their vital interests were at stake when considering any new proposal – precisely the sort of approach that could describe the workings of the Council of Europe.[30] Hence the Conservative government, like its Labour predecessor, presented the EEC as if it wasn't a sovereignty-sharing body. Like its Labour predecessor, it ignored the fact that the veto which could apply to any new legislation did not apply to what had already been agreed and the method by which it was implemented, namely European Law which was binding upon member states, and which overrode national law in the areas to which it applied. That system still stood. Moreover, if the Community resolved to abandon the principles of the Luxembourg Compromise in times to come, then the system of binding European law was in place to make future decisions binding upon member states too. This is precisely what happened – ironically, under Margaret Thatcher. It is a mark of the consistent failure of the UK to understand exactly what it had become a part of in joining the EEC that the most important 'relaunch' of a system that might override the national veto came when Mrs Thatcher was Prime Minister.

In the event, so far as the application to become a member of the EEC was concerned, it was third time lucky for the British, who finally joined under the Conservative Prime Minister, Edward Heath, in 1973. However, not even Heath's government, which took the UK into the Common Market without a referendum, made clear precisely what sort of arrangements the UK was signing up to. Heath talked about the Treaty of Rome as 'a voluntary undertaking of a sovereign state to observe policies which it has helped to form. There is no question of any erosion of essential national sovereignty.'[31] This is not (apart

---

30   The White Paper was entitled 'The United Kingdom and the European Communities (Command Paper No. 4715)'. White papers are called 'command' papers because issued at the 'command' of the monarch. Once again, the debate about the White Paper is worth reading. See https://hansard.parliament.uk/commons/1971-07-21/debates/45c8 5d47-d893-419f-a9b4-ad18f6348f1d/UnitedKingdomAndEuropeanCommunities

31   See May, Alex *Britain and Europe since 1945*, p. 108. The Seminar Studies in History series has a useful set of extracts from official documents at the end. This quote comes from the White Paper on The United Kingdom and the European Communities in 1971, shortly after Edward Heath had unexpectedly won the election in 1970.

from being innately wordy and complex) quite correct. It is true that states can come and leave the EEC – in that respect, unlike for instance joining the USA, it is a voluntary undertaking. One can walk in; one can walk out. Greenland left the EEC; the UK has now left the EU. And it is true that the policies a member state observes are policies it has helped to form.

But it is also true that a member state is bound – legally bound – to comply with policies that are passed into European law, even if it does not itself agree with them, for as long as it is a member of the European Union. In this sense, whatever Edward Heath might have said, there is obviously an 'erosion of essential national sovereignty', for the simple reason that the UK would be bound to implement European Law even if it clashed with national law.

If Heath was going to argue his case effectively, he could have tried to make it clearer what joining a supranational body meant. He could have said that both the experience of war and the close interconnection of European states in the post war world meant that it made sense to have some rules which were binding at the European level and to which member states had to adhere, just as there were rules at the national level which were binding upon regions and localities. He could have said that we were agreeing to be bound by certain laws which we helped to make at the European level, though doing it only in some policy areas, just as regions (or in the USA states) were bound by certain federal laws despite a considerable measure of autonomy at the regional or state level. He could have said that the UK Parliament was used to devolving power to local authorities (and as we shall see later was beginning to realise that it would have to consider devolving much more power to Scotland and Wales). In a similar way it made sense for some powers (for instance over customs duties) to be determined at the European level, so that the Community could develop into an effective trading bloc on the international stage (a familiar argument in the 2020s). The need was to integrate the nation-state into a system of multilateral governance, not to pretend that it could go on doing what it liked.

But this is not the explanation he gave. Nor is it what Labour's Harold Wilson had said when in government. Indeed, it is not what was said by any of the three prime ministers involved in the UK's arduous process of joining the Community. Nor was it the way in which the UK's most ardent critic, General de Gaulle, spoke of the Community in response to the UK's efforts to join it. Heath was therefore in good company when instead of presenting in a clear and coherent way what the sharing of sovereignty meant, he tried to keep the discussion away from sovereignty altogether. But this made it altogether unsurprising when his opponents thought they could see through his words and repeated time and time again that sovereignty was simply being 'given away' rather than shared.

Accession and the first referendum

The votes on entering the EEC in the UK House of Commons were narrow, because though the motion to join in principle was carried by a fairly large majority (356 to 244), the votes on the detail were often much closer, carried by single-figure majorities.[32] It all contributed to a sense of being railroaded rather than persuaded into something. In one sense (though his character was very different) Heath was an appropriate person to take the UK into a system devised by Monnet. He would use Parliament and avoid the referendum other states were having. He did not spend too much time thinking of how he could take the people with him or best explain what the Community was about. He probably thought they'd catch on in time. His idea of being Prime Minister was that you were like the CEO of a large company whose staff more often than not needed to be led by the nose. Just like Monnet and Schuman, he didn't sufficiently acknowledge that even the best ideas need popular support.

After joining the EEC, the Conservative government had to launch itself into negotiations for the first time as a new member, and soon found out that the hopes some people on both sides of the political spectrum had entertained in the 1960s of being able to bend the Community to the UK's will were impractical. Instead of a leadership role, the UK found itself to be one among many squabbling states.

In the early 1970s the Labour Party had unexpectedly moved back into opposition after losing the 1970 general election. It was not inclined to welcome Britain's entry to the EEC. When it returned to power in February 1974, the new Labour government decided to hold a referendum on whether to stay – after all, its predecessor had refused to hold a referendum on whether to join. But

---

32   May, Alex *Britain and Europe since 1945*, p. 53. Sometimes, May records, the majorities in favour were no more than four votes. He quotes Roy Jenkins, the former Labour Home Secretary and Deputy Leader who led the Labour pro-marketeers in a deeply divided party, saying that there were always enough 'old men who had decided their political fate no longer mattered and young men with the gallantry of 1916 subalterns' to ensure that the Treaty of Accession passed into law. See Jenkins, Roy *A Life at the Centre*, p. 338.

it explained that it would hold such a referendum after certain 'renegotiations' that many at the time regarded as spurious.[33]

As the referendum approached, the question of the future European Parliament, Monnet's insufficiently recognised or supported 'assembly,' came up time and time again in arguments about 'sovereignty'. Hostility from certain key politicians in 1975 towards the prospect of a European Parliament was very similar to their hostility to an elected House of Lords. As a revising chamber of the 'great and the good' (however undemocratic) the Upper House was no threat to the powers of the Lower. But as an elected body it would be bound to take some of the powers of the Commons – or why have it at all? Precisely the same threat was posed by the prospect of an effective parliament at the European level. The pro-Marketeers were in a bind. If they made too little of the European Parliament, they seemed to be supporting an 'undemocratic' set of European institutions. However, if they made too much of it, they seemed to be suggesting something that was bound to take over the functions of the 'mother of parliaments.'

The root of the problem was that both Left and Right bought into a view of the sovereignty of the Westminster Parliament that essentially excluded the sharing of power with any other Parliament, be it a revamped House of Lords, the European Parliament in Strasbourg or (later on) the Scottish Parliament at Holyrood. The opponents of staying inside the EEC were perfectly justified in returning constantly to this issue. Those taking the opposite view remained unwilling to make clear that becoming part of the EEC meant upending the principle that Parliament alone was sovereign.[34] As we shall examine later, the principle behind the UK's unwritten constitution, that whatever the sovereign decides in Parliament shall be law, cannot be reconciled with the principle that the decisions of the European Court take precedence over national law when the two are in conflict. The fundamental principle that nations voluntarily agree to be bound by laws which they jointly make is incompatible with the sovereignty of Parliament as it has traditionally been understood in the U.K.

---

33   See Uwe Kitzinger's chapter 'Entry and Referendum Revisited' in Broad, Roger and Preston, Virginia (eds.) *Moored to the Continent? Britain and European Integration*, pp. 79–94. Kitzinger entitles the section on the Labour government's renegotiation of the treaty before the 1975 referendum 'the so-called renegotiation 1974–5' (p.86). Anything substantial would have required an amendment to the Treaty of Rome or to the UK's Treaty of Accession. Neither happened.

34   See Vernon Bogdanor's chapter 'Europe and the Sovereignty of Parliament', in Bogdanor, Vernon *Beyond Brexit: Towards a British Constitution*, pp. 51–87.

Since the Luxembourg compromise, France had turned the EEC into a mixture of inter-governmentalism (in terms of new legislation that could be proposed) and supranationalism (in terms of the institutional structures, like the Court of Justice and binding European Law that were in place to implement legislation already agreed). The UK was effectively joining a hybrid, and it could have developed in a number of ways. It might, for instance, have given up supranationalism altogether and ended the primacy of European Law in any policy areas at all. Or it might have decided to move further towards supranationalism by unlocking the veto on new legislation. In the end it chose the latter course, strongly supported, as we have said, by Margaret Thatcher. But none of this was clear when the UK joined.

This is the context in which we should consider the way de Gaulle referred at the time of his first veto to that 'insular' and 'maritime' country over the water.[35] In a sense he had a point. One had only to look at Wilson and Heath, the two leaders who battled it out during the crucial period from 1964–1976 during which the UK finally managed to join the EEC. Wilson, for all his interest in the 'foreign stage', was certainly insular. Simple home cooking with a good dollop of HP sauce, pride in his Yorkshire origins unlike all those Southern toffs born with silver spoons in their mouths, holidays in the Scilly Isles and as little time abroad as was consistent with his international obligations. At the moment when the UK acceded to the EEC, he decided that the day was best spent attending a football match, anticipating a later Labour Prime Minister, Gordon Brown, who found a 'pressing engagement' that kept him from attending the signing ceremony for the Treaty of Lisbon.[36] Heath was maritime enough to

---

35   See Blair, Alasdair *The European Union since 1945*, p. 106. As one of the *Seminar Studies in History* series, this has a useful set of documents at the back. This document is a translation of an extract from de Gaulle's speech casting a veto against Britain's first application for EEC membership. De Gaulle said that 'England is, in effect, insular, maritime, linked through its trade, markets, and food supply to very diverse and often very distant countries. Its activities are essentially industrial and commercial, and only slightly agricultural. It has, throughout its work, very marked and original customs and traditions. In short, the nature, structure and economic context of England differ profoundly from those of the other states of the continent.' De Gaulle referred to the UK as *Angleterre* (England), never quite realising (or affecting never to realise) that there were other parts of the UK who were more agricultural and, through their traditional links to the continent, less insular.

36   Wilson was invited to attend the ceremony in Brussels by the Conservative Prime Minister, Edward Heath. See Bogdanor Vernon, *Britain and Europe in a Troubled World*, p. 72. For some of the flavour of Labour vacillations over Europe, see Vernon Bogdanor's ex-

be a champion yachtsman and had much more awareness of mainland Europe from the time of his cycling tours through Germany and elsewhere in the 1930s (which certainly alerted him to the perils of fascism). But in his own way he was as abrasive as his successor Margaret Thatcher in his dealings with other people, including Community leaders.

However, none of this detracts from the fact that it was the UK that came closest to seeing the EEC in the way General de Gaulle wished to see it, as an essentially inter-governmental arrangement. Had he wished to ensure that it became the sort of organisation he believed it should be, he would have welcomed the U.K. into the fold from the beginning. This was the irony Macmillan understood back in the early 1960s, when he recognised the way the general sought *L'Europe à l'anglais sans les anglais* (A Europe the way the English wanted it but without the English being part of it).[37] It is arguable that de Gaulle himself recognize the point towards the end of his period in office, when in February 1969, after issuing (in 1967) his second veto on Britain's application to join, he approached the UK with an offer to recast the EEC as an intergovernmental free trade area with the UK inside it.[38] Eight years earlier the U.K. might have leaped at the idea. Now it knew that de Gaulle's days as president were numbered and doubtless two vetoes had bred a degree of resentment. The foreign office reported de Gaulle's offer to the other members of the Six and their consternation helped to hasten the end of de Gaulle's presidency (he resigned three months later). Thus when the U.K. finally managed to get the offer it had always hoped for, it acted as if it didn't want it.

The referendum in 1975, which one might call the first referendum on membership of the EEC/EU, produced a decisive result, with a vote of 2:1 in favour of staying in. The result owed a great deal to the fact that the media (including the *Daily Mail*) weighed in on the side of a 'yes' vote, together with all the

---

cellent six-part lecture series delivered at Gresham College and entitled Britain and Europe since 1945. The 4th is entitled Entry into the European Community 1971–73. ht tps://www.youtube.com/watch?v=zL5XvrHbwBc

37   See Macmillan, Harold *At the End of the Day*, p. 118. See the discussion in Andrew Duff's *On Governing Europe: A Federal Experiment*, p. 59. Duff, who was a Liberal Democrat MEP from 1999–2014, points out that 'The irony is that the British perception of Europe was always – and is to this day – much closer to the Gaullist concept than it was to that of Monnet.' (p. 59). A study of the relations between de Gaulle and Macmillan, stretching back to wartime collaboration, can be found in Peter Mangold's *The Almost Impossible Ally: Harold Macmillan and Charles de Gaulle*.

38   Alex May, *Britain and Europe since 1945*, p. 45.

major party leaders.[39] It was hardly the situation that applied during the 2016 referendum. And yet it was a 'yes' vote that was more overwhelming in terms of numbers than of sentiment. After the vote the radical left-wing MP Tony Benn spent a year wearing a black armband. He lived a very long time, almost into his nineties. Had he lived a few years longer, he could have thrown that armband away and sported something more colourful.

Conclusion

By describing the process leading to the formation of the European Economic Community, the early part of this chapter outlined the UK's attempts to strangle supranational organisations at birth by suggesting alternatives like the Eden Plan and the European Free Trade Association. Interestingly, it was the US rather than the UK that was willing to support supranational initiatives if they helped to ensure Western European unity against what it perceived as the threat from Communism.

None of the UK's counterproposals worked, so it ended up trying to join the organisation it had failed to manipulate from outside. Some felt that this provided an opportunity instead to manipulate the EEC from within, but that opportunity receded with the fourteen long years between the initial application from the UK to join and its eventual confirmation, in a referendum after entry, that it was there to stay (at least for a few decades). The structures were too well-established by the 1970s for the UK to simply disentangle the supranational web and create an alternative form of organisation. At the same time, the actions of France under de Gaulle had removed the supranational edge from the institutions of the EEC, at least so far as the possibility of new binding legislation was concerned. The organisation existed in hybrid form, with European law still binding even as the way to new binding laws was effectively cut off. The UK found itself inside an organisation which arguably did not fully understand itself and which it was unable to transform into something it preferred. When it was offered the chance to do so by de Gaulle in 1969, it did not take the offer seriously – and perhaps by then de Gaulle was in no position to make it, since his presidency was beyond repair.

---

39   The cover of Alex May's *Britain and Europe since 1945* has a picture of people reading the newspapers after the referendum result. The Daily Mail's headline, 'YES, We're in business!' can be clearly seen.

In such circumstances an eventual vote to leave was always on the cards. One might see this in a particularly British context and lament the failure of successive Prime Ministers to argue Monnet's case. It is certainly true that neither of the two Prime Ministers who in different ways guided the UK into the European Union, Edward Heath and Harold Wilson, explained clearly what membership entailed, preferring to talk of something called the Common Market. Moreover, precisely because it became clear to both prime ministers that joining the EEC would not enable them to change it into the sort of intergovernmental body they wanted, they had an incentive to remain unclear about the nature of the organisation they had joined. But the fault lies in a wider context too, not only in the machinations of de Gaulle but in the failure of Monnet himself and the politicians whom he influenced to understand that the idea of sharing sovereignty had to be explained and defended in public in order to give it a popular appeal. A sense of popular ownership was an obvious given where a nation-state was concerned, but how was a sense of ownership to be given to the European project? It wasn't going to be achieved by lobbying the 'movers and shakers' through the Action Committee for a United States of Europe. It wasn't about having an anthem or a European passport. It was about making it clear why after nation-states had nearly destroyed the continent by being at each other's throats in a war that had come as the climax of centuries of destructive European conflict, a system of enforceable cooperation needed to be developed, one that was embedded in institutional structures. The hope now is that the value of such structures, whatever their deficiencies (which will be examined later) will be recognised before conflict breaks out all over again, as in parts of Europe it already has. As tensions rise not only inside Europe but within the UK between its different so-called nations, the danger of conflict applies as much to the United Kingdom itself as to flashpoints further East.

Chapter Seven: The long road towards British departure

The Single European Act and the Treaty of Maastricht

At the end of the last chapter, it was suggested that although the vote in the UK referendum of 1975 to remain inside the EEC was overwhelming (two to one), very little had been done to explain what sort of organisation the UK had decided to stay inside. Some tried to say that it was a 'tamed' organisation (after de Gaulle's forcing-through of the Luxembourg Compromise in 1967) that the United Kingdom joined in 1973, one whose supranationalist wings had been clipped.[1] I have argued that since institutions like the Court of Justice continued to do their work in enforcing binding rules upon member-states, such a clipping of the EEC's wings might well only be temporary, as indeed it proved to be.[2]

Even if partially tamed by de Gaulle after the so-called Empty Chair Crisis in the 1960s and the Luxembourg Compromise that finally ended it, the EEC was released from its cage and allowed to roam free again twenty years later, not least through the efforts of Margaret Thatcher. She restored the full measure of the EEC's supranational authority through her support for the Single European Act in 1986, the first significant revision of the Treaty of Rome. This

---

1   Thus Brendan Simms suggests that 'The problem was not that Britain had "missed the European bus" ten years earlier, because the bus was then headed in a supranational direction that she had no intention of taking, but rather that, once it changed course towards a more acceptable destination, the French were taking their time about letting them on.' (Simms, *Britain's Europe*, p. 187). In other words, he thinks the Luxembourg compromise had essentially changed the EEC into the sort of intergovernmental organisation the UK would feel comfortable with, but unfortunately having made the EEC acceptable to the UK, de Gaulle refused to let it in.

2   See chapter 6, above.

measure re-introduced binding decisions taken by majority vote in certain policy areas. In other words, the freeze on important new laws which were to be binding upon member-states was over.

The decade between the oil crisis of 1973 and the first serious negotiations about a single market ten years later has been described as a lost decade of factional disputes within the EEC as countries reeled under the stagflation (simultaneous inflation and rising unemployment) brought about by the supply shock of a quadrupling of oil prices in 1973. But at the same time those same states could see the opportunities available if they worked together. By the time Spain and Portugal finally joined (1986) the EEC, it would have the same population as the USA and its GDP would exceed that of Japan. Inevitably people started to think about what could be achieved if these member states formed an effective single market. Throughout that difficult decade which had just passed, the Court of Justice had been making binding rulings which forced member states to open up their markets to others. It was not just a question of customs duties – these had been abolished ahead of time before the end of the 1960s. It was all those other ways of keeping out the goods of your neighbours that had 'equivalent effect' to customs duties, such as regulations about how products were defined, certified and even packaged.[3]

Margaret Thatcher realised that the economic liberalisation which she sought – and business in the UK demanded – could only be achieved by removing restrictions, a removal that would not be effective unless they were subject to new EU legislation which was binding and enforceable. However, unless that legislation could be voted through by majority vote it was not likely to be passed. She supported the appointment of a British man, Lord Cockfield, as the Commissioner in charge of the Single Market initiative, and he set to work preparing legislation to remove technical obstacles to further integration. By the end of the 1980s about three hundred directives had been transposed into the legislation of the member states (in other words, 300 new European Laws had been made part of the national laws of those states).[4] The most substantial increase in the number of laws applying in the UK that were 'made in Brussels,' one of the frequent complaints of those who later sought UK withdrawal, was made on Mrs Thatcher's watch.

---

3   The overwhelming economic arguments were made by the Ceccini report on the economic benefits of the single market, *The Cost of Non-Europe*, named after the Italian economist Paolo Cecchini. See Dinan, Desmond *Europe Recast*, pp. 218–219.

4   See Dinan, *Europe Recast*, pp. 216–217.

Margaret Thatcher was not one of those politicians who had little under-standing of the workings of the EEC. When she became leader of the Conser-vative Party in 1975, she was a strong supporter of the campaign to stay inside it. In an article for the *Daily Telegraph* entitled 'Europe: the choice before us,' she declared:

> I believe the Common Market makes a constructive contribution ...Today Eu-ropean peace is taken for granted. But human nature has not changed...Pre-vention (of domination by another nation) lies not only in the willingness of peoples to be vigilant in the defence against tyranny; it consists of being prepared to live our lives together, in their becoming so enmeshed through trade and cooperation that to turn on one another would be unthinkable and impossible...[5]

This is a classic statement of the ideas behind Monnet's supranationalism, namely that precisely because there will always be a bad as well as a good side to human nature, action must be taken at the institutional level to ensure that the conflicts into which nation-states so easily fall become less likely (they can never be made impossible) because of the closeness of the cooperation between them. 'Enmeshed in trade,' as Thatcher put it, they will find it much more dif-ficult to go to war with one another, a view which can be traced back at least to Montesquieu. Margaret Thatcher's summary of the benefits of the Common Market is far more effective than anything managed by her predecessor, Ed-ward Heath. Monnet had the same idea of enmeshing them when he suggested that coal and steel, the industries that had once fuelled the war effort, should be subject to peaceful cooperation managed by a High Authority. More weaving of the Teuton and the Gaul, as Churchill had once put it.[6]

Margaret Thatcher makes it clear in her memoirs that she knew exactly what was doing. She was not being tricked:

---

5   Thatcher, Margaret. 'Europe: the choice before us' *Daily Telegraph*, 4th June, 1975.
6   The best description of such enmeshment came from the British diplomat who said that France and Germany would be 'in an embrace so close that neither could draw back far enough to hit the other.' See Bogdanor, *Britain and Europe in a Troubled World*, p. 13. The quote by Winston Churchill, 'If we could only weave Gaul and Teuton so closely to-gether economically, socially, and morally as to prevent the occasion of new quarrels, and make old antagonisms die in the realisation of mutual prosperity and interdepen-dence, Europe would rise again,' comes from his memories of the Second World War, Volume 1: *The Gathering Storm*, p. 16.

The price we would have to pay to achieve a Single Market with all its economic benefits, though, was more majority voting in the Community. There was no escape from that, because otherwise particular countries would succumb to domestic pressures and prevent the opening up of their markets. It also required more power for the European Commission: but that power must be used in order to create and maintain a Single Market rather than to advance other objectives.[7]

Back in 1975, Thatcher had argued that '…being in Europe, we gain access to a tariff-free market of 250 million people.'[8] A decade later she recognised that the only way of ensuring the free movement of goods and services within that market was to give the European Commission, the heir to the High Authority, powers of enforcement. There was a role for the 'bunch of intrusive middlemen' after all.

In the end Thatcher succeeded in ensuring that the Single European Act did not introduce majority voting in areas like taxation, frontier controls and employment law. By the end of her term of office (in 1990) she certainly felt that the European Economic Community had strayed too far beyond its remit – its concerns had ceased to be exclusively economic. People remember her famous 'Bruges Speech' in 1988 when she warned about attempts to 'suppress nationhood and concentrate power at the centre of a European conglomerate.' Yet she remained committed to membership and insisted that Britain 'does not dream of some cosy, isolated existence on the fringes of the European Community. Our destiny is in Europe, as part of the Community.'[9] As Stephens puts it, 'the flavour of her speech was Gaullist rather than anti-European.'[10] Margaret Thatcher was just like other national leaders in appreciating the value of a European level of governance in some areas while rejecting it in others.

---

7   See Thatcher, Margaret. *The Downing Street Years*. Quoted in Alex May, *Britain and Europe since 1945*, p. 115.

8   She made the remark in an article for the *Daily Telegraph* entitled 'The Choice Before Us,' published on 4th June, 1975. The choice was whether or not to vote Yes or No in the coming referendum on whether to stay in the European Economic Community. Thatcher was an ardent campaigner for staying in.

9   Extracts from the speech can be found in Document 14 at the back of Alex May's *Britain and Europe since 1945* (pp. 115–6). The whole speech can be found in Stubbs and Nelsen, *The European Union: Readings on the Theory and Practice of European Integration*, pp. 45–50.

10   Stephens, Philip. *Britain Alone: The Path from Suez to Brexit*, p. 251.

After her fall her successor, John Major, kept the same close control over areas where sovereignty-sharing was not appropriate. He oversaw the controversial Maastricht Treaty, which was eventually ratified in 1993, and which saw the UK obtain opt-outs from the plan for monetary union (a single currency) and the so-called social chapter, a series of social provisions on (among other things) workers' rights within what now became the European Union. The generation since that treaty was ratified has arguably shown how wise the UK was to retain its own currency – but that is just the point. The UK was able to define the areas in which it was prepared to share sovereignty and the areas where it was not prepared to do so.

It is true that the UK's humiliating exit from the Exchange Rate Mechanism in 1992 was a disaster from which the Conservative government of John Major never managed to recover and fuelled the claims of Eurosceptics that it was when the UK managed to tie itself to EU initiatives that its economy went into a tailspin. But such disasters didn't alter the fact that the UK secured an opt-out from the planned single currency and could perfectly well continue as a member of the EU outside the Exchange Rate Mechanism (ERM). Whether you concluded that it was hopelessly half-out of the EEC/EU or sensibly half-in, it had settled into a comfortable position from which it couldn't be removed. It had secured its opt-outs and any new treaties would require unanimous agreement by all the member-states. In some ways it is understandable that Major should have felt that the Treaty of Maastricht had 'settled' the European issue, allowed the red lines beyond which the UK was not prepared to go to be drawn in the sand and that only the 'bastards,' as he was heard to describe the Eurosceptics in his ranks, tried to pretend that there was anything left to discuss.[11]

The social market

The 1990s provided both an opportunity and a problem for politicians in the UK when dealing with what was now the European Union. They could continue to support and deepen the effective single market that had been created with the help of binding European Law. Business would be pleased with the opportunities provided by the single market. This was how Margaret Thatcher had

---

11   Major made his comment to a journalist at the time of a debate in July 1993 when he
      faced a 'no confidence' motion. See May, Alex *Britain and Europe since 1945*, pp. 85–86,
      the section entitled 'The Conservative Party Divided'.

become reconciled to supranationalism, and it was also the basis for the Left's hostility to the EU as something that they believed had begun as a cartel and then developed into a capitalist club.

But another approach was possible. It was already implied in part of Margaret Thatcher's famous speech at the College of Europe in Bruges in 1988, when she declared that she was not prepared to accept that, having 'rolled back the frontiers of socialism' in Britain, she should have to see them re-imposed by Brussels.[12] Had she recognised something that the Left hadn't? In the same year that Margaret Thatcher produced her Bruges speech, Jacques Delors, now President of the European Commission, addressed the trade unions at their annual conference. He tried to convince them that there were benefits to be had as part of the EEC in the social area, on matters like protection in work and social benefits. It was this address that arguably led Margaret Thatcher to deliver her Bruges speech. Delors was arguing that the single market was not simply being built around deregulation; there had to be better conditions for workers too.[13]

An example. A ruling of the Law Lords (on 3rd March 1994) during John Major's premiership established that procedures over redundancy pay and unfair dismissal were discriminatory and breached European law. The United Kingdom had a 16-hour-per-week threshold for all employment protection legislation. But as the Equal Opportunities Commission pointed out in bringing the case, the numbers of part-time workers beneath the threshold had grown significantly during the 1980s and made up more than 10% of the labour force.[14] Moreover, this rise in part-time working particularly concerned women. In 1994 38% of women part time workers, amounting to 1.9 million people, were under the threshold. The Equal Opportunities Commission therefore argued that rules over redundancy pay and unfair dismissal were discriminatory and breached EU law. The House of Lords upheld this and ruled that the hourly threshold contravened the EU law on equal treatment of men and women. Here was a clear example of ways in which the primacy of EU law could be of significant practical importance to a very large number

---

12   See the extract from the speech published as Document 14 at the back of Alex May's *Britain and Europe since 1945*, p. 115.

13   See Andrew Duff's *Britain and the Puzzle of European Union*, pp. 45–46.

14   See *Regina v. Secretary of State for Employment, ex parte Equal Opportunities Commission*. A very good account of the constitutional impact of EU membership is given by Colin Turpin in Broad and Preston, *Moored to the Continent?*, pp. 127–144.

of (in most cases) low-paid workers and in particular to women. And since it was incumbent upon national governments to implement EU law even if it contradicted national laws, EU social legislation could even be a means of restraining or in some cases overturning government legislation that sought to limit workers' rights.

The ruling cited above was not an isolated incident. If one examines the cases dealt with by the European Court of Justice, one can find many examples of social legislation which had been made binding upon member states and had helped to protect workers' rights.[15] Could the EU be made to appeal to a wider section of the UK population by stressing the benefits of binding social legislation? This might win it support on the Left, even as it triggered complaints about more 'interference' from the Right. After all, it is not surprising that many on the Left had come to see the European Economic Community as a capitalist club in the early years of its existence, when all its member-states were relatively wealthy. When people on the Left thought of the rulings of the European Court of Justice, (ECJ) they cited the *Costa* case of 1964, when the ECJ supported an Italian citizen who had refused to pay his electricity bill on the grounds that the Italian state had nationalised the electricity business and had thereby created a monopoly, infringing community laws on competitiveness.[16] Though ECJ rulings did not in fact prevent member states from nationalising industries, the perception that the EEC was a threat to the socialist policies of member states was important. It was certainly apparent on the Left from the beginning, in the Attlee government's suspicion of the projected Coal and Steel Industry. It lived on even in some of the reservations about the European Union expressed by Labour leader Jeremy Corbyn at the time of the Brexit referendum.[17] But the accession of less affluent countries like Greece, Spain and

---

15   This included social legislation incorporated in the Charter of Fundamental Rights. After the BREXIT referendum, but before the UK formally left the EU, Lord Sumption ruled that a Sudanese official employed by the Sudanese embassy in the UK was entitled to compensation for unfair dismissal, failure to pay her the minimum wage and holiday pay. The embassy had appealed to the UK's State Immunity Act of 1978. Lord Sumption ruled that there was a conflict with Article 47 of the Charter and therefore the UK Act must be disapplied. See Bogdanor, *Beyond Brexit*, p. 149.

16   See Bogdanor, *Beyond Brexit*, pp. 52–54. The case, Bogdanor points out, 'concerned the lawfulness of the nationalisation by the Italian government of the electricity industry' (pp. 52–53).

17   See former Labour Europe minister Denis MacShane in his *Brexit, No Exit*, chapter 12, 'Labour fails to make an impact', pp. 129–144. Corbyn, MacShane writes, 'wanted a so-

Portugal in the 1980s was to change the 'rich person's club' perception, as did the increasing visibility of ECJ rulings in support of the social market.

The shift in perception became noticeable in the 1990s, with increasing Conservative hostility to the EU under John Major, whilst the Labour opposition under Tony Blair became more enthusiastic about Europe. The Labour opposition had actually pledged to withdraw from the EEC without a referendum in its 1983 manifesto, the one on which the future Labour leader Jeremy Corbyn was first elected to the House of Commons. By the end of the 1980s, under Neil Kinnock, withdrawal was no longer in the Labour manifesto. By 1997, now led by Tony Blair, Labour was emphasising the need for the UK to play a leading role in the EU. It was a remarkable turnaround. The Labour government that won a landslide victory in 1997 put its new pro-European stance into practice by signing up to the Treaty of Amsterdam and opting back into the Social Chapter which John Major had secured an opt-out from some five years earlier. It was the one example of the UK opting out of an opt-out, but it reflected a new sense of the value of European legislation. The 'capitalist club' had a chance of being rebranded on the Left as a campaigning organisation for workers' rights, for instance in health and safety, working hours, holiday and pension entitlements, trade union recognition and representation on company boards. All of these matters were now subject to European law, while there was recognition of the need to avoid a 'race to the bottom' which led to a minimum of welfare provision.[18]

The EU was also attractive to those (who tended to be on the political Left) who were increasingly concerned about the environment in general and climate change in particular. After all, pollution knows no boundaries, a chemical discharge into the Danube (say) in one country can affect several others and only binding legislation across borders can be effective in preventing it. It was obvious that a group of more than a dozen (and soon to be more than two dozen) states acting together and being bound to comply with various forms of environmental protection legislation on everything from untreated sewage to the protection of endangered species could achieve much more than each state acting on its own.

---

cialist Europe in which trade unions were strong, while open markets trading arrangements and enforced competition rules were suspect' (p. 133).

18   As the former Liberal Democrat MEP Andrew Duff concedes in his *Britain and the Puzzle of European Union*, 'Tony Blair's first and most positive contribution (to the Treaty of Amsterdam) was to agree that the UK should sign up to EU social policy' (p. 54).

The spin-off from the economic liberalisation of the Single European Act into social and environmental areas that would prevent economic liberalisation from increasing pollution or exploiting workers, helping to form what was called 'the social market', had provided an opportunity for the European Union to appeal to the Left. In the 2001 election, Labour won another landslide majority against a Conservative opposition under William Hague whose unsuccessful campaign was centred around 'saving the pound.' This was hardly likely to prove a major issue when the UK had its opt-out to stay out of the euro, which was clearly the preferred policy of the Labour chancellor, Gordon Brown. The United Kingdom Independence Party (UKIP) received just 1.5% of the vote, 1% less than the Referendum Party led by James Goldsmith had won in the general election four years earlier.[19]

It might have been concluded at the beginning of the new century that Euroscepticism was far from being a vote winner in the UK, particularly among left-wingers. Two developments in the new century changed the situation. One was the eurozone crisis. The other was immigration.

Hung, drawn and troikered

Whether or not they were recognised by the Commission itself, and whether or not the blame lay with Greek over-spending or unfair practices by the so-called Troika of lenders, the sufferings caused by the crisis in the eurozone were visible to the public in countless news broadcasts and were analysed in the UK media during the years running up to the 2016 referendum.[20] A great deal of this was simply hostile propaganda, but not all of it. For instance, one could hardly accuse the BBC's Europe correspondent, Gavin Hewitt, of tabloid irresponsibility. Yet the book he published in 2013 provides an account of the 'eurodrama' which shows just how destructive the eurozone crisis was for those with a belief in the values of the 'European Project.'[21] Indeed, what happened inside the eurozone had a particular effect on the thinking of the Left in the UK. All

19   See https://commonslibrary.parliament.uk/research-briefings/cbp-7529/ for an analysis of all elections during the last century.

20   Many of them by the BBC's Europe editor Gavin Hewitt who later wrote an account of the crisis entitled *The Lost Continent*, published in 2013.

21   Hewitt, Gavin. *The Lost Continent*.

those ghosts of the capitalist rich man's club, which had been the Left's perception of the EEC in its early years, came rushing back. So many of the less well-off countries that had made the EU genuinely representative of a range of European nations, rich and poor, now appeared to be suffering systematic financial abuse from the rich countries. The redistributive intent that was clearly present in the EU's regional policy was overwhelmed by a punitive approach towards the debt-ridden members of the eurozone that was having precisely the opposite effect.

As the referendum approached in 2016, few people on the Left in the UK wanted to discuss whether the EU was an overweening supranational organisation interfering with the sovereign rights of nation-states. But they had seen the demands being made that a poor country inside the EU cut its pensions. Probably a few people in the run-up to the 2016 referendum confused being in the EU with being in the eurozone. But what did that matter? Although they were aware that the Troika could never come knocking at the UK's door even if it remained part of the EU, their news bulletins provided constant reminders of what being in the eurozone might mean. Greeks struggling to survive on reduced benefits. Forced privatisations. Cypriots unable to get to the bank and money being flown out to UK troops stationed there. A proposal (later withdrawn) that even holders of small bank accounts (under 100,000 euros) in Cyprus would suffer a 'haircut' and lose a percentage of their savings (many British people with savings in Cyprus were affected by this idea of a 'bail-in' rather than 'bail-out').[22] It all seemed to add up to an extreme version of the austerity programme that was becoming increasingly unpopular back in the U.K, but this time being imposed upon a country from without by the bureaucrats from Brussels. The poorer countries that had been embraced by EU entry and later by the eurozone were being made to suffer by the richer members. It was just a capitalist club after all. The support from the Left which had been built up through appreciation of the 'social market' was being whittled away.

In the summer of 2015, the Greeks held a referendum on the latest bail-out proposal from the Troika and voted to reject it. The BBC reported as follows:

> Just over a week ago, Alexis Tsipras stepped on to a podium in Syntagma Square in Athens. In his trademark open-necked white shirt, his sleeves rolled up, he punched the air.

---

22   One of the best accounts of the privations involved is given by Jospeh Stiglitz in *The Euro. How a Common Currency Threatens the Future of Europe.*

"I call on you to say a big 'no' to ultimatums, 'no' to blackmail," he cried. "Turn your back on those who would terrorise you."

His thousands of fans roared in approval. The Greek public followed his lead and 61% voted "oxi" ("No").

Roll forward seven days and Greece's prime minister signed the very measures he had fought against. Corporate tax and VAT will rise, privatisations will be pursued, public sector pay lowered and early retirement phased out.[23]

The BBC was able to give its report the headline: *Greek debt crisis: What was the point of the referendum?* The left-wing leader of the Greek government, Alexis Tsipras, had accepted a deal that was even worse than the one rejected in the referendum. His finance minister, Yanis Varoufakis, who was willing to explore alternatives that might fall short of leaving the eurozone (like adopting a parallel currency) then lost his job. Varoufakis has written a great deal on this subject.[24] The question asked here is simply whether it is so surprising, in view of what happened when the Troika went to Greece, that a significant part of the Left in the UK decided to vote to leave the EU in 2016. What did national sovereignty mean if a people could reject privatisation, lower public sector pay and a later retirement age, only to see the measures re-imposed because (it must have seemed) the 'Troika' had everyone in its grip? People didn't need to understand what the 'Troika' was. They just had to understand that the Greeks had been bludgeoned into something they didn't want and hadn't voted for. Furthermore, is it so surprising that for four years (after the referendum in 2016) many on the Left in the UK held their leaders to respecting the result of their own referendum, unlike Tsipras who had ignored the democratic mandate he'd asked for in Greece? The reaction was that even if Tsipras bottled it, we weren't going to. It was the will of the people. In the end they were even being prepared to get the job done by voting in someone who from a Left point of view was nothing but an obstacle to progress, Boris Johnson.

A decade earlier, the Left had recognised that significant parts of a left-wing agenda could be advanced from within the EU. The eurozone crisis killed that perception off. It looked like a return to the neo-liberal agenda that had

---

23   The BBC report was on 11th July 2015. See https://www.bbc.com/news/world-europe-3 3492387

24   See *And the weak suffer what they must? Europe, Austerity and the threat to Global Stability* and *Adults in the Room: My Battle with Europe's Deep Establishment.*

attracted Margaret Thatcher in the 1980s, breaking down the barriers to free trade and building everything around unrestrained competition enforced by European Law, with the weak going to the wall. The bridges and gateways on those euro notes, designed to stress 'connection' and the way everyone was linking up together, had become no more than the pipelines along which unfettered currency and trade could flow, producing its inevitable winners and losers. The eurozone crisis didn't quite drive Greece out of the eurozone. But it did a lot to drive the United Kingdom out of the EU.

Immigration

The second reason why euroscepticism proceeded to take root once again inside much of the UK in the new century was concerned with a very practical and controversial issue – immigration.

The immigration debate is not new in the UK, and it is well-known that it became a source of bitter controversy in the 1960s when Enoch Powell made his famous 'rivers of blood' speech.[25] However, it should be noted that the rise in immigration at the time of Powell's speech did not cause any growth in the overall population – it was a time of net emigration. Insofar as the focus was about immigration in the 1960s, it concerned the fear of having a lot of incomers from other parts of the world (particularly if they were a different skin colour) rather than the fact that the population was growing too quickly.

However, the increase in population in the UK which averaged out at about half a million a year over the decade between 2005 and 2015, undoubtedly was heavily influenced by net immigration. Immigration from the EU played a significant and increasing part in the overall rise of the UK population during that decade, though its extent should not be exaggerated. It was never the cause of more than 25% of that rise. Half or more of the immigration to the UK came from outside the EU, and half of the rise in the UK population had nothing to do with immigration. If a post-Brexit government were to forbid all immigration

---

25   The speech was delivered on 20th April, 1968 to a meeting of the Conservative Association in Birmingham. It spoke out against mass immigration, particularly from the Commonwealth. Powell, once a classics professor, quoted a passage from Virgil's Aeneid where there is a reference to the Roman being 'filled with foreboding.' Others finished the line for him – 'I seem to see the River Tiber foaming with much blood.' Hence the description 'rivers of blood' speech, which Powell didn't actually say but may well have implied from his use of the earlier part of Virgil's passage.

from EU countries, that would perhaps reduce immigration by one half and slow the increase in population by one quarter. Nevertheless, that would still be a significant amount, and migration from the EU certainly did fall sharply after the 2016 vote (which is not to say that this was a desirable thing).[26]

The immigration concerns that hit the headlines through Powell's speeches came at a time when more people were leaving than arriving. It was also a time when there were not only low levels of unemployment, but wages were growing in real terms. The concern was with the cultural and ethnic make-up of the incomers and the perception that this would change the nature of the UK, a concern that was usually blatantly racist.[27] In the case of immigration from other parts of the EU in the 2010s, though there can be discussion of how much superficial assumptions about appearance played a part, the sort of racism that could be discerned in people reacting to a different skin colour was not so evident. EU migration was as large as that from the Commonwealth, it came at a time when real wages were stagnant or falling and it was part of a very rapid increase in the overall population. It was hardly surprising that 'take back control', with its images of raising the drawbridge and holding back the flood, was to prove such an effective campaign – and not only on the Right. As Bogdanor points out, for many in the poorer sections of the country 'immigration seemed primarily to have benefited the elite, who were able to hire Polish builders and Lithuanian au pairs inexpensively.'[28]

With an opt-out from Schengen, the UK did not face demands to implement a common asylum policy. One of the obvious implications of abolishing *internal* border controls was that you had to have effective and mutually agreed *external* border controls. You also had to have clear policies for handling refugees who would arrive in member states on the borders of the EU. You would need to help member states who had to accommodate them while being assessed. You would have to have a common procedure for assessing their claims and deciding where they would stay if accepted. When, in 2015, a large number of people started crossing the Mediterranean from Turkey and (to a

---

26   These figures come from the Migration Observatory at the University of Oxford. See https://migrationobservatory.ox.ac.uk/resources/briefings/long-term-international-migration-flows-to-and-from-the-uk/

27   The figures from a research briefing for the House of Commons library make it clear that in the 1960s and 1970s there was net emigration and not inet immigration. More people were leaving than were coming. (https://commonslibrary.parliament.uk/research-briefings/sno6077/)

28   Bogdanor, Vernon. *Britain and Europe in a Troubled World*, p. 98.

lesser extent) North Africa, it was clear that none of this had been agreed between member states. Intense debate has continued ever since among members of the Schengen area over whether they should be required to take a quota of migrants or even any at all. No effective common asylum policy has been implemented so far and crowded, insanitary refugee camps continue to exist both inside and just outside the borders of the EU.[29]

For the UK, on the other hand, it was always possible to argue that since it had not opened its borders in the first place, there was no need to observe a jointly agreed policy for receiving migrants. This is not to take a position on the ethical issues involved one way or another. It is simply to say that membership of the European Union in no way forced the UK's hand. No one could say that the country was being 'forced by Brussels' to accept Syrians or Afghans. The clearest indication of this was the way that the Leave campaign concentrated not on Syrians arriving but Turks, supposedly on the basis of Turkey becoming a member of the EU (which it couldn't do without the unanimous backing of every member state, including the UK).[30]

The Leave campaign argued that the UK's hand was being 'forced' by internal migration, people moving from one part of the EU to another. In the run-up to the second referendum vote in 2016, the issue was Romanians and Poles, (and potentially Turks), not Afghans or Syrians. In this area there were no opt outs, meaning that EU membership did appear to take border control away. Since the free movement of people was always seen as one of the unassailable 'four freedoms' that enabled the single market to function effectively, it was not possible for the UK to put a lid on the number of EU citizens settling in the country while remaining a member of the Community.

---

29   The European Commission has useful websites for all its different departments ('directorates-general', as it calls them). The one on Migration and Home Affairs has a useful account of its attempts to devise a common asylum policy. Under the EU system, the Commission can only initiate legislation; the Council and Parliament alone can pass it. Many proposals have come from the Commission in this area and have been drastically changed or knocked back by the other EU institutions. See https://home-affairs.ec.eu ropa.eu/policies/migration-and-asylum/common-european-asylum-system_en

30   As Philip Stephens points out, 'The Brexiters cast Turkey as the threat: Johnson and Gove made the entirely false claim that it would soon join the European Union.' See Stephens, *Britain Alone*, p. 372. He records (p. 373) that Labour MP Gisela Stuart even warned of the effects of 88 million people (the whole population of Turkey) being given access to the NHS.

If one moves beyond the UK for a moment and looks at figures for net emigration and immigration throughout what was then the EU-28, one finds that during this decade (2005–2015) there were significant increases in the population of some countries but significant falls in others (Romania, Bulgaria, Latvia and Lithuania). Indeed, since independence in 1991 Latvia and Lithuania have lost about one fifth of their population. In the decade after Bulgaria joined the EU in 2007, its population fell from about 9 million to around 7 million – in other words, about one quarter of the population was lost.[31] Since these are often the brightest citizens, young and dynamic and therefore on the move, their countries do not want to lose them. At the very least, even if they cannot prevent their nationals from leaving, they would like to find a way of attracting them back again after a few years abroad.

Since a degree of balance was in everyone's interest, arrangements to control significant movements from one member state to another, or at least to limit the time away in another member state (brain circulation rather than brain drain) might have been welcomed by both 'sending' and 'receiving' countries. But freedom of movement was and is an essential part of the single market (of which the UK had always been a great supporter).

Yet if the free movement of people was untouchable, the legislation to ensure that it did not mean exploiting workers arriving from elsewhere in the EU appeared to be very flexible. Whatever the efforts made to manage the free movement of people to take up jobs in other member states, it did not lead to the adoption of enforceable rules which would make it impossible for workers coming from another state to be paid lower wages or accept poorer conditions of work than workers from the home state.[32] The result – on the ground, if not in the ivory towers of EU officialdom – was a strong element of resentment as

31   The figures come from the excellent EU statistics agency EUROSTAT. It is possible to see the point very clearly from a detailed description of the period from 2015 to 2021. The population of Bulgaria fell every year and by 2021 was about 300,000 less (out of a population of about 7 million). In the same period, the population of Ireland riose every year to go up by 300,000 (to just over 5 million). The population of Romania fell each year and after 6 years there were about 700,000 fewer out of a population of around 19 million. The population of the Netherlands meanwhile rose by about 600,000. The change was not of course due simply to movements of people inside the EU, but the figures make clear that some countries of the EU are experiencing significant falls in population while others are experiencing significant increases. See https://ec.europa.eu/eurostat/databrowser/view/demo_gind/default/table?lang=en.

32   Wagner, Ines. *Workers without Borders: Posted Work and Precarity in the EU.*

local workers noted that whatever was the case in theory, in practice they were being undercut by migrants. This was a further way in which support for the EU was being undermined on the Left, encouraging the sort of pincer movement that finally produced a vote from both ends of the political spectrum in favour of leaving the EU.

Conclusion

The point of the last two chapters has not been to attempt yet another analysis of why the UK joined the EEC and then left its successor, the EU. Instead, the book has tried to focus upon the extent to which the sharing of sovereignty, the key ingredient in the form of cooperation between nation-states devised by Monnet and first implemented by Schuman, was understood and received by the United Kingdom. The last chapter suggested that it was strongly opposed from the very beginning by post-war UK governments, and certainly not explicitly supported even by those who took the UK into the EEC in the 1970s. Nor, this chapter has suggested, was the sharing of sovereignty ever the focus of discussions among those who debated later in the century whether the UK should remain in the EU.

One surprising conclusion from reading her speeches is that the leader who came closest to understanding the merits of sovereignty-sharing was Margaret Thatcher. She became Prime Minister four years after the referendum confirming UK membership of the EEC, in which she campaigned for a 'Yes' vote. As Prime Minister she did not challenge the supremacy of EU Law in particular policy areas (though she wanted these areas strictly controlled) and more importantly she opened the door to majority voting in the Council of Ministers by agreeing to the Single European Act in 1986. She even defended sovereignty-sharing as a way of curbing the excesses of nationalism. All this was perfectly consistent with emphasising 'thus far and no further' and insisting upon red lines, just as other EU leaders (and her successors as Prime Minister) did. While she was the head of government she never took the sort of view taken by the Conservative government of Boris Johnson today that it is better for the UK to make its own trade agreements and be free of the binding decisions of the Court of Justice altogether. Such a position would have made no economic sense to her – at least while she was Prime Minister, though she changed her views in retirement.

It was not Margaret Thatcher who lit the fuse that led to the eventual with-drawal of the UK from the European Union. In fact, her reservations about the EU were a far less significant factor than the problems of immigration and the crisis of the eurozone that particularly affected UK governments in the early twenty-first century. It was these events that re-awoke traditional fears on the Left that the EU was simply a capitalist club, whereas in the 1990s there had been a growing appreciation on the Left of the social dimension to the single market – something that had worried Thatcher and her successor as Prime Minister, John Major.

From the perspective of this book, the underlying problem was that UK governments never spelled out clearly what sovereignty-sharing meant. Thatcher and Major were not alone in this respect, since none of their predecessors in office, including those who applied for membership and eventually took the UK into the EEC, made it clear either. It is even arguable that on the one or two occasions where the system did lead to a real conflict between national laws and Community law, Community law prevailed without much protest in the UK. It seemed that UK leaders, whether from Left or Right, rarely grasped that the Community represented a new way of conducting international relations. Often they just thought of a new set of instructions, this time coming from Brussels, as part of their membership of the 'Common Market'.

The UK was not uniquely unaware of the arguments about the sharing of sovereignty. There was little discussion of the benefits in France and Germany either. It was probably best appreciated by the smaller countries that became part of the original Six, like Belgium, which has always linked the institutional structures of the EU to its own complex federal system. The UK was simply the place where failure to grasp those arguments had unexpectedly bad consequences, largely because of measures that the EU introduced in the new century to deal with the eurozone crisis and with internal and external migration. The eurozone crisis gave many in the UK the impression that member-states no longer had the right to manage their own economic affairs, even though the UK was not itself part of the eurozone. The debate over immigration gave the impression that member-states could no longer manage their borders, because freedom of movement between EU countries was and remains a key principle of the single market. 'Take back control' therefore became a very powerful headline for the Leave campaign, not least because the idea of joint control had never been properly explored.

Few people suggested, during the long debates over Brexit, that by pooling sovereignty nation-states had done something unique in history. Few people emphasise its benefits even now. However, as this book will go on to suggest, the consequences of the UK's withdrawal from a sovereignty-sharing system extend to the future of its own union, since a version of the structures it has renounced in leaving the EU may be the only way of maintaining the United Kingdom intact. The benefits of sovereignty-sharing may at last come to be appreciated on this side of the Channel, simply because there can be no other way of maintaining a United Kingdom. The rest of the book will apply itself to this question.

Chapter Eight: Invasion and Expansion on the Isles

It is time to take a closer look at the 'multinational state' that has emerged in Britain and Northern Ireland. The history of these nations has been characterised by centuries of constant migration and this book does not pretend to understand all the complexities of the changes involved. Nevertheless, it seems reasonable to suggest that since we have noted the narrative arc which traces the inseparability of England (later Britain) and mainland Europe, a further question arises. What about the arc tracing the development of the Isles themselves, and particularly the different relationship England was to have to Wales, Scotland and Ireland?

What did the Romans ever do for us?

Before discussing the different forms which English expansion into the rest of the Isles took, we should consider two invasions which are crucial to the history of the two islands when seen from an English perspective.

The first was the Roman conquest in the first century. Perhaps because of a later attempt to reproduce Rome's imperial reach themselves, there is a tendency for the English in particular to put positive spin upon their 'Roman origins.' Not only does this often mean beginning their history with the Roman occupation but it also means seeing Roman rule as a civilising mission (presumably for the Welsh as well, since Wales was also made part of Britannia) which brought wine, olive oil, togas, baths, and villas with underfloor heating, not to mention straight roads. However, the Romans stopped short of trying to civilise the 'barbarians' in the far north (hence Hadrian's wall, frequently misunderstood as representing the border between England and Scotland) or across the Irish sea.

According to this conception, the Romans are seen as realising their 'civilising' mission in the parts of the isles they occupied, leaving unmistakable traces on the generations to come (at least in England and Wales) and even falling in love with their 'adopted homeland.' The leading imperialists of the modern world found it easy to make common cause with the leading imperialists of the ancient world.[1] We can see this in Rudyard Kipling's famous poem about the Roman centurion reluctantly ordered back to Rome:

> Legate, I come to you in tears – My cohort ordered home!
> We served in Britain forty years. What should I do in Rome?
> Here is my heart, my soul, my mind – the only life I know.
> I cannot leave it all behind. Command me not to go.[2]

The story of Romans spreading civilisation wherever they went and becoming enamoured of a population that was willing to be uplifted creates the idea that some sort of cultural and social framework must have been passed on when they departed, so that England-and-Wales-to-be must have been able to preserve structures that made it superior to the rest of the Isles.

Quite apart from the way in which this approach undervalues the cultures of those the Romans chose not to 'civilise,' does it overstate the effect of Roman occupation itself on the majority of Britons in the lowland areas who spent four centuries under Roman rule? This is hard to assess. On the one hand, Peter Salway in his *History of Roman Britain* refers to the fact that by the time the Romans departed 'Britain had become so fundamentally integrated into the late Roman state that separation was fatal'.[3] Similarly, P. H. Sawyer in his *From Roman Britain to Norman England* lists many changes that came about through Roman occupation, not only the obvious ones like 'monumental architecture, well-engineered roads and regularly planned towns and farms' – the things an archaeologist can examine to this day – but less easily identifiable aspects like

---

1   Davies, Norman. *The Isles: A History*, p. 126.

2   See Jones, Hayhoe and Jones, *Roman Britain*. The three editors, in a book essentially written for use in schools, have brought together a number of poems and short articles in order to give an impression of life in Roman Britain. The last section, entitled 'The Romans Leave', contains Kipling's 'The Roman centurion's song.' Essentially it conveys the idea of the imperialist falling in love with the land he occupies, a sentiment that was certainly to cause a great deal of trouble where the British Empire was concerned, because it is a large settler population that makes withdrawal from empire most difficult.

3   Salway, Peter. *A History of Roman Britain*, pp. 354–355.

the 'machinery of government', such as systems of assessment used for the collection of tribute, the rights and prerogatives of power, the means of exchange (coinage), law-codes, language and religion. In Sawyer's view 'the Romans did [...] impose a degree of stability on the political divisions of Britain'.[4]

On the other hand, there are other writers who have played down the Roman influence upon the parts of the Isles that they conquered, perhaps because they do not write from an 'English' perspective. 'The demise of the Roman Empire has been mourned to excess', suggests John Davies in his *History of Wales*.[5] 'Its essence was violence,' he continues, 'and its accomplishments were fundamentally second-rate. Its achievements in the world of science and technology were few; what need was there for new inventions in a society which had an abundance of slaves? Its literature and fine arts were a pale reflection of the splendours of classical Athens.'

Davies also plays down the social impact of Roman occupation upon the part of the Isles which was to become England and Wales. Unlike their counterparts in Gaul, the Romans in Britannia lived in walled towns. A hundred or so of these contained perhaps one-tenth of Britannia's population.[6] When military garrisons and a few thousand villa estates are thrown in, the total comes to no more than a quarter of the population. In Britannia, in other words, the 'Romano-British' had a sense of being a minority surrounded by the 'barbarians within.' They were effectively a gated élite. For most people living inside Britannia the Roman occupation had little effect on their lives; it was hardly the moment when 'civilisation' emerged, even in the parts of the Isles that experienced direct Roman rule.

The Romans had much less influence in Britannia than in neighbouring Gallia, where Frankish developed as a variant of Latin after they left. Indeed, much of the influence the Romans did have on Britannia was via visitors from Gaul (anticipating later French influence on English culture). When in 410 they left Britannia to its own defences, they were much more concerned about the Visigoths in Italy (Alaric sacked Rome in the same year) than about retreating from an outpost of empire acquired in a whim and managed half-heartedly. In

---

4   Sawyer, *From Roman Britain to Norman England*, p. 73.

5   Davies, John *A History of Wales*, p. 43.

6   'It is hard to see how the Romano-British could have reached more than one-fifth, or at most one quarter of the whole. The proportions are quite different than in the Empire's continental provinces.' Davies, Norman *The Isles*, p. 118.

the previous century there had been a tendency for the army to crown generals in Britannia and then set off with bands of troops to try to get them made emperor in Rome – in other words, they were looking for a passport back to 'civilisation,' whatever Kipling's centurion might have suggested! In the years before the Romans' final departure, while Honorius was trying to entrench Roman power in Britannia, there were attempts to elevate three generals to the purple, as the making of emperors was termed. One of them, Constantinus, was successful, and Honorius had to cede control of Britannia and Gaul to him. When Constantinus died, Honorius had a chance to take back control, but he settled for concentrating upon Gaul instead.[7] One might conclude that even before Alaric sacked the city, many of those in Britannia were far more interested in what was happening in Rome or even Gallia than what was happening in a northern outpost of the empire. Britain slipped from the grasp of Rome while Rome was concentrating on other things.

The Roman invasion of parts of the Isles was perhaps understood less well by Kipling than by the Polish writer Korzeniowski, better known in England as Joseph Conrad for books which he wrote in his third language, English. Conrad drew on the experiences of his native Poland, which had been parcelled out among three occupying powers for most of his life, and his experiences in the French and British merchant navies. Few people had a better insight into the imperial conquests that both affected the rest of the world and expressed themselves in terms of historical developments within Europe itself. There is a famous passage in the opening chapter of Joseph Conrad's *Heart of Darkness*, written at the turn of the twentieth century (1899) at roughly the same time as Kipling's tearful centurion asking not to be sent home. In the passage, Conrad's character Marlow comments as follows while sitting in a small boat on the Thames watching all the vessels pass by heading for distant outposts of the British Empire:

> I was thinking of very old times, when the Romans first came here, nineteen hundred years ago—the other day ..... Imagine the feelings of a commander of a fine—what d'ye call 'em?—trireme in the Mediterranean, ordered suddenly to the north; run overland across the Gauls in a hurry; put in charge of one of these craft the legionaries—a wonderful lot of handy men they must

---

7   See Davies, John *A History of Wales*, p.41. At the same time 'barbarian' attacks meant a gradual movement of the centre of gravity of the Roman Empire southwards. See Salway, Peter *A History of Roman Britain*, p. 320.

have been, too—used to build, apparently by the hundred, in a month or two, if we may believe what we read. Imagine him here—the very end of the world, a sea the colour of lead, a sky the colour of smoke, a kind of ship about as rigid as a concertina—and going up this river with stores, or orders, or what you like. Sand-banks, marshes, forests, savages,—precious little to eat fit for a civilized man, nothing but Thames water to drink. No Falernian wine here, no going ashore. Here and there a military camp lost in a wilderness, like a needle in a bundle of hay—cold, fog, tempests, disease, exile, and death—death skulking in the air, in the water, in the bush. They must have been dying like flies here. Oh, yes—he did it...They were men enough to face the darkness. And perhaps he was cheered by keeping his eye on a chance of promotion to the fleet at Ravenna by and by, if he had good friends in Rome and survived the awful climate. Or think of a decent young citizen in a toga—perhaps too much dice, you know—coming out here in the train of some prefect, or tax-gatherer, or trader even, to mend his fortunes. Land in a swamp, march through the woods, and in some inland post feel the savagery, the utter savagery, had closed round him—all that mysterious life of the wilderness that stirs in the forest, in the jungles, in the hearts of wild men...[8]

Heart of Darkness focuses upon the British in Congo, but in Conrad's opening chapter the idea of imperial mission is reversed. Instead of civilisation trembling at the approach of the 'dark continent,' as all those ships left London for Congo and other parts of the British Empire, we have Romans trembling at the wet, marshy outlines of what to them might well have seemed the boondocks of their own empire. Natives with bones through their noses looking out from behind trees at the British become natives covered with woad looking out from the grim marshland at the Romans. Unmanageable jungle becomes unmanageable swamp. These Romans were not settlers happy to pass on their 'grandeur' to natives they had learned to love, but people who for one reason or another had drawn the short straw, most of whom would soon be looking for ways of returning to 'civilisation.' Perhaps they had been banished from Rome or had fallen out of favour there, but they would still dream of returning with one of their generals who, once elevated to the purple and able to depose those in power in Rome, would reward them.

---

8   Conrad, *Heart of Darkness* (London: Penguin Classics Edition, 2014), p. 3. The book was originally published in 1899.

Norman Davies suggests in *The Isles* that 'Britannia was neither evacuated, nor stormed, nor ceded by treaty. It was left to its own devices for a temporary period which, in the event, turned out to be permanent.'[9] So, what exactly was left behind when the Romans left? There is a well-known story, recorded by the 6th Century cleric Gildas, of how Vortigern invited the Saxons to come and protect the Romano-British and they then proved to be something of a cuckoo in the nest, an account repeated in Bede's 8th Century *Ecclesiastical History of the English People*.[10] Whatever its consequences, Vortigern's policy is hardly a surprise. If he yielded land to Saxon mercenaries, then he was acting as Rome itself often did, providing land for those who would defend its borders. But it seems that the Saxons, unlike those whom the Romans had used as buffer states, started to spread themselves westwards, moving out of the coastal regions into the interior and meeting little resistance, at least in the lowlands. John Davies argues that what is striking about the Saxon colonisation of England is the way in which it differed from other forms of colonisation in Europe.[11] Unlike in Gallia, where ex-Roman forces still maintained some infrastructure, Britannia had imploded, and there was no unified resistance to invaders from abroad, some of whom were plunderers in transit and some of whom sought to settle.

In many places the so-called 'barbarians,' who are so often pictured storming the various gates of the Roman Empire, willingly adopted the culture of those they displaced. In Gaul the Gallo-Roman culture was effectively taken over by the Franks, who spoke a form of Latin that can be described as proto-French. But across the Channel the Saxons did not adopt the culture of those they displaced to the same extent. Were Roman structures perhaps less firmly established than in Gaul? That might suggest that the Romanisation of Britain was in fact rather shallow. Where the Gauls had a Gallo-Roman culture that survived the departure of the legions in a sufficiently strong form for the invaders to adopt it, the Saxons found something much less established, a Romano-British culture that was not evident throughout the country. The Saxons did not adopt it on the island. A few of the Romano-British decided that

9   Davies, Norman. *The Isles*, p. 147.

10   See the account in Sawyer, *From Roman Britain to Norman England*, pp. 76–91: 'Britain after the Romans'.

11   See Davies, *A History of Wales*, p. 36. Davies suggests that Romanisation 'did not penetrate into the marrow of the population of Britain (and even less so that of Wales) as it did in the greater part of the Western Empire.'

the best solution was to emigrate to what is now France, creating a 'Britannia' (Brittany) which had to be distinguished from 'Great Britain' (the larger Brittany) across the water, one which could at least make use of a more established infrastructure than the chaotic world they had abandoned.

From the perspective of an empire established more than a millennium after the Roman Empire ended, it might appear that the Romans in Britannia were more like the British in India than the British in Australia or New Zealand. After they left, Britannia reverted to a state of incessant warfare – just as happened to British India, which collapsed into civil war after the British departed (not least because of the 'divide and rule' policy which had previously encouraged divisions). Celts fought Saxons, but Celts also fought Celts and Saxons fought Saxons, the whole mix constantly stirred by a chain of migrations and resettlements.

Whatever the important social and cultural developments that happened in those parts of the Isles that were never touched by the Romans, like Ireland, it is not clear that even when the Romans did occupy the land their influence was as great as has often been supposed. The most noteworthy aspect of the Roman 'heritage' in England and Wales was that it was not embedded enough to be passed on. Yet there remains an enduring tendency for the English to play up the Roman influence upon their national formation, an earlier imperial power which provided the inspiration for its successor, rather than the European influence that followed the final departure of the legions. Writing on the cusp of the creation of the European Coal and Steel Community, the historian Christopher Dawson observed a tradition of education in which European nations learned about a lost world order associated with ancient Rome.[12] This applied above all, he felt, to England, where Gibbon's famous *Decline and Fall of the Roman Empire* was digested alongside their own national past. As a result, the existence of Europe as a social reality was underplayed or ignored.

1066 and all what?

Unlike the Romans, the Vikings and Danes did not simply arrive in the South-East of the country. Julius Caesar might have thought in terms of crossing from

---

12   Dawson, *Understanding Europe*, pp. 3–20: 'How to Understand our Past.' Dawson was concerned, however, primarily with the loss of a Christian rather than a classical heritage. The text first appeared in 1952.

Gaul, but for the Vikings from further North it made sense to go to other parts of the Isles. The busiest seaway became that between what is now Ireland and what is now Wales and Scotland. The importance of the 'Celtic Mediterranean' had been insufficiently acknowledged during Roman times and in the decades after the departure of the legions. It was made even more important by the invasions from the North. The Vikings, unlike the Romans, moved into Ireland as well as modern-day Britain from the end of the eighth century, and Ireland proved an important trading-post between Scandinavia and what is now Spain. Economic activity, such as there was, became concentrated away from what is now England.[13] There was none of the present-day perspective from which nothing can match the size of London or the economic dominance of the 'home counties.'

Given the significance of both cultural interaction and trade in the West and North, there is no reason to suppose that developments in what is now Ireland, Scotland and Wales were any less significant than developments in what is now England. Yet 'British' history concentrates on the date 'everyone knows,' 1066, when the successors of Alfred succumbed to invasion. The successful Norman invasion of 1066 took place in a year which saw a scramble on several fronts for the final Viking spoils. A 'Danish' invasion force was repelled by Harold at the Battle of Stamford Bridge in the North. Meanwhile a 'Norwegian' force never arrived and then a force from Normandy overcame Harold at the Battle of Hastings. The focus had returned to the South of England.

The Normans had been moving South on the European mainland since the ninth century and had already fought a series of battles in what would now be France. King Charles III of France decided that the best way to deal with his Scandinavian squatters on the Seine when they migrated South was to adopt them. In 911 the Treaty of Saint-Clair-sur-Epte ensured that they were given land (Normandy), made to accept Christian baptism and became vassals of the King.[14] They accepted feudalism and gave up Viking laws and institutions. It was a similar practice of assimilation to that seen in the case of the Gallo-Roman communities dealing with the Franks.

---

13   '...in the post-Roman era the western seaways thrived. With Roman coastal defences abandoned and turmoil on the landward side, the Celtic Sea returned to its earlier function as the great open conveyer of goods, people and culture.' Davies, Norman *The Isles*, p. 175. Indeed the arrival of the Vikings intensified a process which had already begun in the post-Roman period.

14   See Davies, *The Isles*, p. 234.

Victorious though they had been against Harold in 1066, the Normans in England remained culturally and socially attached to French-speaking Normandy. They accepted that the arrangement made with Charles III a century before meant that they remained feudal vassals of the King of France. The Norman and subsequently the Plantagenet Kings did not just think 'in continental terms' because they wished to ensure that England was well-protected against external threats. They thought in such terms because this is where they kept their legal obligations and their cultural roots. They retained towns, titles and connections subordinating them to French monarchs. Every English King up to and including Edward III (in the fourteenth century) paid homage to the French King. The mainland was where their focus lay. Even in the late twelfth century, more than a century after the Norman invasion, Plantagenet Kings were only spending about one-third of their time in England. They travelled through all their lands extracting tribute from their tenants-in-chief and dealing with disputes. If this was an 'Empire', it wasn't an Empire centred upon England in the way that the British Empire was centred upon Britain or the Roman Empire upon Rome. It was centred upon Normandy. The ten-year reign of Richard the Lionheart (1189–1199) saw him spend just six months in England. Unsurprisingly, when Queen Victoria requested that the remains of the many Plantagenet Kings buried in France be returned to England, she was reminded that so far as these monarchs were concerned by having their last resting-place outside England they had merely come home![15]

Nevertheless, despite their attachment to Normandy, the Normans did begin to expand into other parts of the Isles. This was partly a defensive action.[16] They were keen to rein in some of their followers who sought independent lordships or who launched freelance operations, for instance from Wales into Ireland. By trying to keep their supporters under control they found themselves

---

15   Davies, *The Isles*, p. 290. It was the Prefect of Maine-et-Loire who reminded Victoria of this. The important point is that the primary attachment of the Plantagenets was to France. Davies points out that there is no evidence that they could speak a word of the English language.

16   We see here the beginnings of the idea that Scotland, Wales and Ireland, which he chooses to call 'peripheral polities,' might be used as a 'back door' by European enemies. Of course, immediately after the Norman invasion the enemies were more groups like the Marcher Lords who were ostensibly allies of the Normans. See Simms, *Britain's Europe*, p. 6 and for the Marcher Lords Davies, *A History of Wales*, p. 106. The Marcher Lords had to be weak enough to be under the control of the English monarch, but strong enough to keep the lid on the Welsh to the West.

extending their range. From this perspective the Normans really wanted to concentrate on mainland Europe but found themselves drawn further and further in the other direction. The constant European attachment associated with the importance of Normandy to England's mediaeval rulers, came alongside a growing association of other parts of the Isles with military adventurism and sedition.

This perspective affected later attitudes towards different parts of the Isles. The areas left untouched by Roman 'civilisation' became, in Simms' oft-repeated imagery, the 'back door' that can never be kept secure, the 'supply store' where resources can be found for campaigns on the European mainland, a kind of tradesmen's entrance for deliveries from the wilder parts of the Isles. He quotes the writer of *Robinson Crusoe*, Daniel Defoe, saying that England's considerations for uniting with Scotland in the Act of Union between the two countries in 1707 were 'peace, strength and shutting the back door of continual war and confusion from the North'.[17] The parts of the Isles away from England became a potential entry-point for foes seeking to attack. Just as the mediaeval historians who talk about Norman expansion present it as an attempt to control unruly followers like the Marcher Lords who pursued freelance operations in the 'Wild West', so the later development of the United Kingdom is presented by Simms as a way of cutting off the possibility of invasion by the back door, by Louis XIV in the case of the Union with Scotland and by Napoleon in the case of the Union with Ireland. An internal empire is developed for purely defensive reasons. The wilder edges of the isles are suppressed out of necessity and a religious gloss is thrown over their supposed backwardness by their reluctance to adopt the religious settlement that emerged with the Henrician Reformation. The un-Romanised 'outer Britain' that was only gradually brought into the fold and civilised had been turned into those in the 'Celtic fringe' who denied the Anglican establishment.

Three kingdoms, four nations

There are two things you can do with your enemies. One is to create a barrier between yourself and them; the other is to take them over and subdue them. In the case of Wales, William the Conqueror chose the former option. He did this through providing land and honours to some of his kinsmen in the 'marches,'

---

17   Simms, Brendan. *Britain's Europe*, p. 47.

the border areas between England and Wales which were collectively known in mediaeval Latin as the *marchia Wallia*, while the native Welsh lands to the west were considered Wales Proper (*pura Wallia*). William's kinsmen in the Welsh Marches were to become the Marcher Lords. They came from far and wide, including Flanders and Brittany. It was people from Flanders rather than England who initially gave Pembroke the reputation of being 'Little England beyond Wales.'

By the 12th Century a 'lawless frontier' was in place, where the robber barons of the Marches administered their own law as they saw fit. As the rulers of *marchia Wallia*, they were the lords of No Man's Land, or what John Davies calls 'a cordon sanitaire of Norman lordships between his (The King of England's) kingdom and the territories of the Welsh rulers.'[18] A similar creation of barriers could be observed in Scotland and Ireland. The Marches were created to keep the Welsh at bay, the lowlands of Scotland were used to keep the Highlanders at bay and the Plantagenets established the 'Pale' in Ireland to keep out those who were 'beyond the Pale.'

It was an attitude that might be compared to that of the Romans towards their borders, which were best secured not by barriers (as said, Hadrian's Wall on the Northern frontier is misunderstood if seen in these terms) but by making use of sympathetic 'barbarians' who could protect the edges of the Empire. It was not a policy without risk. Those who were installed to defend borders could prove troublesome for those on either side of them. They also tended to see themselves as superior to those they were created to manage, a view that has had echoes down the centuries. Professor Vernon Bogdanor, in a lecture given in Gresham College on the former Labour Chancellor and Home Secretary Roy Jenkins, records that when an undergraduate in Oxford the young Jenkins was thought snobbish because he liked to say that he was 'from the Marches' rather than from Wales!'[19]

In the case of Wales, the barrier was broken down decisively in the late thirteenth century by the English. In 1277 King Edward I mobilised not just the feudal knights of England but a mercenary army and a fleet of ships from Gascony and elsewhere across the Channel. It was the largest army to have been

---

18   Davies, John *A History of Wales*, p. 106.

19   The lecture was one of six given by Professor Bogdanor at Gresham College, London, on politicians who helped to shape 20th Century UK politics but never became Prime Minister. This was the third and was called 'Roy Jenkins, Europe and Civilised Society.' https://www.youtube.com/watch?v=dimAWlJfNOY

mobilised since the Norman invasion in 1066. It may have begun as a punitive expedition, but it soon became an invasion. Edward took not just soldiers with him but other trades, such as carpenters and stonemasons to put together the infrastructure of occupation, not to mention 360 reapers to seize the grain harvest in Anglesey. He built roads and castles which (before the age of gunpowder) were impregnable and served as bases from which his forces could ride out and hunt down 'rebels.'[20] The Edwardian castles have remained in Wales ever since as 'the magnificent badges of its subjection,' as Thomas Pennant called them.[21]

Hence, though it was in 1901 that people first began to talk of a statute passed during the reign of Henry VIII as an act of 'Union' between England and Wales, this was hardly an accurate description. Earlier invasions and the reforms passed in their wake had effectively removed anything for the English to unite with. The Welsh Act was passed by England alone, without any members from Wales; indeed, one can see this from its preamble which claimed that union between Wales and England already existed at the time of the act:

Wales...is and ever hath been incorporated, annexed, united to and subjecte to and under the imperialle Crown of this Realme as a verrye member...of the same.[22]

It was effectively an act of annexation rather than union. The Tudor reorganisation of England and Wales under Henry VIII resembled the way in which seven European powers carved out the shape of what were to become fifty African countries in the nineteenth century, without consideration of where ethnic groups were located or traditional boundaries lay. The act of 1536 made no use of Offa's Dyke, the eighth-century earth embankment designed to mark off the border with Mercia, much of which is still visible today.[23] That was a way of marking off two kingdoms, whereas what happened during the reign of Henry VIII was a way of reorganising one kingdom. As with the meandering line that later divided 'North' from 'South' in Ireland and which remains so controversial today, any border created in 1536 was not intended to mark a boundary between nations.

---

20   See Davies, *A History of Wales*, pp. 151–152.

21   See Davies, *A History of Wales*, p. 167. An eighteenth century writer, Davies calls Pennant 'the most learned of the Welsh antiquarians of his age' (p. 336).

22   See the Laws of Wales Acts of 1535 and 1542, sometimes called 'Acts of Union' but this is not like the Act of Union with Scotland, being more of an annexation. See Johnes, Martin *Wales: England's Colony?: The Conquest, Assimilation and Re-creation of Wales*.

23   This is explored further below in Chapter 10, 'Home Rule for Northern Ireland?'

It was different in the case of Scotland. By the end of the seventeenth century, the need to settle the relations between England and Scotland had become crucial. As the eighteenth century dawned, the War of the Spanish Succession was making England acutely aware that it might have its own war over the succession to the three kingdoms of England, Scotland and Ireland. Scotland wanted the succession to go to the Stuarts and Louis XIV, the King of France, backed James' exiled son James III, the so-called 'Old Pretender', as the rightful heir to the throne. The heir was now a teenager and the Auld Alliance (of Scotland and France) was starting to look threatening once again.[24] In England the Act of Settlement in 1701 was passed overruling the rights of the House of Stuart for those of Hanover. However, two years later the Scottish Parliament passed its own Act of Security which claimed the right to determine the succession and not have it imposed from Westminster. An Act of Union had to be secured if there was not to be a War of the Stuart Succession.

Unlike the annexation of Wales, the Act of Union between England and Scotland was an agreement between two parliaments, one which left Scotland with a degree of autonomy denied to Wales, in terms of retaining its own legal system, its own education system and its own 'established' presbyterian church. Nairn talks of 'a nationality which resigned statehood but preserved an extraordinary amount of the institutional and psychological baggage normally associated with independence.'[25] There was intense pressure from the English, who had demonstrated that they could elbow Scotland out of the acquisition of colonies and hamper her trade with the rest of Europe. Yet this rivalry ended up making the union more likely rather than less. Scotland had designs on creating an empire overseas but lacked the means. The Scottish Parliament created the Company of Scotland in 1695 which funded a settlement to be called New Caledonia. It was a disaster. Sickness, storms and siege decimated the settlers and English governors in nearby colonies had no desire to help what at the time was a rival nation with its own imperial designs. They treated the Scots as they would the Spanish or the French. The result was a significant number of Scots willing to concede independence in return for the benefits of trade and the possibility of participating in an Empire that the resources of a combined British

---

24   See Simms, *Britain's Europe*, p. 47. He quotes Daniel Defoe's remark about 'shutting a back door' – that familiar image – and suggests that the Whig elites both North and South of the border were prepared to settle their differences in order to combine against Louis XIV.

25   Nairn, Tom *The Break-Up of Britain*, p. 119.

Union could manage. Scotland's willingness to support the Act of Union in 1707 was therefore linked to its abortive attempt to colonise Darien in Central America in 1698. This was the beginning of a century in which what was to become British overseas expansion took off, from the time of the Treaty of Utrecht in 1713 to the enormous 'gains' in India and Canada in mid-century.[26]

The Act of Union provided Scotland with the benefits (as they were believed at the time) of imperial expansion and in the following century the benefits of industrial expansion. It was a question of receiving a share of the spoils, and to this extent, despite the ways in which the English were arm-twisting their northern neighbour, a matter more of partnership than annexation. As Nairn puts it, 'during the prolonged era of Anglo-Saxon imperialist expansion, the Scottish ruling order found that it had given up statehood for a hugely profitable junior partnership in the New Rome.'[27] Arguably one can see in Scottish attitudes to England at this time an early version of the UK's attitude after the Second World War, as it also came to accept that it could no longer manage an empire and chose instead to be a junior partner of the USA.

This by no means implies that Scotland would be any less reluctant to opt for independence in the twenty-first century, when the loss of empire and industrial decline of Britain make those spoils much less alluring. In fact, some Scots would say that the 'spoils' started travelling in the opposite direction half a century ago, when England began receiving the benefits of offshore oil deposits in the 1970s, the decade when the Scottish National Party first became much stronger (campaigning under the slogan 'It's Scotland's oil') and books appeared predicting the end of the union, like Tom Nairn's *The Break-up of Britain*, first published in 1977. Partly influenced by this decline of Britain, a number of books appeared over the next two decades exploring Scottish identity.[28]

Scotland has a stronger sense, as Bogdanor puts it, that the Act of Union sets down certain parameters within which the new British parliament must operate.[29] Scotland is particularly aware of limitations to the idea of Parlia-

---

26   See the first part of 'The British Imperial Isles,' Chapter 9 of Norman Davies, *The Isles*, pp. 553–584.

27   Nairn, Tom *The Break-Up of Britain*, p. 119.

28   For instance, David McCrone, Stephen Kendrick and Pat Shaw (eds) *The Making of Scotland: Nature, Culture and Social Change*, which appeared in 1989 and David McCrone's *Understanding Scotland: The Sociology of a Stateless Nation*, which appeared in 1992.

29   See Bogdanor, *Beyond Brexit: Towards a British Constitution*, esp. the chapter 'Brexit and Devolution: The Future of the United Kingdom'.

ment's sovereignty, not least because the Scottish Parliament preceding the Act of Union was never fully sovereign (some in Scotland claim that the idea of loyalty to the Scottish Parliament was merely conditional goes back to the Declaration of Arbroath in 1320) and therefore was not in a position to give its sovereignty away to the new British Parliament. At the very least it could be taken to suggest that the Act simply meant that Scottish representatives were admitted to the parliament of England. Moreover, the idea that parliamentary sovereignty means that Westminster can do what it likes appears to clash with the explicit agreement at the time of the Act of Union that in certain respects Scotland could go its own way. It retained its own legal, educational and religious system under the 1707 Act of Union. From a Scottish perspective, these constraints agreed upon at the time of the Act of Union must necessarily mean that the new British Parliament can't do what it likes where cultural and legal arrangements north of the border are concerned. However, no machinery has been established in order to enforce this or to work through, in detail, how it can be squared with the idea of parliamentary sovereignty. In practice, the new British parliament passed, for instance, certain laws concerning the Presbyterian church that might have been challenged for being unconstitutional on the grounds that such matters could be decided by Scotland alone. This is a situation in which a degree of sovereignty-sharing can not only help to strengthen a British Union post-Brexit but help to formalise the Act of Union through which England and Wales first joined with Scotland to form Great Britain.

Scotland's willingness to support the Act of Union in 1707 was linked, as we have seen, to its abortive attempt to colonise Darien in Central America in 1698. A rival was cajoled into becoming a partner. In the case of Ireland, it was different. Simms suggests that the same concern for French exploitation of the 'back door' at the time of Napoleon led to a further Act of Union in 1800, drawing Ireland into Britain by merging the Parliaments.[30] Thus, Napoleon forced Britain and Ireland together, just as a century earlier Louis XIV had forced England and Scotland together. But if so, they were forced together in very different ways.

From the time of the Hanoverian succession in 1714 all Kings of Britain were automatically Kings of Ireland, but here there was no sense of participation either in the spoils of empire or (after the mid-eighteenth century) the benefits of the industrial revolution. There was no equivalent in Ireland outside Ulster, where what Peter Gibbon calls 'the great industrial triangle of the valleys of the

---

30   Simms, *Britain's Europe*, p. 112.

Mersey, the Clyde and the Lagan[31] helped to set what was to become Northern Ireland apart and created a strongly unionist working class. Ireland remained a country whose economy was based on agriculture.

The Irish were not only kept from industrialising, they did not have control of the agriculture to which they were largely confined. Absentee landowners enjoyed the profits from the land and determined how it would be administered. Though its population grew in the eighteenth century, rising from about two million to four by the end of the century, most of them were very poor, housed in little cottages called 'cabins' – the word an indication of how cramped they were.[32]

Hence, when in 1800 a further Act of Union created a United Kingdom of Britain and Ireland, it was hardly an invitation to Ireland to share in the benefits of industrial and imperial expansion. As with Scotland, this further Act of Union reaffirmed the sovereignty of the Westminster Parliament and ignored the pre-Union Irish Parliament's repudiation of it, later taken up by Irish Repeal movements. Yet though Scotland, like Ireland, was confronted by the supremacy of the Westminster parliament and was also a country whose people overwhelmingly rejected Anglicanism, and though it also suffered a measure of economic oppression from England itself, for instance at the time of the so-called highland clearances, its economy did benefit from the industrial revolution. Scotland was partner as well as victim when it came to English expansion. Ireland was never more than a victim.

Religion was a crucial ingredient in the way Ireland was never drawn into partnership with Britain even after it became part of the UK. In the nineteenth century the Irish could no more control the churches they might have expected

---

31   Nairn, Tom *The Break-Up of Britain*, p. 224. The original article by Peter Gibbon was published in New Left Review, I/55 May/June 1969 and was entitled 'Dialectic of Religion and Class in Ulster'.

32   Arthur Young, in his famous *A Tour in Ireland 1776–1779*, described Irish dwellings in the following terms (pp. 25–6): 'The cottages of the Irish, which are all called cabbins, are the most miserable looking hovels that can well be conceived: They generally consist of only one room: mud kneaded with straw is the common material of the walls; these are rarely above seven feet high, and not always above five or six; they are about two feet thick, and have only a door, which lets in light instead of a window, and should let the smoke out instead of a chimney, but they had rather keep it in especially when the cabbin is not built with regular walls, but supported on one, or perhaps on both sides by the banks of a broad dry ditch.' They remained in this state for much of the nineteenth century.

to worship in than the fields they cultivated. The established Anglican church maintained control over these, while the mostly Catholic inhabitants were forced to worship in fields through so-called 'hedge masses'. Scotland had a different brand of Christianity to the Anglicans too, but its established Kirk had a degree of recognition that the Catholic Church in Ireland did not have. Technically, the present monarch may not be a Catholic, but attends Presbyterian church services when in Scotland and is duty-bound to protect that Church under the terms of the Act of Union.

More than that, Ireland could be treated more as a colony ripe for settlement than as a part of the UK ripe for development. An earlier example of this approach, but one with huge significance in later centuries, was the so-called 'plantation of Ulster.' Though with English supervision, this was carried out by Scots. At the start of the seventeenth century Ulster was the most Gaelic, Catholic and traditional province in Ireland. Its nature was radically changed by 'plantations.' It became an equivalent to Massachusetts which was created for a similar reason, to maintain a 'purer' religion than that which was practised in the home country.[33] The Puritans who travelled away from Plymouth on the Mayflower in 1620 were looking for a 'new Eden' away from bishops and what they saw as other Anglican compromises with papacy. The Scots who went to Ulster in the earlier part of James I's reign were similarly looking to escape the impositions of Anglican rule on Presbyterian Scotland and sought to implant their idea of a pure form of Protestantism. Norman Davies reminds us that:

> The Ulster Plantation was planned at exactly the same time as the third attempt to plant a colony in Virginia. Derry, renamed Londonderry, was to be the Irish Jamestown. The native Irish were to play the same part as the native Americans.[34]

And since the Irish were meant to play the role of 'Red Indians,' as the native Americans were called, they were treated as such. When they rose up and killed 2,000 settlers in 1641, this was seen as a 'native uprising' and ruthlessly put down.

Davies describes the way in which the new settlers organised their lives:

---

33   See Davies, *The Isles*, pp. 478–482.
34   Davies, *The Isles*, p. 479.

> From the outset, therefore, the new settlers of Ulster operated a system of social and cultural apartheid. The principal leaseholders were usually English servitors, that is, former soldiers or crown servants, but the mass of tenants were preponderantly Scots. They built neat new towns and villages of timber-framed or stone cottages, which they fortified like frontier posts and adorned with English names.... They built their own churches ... they cleared the land, cut down the forests, and applied themselves to arable farming on a scale never seen before and they rapidly organised a prosperous trade in timber, cattle and flax. They had no contact with the native Irish except those who worked for them as labourers or servants...[35]

It is a description which might be replicated in terms of many overseas settlements. The same distance from the 'natives', except in so far as they are needed as servants, the same creation of secure, fortified compounds designed as if they were being built back at home. And eventually the same question that arose in all those colonies which it was difficult to leave because they had so many settlers, such as Rhodesia (later Zimbabwe) and South Africa. In this sense it was not difficult to link the Unilateral Declaration of Independence by Ian Smith in Rhodesia in the 1960s, where the white settlers in the future Zimbabwe declared that they were now the rulers, with the carving out of a slice of Ireland in 1922, comprising six of the traditional nine counties of Ulster and saying that they should be cut off from the rest of the island and run by the Protestant majority in that particular part of it. If one tries to imagine how, in 1922, the UK was able to accept the loss of one-third of its territory – more than Germany was forced to lose after its defeat in the First World War – the reason lies in the fact that what became the Irish Free State was seen more as a colony or dominion demanding independence than as a part of the UK precipitating a civil war. As Robert Skidelsky put it:

> historians mislead if they also see 1916 (the date of the Easter Rising) as the start of the dissolution of the British state. Ireland was part of the empire, Scotland was not.[36]

---

35   Davies, Norman. *The Isles*, p. 480.

36   Skidelsky *Britain since 1900: a success Story?* pp. 180–181. See also Stephen Howe, *Ireland and Empire: Colonial Legacies in Irish History and Culture*.

The dynastic umbrella

The UK as a multinational state has hardly emerged in any smooth or logical manner. It has instead been created by successive unions, each one taking a different form. Over a century ago Seeley's standard textbook referred to *The Expansion of England*,[37] and in the twentieth century many continued to see it in those terms, including the great social historian George Macaulay Trevelyan in his *History of England*, seeing English expansion as partly a mission to bring the 'Celtic fringe; into the embrace of 'civilisation'.[38] This is partly why the Scottish reference to themselves as 'North Britain' after the Union of 1707 never found a response in England, for if they were to call themselves 'South Britain' it would undermine the idea of England simply spreading itself into other parts of the Isles. Others have stressed the importance of the Protestant religion in building a Union, but apart from the fact that this could only apply to Britain, Protestantism took very different forms in Britain itself, whether Welsh nonconformity, Scottish Presbyterianism or the Church of England. Somewhere at the back of this idea may be the idea of a liberalising Protestant Spirit that swept through the land, but there was nothing very liberalising about some of the forms which Protestantism took in the Isles or in the way in which the Act of Union with Ireland in 1800 failed to introduce Catholic emancipation, which had been promised. Norman Davies goes so far as to deny that the United Kingdom has ever been a nation-state at all, although of course it depends on how you define the term. It remains essentially, he argues, a dynastic conglomerate. His view is that it is what became the British monarchy that provides an umbrella to cover a multiplicity which contains no unified legal system, no centralised education system, no common religion (the Act of Union enshrined that England and Scotland went their different ways in these three areas) and no common history.[39]

---

37   Seeley, *The Expansion of England* was published in 1883, at the height of Empire.
38   Trevelyan's *History of England* came out in 1926. For analysis of this way of thinking see Colls, *Identity of England*.
39   This is his conclusion in one of his most interesting books, *Vanished Kingdoms*, which examines lands that have failed to survive, or have been transformed out of recognition, like the former USSR. Davies believes 'that the United Kingdom will collapse is a foregone conclusion' (p. 679). He is arguably too influenced by what he sees as other empires trying and failing to decentralise like Austria-Hungary. See *Vanished Kingdoms*, pp. 679–685.

A famous case from the year that Elizabeth II was crowned, *MacCormick v Lord Advocate*, considered whether Queen Elizabeth should be known as Elizabeth II in Scotland when the nation had no Elizabeth I. The court dismissed the case, but the point about the role of the monarch as part of the glue holding the UK together (Elizabeth I, of course, was no more Queen of the UK than she was Queen of Scotland) is illustrated by these concerns at the time of her coronation. Seventy years on, no one could have failed to notice how the carefully choreographed and long-drawn-out obsequies after the death of Elizabeth II took in each of the 'four nations' in turn. Once the British monarchy had lost real power, it was able to exercise symbolic power. It took until the latter half of Victoria's reign before, as Cannadine argues, the ceremonial existed 'to exalt the crown above the political battle, to that Olympus of decorative, integrative impotence which it was later to occupy'.[40]

Cannadine points out that where other countries in the late nineteenth century (for instance Russia) were still parading ritual in order to exalt royal power, in the UK such ritual was made possible by growing royal weakness. The monarch moved from being the head of society in the early nineteenth century, part of an aristocratic elite that moved around in horse-drawn carriages, to being the head of the nation at the end of the century and even the head of the empire. Disraeli made Victoria Empress of India in 1877 and twenty years later Joseph Chamberlain roped in colonial premiers and 'exotic' representatives of different parts of the empire to mark the Queen's Diamond Jubilee.

The monarch was still in a horse-drawn carriage while the rest of the population had moved to bicycles and, to a growing extent, buses and even private motor-cars. But this was what made royal ritual so popular and gave it a 'fairy-tale' quality which endured through the twentieth century and the transformation of the Empire into a Commonwealth:

> In the world of the aeroplane, the tank and the atomic bomb, the anachronistic grandeur of horses, carriages, swords and plumed hats was further enhanced.[41]

Yet even if the UK was increasingly held together by its royal sovereign in the manner of the Habsburg Empire of Austria-Hungary, the fate of that empire alone would show that it needed to develop more than a line of imported

---

40   See David Cannadine's chapter in Hobsbawm and Ranger, *The Invention of Tradition*, pp. 101–165. The quotation is on p. 116.

41   Hobsbawm and Ranger, The *Invention of Tradition*, p. 143.

monarchs to maintain the identity of a multinational state. It is noteworthy that when Elizabeth II died in 2022, many commentators fixated on the possibility of the former 'dominions' following Barbados in the direction of declaring themselves republics, rather than addressing the question of how far Charles III would be a less effective head of the British Union than his predecessor.[42] A more careful analysis of the prolonged funeral celebrations, with the carefully stage-managed visits of Charles to Scotland, Wales and Northern Ireland, would suggest that it is not Jamaica that is a source of concern to those who fear for the future role of the monarchy but nations closer to home – indeed the nature of home itself.

Conclusion

The chapter began by looking at the way English self-perception has been affected by two invasions. In the first place there is the Roman invasion, about the significance of which there remains some argument, both about the extent to which it was a 'civilising' mission and the extent to which, even if it was, it had a significant effect on the lives of most Britons. There are those who think that the most noteworthy aspect of the Roman 'heritage' in England and Wales was that, unlike in Gaul, it was not embedded enough to be passed on.

The second invasion, the Norman conquest of 1066, attached England to the continent, as Chapter Two sought to emphasise in terms of the continuing importance of mainland Europe to British identity and affairs. But in doing so, it led to a shift of focus to the South of England and the idea that expansion to the rest of the Isles was a defensive manoeuvre to ensure that the less 'developed' parts of the Isles did not provide a platform for rebellion or further invasions.

The chapter suggested that the narrative arc through which the British Union was built up took different forms in Wales, Scotland and Ireland. The suggestion of annexation in the case of Wales, partnership in the case of Scotland and colonisation in the case of Ireland is an over-simplification,[43] but it

---

42   The BBC produced a report on 13th September 2022 under the headline 'Will Jamaica now seek to "move on" and become a republic?' See https://www.bbc.com/news/world-latin-america-62846653

43   Though not, perhaps, too much of an over-simplification. Note Brendan O'Leary's trilogy on Northern Ireland, whose volumes are entitled 'Colonialism', 'Control' and

at least points up the different ways in which the United Kingdom was put together. The result is that the Isles are now made up of two nation states, one of which is a conglomerate or 'multinational state,' to give it the description used by Vernon Bogdanor, comprising four different parts that have been variously described as nations (or the 'home nations'), countries, regions and principalities.[44] 'Conglomerate' might not be a very attractive word, but it needs to be pointed out that 'the United Kingdom' (which has to be spelt out on passports as 'The United Kingdom of Great Britain and Northern Ireland') is a wordy description which would befit a conglomerate. It has been argued that there is little to unite it beyond the symbolic power of the monarchy, which is itself subject to change now that Elizabeth II is dead. The death of Elizabeth might help to make clear that the UK needs to go further than relying on the symbolic power of monarchy in order to maintain its unity as a single nation-state.

'Consociation,' the last a new term to add to the list of possible ways forward for governing the Isles.

44   See his *Beyond Brexit: Towards a British Constitution*.

Chapter Nine: Saving the UK4

The failure of Home Rule All Round

The last chapter looked at the way in which the UK was formed. But now that we are in the twenty-first century, how is the UK to be held together? Some form of devolution for the 'four nations' of the UK has been a regular part of political debate over at least the last generation. But how seriously has it been implemented? G. K. Chesterton said of Christianity that it had not been tried and found wanting but found difficult and consequently not tried.[1] The same, this book will argue, can be said of devolution. The same insouciance, where the constitutional implications of belonging to the EU is concerned, now applies to the status of the 'four nations' within the UK.

Proposals for devolution go back a long way. They originally concerned the area created by the Act of Union of 1800, in which the whole of Ireland was incorporated into the UK. The Irish MP Isaac Butt proposed 'Home Government' in 1870, with parliaments in Scotland, Ireland and 'England plus Wales' (hence no separate parliament for Wales), all subordinate to Westminster. Gladstone supported Home Rule for Ireland as a way of preserving both the Union and the sovereignty of the Westminster Parliament but opposed the idea of the Irish MPs remaining in Westminster.[2] To his opponents, including those who broke away to form the Liberal Unionists, allowing Ireland a separate parliament would be the beginning of a move towards independence, and it is true that both the Act of Union in 1707 and that of 1800 had involved the abolition of the Scottish and Irish parliaments respectively.

---

1   It is a quote from Chesterton's *What's Wrong with the World*. It is found in Part One, 'The Homelessness of Man,' Section V. 'The Unfinished Temple'.
2   See Keating, *State and Nation in the United Kingdom*, p. 32.

The Liberal Unionist Joseph Chamberlain, who had split with Gladstone on precisely this issue, had his own idea for 'Home Rule All Round,' with Irish representation at Westminster continuing whatever was granted to Ireland in the way of home rule. This was subsequently backed by Gladstone's successor, the Earl of Rosebery, Liberal Prime Minister in 1895 (as it was at the time by the Welsh MP and future Prime Minister, David Lloyd George).

'Home Rule All Round' obviously referred to all the nations of the UK, including Wales. But given the fact that at the end of the nineteenth century the most pressing concern was Ireland, it was in the context of the future of Ireland that 'Home Rule All Round' came to a head towards the end of the First World War. What is noticeable from the constitutional debates of the time is that they raised precisely the issues that were raised at the end of the last century over devolution. Was Home Rule a way of avoiding independence or would it make it more likely? Why should Irish MPs be able to vote in Parliament on matters that concerned English, Welsh and Scottish MPs, while they would be unable to vote on matters that concerned the Irish Parliament alone (the West Lothian question associated with Tam Dalyell goes back a century further). The main difference is that for 'liberal imperialists' like Joseph Chamberlain 'Home Rule All Round' was seen in terms of the wider Empire and the role of the dominions in particular.

The early twentieth century was a time when people from all parties talked about some form of 'federal devolution' in the United Kingdom. Home Rule for Ireland was on the statute book from September 1914, but implementation was to be delayed until the end of the war. It was made more difficult by the Ulster Unionists, who resisted any form of Home Rule for the whole of Ireland, and by the Easter Rising in 1916. But perhaps more important was the effect of over a century during which, as the last chapter pointed out, Ireland had been incorporated into the United Kingdom but had seen its population remain stagnant and had been largely unaffected by the industrial revolution taking place elsewhere. On top of that was the effect of the famine in the 1840s, during which a million died and a further million were forced into emigration. Ireland's population of about four-and-a-half million on the outbreak of World War One was hardly any higher than its population at the time of the Act of Union with Britain in 1800.[3] The island of Britain, on the other hand, had seen its popula-

---

3   The figures are striking. Cormac O'Grada published an article in 1979 entitled 'The Population of Ireland 1700–1900: A survey,' *Annales de Démographie Historique* 1979, pp. 281–299. It contains a table of the population of the whole island of Ireland dur-

tion treble during the same period, mostly in England. Two results of this are often under-estimated. One was the fact that three times as many citizens of Irish origin ended up in the USA than lived in Ireland itself, a major influence upon US opinion and a contributing factor to its reluctance to become involved in wars between 'colonial powers' in the twentieth century. The other was an obvious reduction (insofar as seats were proportional to population, which was only partly so) in the influence of Irish MPs on the Westminster Parliament, even though Irish MPs did sometimes end up sustaining Liberal governments in power. They did so in 1885 and, most notably, in 1910, when Irish votes allowed the reforming Liberal government first elected in 1906 to continue in office after an election in which Conservatives and Liberals won the same number of seats.[4]

Modern discussions of devolution frequently point to England as the 'elephant in the room' and explain that something like five-sixths of the UK population is located there. At the time of the Act of Union (when of course the whole of Ireland was included in the UK) England represented only slightly more than half the UK population. Had anything like 'Home Rule All Round' been implemented at that point, England's dominance might have been much less marked. The island of Ireland, had it grown at the same rate of Britain, would have had about fifteen million inhabitants by the time of the First World War – about double the number of inhabitants that it has now.[5]

---

ing those two centuries (p. 283). He gives a population of about 4 million in 1781, 7 million in 1821, 5 million in 1881 (after the famine and emigration) and 4 million in 1926. The population of the whole island is now about 7 million, roughly what it was two centuries ago. By way of contrast, the population of Britain roughly trebled in the period between the mid-eighteenth and mid-nineteenth century, from 6–7 million to about 20 million, doubled again by the end of the century to around 40 million and then added another 25 million in the course of the 20th Century to its present (approximately) 65 million. Nowadays the Western Isle has only about one-tenth of the population of its Eastern neighbour.

4   The Liberals and Conservatives each won just over 270 seats. Labour had 42 and the Irish Nationalists 74. Thus the Liberals had a comfortable majority with the support of the Irish. It might be compared to the situation in 2010 when the Conservatives had a comfortable majority by governing in coalition with the Liberal Democrats. Electoral Calculus publishes results for all elections since 1900. See https://www.electoralcalculus.co.uk/commentary.html The House of Commons Library publishes results for all elections since 1918.

5   As the article by O'Grada shows, the population of Ireland was about 7 million in 1820, at a time when that of Britain was perhaps 12–15 million. If it had more than doubled

The decreasing significance of the Irish vote and the long history of neglect and under-investment that made Ireland for a century more a victim of UK economic expansion than a partner in it, affected the willingness of Ireland to be satisfied with Home Rule. The Easter Rising and the brutal reaction to it by a government that thought such actions unconscionable at a time of world war were important factors too, but Home Rule all Round was still thought to be a practical proposition by many when the First World War ended. Moreover, in the early twentieth century the UK not only had a problem of how much power should be devolved to England, Scotland and Wales, but also how much should be devolved to its imperial possessions overseas, its colonies and dominions. The approach of Woodrow Wilson, the U.S. President, with his emphasis upon national self-determination, created obvious difficulties for European powers with colonial possessions.[6] The principle of self-determination was busy carving new states like Czechoslovakia and Yugoslavia out of the former Austro-Hungarian Empire. New states would arise from the declining Ottoman Empire. Must not the same thing happen to the other European empires? It was already clear that the so-called dominions like Canada and Australia were calling for greater autonomy and disliked the way in which they had simply been 'summoned to war' in 1914 on the basis of an imperial edict issued by George V. The governments and parliaments of the dominions and colonies were not consulted. As Taylor puts it:

> Some 50 million Africans and 250 million Indians were involved, without consultation, in a war of which they understood nothing against an enemy who was also unknown to them.[7]

---

as the population of Britain did over the next century, 15 million is a reasonable estimate. It would also have meant far more Irish MPs in a UK parliament and thereby more influence.

6   Consider Wilson's 'fourteen points,' from 8th January 1918. Point 10 declared that 'the peoples of Austria-Hungary... should be accorded the freest opportunity of autonomous development.' But what about India? What about Egypt? Point 5 talked about a 'free, open-minded and absolutely impartial adjustment of all colonial claims,' but then went on to say that 'the interests of the populations concerned must have equal weight with the equitable claims of the government whose title is to be determined.' What if the populations concerned demanded autonomy like the newly-born nations of Czechoslovakia and Yugoslavia in order to serve 'the interests of their populations'? See Taylor, *English History 1914–1945*, p. 119 for a list of the 14 points.

7   Taylor, A.J.P *English History 1914–1945*, p. 3.

Australians and New Zealanders had fought and died in large numbers in the Dardanelles and elsewhere. Indians had fought in the trenches. Thousands of Canadians had died in the battle of Vimy Ridge in 1917. With talk of self-determination in the air when the War finally came to an end, it was clear that the future of Great Britain would be inseparable from the future of the British Empire. India had been promised 'responsible government... as an integral part of the British Empire.'[8] What was that responsible government going to mean? Was this Home Rule? How would it differ from the sort of responsible government to be offered to Wales, Scotland and Ireland? Home Rule All Round could represent Home Rule all round Britain or Home Rule All Round the Empire, with Westminster retained as an Imperial Parliament, where the Empire would be represented in a United States of Greater Britain or some kind of Britannic Commonwealth.

Britain had already been down a road which was similar to that explored by the European Economic Community half a century later. Joseph Chamberlain, the champion of the policy of Empire Free Trade, recognised the problems involved in trying to unite the Empire around a common defence and foreign policy. But he had high hopes of being able to unite it around a trade zone with a common external tariff on goods from outside the Empire. It proved to be a task beyond him, partly because some of Chamberlain's colleagues feared that his ideas were a threat to the principles of free trade. Another reason was that the dominions increasingly wished to develop their own industrial strength and did not want a system where they were given preference in supplying raw materials to the 'mother country' in return for preference being given to her manufacturing exports.[9] Though some forms of imperial preference were eventually put in place and were a bone of contention during the discussions about joining the EU in the 1960s and 1970s, the dream of an economically self-sufficient empire was not fulfilled. But in its attempt to strengthen the bonds of Empire through a common economic policy, Chamberlain anticipated a route to be taken later by those who moved on from the failure of the European Defence Policy to the development of the European Economic Community.

---

8   See Taylor, *English History 1914–1945*, p. 152. The promise was made in 1917, by which time hundreds of thousands of Indians had died from participating in a war which they were commanded to take part in on the basis of a proclamation by their viceroy.

9   Empire Free Trade failed because the dominions wished to industrialise themselves. This became clear at an Imperial Conference held in Ottawa in 1933. See Taylor, *English History 1914–1945*, p. 333.

The hope after the First World War, then, was that some form of autonomy would be an alternative to independence, not only within the UK but within the British Empire. The government was aware that not only the 'dominions' like Canada and Australia, but countries like Egypt and India, not ruled by settlers but with powerful voices calling for independence, were demanding more control over their affairs. Both within the British Isles and the British Empire Westminster was preparing to concede a little in the hope that it would not have to concede too much.

In the last year of the First World War, several Conservative MPs declared support for a 'system of federal devolution for the United Kingdom.' There was therefore a measure of all-party support for devolution, including Arthur Henderson, General Secretary of the Labour Party, who came out in favour of Home Rule All Round in June 1918. However, despite a vote in favour of devolution in 1919 and a Speaker's Conference being set up on how to deliver it, its final report the following year was ignored. It appeared to lose its significance almost as soon as it was proposed.[10]

The reason had a lot to do with developments both in Ireland and in the Empire in the aftermath of the First World War. Following the Easter rising of 1916 Lloyd George, who was not yet Prime Minister but had set his sights on becoming so, tried to negotiate immediate Home Rule for all of Ireland except for the six counties which formed part of historic Ulster. This was difficult for the Nationalists to accept, since it was Home Rule for the whole of Ireland that had been agreed and which was already on the statute book. Lloyd George proposed that the six counties remain part of the United Kingdom 'until after the war.'[11] It was the familiar expedient repeated later, assuring one side that the six counties represented a temporary expedient bound to fail and the other side that it was a viable proposition bound to succeed.

The negotiations nearly succeeded, but when they eventually didn't the supporters of constitutional reform rather than armed resistance found their position weakened. Sinn Fein began to triumph in by-elections and in the elections to the Dáil (the Irish Parliament) in 1918 Sinn Fein won 73 out of 103 seats.[12]

---

10   See the excellent blog by Andrew Green, https://gwallter.com/history/the-home-rul
      e-all-round-movement.html. Half English and half Scots, Andrew Green is a fluent
      Welsh speaker who now lives in Swansea.

11   See Note B, 'The Proposed Irish settlement, 1916' in Taylor, *English History 1914–1945*,
      pp. 71–72.

12   Though they received less than 50% of the votes.

They proceeded to proclaim a Republic and act as if it already existed, levying taxes and setting up republican courts. A similar strategy had been pursued by the Hungarians half a century earlier with agents of the Austrian Empire.

The strategy was soon undermined. The IRA (Irish Republican Army) launched a war without any authorisation from the Dáil, while the British brought in brutal irregulars who acted as terror squads. The death toll mounted on both sides. Once more Lloyd George tried to reach a settlement, again seeking to square the circle by ruling in a United Ireland while ruling out any coercion of the six counties to accept it. The Government of Ireland Act in 1920 devised two Home Rule Parliaments, one based in Dublin and the other in Belfast, together with reduced representation in the Westminster Parliament and a Council of Ireland drawn from the two parliaments to reflect the unity of Ireland. Sinn Fein refused to accept the Southern Parliament, while the Ulster Unionists rejected the Council of Ireland but accepted their own Parliament. Ironically, this meant that the one regional level of government in the UK after 1921 was the Unionist-dominated Northern Ireland Parliament.

There was a similar lack of progress in the Empire. In India a few provincial constitutions and much-trumpeted elections did not dent the power of the viceroy or the India office in London, while 1919 saw the bloody massacre at Amritsar where General Dyer oversaw the killing of nearly 400 members of an unarmed crowd. Perhaps because of the brutalising effect of four years of warfare, the excesses being displayed in Ireland seemed to be replicated elsewhere and with the same results. From that point nothing short of independence was acceptable. The India National Congress launched a campaign of civil disobedience in order to secure it.[13]

Home Rule All Round therefore took off neither in the Empire nor in the United Kingdom. Where the Isles were concerned, the creation of the Irish Free State in 1921 after two years of violent conflict suggested that it was impossible to concede anything less than almost total independence. When a settlement was finally reached, the Republic achieved Dominion status on a par with Canada, meaning that it could move towards full independence if it chose (which it eventually did). It had far more independence than the early home rulers had ever dreamed of, amounting to complete autonomy in finance, justice, administration and education. But in order to secure this it had had to

---

13   It should also be noted that India suffered disproportionately from the influenza outbreak of 1918, which accounted for over ten million deaths in the country, more than any other country.

give up the six counties, over the future of which a bloody civil war was fought in 1922–3. In 1925 the Council of Ireland that was meant to represent the whole island was formally abolished.

Hence the one instance of home rule to emerge from the events of the early twentieth century was the Northern Ireland Parliament – and it was hardly a good instance, since it was accused of using its powers to rig constituencies, create a police force that was not representative of both communities and tolerate discrimination against the Catholic minority (which made up one-third of the population of the six counties) in housing and employment allocations. Home Rule All Round had ended up as Home Rule in One Place Only, the results of which were to generate protests and later violence in the North for thirty years in the second half of the century.

Unsurprisingly, many concluded that whether it was Ireland or India, the nation state appeared to be the only kid on the block. Solutions in terms of increased autonomy, however defined, were a useless halfway house between regional status and full independence. Support for a wider federal settlement for the two islands that after 1922 made up the UK and the Irish Free State started to fade. This did not mean that interest in more autonomy went away. A petition asking for Home Rule for Scotland, for instance, presented to Parliament in 1949, was signed by some two million Scots (perhaps 40% of the population at that time). However, the so-called Scottish Covenant provoked little reaction in Westminster.[14] The halfway house between independence and regional or provincial status seemed unable to provide a viable option. At the time of the Scottish Covenant a Labour government elected after the Second World War was increasingly aware of the fact that nothing short of independence could follow the Empire. British India had just collapsed into different independent nations (more were to follow), with over a million dead. Doubtless a policy of 'divide and rule' on the part of the British themselves was partly to blame for this bloody civil war, whose consequences continue to this day. Nevertheless, it seemed clear that the only option for the future was the jostling pack of independent nation-states, the Hobbesian 'state of nature' transposed to the international realm as outlined earlier in this book.

Hence the development of a sovereignty-sharing system between member states of European Coal and Steel Community and later the European Economic Community did little to make the UK rethink the structure of its own in-

---

14   See Jack Brand, *The National Movement in Scotland*, originally published in 1978 but re-issued in 2021.

ternal union. As earlier chapters suggested, it was hostile to a system in which sovereignty was shared and did not think that there were lessons to be learned from it. Hence when in the 1970s, shortly after it had joined the EEC, the UK government began to interest itself in forms of devolution for Scotland and Wales, it did not for a moment consider the way power was shared between the UK, France, West Germany and the other countries in what by 1973 was the nine members of the EEC as a springboard for developing new approaches to power-sharing within the UK.

Devolution

One of the reasons why new approaches to power-sharing within the UK failed to connect with those outside it in the newly formed EEC was that the pioneers of such approaches were deeply hostile to the EEC. The 'original manifesto', as McBride calls it, for a 'four nations' approach to the future of the UK came from a New Zealander, J.G.A Pocock, whose 'British History: A Plea for a New Subject', was first published in 1975. As McBride explains:

> The 'Plea for a New Subject' was occasioned by the United Kingdom's entry into the European Economic Community (EEC) in January 1973 and the consequent demise of the system of imperial trade preference that discriminated in favour of British producers—even if the British in question lived on the other side of the planet.[15]

The impact of the Common Agricultural Policy on Commonwealth producers was a hotly debated topic at the time of Britain's entry to the EEC. Since the basis of the CAP was to support farmers through a guaranteed floor price together with a common external tariff to prevent that guaranteed minimum price being undercut by cheap imports, joining the EEC would effectively mean making the UK buy more expensive food from Europe rather than cheaper food from the Commonwealth. To those with memories of Empire Free Trade this went against a tradition reaching back nearly a century, where the aim was that Britain's manufacturing exports were received at a discount by her Empire and in return food from the Empire was received more cheaply by the 'mother country'. The economic model upon which this system was based was always a con-

---

15   McBride, Ian 'J.G.A. Pocock and the Politics of British History,' in Lloyd-Jones & Scull, *Four Nations Approaches to Modern British History: A (Dis)united Kingdom?* p. 40.

troversial one and never fully implemented, since it threatened to discourage industrial development in the Empire outside the UK. But as McBride makes clear, the system could still exert a romantic appeal:

> Emotional ties between New Zealand and Britain were strengthened by the islands' unique reliance on the export trade with Britain. Hundreds of thousands of tons of refrigerated mutton and dairy products were sent to Britain annually by steamship. In return, ships from Britain carried books, newspapers and mail to the dominions. More than ever before, the dominions were cultural provinces of London, co-owners—not mere subjects—of the world's largest empire.[16]

Pocock's concerns about the future of the United Kingdom were therefore tied up with his own sense of being 'British' as a New Zealander. The very fact that Pocock derived so much of his own sense of identity from Britain would now be seen as a failure to appreciate a culture that the settlers had undermined and that deserved to be part of a distinct identity formed in the South Pacific. But one can still see how his desire to untie the complex intricacies of 'Great Britain' might be linked to his awareness of an unravelling 'Greater Britain' that included the former dominions. The last thing he was likely to turn to was the sovereignty-sharing system that had come between his own country and Britain and was upsetting the model upon which trade between the two had been based for decades.

In any case, though the first years of UK membership of the EEC coincided with a new interest in some new kind of 'Home Rule All Round', now described as devolution, the interest produced no concrete results. In the 1970s a Labour government held referenda in both Scotland and Wales on the issue. Wales voted overwhelmingly 'no' (by about 4 to 1) while Scotland was deemed to have voted underwhelmingly 'yes'. The establishment of what was called a Scottish Assembly would only be granted if at least 40% of the electorate voted for it and the numbers failed to reach this figure.[17] Resentment over this condition, which was seen as an attempt to stymie the assembly by Labour MPs hostile to devolution, contributed to the Labour government's failure to survive a vote of confidence in 1979 and its consequent loss of power to Conservative governments for eighteen years.

---

16   Lloyd-Jones & Scull, *Four Nations Approaches to Modern British History: A (Dis)united Kingdom?* p. 41.

17   Bogdanor, *Beyond Brexit*, pp. 104–105.

'Four nation' approaches really took off in the 1990s, in writers like Linda Colley, Norman Davies and Tom Nairn, who were particularly conscious not only of the growth in calls for devolution within the UK itself but also of the dangers of states in the process of decomposition. The 1990s was a time when people were conscious of five wars in the former Yugoslavia, causing tens of thousands of deaths and undermining the complacent boast that Europe since the war had seen half a century of peace. Yet though these writers were wary of Pocock's ideas about the detrimental effects of the 'Europeanisation' of Great Britain upon its former dominions, they did not always differ from him in failing to see a positive development in the move towards sovereignty-sharing in Europe's divided continent.

A further – and this time successful – attempt at devolution was made when Labour returned to power at the end of the twentieth century. There were clear political reasons for doing so. The party was highly dependent on votes in Scotland and Wales, which supplied between a fifth and a quarter of its MPs, to sustain Labour in government. It would be very difficult for it to secure a majority based on English votes alone. The failure to make something of Home Rule All Round had been a catastrophe for the Liberals at the beginning of the century. Irish independence meant that 80 Irish MPs who had generally supported the Liberals in Parliament were replaced by a dozen or so MPs from Northern Ireland who supported the Conservatives. The Liberals were never to return to power again (unless one counts the Liberal Democrat-Conservative Coalition government of 2010–2015).[18] Labour was afraid of the same thing happening to its own support, and it was right to be concerned. The rise of the Scottish National Party has had an enormous impact on the Labour Party's hopes of returning to power – unless in coalition with nationalist parties – after more than a decade in opposition.

In the new referenda at the end of the last century both Scotland and Wales voted in favour of devolution, though only by a whisker in the case of Wales. From 1999 some form of Home Rule was therefore established in both countries. Scotland received a parliament under the 'reserved powers' model, with legislative powers over all matters that were not reserved to Westminster.

---

18   Professor Vernon Bogdanor's lecture on 'The Liberal Party and the Liberal Democrats', part of a series of Political History Lectures given at Gresham College, London in 2017. It gives a very good account of the traumatic history of the party, although since 2017 there have been some modest signs of revival that might have tempered Bogdanor's rather pessimistic account. See https://www.youtube.com/watch?v=44ir_D_hD-M

Wales at first received an 'assembly' rather than a parliament, with powers over a prescribed range of policies, the 'defined powers' model, though it was later 'upgraded' to a parliament (*Senedd*) in 2020, while the 'executives' in both Scotland and Wales became recognised as 'governments.' By way of contrast, a special form of devolution through an 'Assembly' and 'Executive' was created in Northern Ireland as part of the Good Friday agreement in 1998, avoiding terms like 'parliament' and 'government' which might suggest that Northern Ireland was moving towards the status of sovereign state, something resisted for different reasons by both nationalists and unionists.[19]

Has devolution been a success this time round? In one sense, no. It has certainly not silenced those who would prefer full independence. If anything, support for full independence has grown. In Scotland it led to a referendum in 2014 when nearly half the population (45%) voted for independence. Opinion now appears to be evenly divided. Support for independence in Wales is less but has been growing, amounting to perhaps 20–25% of the population, (a poll in March 2021 put it as high as 40%, but was perhaps an outlier – Dafydd Trystan[20] has suggested increasing numbers of people who are 'Indycurious' (!) rather than outright supporters of independence) – while in the different situation of Northern Ireland support for reunification with the South has also grown.[21] It is currently favoured by around 40% of the population in Northern Ireland. It should always be borne in mind that more Catholics in Northern

---

19   See Davies, John *A History of Wales*, pp. 673–685 for an account of the arrival of the assembly and its first years of existence (up to 2005). For an interesting account of the ups and downs of the assembly in the first two decades of its existence, see former first minister Rhodri Morgan's *Rhodri: A Political Life in Wales and Westminster*, chapters 6–10. The book was almost completed when he died in 2017. For the last five years there is a shortage of in-depth analysis so far, but the Institute for Government provides a useful short account of how the powers of the devolved body have changed over time. See https://www.instituteforgovernment.org.uk/article/explainer/senedd-cymru-welsh-parliament. There is a very good research briefing of 30th January 2023 produced by David Torrance for the House of Commons Library. It is called 'Devolution in Wales: A Process, not an Event' See https://researchbriefings.files.parliament.uk/documents/CBP-8318/CBP-8318.pdf

20   Trystan, Dafydd. 'Indycurious and Curiouser: New Poll shows Support for Welsh Independence on the Rise'. The poll was in 2019. Welsh independence movements are associated with a much higher level of support for European integration than their counterparts in Scotland, a view reflected in the keen Europeanism of *Plaid Cymru*.

21   Bogdanor, *Beyond Brexit*, p. 237. Bogdanor argues that though Northern Ireland is the only part of the UK that could rejoin the EU without having to re-negotiate entry, even

Ireland are opposed to unification than Protestants favour it, so a simple head-count of the different religious communities will not give you a precise view of how likely it is the North will vote for independence. Brexit may well increase the proportion of Catholics favouring a united Ireland.

However, it would be unreasonable to pronounce devolution a failure on this basis. It has certainly increased its popularity in Wales since the very limited support it received in 1999. The granting of additional powers in the generation since it was first introduced suggests that it is something of which people in Wales and Scotland (though not necessarily, as we shall see, Northern Ireland) want more, even though some insist that nothing short of full independence will do. The possibility of developing a system that satisfies all the nations of the UK without dismantling the UK should not be ruled out.

The English 'problem'

One point that must not be forgotten is that devolution is a matter for England as well as for the other nations. What is often missing from considerations of devolution is an awareness of the level of support on the part of the English for what Gavin Esler called in a recent book the 'end of Britain.'[22] What polls there have been on support for Scottish independence, for instance, suggest that opinion in England on the issue is roughly split down the middle. Hence the end of the Union with Scotland is supported by about half the Scots and half the English. This may not be a majority and the general view may be one of indifference – Lord Ashcroft found in 2019 that about 40% of people cared about what happened in Northern Ireland while 40% didn't.[23] In the same year another survey showed 20% in favour of Scottish independence and 40% against, with 40% indifferent.[24] In England the level of indifference towards or even

---

in 2018, after the Brexit vote, polls showed that a minority in Northern Ireland favoured reunification – in the poll he quotes, a minority even of Roman Catholics.

22   Esler, Gavin *How Britain Ends: English nationalism and the Rebirth of Four Nations*.

23   Ashcroft, Lord 'England and the Union', Lord Ashcroft Polls.

24   It has to be borne in mind that in England there is a strong perception that the other parts of the UK are 'subsidised' at England's expense. This perception, whether right or wrong, leads many to adopt a 'we'd be better off without them' attitude. Lord Ashcroft makes this point in one of his many useful polling surveys. See https://lordashcroftpolls.com/2019/10/england-and-the-union/

support for the other 'nations' breaking away from the UK is far higher than it is in the equivalent majority parts of Canada or Spain.

It is not only 'English nationalists,' or those convinced that without the other nations England would be richer, who support the end of the Union. Some who certainly couldn't be called 'right-wing nationalists' seem to think that being on its own could be a wake-up call to bring England to its senses as a post-imperial medium-sized European state. Such a view has been put forward, for instance, by Professor David Edgerton in a podcast broadcast in April 2021,[25] even though in *The Rise and Fall of the British Nation: A Twentieth-Century History* he made much of the idea that the post-war generation's emphasis upon planning and a strong welfare state had intensified a sense of social citizenship at the UK level, since all parts benefited from the investment and welfare provision on offer. This view would have to be reconciled with Keating's point that a growth in support for self-government has been associated with good times while depressions increased dependence upon the centre.[26] One could also suggest that the last quarter of the twentieth century, when right-wing UK governments under Thatcher and Major tended to prefer the idea of the welfare state as a safety net for the poor to the idea of its expressing a clear sense of social citizenship, was a time when that central planning could be maintained only by being transferred to countries – like an independent Scotland – which were intent upon preserving it to its full extent. In any case Edgerton's suggestion in his podcast seemed to be a different one (if just as questionable), namely that cutting out Wales, Scotland and Northern Ireland might help to cut England down to size and enable it to feel at ease with itself.

One reason why it is difficult to think of the UK as a 'multi-national state' is that England is so much bigger than the other three parts of it (five-sixths of the UK population live in England). Vernon Bogdanor points to the situation in Canada as the 'nearest equivalent' where about 40% of the population live in Ontario.[279] The much greater size of England's population has meant attention is often focused upon how to give extra powers less to the whole country than to parts of England, perhaps through regional assemblies, each of which might

25   https://euromovescotland.org.uk/podcast/brexit-ideology-and-the-decline-of-the-br itish-state/

26   See Keating, Michael *The Independence of Scotland: Self-Government and the Shifting Politics of Union.*

27   Bogdanor, Vernon *Beyond Brexit: Towards a British Constitution*, p. 185.

be considered roughly the same size as the other three non-English nations.[28] Progress in this direction has been mixed. In 2004 a proposal for a regional assembly in North-East England was rejected overwhelmingly (by almost 4:1 on a turnout just short of 50%).[29] Some people said that the proposal to have the assembly's headquarters in Newcastle alienated other cities in the North-East, but even in Newcastle the vote was 2:1 against. Behind the rejection was a perception that it lacked real powers, in which case it would only add another layer of taxpayer-funded bureaucracy to the administration of the area.

Much more successful has been the creation of 'metro-mayors' by the Conservative government elected in 2015 (with shades of the old metropolitan county councils abolished by the Conservative government led by Margaret Thatcher in 1986, and which in turn had been created by a Conservative government led by Edward Heath in the early 1970s – Conservative governments are rarely sure how much power they wish to allow local councils in England). Combined local authorities agreed to a directly elected mayor who would have substantial new powers in certain parts of the country. The metro mayors, like the mayor of London, have managed to raise their profiles, often leading the way in insisting that their areas had special needs (or that their needs had been neglected) during the coronavirus pandemic. They do not have the taxation or legislative powers of the nations outside England in the UK. However, some metro mayors have been able to convince voters that they have a strategic role in bringing together an area (a 'city region' such as Greater London or Greater Manchester) which has not been sufficiently recognised in the past.

Moreover, they raise important economic questions about the distribution of wealth and inequality within England itself which has sometimes led to talk of 'internal colonialism.' Though this charge has traditionally been levelled at the treatment of the nations outside England (for instance in Michael Hechter's revealingly titled *Internal Colonialism. The Celtic Fringe in British National Development 1536–1966*), written in the 1970s as the first moves towards devolution were being taken, one could also consider how far 'internal colonialism' applied within England itself, dominated as it is by the capital and its sprawling home county surroundings. In terms of broad economic strategy,

---

28   Bogdanor points out that the new metro-mayors introduced mostly in May 2017 made this a more plausible option. See *Beyond Brexit*, pp. 204–206.

29   As Bogdanor points out, this was despite the Labour Party being in favour of the assembly and despite the fact that Labour was the dominant party in the North-East. See Bogdanor, *Beyond Brexit*, p. 106.

there were certainly efforts at both the national and European levels to deal with regional disparities. UK plans included English regions as well as what are now the devolved nations, but there was also growing attention to regional disparities within the EEC (European Economic Community) and later the EU. When in the early 1970s Edward Heath's Conservative government led the UK into the EEC, he laid particular stress upon the need to support what came to be called 'cohesion' policies, addressing the needs of poorer regions with EEC funds (matched funding by national governments was necessary).[30]

By the 1990s centrally directed planning had fallen out of favour in the UK, and regional development was devolved with all the emphasis on local initiatives and competition for investment from overseas. EU regional policy, on the other hand, continued and two regions within the UK came to be particular beneficiaries of EU regional support. One was the West of Wales, but the other, Cornwall and the Scilly Isles, was at the South-Western tip of England. UK governments remained unwilling to embrace cohesion funds, seeing them as another bad example of central planning – despite the fact that the EU sought desperately to involve regional bodies in decision-making on the funding, often to come up against resistance from national governments, especially in highly centralised member-states like the UK. In the end the main beneficiary of such funds in England, Cornwall and the Scilly Isles, voted heavily for Brexit, partly because UK governments, determined always to focus on the money that was going *to* Brussels rather than the money that was coming *from* it, did very little to explain where the funding was coming from (and did their best to hide the plaques which recorded EU involvement and spending).[31] Meanwhile over the last decade a number of dinky little high-profile schemes with names like 'city deals' have reflected attempts to raise the profile of central government initiatives both in the regions and the devolved nations, but the amounts involved have been very small. The key point is that regional disparities inside

---

30   Heath left the details to be worked out after the UK became a member. As Duff points out, Heath remained 'optimistic that once inside the Community the UK could begin to effect much-needed reform.' Duff, *Britain and the Puzzle of the European Union*, p. 26. But soon after UK accession he was out of power in the UK. Hence it was the new Labour government that in December 1974 reached agreement on the shape and size of the regional development fund (Duff, p. 31).

31   That said, there were numerous high-profile characters who recognised the importance of EU funding. This is a YouTube video of celebrity chef Jamie Oliver thanking the European Regional Development Fund for help in training young people as chefs in Cornwall: https://www.youtube.com/watch?v=EgJAY106oz4

the UK remain – the OECD ranks it as having the highest territorial disparities among its member states.

What seems clear is that people have a greater sense of belonging where
the city regions are concerned than they do in the case of wider geographical
regions. 'I'm from the North-East' means much less than I'm from Newcastle'
or 'I'm from Tyneside.' If there isn't a sense of belonging or at least something
similar to the national feeling that motivates people in Wales and Scotland to
call for more powers, then administrative reorganisation may bring benefits
but is unlikely to excite passions. Many people have heard of the old saying:
'You can take the boy out of Liverpool, but you can't take Liverpool out of the
boy.' It is more difficult to imagine someone saying: 'You can take the girl out
of the North-West region, but you can't take the North-West region out of the
girl.'

What one can conclude from this is that it might not be impossible to divide
England into regional blocs of some kind, some of which might be of roughly
the same size as Scotland or Wales (London, of course, would be much bigger,
but there are issues there over how London should be defined.)[32] Regional parliaments would then presumably be put together with the parliaments from the
devolved nations. That would avoid the need to create an English Parliament
which might look too much like a replication of the Westminster Parliament.

So far little has been done to bring together the devolved nations and the regions, although there has been some talk of the Upper House (House of Lords)
being reformed in this direction. Instead, what has been attempted is a policy
of giving English MPs a separate identity within the Westminster Parliament.
The focus has been on the so-called EVEL principle (English votes for English
Laws) where English MPs could accept or veto legislation affecting their constituents before it passed to a third reading, its final Commons stage, at which
point it would be voted on by the whole House.[33] Introduced by a newly-elected
Conservative government in October 2015, EVEL was finally abandoned by another Conservative government in July 2021 – arguably a testimony to how ill-
thought out the proposal was.

---

32   Vernon Bogdanor provides a wonderful summary of this impossibly tangled issue in
      one of his Gresham College lectures. See https://www.gresham.ac.uk/watch-now/futu
      re-london-government-mayor-and-london-boroughs
33   See Bogdanor, *Beyond Brexit*, pp. 203–204, where he explains how EVEL worked and
      some of its drawbacks.

Not the least of its problems was the difficulty of knowing which piece of legislation applied to England (or in some cases England and Wales, and in a few cases England, Wales and Northern Ireland) alone. At first sight it shouldn't have been too difficult. The issue first became controversial after a vote in 2004 over the issue of university top-up fees. These were only to apply to students in England, and yet the imposition of such fees was carried very narrowly (by five votes) in the House of Commons. It was clear that the support of Scottish Labour MPs had been enough to ensure that the bill was passed, and yet the bill would not apply North of the border, where the devolved Scottish Parliament had decided against such fees. Unsurprisingly, the reaction was to feel that this was an injustice that could only be righted if there was some mechanism by which only MPs representing English constituencies could vote on matters affecting England alone. At the same time the increase in powers for the Welsh *Senedd* and Scottish Parliament made it likely that there would be more and more issues which the devolved Parliaments would be dealing with. The more powers that were devolved, the more the 100 or so MPs in the Commons representing constituencies outside England would be dealing with matters that related only to England.[34]

There were several problems with EVEL. There was the question of identifying what was to be considered England-only legislation, a task which was assigned to the Speaker. The decision might have seemed straightforward, but apparently England-only legislation could have knock-on effects for other parts of the UK. For instance, some argued that according to the so-called Barnett formula, levels of spending on services like health and education in the devolved regions depended upon the levels in England. Therefore, a measure which had the effect of raising or lowering health or education spending in England would not be entirely an England-only matter, since it would affect the overall level of health spending in Scotland and Wales. This argument was used to suggest that in practical terms it was far more difficult to isolate 'England-only' issues than it might seem to be.

A second problem was that EVEL was in practice more an English veto than an English voice. It gave English MPs the right to stop legislation but hardly provided a forum within which they could discuss 'English issues.'

---

34   Keating suggests that EVEL arose because the UK Prime Minister David Cameron, having promised more powers for Scotland at the time of the Scottish independence referendum in 2014, had to promise 'something to England to compensate for the attention given to Scotland,' Keating, *State and Nation in the United Kingdom*, p. 84.

There wasn't even an English Affairs Committee in Westminster to match the Scottish Grand Committee. English MPs could pile in to stop something being passed but they didn't develop a sense of what 'English concerns' were. They didn't even have 'English-only days' in Parliament. The obvious reason for this lay in the fact that there was no English Parliament to match the Scottish Parliament or the Welsh *Senedd*. English concerns were effectively being tacked on to a body whose primary purpose was to consider the interests of the UK as a whole. One of the most effective criticisms of EVEL was that it would create two classes of MP, those representing English constituencies and those representing other constituencies who would be half-in and half-out of the law-making process. This was inevitable if there was an attempt to create an English Parliament inside the Westminster Parliament rather than separate from it.[35]

EVEL was condemned as a halfway house towards creating an English Parliament, or what the SNP MP Pete Wishart called a 'quasi-English parliament squat in the UK Parliament', a procedure that satisfied no one.[36] It would have made more sense to have established a separate English Parliament somewhere in the middle of the country rather than at its south-eastern edge, a development which would certainly have helped to counter the accusations of 'London-centrism' which leads to the occasional decampment of broadcasters, civil servants and other public officials to other parts of the country. But there is little sign that MPs have thought seriously in these terms, not least because the one thing that would force a re-defining of the sovereignty of Westminster, even more than a reformed and therefore potentially much more powerful House of Lords, is the creation of an English Parliament. If the system is left as it is at present, then 500 or so English MPs can effectively dominate the Westminster Parliament. However, if they were to have a separate Parliament, the Westminster Parliament would have to be reconfigured on federal lines to be a forum for joint working between the different nations. Ironically, the real reason why English MPs don't want an English Parliament is that they fear it would mean a loss of power for them.

---

35   See Glover, Daniel and Kenny, Michael. 'Answering the West Lothian question? A Critical Assessment of 'English Votes for English Laws in the UK Parliament'.

36   Wishart made the remark on 13th July 2021, when the government had decided to scrap the law it had introduced 6 years earlier. His speech to the House of Commons, before members in various masks to remind us that it was during the COVID crisis, can be found on YouTube: https://www.youtube.com/watch?v=NoVi8erLScY

Conclusion

The chapter began with a survey of 'Home Rule All round' over the last century. It argued that the failure of early schemes to keep both Britain and Ireland inside the United Kingdom, not to mention attempts to maintain the unity of the British Empire, led many in the UK to think that there was no halfway house between a centralised multinational state and independent nations breaking away. Devolution, they came to think, was more likely to encourage separatism than to restrain it.

The forms of governance emerging on the continent through the Coal and Steel community might have suggested this wasn't the case, but those who began to interest themselves in the idea of 'four nations' inside the UK did not – and do not – see much to encourage their efforts at devolution in the emergence of the institutions that eventually became the European Union.

The chapter emphasised that devolution cannot be discussed without considering England. It examined English attitudes, mindful of Keating's remark that 'this combination of Euroscepticism with Englishness would appear to be one of the strongest challenges to the Union.'[37] Much of the attention where England is concerned has been upon the installed and then rejected policy of 'English votes for English Laws'. This was too much like trying to graft an English Parliament onto Westminster, perhaps as a way of avoiding a separate English Parliament that might have been seen as a rival to Westminster. As a later chapter will look at in more detail, the most logical way of making devolution effective would be a body (perhaps a reformed House of Lords) bringing together the devolved parliaments and those of English regions or 'city-states' like London and Greater Manchester. Instead of wondering about how to set up an English Parliament, the focus would be upon how to establish a system whereby a dozen parliaments, regional and national, could jointly develop a system for managing the British Union. Joint working, however, is precisely what many fear most. To this point the book will return.

Where progress made to date is concerned, this may appear to be a rather negative conclusion to reach. However, the next chapter will suggest that, perhaps counter-intuitively, the one part of the United Kingdom where devolution has proved most difficult might provide the best indication of how it could be made effective at the UK level in the future.

---

37   Keating, *State and Nation*, p. 191.

Chapter Ten: Home Rule for Northern Ireland?

In the last chapter it was pointed out that the one instance of home rule to emerge from the events of the early twentieth century was the Northern Ireland Parliament. Quite apart from its origins, it has always been controversial in its workings, accused of acting on behalf of the Unionist majority, manipulating electoral districts to promote unionist representation, and ensuring discrimination in housing and employment. For many in Northern Ireland, it was seen as a case where removing a higher level of government allowed a lower one to act in an irresponsible manner.

Currently the Republic of Ireland consists of 26 of the 32 counties of Ireland. The other six are often known as Northern Ireland or Ulster. Neither term is quite accurate. Historically Ulster consisted of nine counties, only six of which were separated in 1922 when Ireland was partitioned. Of the three that remained in the Republic, one of them contains the northernmost tip of the island. On any geographical definition, part of Northern Ireland is in the Republic.

In fact, geography reflects the lack of solidity, the unavoidable fluidity of what is called 'Northern Ireland.' Its border with the Republic is a meandering worm with no apparent logic to it. It wiggles its apparently unplanned way for nearly 500 miles through lakes, woods, parishes, farms and even homes. But it was designed originally to be the dividing line between the two areas of Home Rule within a single United Kingdom. Lloyd George, Prime Minister when the Irish Free State, as the 26 counties were called at the time, was brought into being, promised those opposed to the division that the six counties would prove to be unsustainable, and the meandering line seemed to reflect that conviction.[1] It ended up, however, as an international border between two countries,

---

1   See Roy Hattersley's biography of Lloyd George, *The Great Outsider*, ch. 33 'God Help Poor Ireland', pp. 530–546. Hattersley suggests that Lloyd George redrew the boundary be-

the Republic of Ireland and (to give it its full title) The United Kingdom of Great Britain and Northern Ireland, making it clear that Northern Ireland is an addition to Britain (however much Unionists in Northern Ireland wish to emphasise that they are British).

What lay behind the wiggling line of the border was the desire to create an area in which Unionists had a majority, something they clearly did not have on the island as a whole. The eventual creation of the six counties made it inevitable that there would be a substantial minority (one-third to two fifths) who would be opposed to the creation of Northern Ireland despite having to live there and who would wish to be united with the rest of the island. That clearly coloured the politics of this part of the UK in a way that didn't apply in the other devolved areas.[2]

Hence, whereas in the case of Wales and Scotland, or London and the city-regions of England, there was a majority desire for more powers to be conferred, in the case of Northern Ireland there was resistance to any conferral of additional powers. From the point of view of the Nationalists, the Unionists only wanted more powers if they could use them to discriminate even more against the minority. From the point of view of the Unionists, it would have the effect of detaching Northern Ireland further from Britain. The situation of Northern Ireland therefore makes it difficult to talk of it as one of the 'four nations' of the United Kingdom (a reference that had become familiar by 2022, for instance when discussing policies to combat COVID-19).[3] One can see why Professor Bogdanor refers to 'three nations and a contested province.'[4] Nationalists in Northern Ireland do not wish it to be a nation, because that would complicate its future as part of a united Ireland. Unionists would not want to be part of a separate nation, if being a nation was going to cause it to drift away from Britain and the rest of the UK. Technically, as we have seen, the UK is a

tween the Six Counties and the Irish /Free State in order to make the separation 'essentially temporary' (p. 543).

2   As Hattersley points out, Lloyd George seemed to think that this would be an arrangement which ensured that Northern Ireland's existence would be 'temporary'. The result was that 'temporary' meant more than a century and involved a lot of bloodshed North of the border, not to mention the Civil War in the South that followed the agreement.

3   See Bogdanor, *Beyond Brexit*, p. 178. He notes the recent tendency to talk of 'four nations' but argues that Northern Ireland is not a nation, despite the habit of critics of devolution to talk about 'four nations and a funeral'.

4   Bogdanor explains in *Beyond Brexit*, pp. 178–179, why it makes no sense to talk of Northern Ireland as a 'nation'.

United Kingdom of Great Britain and Northern Ireland. But for many Unionists the emphasis is upon their being British. The last thing they want is to drift into a kind of No Man's Land where they are neither British nor Irish, although this has always been a possibility. In Nairn's words, 'they were always, and they still remain, profoundly and embarrassingly different from the society they imagine they are a frontier of.'[5] A Protestant U.D.I. remains the last resort that no one wants but which can never be entirely ruled out, 'an almost apocalyptic answer to British perfidy, the awesome threat at the end of the line.'[6] Interestingly, there were hints of such a move after the collapse of the Sunningdale Agreement in 1974, when some Protestant paramilitary groups talked of an independent Northern Ireland and even spoke of Catholic participation in the Cabinet. It was a kind of power-sharing from within rather than one imposed from without, hinting perhaps that even Catholic treason would be more acceptable than British perfidy.[7]

It was the Unionists themselves who brought down the power-sharing Northern Ireland executive put in place by the UK government in the Sunningdale Agreement of 1973 and made it necessary to restore direct rule from Westminster. Unlike in Scotland and Wales, their priority was not for more power to be devolved to their 'nation,' but for their existence as part of the United Kingdom to be guaranteed. The approach was reflected in an election poster on behalf of the Unionists in the election of February 1974 which declared that 'Dublin is just a Sunningdale away.'[8] In other words, the form of devolution being offered to Northern Ireland was likely to move it into the orbit of the Republic. The remit of the Council of Ireland, resurrected by the Sunningdale Agreement, was limited to tourism, conservation and animal health, but this was regarded by Unionists as the thin end of the wedge and indeed there were some on the Nationalist side who saw it in precisely those terms, such as SDLP (Social Democratic and Labour Party) Councillor Hugh Logue, who called it 'the vehicle that would trundle unionists into a united

---

5   Nairn, Tom *The Break-Up of Britain*, p. 224.
6   Nairn, Tom *The Break-Up of Britain*, p. 231.
7   See Nairn, *The Break-Up of Britain*, p. 244. The whole chapter, 'Northern Ireland: Relic or Portent?' is worth reading.
8   See the research paper for University College, Dublin written by P.J. McLoughlin and entitled '"Dublin is Just a Sunningdale Away?": The SDLP, the Irish Government and the Sunningdale Agreement.'
     It can be read online at https://researchrepository.ucd.ie/entities/publication/389d38 ad-7e4e-40eb-88e0-469fc5257da4/details

Ireland.'[9] Unionists also welcomed the fact that the end of Sunningdale and restoration of direct rule led to an increase in the number of Northern Irish MPs from 12 to 17. This reflected another approach to dealing with the problem of England not having its own Parliament unlike Scotland and Wales, one which suggests that devolved nations should have fewer MPs at Westminster. Instead of having MPs from the devolved regions voting on fewer issues than their English colleagues, one would simply have fewer MPs from the devolved regions. But it was also welcomed by Unionists who directed their efforts (successfully) towards more power at Westminster as the reward for less power at Stormont.

The significance of the Belfast Agreement

The breakdown of Sunningdale, the problems of direct rule and the prospect of 'Protestant U.D.I' demonstrate what a very important advance was made in Northern Ireland by the Good Friday agreement of 1998. Coming a generation after Sunningdale, there was a tendency to dub it 'Sunningdale for slow learners', but in important respects it was different.[10] One key provision was that it made power-sharing in the Northern Ireland executive mandatory, ensuring that it would no longer be possible for the majority to impose its will on the minority.

The most important part of the agreement lay in its constitutional provisions. Effectively, it enshrined the view that the future of Northern Ireland was an issue for both parts of the island, Northern Ireland and the Republic. Indeed, the Good Friday agreement itself was subject to referenda on both sides of the border. Any further change to the status of Northern Ireland would also have to be subject to referenda both North and South of the border. Essentially, the Irish government recognised that without the consent of both sides a united Ireland would not come about, whilst the UK government accepted that with the consent of both sides it *would* come about. In this respect both governments, the UK and the Irish, were making an important concession. London accepted that the Irish Republic becoming a single 32-county island state was

---

9   He made these controversial comments in Trinity College, Dublin at the time of the Sunningdale Agreement.

10   The comment came from Séamus Mallon, Deputy First Minister of Northern Ireland from 1998–2001.

acceptable if a majority in both Dublin and Belfast wished it. The Irish Republic accepted – and amended its own constitution to this effect – that a united Ireland could not bypass the wishes of a majority in Northern Ireland.

The Good Friday agreement was a breakthrough after decades of killing on both sides. The brilliance of its design lies in the fact that it has not depended upon persuading one of the two sides that it is wrong or even on securing the sort of settlement where a compromise is reached because both sides give a little. It is more an agreement which allows both sides to proceed as if their position has been vindicated. This applies especially to the border. It has already been pointed out that the border between the six counties and the rest of Ireland wiggles its apparently unplanned way for nearly 500 miles through lakes, woods, parishes, farms and even homes. Vernon Bogdanor is probably correct to say that 'the real border in Ireland is not a line on the map but a border in the mind,'[11] but the question is how to deal with it. Faced with two apparently irreconcilable positions, one of which insisted that the six counties must be part of a united Ireland and the other that they must not, the 'solution' in the Good Friday agreement was to make the border of as little significance as possible so that both sides could act as if their position was the real one. A Nationalist, whether or not she took advantage of the option of having an Irish passport, could move seamlessly around the island that she saw as her homeland with access to jobs and benefits like anyone else. A Unionist could tell herself that she was still part of the United Kingdom, a subject of the King, her local MP represented in the Westminster Parliament. The solution to two irreconcilable positions is not to come down on the side of one or the other but to find a way of being able to maintain both.

By and large this has worked. The violence has largely stopped, investment has begun to move in and power-sharing has proved – from time to time – successful. Stormont has received a steady increase of powers, including control of policing and criminal justice powers in 2006 and a right to vary the rate of corporation tax in 2014.[12] The problem is that there is such a fundamental divide between the two main parties, the Democratic Unionists and Sinn Fein, who dominate the politics of Northern Ireland (although the recent successes of the Alliance Party have demonstrated a few cracks in that edifice), that power-sharing sometimes breaks down, causing regular suspensions of the assembly. But for the most part there has been a generation of peace.

---

11   Bogdanor, Vernon *Beyond Brexit: Towards a British Constitution*, p. 243.
12   Bogdanor, *Beyond Brexit*, p. 183.

The trouble now is the aftermath of Brexit. The border has become much more significant as a border between two countries, one of which is a member of the EU and one of which isn't. The meandering line has been forced to become a demarcation point of significance, raising all the questions concerning border and customs checks and whether they can be all be done 'electronically' that characterise discussions of trade between the two parts of the island today. Endless discussions are currently going on about whether and how to shift the border to the Irish Sea, so that Northern Ireland effectively has to follow the rules of the EU internal market and ceases to have the same trade rules as the rest of the UK.[13] It is still unclear, with the assembly once again suspended until this problem is solved, what the outcome will be. It might seem as though the problem is a trade issue to which a sensible solution can be found (perhaps through modifying the so-called Northern Ireland Protocol) without endangering the future of peace in Northern Ireland. But such is the sensitivity over the border which the Good Friday agreement sought in its own way to dampen down and even marginalise rather than solve, that anything which forces people to focus once again on the line of separation between those on one side of the border and those on the other is bound to threaten peace.

Furthermore, Brexit has removed the broader perspective within which the 'Northern Ireland problem' could be viewed in European terms as a problem between two member states. The EU has plenty of sensitive borders which are a product of conflict, such as those between different parts of the former Yugoslavia, some of which are part of the EU (Slovenia, Croatia) and some of which are not. EU membership has helped to dampen tensions, if not to remove them. Croatian membership helped to resolve the dispute between Slovenia and Croatia over access to the Adriatic Sea. There are plenty of EU countries with minorities that were once part of other member states (for instance Hungarians in Transylvania, now part of Romania) and which campaign, for instance, over rights to their language and its use in schools. There are similar arguments from Russian speakers who make up a substantial part of the population of Latvia, not least because the Baltic states were actually part of

---

13   The whole issue continues at the time of writing with the so-called 'Windsor Framework' supposed to make the situation more acceptable to unionists. A BBC report in April 2023 gives a snapshot summary of developments. See https://www.bbc.com/news/explainers-53724381. However, the problem was clearly recognised five years ago by former Europe minister Denis MacShane. See *Brexit, No Exit*, ch.18: 'Brexit spells danger for Ireland and concern in Scotland', pp. 214–224.

the Soviet Union and not mere satellite states of it like the Hungarians or the Czechs. The EU also has to manage the border between the Turkish-occupied part of Cyprus and the rest. When problems arose over the question of how the border between the Republic and the UK could be managed after Brexit, members of the UK government were quick to study the border between the USA and Canada. They were less keen to study the practices of the Union from which they had just decided to depart. Yet the special arrangements for the border between independent Cyprus and the Turkish-occupied part of the island, or those in the Balkans between Croatia (which is inside the EU) and Bosnia (which is not), would arguably have been more helpful. From an EU perspective, the Irish border is just one of many 'little local difficulties', and one of the advantages of EU membership is that it provides a wider context within which people can set their particular concerns. That advantage has now been closed down by Brexit.

The Future of Northern Ireland

There are many reasons for supposing that the situation in Northern Ireland is the one that most threatens the continued existence of the United Kingdom, despite the narrowness of the result of the referendum over the future of Scotland in 2014. Most of the attention recently has been on trading arrangements. However, the problems over trade are arguably symptomatic of something that goes much deeper.

For one thing, it would be much easier for Northern Ireland to become part of the EU if it seceded from the UK than for Scotland to do so. Scotland would have to apply as a candidate country, requiring the unanimous consent of all the existing EU members – including Spain, which would be mindful of the possible repercussions for the independence movement in Catalonia. When the President of the European Commission was interviewed on British television shortly before the referendum on an independent Scotland José Manuel Barroso declared that it would be 'extremely difficult, if not impossible' for an independent Scotland to join the EU.[14] Barroso (who retired a few months later)

14   He was interviewed on the Andrew Marr Show on 16th February. The comments (naturally welcome to the British government) caused quite a stir. See Corner, *The EU: an Introduction*, p. 43. The former DDR became part of a united Germany without requiring the unanimous approval of existing members, which would be necessary in the case of

probably exaggerated, but there would certainly be difficulties. Though the EU emphasises the need to protect minorities within its member states, it does not support them when they seek to secede. Northern Ireland, on the other hand, would not have this problem. It could simply become part of Ireland, just as the former DDR (*Deutsche Demokratische Republik*), as East Germany was called, became part of a reunified Germany in 1990, bypassing the need to apply as a candidate country.

The currency issue is also less problematic. Northern Ireland would automatically join the Republic as part of the eurozone. Scotland, on the other hand, would be faced with a difficult situation. It would have three choices. It might remain with sterling, which would be bizarre given the fact that it had just voted to be an independent country. It might receive some kind of dispensation to adopt the euro whilst outside the eurozone or even the EU (in the manner of Montenegro). It might adopt a new currency, perhaps the 'Scottish pound', before applying (as a new member state must) to become part of the eurozone. None of these options is simple.

For these reasons, we can see that if one ignores the bitter and possibly violent consequences of such a decision, it remains the case that it would be simpler for Northern Ireland to leave the United Kingdom and rejoin the European Union than for Scotland or Wales (which in any case voted to leave the EU in 2016) to do so. The attraction of being once again a part of the EU, which for Scots would involve all sorts of practical difficulties, would in the case of the Northern Irish be relatively straightforward.

Yet even though the easiest route back into the EU following secession from the UK would be the one taken by Northern Ireland, the Good Friday agreement provides important pointers towards a future constitution of the UK4. Northern Ireland shows how crucial an increased measure of autonomy for the members of the UK will be. Ironically, the very fact that Northern Ireland is the likeliest part of the UK to leave has already meant accepting a degree of autonomy for Northern Ireland which does not exist elsewhere.

In 2017 the UK Supreme Court unanimously held that the consent of Northern Ireland voters was not required to leave the European Union. It had just decided in the Miller case that the consent of the UK Parliament was necessary in order to leave the EU, a majority decision that earned it brickbats of

---

any applicant country. There was talk at the time of a possible UK veto, just as there is talk now of a possible Spanish veto to an application from an independent Scotland. A re-united Ireland, like a reunited Germany, could avoid any possible veto.

a 'the judges versus the people' kind in the press.[15] Yet it did not see why this principle should be extended to the parliaments based in Edinburgh, Cardiff and Stormont (Wales, as said, voted narrowly to leave the EU). Devolution had made it perfectly clear that matters of foreign policy were reserved to the UK Parliament alone.

This was an understandable position, and yet the Good Friday Agreement had taken the decision on the future of Northern Ireland out of the hands of the UK as a whole and had made it a decision in a referendum for the two sides of the Irish border alone. If the continuation of Northern Ireland as part of the United Kingdom is a matter in which Northern Ireland is effectively allowed a veto on its future, shouldn't it have been allowed a veto on its continuing to be part of the European Union? The logic of Good Friday is that decisions on the future of this 'nation' should be subject to the agreement of both the Irish Republic and Northern Ireland. In other words, both could exercise a veto on the agreement. Surely it would make sense to apply the power of veto to other decisions with profound implications for Northern Ireland, such as member-ship of the EU. It may be too late to advance that particular argument now, but it is not too late to point out that veto powers for the devolved bodies should be part of any future constitutional changes.

The provisions in the Good Friday agreement anticipate the form which a degree of shared sovereignty might take, both in a future united Ireland and within the United Kingdom. The first of these two is being discussed in the Irish Republic, where a new Citizens' Assembly may be asked to look at the question of a fresh border poll on re-uniting the island. Though in the sum-mer of 2022 the Irish foreign minister declared that such an assembly was not 'on the radar,' and even less so a referendum on the issue, it has not been ruled out further down the road.[16]

Just as it was recognised in Northern Ireland that only a radical form of power-sharing could make sense in the context of administering the North, so it is recognised in the Republic that only a radical form of power-sharing could

---

15   See Keating, *State and Nation in the United Kingdom*, p. 69.

16   The Irish Foreign Minister Simon Coveney made the remark after elections to the Northern Ireland Assembly had given Sinn Fein more seats than the DUP. On the other hand, as Coveney pointed out, the party that made the most gains in the election was the Alliance Party who tried to steer a middle ground. See https://www.breakingnews.ie/ireland/coveney-says-citizens-assembly-on-borde r-poll-not-even-on-the-radar-1301695.htm

make sense in the context of a United Ireland. Neale Richmond, TD, a Fine Gael politician in the Irish Republic, presented a paper *Towards A New Ireland* at Sidney Sussex College, Cambridge University, in April 2021, which described itself as setting out a vision 'for a new political system that would retain elements of the power-sharing dynamic in Stormont'.[17] It proposed to use some of the ideas for power-sharing in the North of Ireland for power-sharing in a United Ireland. Rather than people from Northern Ireland just entering into the existing Irish state, a new Ireland would be created with power-sharing at its core. A devolved administration would continue in Belfast for 10 years, in parallel to an all-island parliament in Dublin. In a manner that replicated power-sharing in the North, this parliament would elect a speaker and deputy speaker, one of whom would come from Northern Ireland, with the same principles applying to the chairs and vice-chairs of parliamentary committees. If Sinn Fein can sit down with the Democratic Unionist Party in the North of Ireland, then could it not do so in a United Ireland?

Most significantly for the future of the Isles as a whole, the second area in which the Good Friday agreement is important concerns the form power-sharing might take inside the UK. Ironically, given the way in which the English constantly described the EU as encroaching upon national sovereignty, what could be learned from the EU in this instance is the point of allowing all members of the UK Union, small and large, a power of veto in certain policy areas. The Good Friday agreement referred to the UK and the Republic of Ireland as 'partners in the European Union'. Constitutional reform might allow the 'four nations' to act effectively as partners in a British Union. However, this will only be possible if the members of the British Union have powers that at present they lack, such as the power of veto where vital constitutional matters are concerned.

Furthermore, the Good Friday agreement facilitates power-sharing in a way that the UK has often presented itself as constitutionally averse to. The UK declares its preference for the so-called First Past the Post System and its aversion to coalitions.[18] The system in Northern Ireland is an enforced coalition.

---

17   The paper appeared in *The Political Quarterly*, Vol 94, No 1 (Jan/March 2023), pp. 115–121. https://www.finegael.ie/app/uploads/2021/04/Towards-a-new-ireland-Neale-Richmond-2021.pdf

18   See Bogdanor, *Beyond Brexit*, pp. 190–198. Bogdanor points out that 'Coalition government in Northern Ireland is not, as is normally the case in parliamentary systems, a voluntary choice, but is required by statute' (p. 191).

The first minister comes from the largest party (which used to be the Democratic Unionist Party and is now Sinn Fein) while his or her deputy comes from the second largest party (currently the Democratic Unionist Party). At a time when members of the two main parties in the Republic, Fianna Fail and Fine Gail, were considering whether they could possibly sit down with members of Sinn Fein, such collaboration was being forced on the Northern Ireland executive by the Belfast Agreement. As pointed out above, the structure has had its difficulties (not least a three-year suspension of Stormont from 2017–2020), but it represents an attempt to bridge apparently uncrossable divides which might be compared to the coalition-building approach favoured in many of the countries of the European Union and in some of its own institutions (for instance the Parliament). It could therefore be that a Council including the whole of the UK, or even one encompassing both the Isles and including the Republic, could be managed on this basis. Indeed, there is already such a body established as part of the Belfast Agreement, a British/Irish Council (and a British/Irish Inter-Governmental conference), comprising not only the British and Irish governments but those of Scotland, Wales and the so-called 'Crown dependencies', the Isle of Man, Jersey and Guernsey. Set up to promote 'the harmonious and mutually beneficial development of the totality of relationships among the people of these islands,' the Council could be the launching-pad for a serious discussion of how the four nations and two nation-states might give constitutional form to that 'harmonious and beneficial development.'[19]

The EU has no difficulty being made up of 27 states some of which are large (Germany has 80 million inhabitants) and some of which are small (the smallest, Malta, has a population of 400,000, 200 times smaller than that of Germany). Its institutional structure gives added weight to smaller countries in the voting systems adopted (so-called 'degressive proportionality'), in the rotating six-monthly presidency, in the provision of one commissioner per member-state whatever its size and in the need for unanimity on many key issues such as admitting new members or agreeing a new treaty.

It is clear that if UK governments wanted to devise a constitution for a British Union influenced by the structures of the European Union, they would have to give their own 'member nations' far more autonomy than they give them at present. Yet their image of the EU is of an oppressive power threatening national sovereignty which had to be escaped before the UK became a

---

19   See its website at https://www.britishirishcouncil.org . As Bogdanor points out, it has no member from England (*Beyond Brexit*, p. 198).

mere region of an overweening superstate. Hence the irony of the fact that if a constitutional settlement is to be achieved and the break-up of the UK avoided, Westminster needs to secure the autonomy of its member nations in the way the EU secured the autonomy of its own member states. Such an irony is naturally hard to bear for those who pulled the UK out of the EU claiming that they were being turned into the powerless victim of a centralised EU machine.

The relation of the UK to the Republic of Ireland

The last chapter pointed out that the failure to achieve a devolution settlement for Ireland had a considerable impact upon attitudes towards devolution (or Home Rule All Round as it was called) in Westminster. The creation of the Irish Free State was part of a process of winning independence in stages. At first it was effectively another dominion, a constitutional monarchy with George V as its King and a governor-general, whose approval was needed for whoever was elected prime minister to take office. It was a halfway house, more than home rule but less than full sovereignty. It needed the Statute of Westminster of 1931, which restricted the rights of the UK to legislate for its dominions, in order to acquire full sovereignty for itself by effectively neutering remaining powers like that of the governor-general and appeals to the privy council. It made use of the crisis over Edward VIII's abdication to abolish the oath of allegiance to the Crown (George VI became 'King of Great Britain and Northern Ireland') and through the External Relations Act to deny the UK any control over its foreign affairs. In 1938 it regained control of three treaty ports which had been occupied by the Royal Navy since 1922 and which on the grounds of strict neutrality it refused to make available to the UK during the Second World War. Finally, in 1949, it left the Commonwealth, so that any residual influence of the 'mother country' and its monarch as 'Head of the Commonwealth' was finally done away with.

However, a timeline such as this can be misleading about the relationship between the two nations. The Republic of Ireland is, of course, an independent nation-state, just as France and Germany are independent nation-states. It has its own foreign policy which means that it has chosen not to be part of NATO and yet to remain part of the European Union. Yet the impact of its former ties with what is now the UK remains and is woven into the constitutional arrangements of both nation-states. As Hobsbawm points out, 'the independent Irish

Republic, while insisting on its total political autonomy from Britain ... in practice accepts considerable mutual involvement with the United Kingdom.'[20]

Between the UK and the Republic there exists a common travel area which means that people in the UK can travel freely to the Republic and vice versa, seeking employment and receiving benefits, access to health care and voting rights. EU citizens lost this right after Brexit, but the UK made a specific exemption for members of the Irish Republic. In a similar manner, even when Ireland left the Commonwealth in 1949, Parliament treated her citizens as Commonwealth citizens with free right of entry to the UK. When curbs were introduced on immigration from the Commonwealth in 1962, the Republic was exempted from them. Ireland's special status preceded the time when it and the UK entered the EEC/EU and will continue after Brexit.[21] The UK allows a degree of inter-governmental cooperation in the case of the Republic of Ireland which it has rejected in the case of other EU nations. One arrangement from which it was determined to seek an opt-out when inside the EU, the Schengen agreement on visa-free travel, was effectively applied to the one neighbour with which it had a land border.

The Good Friday Agreement contained provisions for North-South cooperation and at the very least a consultative role for the Republic. A consultative role means that there is nothing binding in these arrangements, but certain other provisions in the agreement suggest that cooperation may have to go further than this. People in Northern Ireland can choose whether to have British or Irish citizenship or both. If they choose Irish citizenship, they are EU citizens and should be covered by the provisions of the EU Charter of Fundamental Rights, which the UK has not incorporated into UK Law. They would therefore seem to have rights which they cannot exercise in practice. It is difficult to see how this problem can be resolved without some kind of All-Ireland Charter of Rights about which there are ongoing discussions between the UK and Irish governments. Whatever the emphasis put upon the merely 'consultative' links between the two parts of the island, the connections between them, whether in relation to tourism sport, environmental management or even trade union and banking arrangements, are strong enough to make joint decision-making in some areas inevitable. Indeed, it should be borne in mind how many Unionists support these links without wanting a United Ireland.

---

20   Hobsbawm, Eric *Nations and Nationalism since 1780*, p. 188.
21   See Bogdanor, *Beyond Brexit*, pp. 238–241.

The focus in the early 2020s is still the so-called 'Northern Ireland protocol' and the problems of maintaining seamless trade between the UK and the Republic when one country is inside the single market and the other is not.[22] Occasionally recriminations fly between both sides. But it is worth standing back from this and considering the wider picture. One important point concerns the general reliance of the Republic on trade with the UK. This is important, but less so than it used to be. When the Irish Free state came into existence a century ago, 99% of its exports went to the UK. By the time the EEC was formed the figure was around three-quarters. By the time the Republic joined the EEC it was still over one half, but by the time of the Brexit vote it was around one-quarter. That is still a significant amount, but the Irish Republic has a much more diversified economy, one much less dependent on the UK than was the case when they both joined the EEC half a century ago.[23] One should therefore avoid presuming that the Republic's trade is exclusively with its Northern neighbour.

The second point concerns the continuing ties between the two despite their increasing economic divergence. The fact is that the UK and the Republic of Ireland, two separate nation-states, with very different foreign and defence policies and different currencies, behave towards each other as if they were both part of the European Union. There may be a problem with the freedom of movement of goods between the two, but the freedom of movement of people has been maintained.

In certain key areas the UK has felt constrained to continue to have the sort of relationship that the two countries would have if both remained part of the EU – indeed a closer one even than that, given the commitment to the common travel area. They may well have to reach a common position on rights, whether in terms of the EU Charter or the European Court of Human Rights

---

22   Now modified by the so-called Windsor Framework. The Egmont Institute based in Brussels provided a short summary of the framework in April 2023, https://www.egmo ntinstitute.be/the-windsor-framework/but it still has to be seen whether it can restore effective government in Northern Ireland.

23   Figures for the 20th Century come from John Bradley's 'History of Economic Development in Ireland, North and South.' For later figures see country profiles from organisations like the World Bank. See the Economics Observatory report which actually traced the level of dependence on the UK since the Republic was formed a century ago. https://www.economicsobservatory.com/irelands-economy-since-independence-what-lessons-from-the-past-100-years

in Strasbourg. The UK has recently had difficulties with this body, despite being a founder member of the Council of Europe, which brought the court into being. Current considerations of whether to introduce a British Bill of Rights to replace the UK Human Rights Act, triggered by the European Court of Human Rights' ruling on the illegality of the UK government's plans to deport certain asylum seekers to Rwanda, must continue to bear this Irish perspective in mind. It is all too easy for UK governments, when they hear about rulings from Strasbourg, to rush to the conclusion that 'foreign judges' are interfering in 'UK affairs.' They need to bear in mind that the minority community in Northern Ireland remembers how their rights lay unprotected by UK governments until protests inspired by the American civil rights marches of the 1960s began to change things. They can clearly perceive that the issue of rights needs to be separated from nationality. The 'Irish question' helps to ensure that this perception will not easily be lost now.

Conclusion

This chapter sought to show that ironically, given the fact that the creation of the Irish Free State was one of the major factors in the failure of Home Rule All Round to succeed, it is what has happened in Northern Ireland that points to a possible way forward towards an effective settlement that might be able to preserve the UK. Devolution to other parts of the United Kingdom arguably began as a way of trying to ensure that they didn't follow the Irish into seceding. Devolution to Northern Ireland under the Good Friday agreement may help to prevent such a secession if certain features of that agreement, in particular the arrangements involving power-sharing, are taken seriously enough to be replicated elsewhere.

The next two chapters will consider in more detail what constitutional arrangements might be adopted by a UK Union. It will pay particular attention to a proposal from Wales, which perhaps because it voted to leave the EU and because support for independence (though growing) is clearly a minority position, has shown a great deal of interest in what constitutional arrangements might hold the UK together in the future.

Chapter Eleven: Wales and the English

The last chapter suggested that paradoxically it is in Northern Ireland, the one part of the United Kingdom to have received some sort of devolution from a very early time and the one area where it seemed to provoke the most conflict, that the most progressive institutional arrangements have been developed, arrangements that might well be applied elsewhere in the United Kingdom. The next two chapters will look at some serious proposals for constitutional reform that have emerged within the UK, most notably from Wales. Before looking specifically at the Welsh proposals for constitutional reform, it is worth considering some of the historical background in a little more detail. This is not a book by someone who can claim detailed knowledge of the history of Wales, but it is useful to attempt some historical background to the current situation.

The chapter on invasion and expansion in the Isles has already mentioned the process whereby the creation of the 'marches,' the border areas between England and Wales, sought to isolate rather than to subjugate Wales. However, subjugation was to come, as mentioned earlier, in the form of an invasion force led by Edward I in 1277. One important effect of Edward's invasion was the loss of the Law of Hywel (Welsh Law) and its replacement by English Law (something that didn't happen in the case of Scotland). The difference in legal systems was particularly important in the context of land tenure. Welsh law contained *Cyfran*, the custom of dividing land among all male heirs; English law made the eldest son the sole heir. The English system, in a way that anticipated the arguments in later centuries for enclosures, essentially the 'enclosing' of common land so that it was in the possession of one owner, was defended on the grounds that a host of scattered scraps in various hands was not economically viable. But 'economically viable' needs careful defining. The Welsh system meant promoting communities of fairly poor small landowners, but communities where everyone had employment and their own patch of land. Under En-

glish law these became communities with a few wealthy estate owners and a
large landless proletariat looking for work.[1]

One advantage of large numbers desperate for work is that they have to
take any job on offer. Many Welshmen were recruited into English armies during the following century. The Romans had been quite prepared to hire 'barbarians' for their armies – many had considerable military prowess – and the
English had a similar view of the Welsh. The outcome of many famous battles in
English history depended on the Welsh, just as Wellington's victory at Waterloo
in 1815 was to be dependent on the presence of the Prussians. 5,000 Welshmen
fought at the Battle of Crécy in 1346 in distinctive green and white uniforms,
while another 5,000 fought in Edward II's army at Bannockburn in 1314. A cynic
might say that from the English point of view it was a perfect outcome. First
you defeat your foes, then you impoverish them and finally you hire them when
they have no alternative but to help you defeat other foes. The process did not
only apply to Wales. Keating quotes Kumar's account of 43% of Crown forces
in 1830 being Irish (an alternative to starving in the potato famine) and 13.5%
were Scots.[2]

As the earlier chapter pointed out, it was in 1901 that people first began to
talk of a statute passed during the reign of Henry VIII as an act of 'Union' between England and Wales, but this was not an accurate description. The Act was
passed in 1536 at the time of the break with Rome that partly inspired it, since
the break increased fears of civil disorder and French or Spanish invasion.[3] 1536
was also the year in which the 'pilgrimage of grace' broke out in Yorkshire before spreading to other parts of the North. Many areas of Wales also rejected
the break with Rome and held fast to the Catholic faith.

In this context a desire to pacify Wales was understandable. But 'Union' was
hardly the right word for what was happening. Earlier invasions and the reforms passed in their wake had effectively removed anything for the English
to unite with. As Chapter Eight explained, what happened in 1536 was an act of

---

1   John Davies makes this point in his *A History of Wales*, p. 183.

2   See Keating, *State and Nation*, p. 27, quoting Kumar's *The Making of English National Identity*.

3   'By breaking with Rome, Henry VIII was challenging the Roman Catholic states of Europe, and the Tudors had particular reason to be aware that the condition of Wales was
such that its coasts were open to invasion.' Davies, *A History of Wales*, p. 219. It was the
usual story of the 'back door' to England, the image used for union with Scotland and
Ireland by Simms in his *Britain's Europe* (p. 112 in the case of Ireland, p. 32 in the case of
Scotland and Ireland together).

annexation rather than union. Some new counties were created and the border between Wales and England which has survived to this day was brought into being. But since no one thought in terms of what was an appropriate border for a country, they did not concern themselves with the fact that some Welsh-speaking districts were put outside Wales or that some diocesan boundaries were not respected by the border. As said earlier, the act made no use of Offa's Dyke, the eighth-century earth embankment designed to mark off the border with Mercia, much of which is still visible today. That was a way of marking off two kingdoms, whereas what happened during the reign of Henry VIII was a way of reorganising one kingdom. Having been penned in by the marcher lords after the Norman invasion, Wales ended up under Henry VIII being transformed into an extension of England. The legal forms used in Wales would be those of English law and Wales would have representatives in the English parliament just like any part of England.

Survival through language and religion

In the long run, the events of 1536 strengthened the importance of the Welsh language. The Scots could define themselves in terms of having a particular legal and educational system. They could talk about historic boundaries of the Kingdom of Scotland. The Welsh, with their unclear border and the absorption of their legal and educational systems into that of England, would find it more difficult to define themselves in these terms, and therefore the Welsh language became central to their sense of identity.[4]

It helped that in matters spiritual Welsh remained alongside English. It was important for preserving the language – and it has to be borne in mind that this was not the secular society of today but one in which everyone was required to go to Church. Welsh versions of the Bible and prayer book were made available in Welsh parishes alongside English versions after the break with Rome. By way of comparison, there was no Irish Bible until 1690 and no Gaelic Bible until 1801.[5]

---

4   Tom Nairn in *The Break-up of Britain* quotes John Cowper Powys' remark that '...the Welsh National spirit has had to bank itself up in the Welsh language for want of being able to express itself politically' (p. 201).

5   See John Davies, *A History of Wales*, p. 238.

Despite its increasing association with the 'lower orders,' the Welsh language survived. As late as the early nineteenth century it is fair to say that over half, perhaps two-thirds, of the inhabitants of Wales were Welsh-speaking. In most cases Welsh was the only language they knew.[6] Could it develop so that Welsh became the national language? This certainly happened in some parts of Europe where the second half of the nineteenth century saw the development of nationalist movements with a distinct emphasis upon language that paved the way for independence later.

The Czech National Revival in the nineteenth century, led by Joseph Dobrovský, Josef Jungmann and František Palacký, is a case in point. This was very much focused on language. German was the official language of the Austro-Hungarian administration and Germanisation of the Czech lands had proceeded apace in the two centuries following the Battle of the White Mountain in 1620. Czech, though an ancient language like Welsh, was soon spoken mainly by the lower classes and in rural areas. It was not seen in schools or universities, in literary and academic publications or in the state administration. Yet a national renewal movement associated with these three individuals managed to reinvigorate the language. Dobrovský published a Czech grammar while Jungmann produced a Czech-German dictionary which included borrowings from other Slavic languages and neologisms designed to ensure that Czech had the terminological resources for the latest scientific research to be produced in that language. Jungmann also provided several translations of the classics – such as the works of England's John Milton and Germany's Goethe – to ensure that the world's literary classics would be available in Czech. He was perfectly clear that 'should a social emancipation of the Czech people occur, it must happen through their language's equalization in the Czech lands.'[7] Palacký (who currently features on the Czechs' one-thousand-crown note, since they have managed to steer clear of the eurozone) ensured that an academic journal was available for publishing in Czech through the 'Journal of the Bohemian Museum,' linked to the National Museum in Prague. The Czech National Revival ensured that when Czechoslovakia became an independent nation-state in 1918 (the

6   Davies, *A History of Wales*, p. 388. He suggests that 2 out of 3 inhabitants of Wales were Welsh speakers in 1850 and most knew no other language. By 1914 there were more Welsh speakers but they now represented less than half the population – because there had been substantial immigration from England, particularly to the coalfields.

7   See 'The Birth of the Modern Czech Nation' Chapter XI of Pánek, Jaroslav et al, *A History of the Czech Lands* pp. 281–309. The quotation is on p. 298.

Czech Republic and Slovakia were formed out of Czechoslovakia in 1993), Czech could function as the official language and the business of state and the latest scientific research, as well as the education system, could be managed in that language.

This is not what happened in Wales. It is interesting to consider why, given the obvious determination of the Welsh to preserve their language and the fact that the process of industrialisation was common to both the Welsh and (for instance) Czech experience of the nineteenth century, besides which, as John Davies points out, '...in the mid nineteenth century, English speakers were hardly a higher percentage of the population of Wales than were German speakers of the population of Bohemia.'[8]

The answer lies partly in the way the economy of Wales developed.

Despite the impact of the loss of the Law of Hywel (Welsh Law) after Edward I's invasion upon employment on the land, there had been other job opportunities apart from joining the ranks of those employed to fight battles for the English. The late mediaeval economy was very much based on wool. Because of its many rivers, Wales filled up with water mills for processing cloth (known as fulling mills). From its farms a lot of Welsh beef made its way to England. With its coastline Wales was an important location for trade, not least with Ireland at a time when a high proportion of 'international trade' took place across the Irish Sea. There was also fishing and on a small scale the extraction of iron, copper, lead and coal, and it was this last that anticipated the industrial revolution to come. Welsh coal went to Ireland and South-West England well before the industrial revolution, but there was an enormous expansion of the coalfields at the end of the nineteenth century.[9]

If the emphasis at the time of the loss of the Law of Hywel was upon the Welsh seeking employment fighting for England against Scotland at Bannockburn or the French at Crécy, the emphasis with the growth in importance of the coalfields was upon the English seeking employment in Wales. Wales was a beneficiary of the economic expansion that came with the industrial revolution and its aftermath, but on terms dictated by England. The mass migration into what became the South Wales coalfields had huge cultural implications. John

---

8   Davies, John *A History of Wales*, p.407; Morgan, K. *Wales: Rebirth of a Nation*.
9   See Davies, *A History of Wales*, p. 186. He writes that the development of the fulling-mill 'gave rise to an Industrial Revolution in the Later Middle Ages'. The coastal trade with Ireland, as well as the south-west and north-west of England, was also important in the 15th century (pp. 206–207).

Davies records how for half a century between 1880 and 1930 between a quarter and one third of the male labour force worked in the coal industry, while the figure can be pushed to about half by including quarrying. Morgan claims that Welsh mines at this time accounted for one-third of all world coal exports.[10] In the first decade of the twentieth century, Davies records, Wales was unique among the countries of Europe in having more people moving in than out. 'In that decade,' he writes, 'only the United States excelled Wales in the ability to attract immigration'. Facilities were stretched and riots broke out. 'With such a flood of incomers, some districts became grossly overcrowded'. Davies quotes *The Times* in 1904 reporting that in the Rhondda there was 'the same oppressive atmosphere that one experienced in the streets of Odessa and Sebastopol during the unrest in Russia in the winter of 1904.'[11]

There were cultural consequences, including consequences for the language. The mines were organised at the British rather than Welsh level, and this was reflected in the concerns of their leaders, including union leaders. At the same time, the influx produced 'anglicisation' and despite efforts by the coalfields to promote the learning of Welsh there was a huge increase in the number of monoglot English speakers. In this context it is hardly surprising that the main threat to Welsh identity and to the Welsh language would be seen as coming from England.

It is true that, as Tom Nairn points out from a Scottish perspective, 'the industrial revolution which so threatened Welsh language and life also gave it a chance of life'.[12] It established the language in the industrial valley communities, whatever their need to speak English, and they often used Welsh in order to maintain links with other industrial sectors through their unions and other associations. It also prevented Welsh being associated with 'primitive' rural communities, 'noble savages' who communicated with one another in a strange tongue. Arguably, Welsh was both buoyed up and overwhelmed by rapid industrialisation at the start of the twentieth century.

By 1914, though the number of Welsh speakers had risen to one million, that represented less than half the population and most of them knew English as well. To reach the majority of the Welsh population it wasn't any longer necessary to know Welsh. By the time of the outbreak of the First World War, five-sixths of Welsh speakers were bilingual. They could be reached by using English

10   Davies, John *A History of Wales*, p. 475.

11   Davies, John *A History of Wales*, p. 478.

12   Nairn, Tom. *The Break-up of Britain*, p. 200.

and material in Welsh no longer had to exist in every subject. In this respect one of the ways in which Welsh speakers contributed to the decline of Welsh was by learning English.[13]

A second difference from the situation in the Czech lands was associated with religion. There was a strong tradition of Nonconformity (Protestantism outside the Anglican Church) in Wales, and its leaders were unwilling to use the Welsh language. They saw their evangelising mission as best conducted in English, especially as this was the language of English incomers. Had not St Paul in the first century spread the gospel by speaking and writing in Greek, not in Hebrew or in Aramaic, the language spoken by Jesus of Nazareth? The demands of the gospel must come before those of the Welsh nation. In the case of the Czechs, it is true that their history was steeped in their own form of nonconformity in the form of the tradition associated with Jan Hus, the fifteenth-century reformer who was burnt at the stake in 1415 at the Council of Constance, and whose fate Martin Luther was keen to avoid when he was 'captured' by friendly knights a century later. Yet the passion for national revival in the nineteenth century was less tied to religious roots in the Czech lands. In Wales, on the other hand, Welshness had been partly hijacked by nonconformity, which not only put an emphasis upon the use of English but forced those who wanted to see the development of a secular Welsh culture to look elsewhere. Inevitably they were drawn more to the secular traditions of the wider world, including those of England.[14]

This led – and continues to lead – to problems in the key sphere of education. By the end of the nineteenth century, the Welsh language had little more than a foothold. Schools did not have to teach Welsh, and if they did so it was added to an English curriculum. Some of them opted to ban Welsh from their schools altogether. After all, it is not so long since speaking Welsh in a Welsh school was a punishable offence, with the so-called Welsh Not, a stick or ruler or something similar that could be used as a cane. The last recorded use of the Welsh Not as a form of corporal punishment to enforce the use of

---

13   Davies makes this point in *A History of Wales*, pp. 482–483.

14   Davies suggests that 'in the second half of the nineteenth century, Nonconformity succeeded in 'hijacking' Welshness and a secular Welsh-language culture did not therefore emerge. As a result, the interconnection between chapel-going and Welshness was confirmed, for those who did not sympathise with the values of Nonconformity could turn their backs upon both.' *A History of Wales*, p. 486.

English comes from the 1940s. Even when such barbarism ceased, the problem was that rather than being the medium through which the whole world of learning was opened up across the full spectrum of subjects, Welsh was becoming another language subject tacked on to the rest of the curriculum, where it obviously seemed less appealing and relevant than learning German or French. The most that this foothold in the education system could do was to save Welsh from virtually dying out in the way Breton did.[15]

Industrial development and English overspill

Since the battles in the nineteenth century to make sure that Wales was a Welsh-speaking nation in its entirety have been lost, it has become difficult to avoid division between a Welsh-speaking Wales and an English-speaking Wales, one which to some extent reproduces the old division between *pura Wallia* and *marchia Wallia*, between 'Wales proper' and the Wales of the Marches. The former, concentrated in the West and North, would clearly support a powerful Welsh *Senedd* and even an independent Wales. The Welsh National Party, *Plaid Cymru*, remains known by its Welsh name rather than any English equivalent, though it is technically the Party of Wales. By way of comparison, few know the Scottish National Party as *Pàrtaidh Nàiseanta na h-Alba*, its name in Scottish Gaelic. But *Plaid Cymru* has its heartlands in Welsh-speaking Wales. In Wales overall it can rarely secure more than 20% of the vote (this was its score in the 2021 *Senedd* elections).[16]

English-speaking Wales, on the other hand, might not consider itself Welsh at all. A far larger part of the Welsh than the Scottish population is made up of people who would consider themselves English even though they have settled in Wales. More than half of the Welsh population lives within 25 miles of the border (the figure for Scotland is 3%). Many of them are more English overspill than Welsh, like the bulging bottom that spreads itself onto the next seat in the train. It is unsurprising that half a century or more ago when there

---

15   See Davies, *A History of Wales*, pp. 443–444.

16   Keating makes the point well: 'Welsh identity has historically been more linked than its Scottish counterpart to cultural markers, including the language and Nonconformist religion. Yet the language has also been divisive, as it is spoken by a minority, too small to demand comprehensive linguistic transformation but large enough to be a political force.' Keating, *State and Nation in the United Kingdom*, p. 180.

were several arson attacks linked with Welsh nationalism, the attacks were particularly on this overspill in the form of second homes bought up by the English and unoccupied outside the tourist season.[17]

This means that people with homes in Wales are not always aware of themselves as living in another country within which they must become assimilated. Some of them might be happy to reflect that England and Wales have a single legal system or that their football teams play in the same league, despite their having different national teams (as became more than clear during the world cup at the end of 2022, when both teams played against each other). Others note that there are county cricket teams based in Wales. They may even take the view that since they don't speak Welsh the language barrier rules out assimilation and they prefer to have nothing to do with it. Thus, where a hundred years ago Welsh children resented being forced to learn English under the rod of the Welsh Not, now English settlers resent their children being forced to attend classes in Welsh. Where the nineteenth-century nonconformists saw Welsh as a barrier to hearing the word of God, English settlers see Welsh as a barrier to hearing the word of science and technology. Even in schools where Welsh is the medium of instruction, only 70% of secondary school subjects are taught in Welsh. A BBC report entitled *About Wales*, aiming to provide a straightforward and unbiased introduction to the country's education system in October 2014, reported that 'some Welsh medium secondary schools prefer to teach science and maths in English, because this is seen as the international language of science.'[18] It is true that the majority of scientific research papers and conferences are in English, but as a reason for teaching maths or science in English this is highly questionable. It feeds the prejudice that there has been no attempt to 'update' the language in the manner of the neologisms introduced through Jungmann to ensure that Czech had the terminological resources for the latest scientific research to be produced in Czech. The assumption seems to be that were children to learn Welsh they would be forced to have endless discussions about how to harness oxen to the plough or the impact of a harvest moon on maidens' hearts. As the Czechs were only too well aware as members of a Habsburg Empire whose officials spoke German, a sense of social and cultural

---

17   See a report of 2018 on the Welsh tax base from the Welsh Centre for Public Policy by Guto Ifann and Dr Ed Gareth Poole. The figure given on p. 12 is a little under 48%, but it has grown slightly since then, https://www.wcpp.org.uk/wp-content/uploads/2018/07/The-Welsh-Tax-Base-_WCPP-Final-180627.pdf

18   https://www.bbc.co.uk/wales/livinginwales/sites/aboutwales/pages/education.shtml

superiority can manifest itself in a view that some languages lack the resources to act as vehicles for sophisticated ideas. Given the way the English language is currently used, one might be tempted to view this as a bizarre reversal of the truth!

It is often pointed out that the existence of uncontrolled levels of immigration from other parts of the European Union was one of the prime factors behind the success of the Brexiteers in the 2016 referendum vote on whether to remain inside the EU. Few of the Brexiteers, including many of those English speakers who were voting in Wales, thought of how uncontrolled levels of immigration from England to other parts of the UK had proved problematic in earlier times. On the other hand, such an association would certainly have occurred to people who feel strongly about their Welsh identity and its close association with their language. It is very unlikely that they would feel that identity threatened by the European Union. They are far more likely to think that it will be crushed by the English.

It is hardly surprising that Wales made full use of the opportunities to promote Welsh provided by membership of the European Union. The language had been supported within the European Economic Community (forerunner of the EU) since the Mercator Project which first became a European project through a resolution passed by the European Parliament in 1988. Wales received support from the 1992 European Charter for Regional and Minority Languages, which entered into force in 1998, and from the European Charter of Human Rights, which emphasises linguistic diversity in Article 22 and in Article 21 prohibits discrimination on the basis of language. After Brexit the European Charter of Human Rights no longer applies (a problem, as we have already seen, for Irish citizens living in Northern Ireland) and various forms of funding support used to bolster the Welsh language have been lost.[19] It is this loss of participation in a wider community of twenty-eight nations with over twenty national languages, and the disappearance of measures to protect minority

---

19   It is difficult to assess the loss of funding after Brexit. The UK government claims that it has stepped in to make up for any losses, the Welsh government denies that this is so, and neutral observers point out that it can be difficult to count the figures anyway. The Welsh *Senedd* produced a report in 2018 entitled 'Brexit, The Arts Sector, Creative Industries, Heritage and the Welsh language' outlining some of the difficulties. See https://senedd.wales/media/ghdecoxo/cr-ld11940-e.pdf. The UK government insisted that it had made up for any loss of funding after Brexit – this, for instance, is a BBC report reporting the government position in February 2022. https://www.bbc.com/news/uk-wales-politics-60332682

languages, that is bound to influence a large body of opinion in the country. This is a perspective that must be borne in mind when considering the history of devolution in Wales and the measures proposed by the Welsh *Senedd* itself for constitutional reform in the UK, measures which will be considered in the next chapter.

The history of devolution in Wales

Before the introduction of legislative devolution, Wales received a degree of executive devolution when a Secretary of State for Wales was created by Harold Wilson's Labour government in 1964. On the whole Welsh secretaries of state were sensitive to national differences, and in particular to the strong support in Wales for the Labour Party, whoever was in power at Westminster. This may have influenced the overwhelming rejection of devolution by the Welsh in a referendum in the 1970s, as did the fact that for much of this time the same party (the Labour Party) was in power in Wales and Westminster (1964–1970 and 1974–1979).

However, this was to change after Mrs Thatcher's victory in 1979 ushered in eighteen years of Conservative government at Westminster. In 1993, after the Conservative Party had been in power in London for fourteen years, John Redwood became the Secretary of State for Wales in the government led by John Major. He was later to challenge (unsuccessfully) John Major for the Conservative leadership and later still became a prominent Brexiteer. This was unsurprising. He was one of those whose attitude to power was that it should exist at only one level, that of London. John Davies describes him as 'an oddity among Welsh secretaries',[20] essentially 'London's viceroy in Wales', his mission 'specifically to carry out his own vision – unfettered competition, low taxes, small government and total resistance to any advance in the powers of the European Union'. Other Welsh secretaries (in the 1980s) had toned down the Thatcherite vision out of respect for the different ideological perspective of many in Wales.

Such toning down was often the case in the parts of the UK outside England, especially when a Conservative government was in power in Westminster, but other parties dominated in Wales, Scotland and Northern Ireland. One thinks of Jim Prior's famous remark when he was Secretary of State for Northern Ireland under Mrs Thatcher, telling visitors from Britain that 'we're

---

20   Davies, John *A History of Wales*, p. 666.

all Keynesians here.'[21] Redwood's vision was different. He was not accommodating himself to the different views of another part of the United Kingdom. He preferred to think of himself as imposing his vision upon the recalcitrant 'natives', from whom he clearly felt he had nothing to learn. During his period as secretary of state, he did not sleep a single night in Wales and an attempt he made to pretend that he knew the Welsh national anthem by mouthing the words during a public meeting was the cause of much derision.

There were other important influences upon Welsh attitudes to devolution in the 1990s. One was local government reorganisation in 1996, which reduced the two tiers of Welsh local government to one (eight county and thirty-seven district councils were replaced by 22 unitary country councils, thereby ending the squabbles over demarcation of powers between districts and counties). This allowed a Welsh assembly to be introduced without introducing a third tier of government.[22] The 'why introduce another layer of bureaucracy?' argument against introducing devolution was therefore less strongly felt.

Another influence was the existence of so-called Quangos (Quasi-Autonomous Non-Governmental Organisations), something that grew up right across the UK in the 1980s and 1990s. These were frequently attacked for taking powers away from elected representatives (in local and regional councils) and giving it to appointees of the government. In Wales this meant groups of people appointed by the Secretary of State for Wales, spending billions of pounds and employing tens of thousands of people. It was understandable that people might prefer that this money be managed by a Welsh Assembly elected by the Welsh people.

As a result, the Welsh, who in the 1970s had rejected the idea of a devolved assembly decisively, voted by a whisker in its favour twenty years later. This was the closest of all referenda – its majority of 50.1 to 49.9 closer even than that of the referendum on leaving the EU. Yet despite the narrowness of the result, it represented a huge shift of opinion in Wales itself when compared to twenty years earlier.

Since the narrow vote in favour of devolution, the 'assembly' (as it was originally called) has steadily increased its powers. In 2006 the Government of Wales Act gave the Welsh government and assembly powers much closer to those of the Scottish government and parliament. A referendum in 2011 on whether to

---

21   Quoted in Philip Whitehead, *The Writing on the Wall* pp. 388–389.

22   This was The Local Government (Wales) Act 1994, which came into effect in 1996.

extend the legislative powers of the Assembly further was passed by 2 to 1, suggesting that the body had grown on Welsh citizens. In 2017 it received 'reserved' as opposed to 'defined' powers, meaning essentially that rather than exercising all powers specifically given to it, it could exercise all powers not specifically denied to it. To recognise its increased authority, it was finally renamed to recognise its increased powers. It became known as the *Senedd Cymru* in 2020.[23] The word might suggest 'Senate' but is essentially chosen as a Welsh word to describe what is called in English the Welsh Parliament, much as the Irish word *Dáil* is used to describe the Irish Parliament.

The problems of sharing power

An earlier chapter mentioned some of the problems raised by devolution in discussing EVEL, the so-called principle of English Votes for English Laws. It argued that the principle of English Votes for English Laws can be difficult to apply when it isn't clear exactly which laws apply to England alone. Decisions that apparently apply only to England have consequences outside England, since under the Barnett formula Scottish and Welsh funding is a percentage of that given to England. Hence a decision that might seem on the face of it to concern England alone may have knock-on effects elsewhere.

The issue obviously crops up in the context of devolution, since there will be arguments over what is properly within the competence of the devolved governments. This is not the place to examine all the different issues over which problems have arisen, but one example will serve to illustrate the difficulties and raises an issue very similar to the one mentioned in the last paragraph concerning EVEL – rail transport.

Towards the end of the nineteenth century people didn't only go in large numbers to Wales from England for work. The coming of the railways brought English tourists to Wales and especially to the coastal resorts. This was another reason for encouraging the learning of English. Knowing English was obviously an advantage in developing the tourist industry, especially in an age when beach holidays were taken in the Isles rather than abroad (which was

---

23   As Bogdanor puts it, devolution in Wales has 'proved to be a process rather than an event'. See *Beyond Brexit*, pp. 192–193 where he summarises the process.

overwhelmingly the case before the Second World War and the expansion of commercial flights through the jet engine).[24]

The shape of the Welsh railways in the 2020s still reflects the nineteenth-century English dash to the coast. The fact that there was no Welsh government to take part in planning the railway network, while all the UK government did was to approve schemes by private contractors, meant that the railway system that emerged was one of connecting populous areas of England with the Welsh conurbations and resorts they wanted to travel to. Lines appeared running West from the Bristol area to the industrial heartlands of the south and then on to the coast. Another set of lines ran Westwards from the Liverpool area to the North Wales coast. But no lines (until after 1860) ran across Wales itself connecting the North with the South. In its own way the rail network reflected the treatment of Wales as an extension of England rather than as a country in its own right, an approach that can be traced back to the annexation of 1536 and beyond.[25]

Because it was not a Welsh network but an extension of the English network, to get to the north of Wales from the South by train you had to go into England and then back into Wales. The system was taking the English to the seaside and back rather than taking the Welsh to other parts of their country. Despite some tweaking of lines, it still looks that way in the twenty-first century. Someone travelling from Cardiff to Bangor, for instance, has to go through England twice. A person frequently making this journey in the autumn of 2021, at a time when COVID-19 policies were to require masks to be worn in Wales but not in England, remarked to me that his journey, where the mask was concerned, was a case of On-Off-On-Off-On.[26] The demand for devolution to the Welsh *Senedd* of all responsibility for public transport has to be seen in this context.

---

24   See Davies, *A History of Wales*, pp. 395–396. In effect the seaside holiday took off with the railways in the mid-nineteenth century and ended a century later with the application of the jet engine to commercial flights.

25   See the maps in Davies, *A History of Wales*, pp. 398–399. More lines had appeared by 1914 (see p. 399), though not all of them are still in existence a century later. But the most noticeable feature is the difficulty of getting across Wales, particularly from North to South.

26   If you try to get from the Welsh capital, Cardiff, to Llandudno on the North coast, the journey takes five hours and goes through Hereford, Shrewsbury and Crewe – i.e. it snakes in and out of England before eventually returning to Wales. It takes rather longer than going from London to Edinburgh.

Twenty years on from devolution, the Welsh government runs the day-to-day operations of the railways in Wales through its operator Transport for Wales, but railway infrastructure remains the responsibility of the UK Government. Many in Wales would like management of the infrastructure to be devolved too, partly in order to develop the *One Wales* policy, which aims to reduce travel time between the North and South of Wales, and partly for financial reasons.

Research from Cardiff University's Wales Governance Centre found that Wales could have received an extra £514 million investment between 2011–12 and 2019–20, had rail infrastructure been devolved. The problem is the UK government's controversial £100 billion (and rising) High Speed 2 (HS2) rail project, which is designated an England and Wales project, despite none of the infrastructure applying to Wales.[27] According to the Barnett formula, funding levels for Scotland and Northern Ireland are based upon the level of funding for England. As mentioned earlier, this was precisely the problem highlighted when discussing EVEL, in that a vote in the House of Commons on some aspect of education or health policy in England alone might nevertheless have ramifications outside England. It might be assumed that policies concerning England alone have 'nothing to do with the devolved nations', but the Barnett formula ensures that they do, because their cost implications will have a knock-on effect on funding levels in devolved nations. The issue of HS2 illustrates the point nicely. Because HS2 is very costly, this means that Scotland and Northern Ireland will get substantial extra funding (because their spending has to be proportionate to that in England). But not Wales, which is excluded from receiving additional funding because the rail infrastructure (unlike in Scotland) is not devolved, and so this is seen as spending in England and Wales combined. Hence the calculation that if the rail infrastructure had been devolved, Wales would have received an extra half a billion over the lifetime of the project, enough to finance some substantial projects within Wales itself (for instance a line from Camarthen to Aberystwyth, or the electrification of the main line from London, which stops at Cardiff because of funding problems rather than being continued as far as Swansea). The response from Westminster that passengers using the HS2 would be able to change at Crewe and enter North Wales

---

27   https://www.cardiff.ac.uk/__data/assets/pdf_file/0009/2508372/ WFA_evidence_rail 2.pdf The report was taken up by Westminster's Welsh Affairs Committee in an attempt to have the HS2 project re-classified as an England-only project.

more quickly using other trains was hardly very convincing.[28] In May 2022 the leader of the Tories in the Welsh *Senedd* declared that he agreed with the argument that Wales should receive such money, but the visiting Prime Minister, Boris Johnson, refused to commit himself.[29] In any case, whatever the final shape of the Welsh railway system and its management, it seems clear that a network put in place above all to serve the interests of England needs to be controlled by Wales in order to ensure that it is gradually transformed into a network primarily designed to serve the people of Wales.

Rail transport may not be the most important item in devolution, but it does illustrate how from a Welsh perspective the country might be seen as threatened more by its forced participation in the British Union than by membership of the European Union. Many aspects of its economy have been determined by how far they have served the needs of England, and over the decades this has limited the capacity of Wales to determine its own welfare. Sometimes it has been overwhelmed by English immigration; at other times its infrastructure has been built up to serve English needs; its culture and identity have been threatened by the English language and to some extent confined to a particular part of the country. It has been pushed back into a corner which has served as 'Wales proper', and then incorporated within a greater whole that has smothered it. It has taken part in the industrial expansion that Britain enjoyed in earlier centuries, but without being able to determine its own part in that expansion.

Compared with this, for many people in Wales the EU has been far more of an opportunity than a threat. For one thing, it has been a source of funding. Indeed, there are fears that the end of the EU Structural Funds programme following Brexit will further limit the ability of the Welsh Government to provide top-up funding for railway infrastructure. The EU's regional spending budget gave support to regions where GDP per head was 75% or less of the EU average, and when the UK was a member of the EU this included two regions of the UK, of which one was the West of Wales. It is not clear that the UK government will be prepared to make up the shortfall, particularly as Brexit rode on the back of government claims that money was being poured into the EU and it does

28   See the BBC report in December 2021 https://www.bbc.com/news/uk-wales-59596529
29   See this report from the BBC in May 2022. https://www.bbc.com/news/uk-wales-polit ics-61495454

not like to admit that substantial sums were travelling in the other direction.[30] In addition, the EU was an opportunity to strengthen Welsh identity, particularly through the support given to its language. Such support can come from a British Union too – there are obvious examples of backing given to Welsh at a UK level too, such as the BBC's support for *Creative Wales*. But in the case of the European Union, it is part of a wider process supporting minority languages right across Europe. More generally, it is important to appreciate how, while the UK was part of the EU, devolved governments were drawn into European policy networks and various pan-European networks of sub-state governments such as RLEG, a joint initiative of European regions with legislative powers.[31] They ceased to be always engaged in bilateral negotiations with the UK. Now that experience of 'multilevel governance' has been severely curtailed.

Conclusion

The chapter looked briefly at the way Wales was first penned in by the Marcher lords after the Norman invasion and then effectively invaded under Edward I, ending up under Henry VIII being transformed into an extension of England. It pointed out that because its legal and education systems were effectively those of England, Welsh identity had above all to be preserved through its language. However, it never managed to make Welsh the language of its people in the way that, for instance, Czech was established as the language of the Czechs. Some of the explanation for this lies in an unprecedented number of migrants from England, particularly in the first decade of the twentieth century. It may also have been affected by the strength of nonconformity in Wales.

The chapter then briefly considered the history of devolution in Wales. It suggested that local government reorganisation, the creation of quangos that handled large amounts of money without local accountability and some rather domineering and insensitive secretaries of state for Wales managed to create

---

30   It can be difficult to know whether the UK has made up the shortfall because it is never a simple question of comparing like with like. It is noteworthy, however, that in April 2023 MPs called for a public inquiry into the economic effects of Brexit. See the BBC report https://www.bbc.com/news/uk-politics-65384431. It is interesting that the government response to the MPs' call was to say that Brexit was the choice of voters, not that it was an economically advantageous decision.

31   See https://rleg.eu

support for an Assembly which was overwhelmingly rejected in an earlier referendum in the 1970s. Though the devolution vote was only passed by a whisker in the 1999 referendum, devolution grew more popular in the new century and the assembly (now parliament/*Senedd*) has been able to increase its powers.

For much of its history, Wales has been able to benefit economically from its association with England, but only on terms dictated by the latter. The problem of railway transport illustrates how Wales lacked control of its own railway infrastructure, which was made to serve English needs. The railway lines conveyed English tourists to the coast, just as the coalfields magnetised huge waves of English immigration. Wales was in control of neither.

The UK turned against the EU partly because it was perceived to be unable to 'keep out' foreigners from the EU. The Welsh had been completely unable to keep out foreigners from England. In 2020 and 2021 there were echoes of this under COVID-19, in the inability to keep out English trippers desperate for a bit of beach life or rural relief after their confinement.

Partly because of the effects of English overspill, for many people living in Wales it is clear why the European Union has been seen more as a means of preserving their identity than as a threat to it. Support came from the EU for the Welsh language and for Welsh rural development, while the expansion of the EU in 2004, when new members included many that were roughly the same size as Wales, demonstrated how small and large countries can co-exist within an EU format. It demonstrated that a nation-state of three million would be perfectly viable. If the Baltic states can manage it, so can Wales.

The points outlined in this chapter provide background to proposals for a reformed UK constitution made by the Welsh *Senedd* which are considered in the next chapter.

Chapter Twelve: Wales and a British Union

Many proposals made by governments in Westminster in the light of devolution have been ad hoc and ill thought out. The English Votes for English Laws idea, rushed into being in the wake of the Scottish referendum, was thrown out six years later by another government of the same political persuasion. Proposals for an English Parliament remain undeveloped. The idea of dividing England up into regional groupings has proceeded by trial and error, rejected in the case of a North-East Assembly, embraced more warmly in some of the areas covered by the so-called 'metro mayors.'[1] The House of Lords, which might be turned into a second chamber providing representation for regions and nations inside the United Kingdom rather in the manner of the German *Bundesrat*, remains unreformed and entirely unelected.

However, there have been some suggestions for constitutional reform in the UK that have been much more clearly thought-out than the piecemeal proposals outlined by Westminster governments so far. Among the most significant is one from the Welsh *Senedd* which appeared in a document originally published in 2019 and entitled *Reforming our Union: Shared Governance in the UK*.[2] The last chapter considered the history of Wales as a nation and then the history of devolution within Wales. This chapter connects that background with the fact that some of the most interesting proposals for constitutional reform in the UK have emerged from Wales.

Because Wales voted narrowly in favour of Brexit, there isn't the same feeling that the country has been pushed out of the EU against its will which understandably embitters some of the Scots and Northern Irish. It is also not dominated by a nationalist party in the way Scotland is. The Labour Party tends to

---

1   See Bogdanor, *Beyond Brexit*, pp. 204–206.
2   See https://gov.wales/reforming-our-union-shared-governance-in-the-uk-2nd-editio n. The document was first published in 2019 and then updated in 2021.

be the most popular party (as the 2021 elections proved, in which Labour took half of the *Senedd* seats). An overwhelming majority of Welsh voters remain Unionist. This has enabled Wales to concentrate more on how to foster Welsh interests inside the British Union than on how to leave that Union. Keating is surely right to suggest that the Welsh Labour government 'is perhaps the only unambiguously pro-devolution government in the United Kingdom and has sought to move towards a form of cooperative federalism in which Wales would be recognised as a full partner in union.'[3] Indeed, other Welsh politicians before Mark Drakeford, the current first minister of Wales, have made similar proposals, including Carwyn Jones, his predecessor as first minister from 2009–2018, who after frequent clashes with the austerity policies of the Liberal Democrat-Conservative coalition between 2010 and 2015 felt that sufficient economic support for Wales could only come through a 'renewed union.'[4]

However, knowing how to foster those interests effectively has proved far from easy. It should be clear from the discussion of rail transport in the previous chapter that the devolution of powers is a difficult process, however well-intentioned both sides might be. Brexit, however, has complicated the process further. Several important economic areas, such as agriculture and fisheries, were devolved in the original agreements made when the UK was not expected to be leaving the EU. Such devolution was more apparent than real because the binding rules of the EU single market effectively meant that decisions in these areas were taken in Brussels, not in London or Cardiff. Post-Brexit, however, these rules no longer apply. The Westminster government is keen to maintain the integrity of a UK single market in order to be able to negotiate the much-vaunted new trade deals that Brexit is supposed to facilitate. It is disinclined to compromise that integrity by repatriating too many powers to Scotland, Wales and Northern Ireland.[5] It therefore feels compelled to exercise some sort of

---

3   Keating, *State and Nation*, p. 51.

4   See Jones, Carwyn. *Our Future Union-A Perspective from Wales* written in 2014 https://w
     ww.instituteforgovernment.org.uk/events/keynote-speech-rt-hon-carwyn-jones-am
     -minister-wales-our-future-union---perspective-wales/ and the Welsh government's
     report of 2017 entitled 'Brexit and Devolution' https://gov.wales/sites/default/files/20
     17-06/170615-brexit%20and%20devolution%20(en).pdf

5   See Bogdanor, *Beyond Brexit*, p.213-214. He concludes on p. 214 by quoting the words of
     the European Union Select Committee of the House of Lords that the European Union
     was 'in effect, part of the glue holding the United Kingdom together since 1997.' 'That
     glue is now becoming unstuck,' Bogdanor concludes.

control over decisions that it has theoretically entrusted to the devolved bodies. For this reason, it can easily seem as though the government would like the devolution process to go backwards after Brexit, with attempts being made to repatriate powers to Westminster.

When the *Senedd* published a second version of its proposals for a reformed constitution in June 2021, it came after the Internal Market Act of 2020. This Act quoted the 'Sewel convention,' which determined that Parliament will not 'normally' legislate for Wales, Scotland or Northern Ireland with regard to devolved matters without the consent of the relevant devolved legislature.[6] The Sewel convention allowed for a different approach to devolved matters if the situation was not 'normal' – and Brexit, it was argued by Westminster in 2020, had hardly produced a 'normal' situation. But who was to decide this? Who was to say what was or was not a 'normal' situation? An outbreak of war? A pandemic? Leaving the European Union? Since it was for the UK government and Parliament alone to decide what circumstances were 'abnormal', the government could proceed with the UK Internal Market Act in 2020, despite overwhelming opposition and the withholding of Legislative Consent by both the *Senedd* and Scottish Parliament. It was not even possible for the Supreme Court to judge whether this interpretation of 'normality' was appropriate. It seemed clear that the 'Sewel convention' was simply a vehicle for trying to reconcile Westminster supremacy with devolved powers and if necessary use the former to override the latter. It was a process described by Michael Foley as an unwritten understanding, something that (in words quoted by Keating) should 'remain understood as long as they remain sufficiently obscure to allow them to retain an approximate appearance of clarity and coherence while... accommodating several potentially conflicting and quite unresolved points of issue.'[7] In other words, one might think, deliberately obfuscating, burying problems in verbiage much as the banks did when their financial malpractices were threatened with discovery shortly before the financial crisis of 2008. As for joint working between all the nations, that would be kept to a minimum. Time and time again the UK government showed that it was prepared to give powers away but could not handle the idea of sharing power, rather like the sort of passive-aggressive introvert who is willing to delegate but baulks at teamwork.

---

6   See the summary of discussions in Parliament at https://publications.parliament.uk/p a/ld5802/ldselect/ldconst/142/14207.htm

7   Foley, *The Silence of Constitutions*, p. 38, quoted in Keating *State and Nation*, p. 64.

Unsurprisingly, the Welsh *Senedd* saw the Internal Market Act less as a 'four nation approach' than one of 'aggressive unilateralism.' Hence the new version of its proposals in the summer of 2021, followed by an announcement in October 2021 that it was setting up an 'independent constitutional commission', following a promise made by the Labour Party in the elections for the *Senedd* in May 2021.[8]

Westminster's reaction had undermined a degree of sympathy for its position where the Internal Market Act was concerned, even on the part of the devolved nations. They themselves recognised that matters concerning agriculture and fisheries had been devolved in theory, but in practice were decided in Brussels as part of the Common Agricultural Policy and Common Fisheries Policy. When these matters were repatriated after Brexit, they should strictly speaking have been returned to the devolved nations under the devolution settlement. But it made sense to avoid having four different agricultural and fisheries policies in the UK, particularly when there were trade deals in the making. In such circumstances the best way forward was certainly to adopt some joint approach whereby trade deals could still be made by the UK, but in such a manner that (because some ingredients of those deals were in devolved areas) they were arrived at by joint decision-making. And that was precisely what the Westminster government appeared loathe to allow.

The issues raised by the Internal Market Act of 2020 show that the problems raised by devolution are not simply a matter of how much legislation should be 'passed down' from Westminster to the devolved bodies. They are also a matter of how decisions might be reached jointly by all the parties involved – in other words how the Westminster Parliament could work with the devolved bodies (perhaps including an English Parliament or representatives of the English regions) on matters where they need to work *together*. This is an absolutely central point, which is constantly overlooked. Discussions of devolution, including so-called 'devo-max', focus on how many (or how many more) competences should be handed down to the devolved nations, rather as if it was similar to a discussion of how much responsibility should be accorded to municipal (local) government. But what is absolutely essential for successful devolution is a mechanism whereby all the nations could work together in areas where it made sense for them to work jointly rather than separately. It is precisely this that

---

8   Mark Drakeford, Labour leader of the Welsh *Senedd*, describes the proposals in such terms in his Foreword to the second edition of 'Reforming Our Union: Shared Governance in the UK,' which was produced in June 2021.

the Westminster Parliament is loathe to recognise, because it pushes towards a system of shared sovereignty.

Furthermore, there needs to be a mechanism – most appropriately a legal mechanism – whereby judgments can be made about when there has been a breach of any constitutional arrangements decided upon. For instance, it might be agreed that a trade deal would be negotiated at the Westminster level but would require confirmation by each of the devolved governments. There is a precedent for this in the European Union. When the EU reached a trade agreement with Canada, it needed to be ratified by all EU governments, but in the case of Belgium ratification was delayed on account of objections from Wallonia, a region of Belgium. Under the Belgian system, ratification must be agreed by the regional parliaments as well as by the federal government. The trade deal with Canada was certainly delayed while Wallonia hesitated before giving its consent, but eventually ratification went through, and the deal proceeded. There was criticism about 'delay' and (that inevitable buzzword) 'inefficiency', but it could also be argued that it was worthwhile to secure consent at the sub-nation state level.[9] Could the same be done by the UK?

In order to take this further, the present chapter will examine the *Senedd* proposals in a little more detail. What constitutional reforms does it have in mind to prevent what the devolved nations see as the cavalier disregard for their concerns shown, for instance, in the case of the Internal Market Act?

Parliament and the Courts

The previous section outlined an alternative approach to devolution. Instead of asking what powers need to be handed down, as if the question was simply one of who owns what, one could ask what powers could be shared by everyone (i.e., by the four nations). This is a key issue, since devolution and even secession need not mean a willingness to share sovereignty. It may simply mean trying to preserve the sovereignty of parliament while reducing the area it covers (from mother country and dominions to mother country, then a reduced

---

9   Though the headlines at the time were of a deal in 'crisis' and EU leaders 'humiliated', it was only a short delay and it is notable that Wallonia was able to use its power to effect significant concessions before the final deal was signed. See https://www.france24.co m/en/20161027-belgians-eu-canada-trade-deal-controversial-reach-agreement

mother country). I have already suggested that this may explain why some conservative commentators are in favour of an independent Scotland. It is an altogether less 'shocking' prospect than a sovereignty-sharing system which might be seen as sharing power with Scots in a wide range of policy areas!

The introduction to *Reforming our Union* describes the 'Whitehall perspective' as one that assumes...

> the default is centralisation of political authority within the UK. But that is the wrong starting point. We should instead start from a presumption of subsidiarity and sovereignty shared within the UK. Then we can focus on how to make the Union work effectively, to join its constituent parts in a shared enterprise of governing the UK.

In other words, the Welsh proposals focus on the fact that it is better to think of the UK as a joint project with shared governance than to think in terms of a centralised government handing down larger and larger morsels from the top table:

> Whatever its historical origins, the United Kingdom is best seen now as a voluntary association of nations taking the form of a multi-national state.

The report continued by affirming that:

> Wales is committed to this association, which must be based on the recognition of popular sovereignty in each part of the UK; Parliamentary sovereignty as traditionally understood no longer provides a sound foundation for this evolving constitution.

The talk of 'sovereignty in each part of the UK' is fascinating, since it is precisely the sharing of sovereignty that lay at the heart of Monnet's proposals for the Coal and Steel Community and later for the EEC/EU.

The document continues by reaffirming that:

> the traditional doctrine of the sovereignty of Parliament no longer provides a firm foundation for the constitution of the UK. It needs to be adjusted to take account of the realities of devolution, just as it was adjusted to take account of the UK's membership of the European Union.

Hence the Welsh proposals expressly link the structure of devolution within the UK to the structure of pooled sovereignty within the EU.[10]

What is this 'traditional doctrine' that needs to be adjusted to take account of the realities of devolution? It was the traditional position that the UK, insofar as it has a constitution, has one that is based upon the sovereignty of Parliament, so that it might be summed up as 'what the King enacts in Parliament is Law.' It is on this basis that the United Kingdom does not have a written constitution, since whatever was written could be changed at will if Parliament sought to do so. The document suggests that parliamentary sovereignty has to give way before what it calls '*the recognition of popular sovereignty in each part of the UK.*'

What is not generally recognised is the fact that Parliamentary sovereignty has *already* given way, when the UK joined the EEC in 1973. That is why the Welsh document connects EU membership with what it calls 'the realities of devolution.' The UK's membership of the European Union meant that European Law must override national law when the two were in conflict. Hence the oft-quoted *Factortame* case where UK legislation concerning fishing rights was disapplied because it clashed with European Law.[11] The Westminster Parliament accepted that its legislation might be disapplied if there was a conflict with European Law. The question therefore becomes one of whether a conflict with laws in Wales, Scotland or Northern Ireland might lead to a similar requirement to disapply Westminster legislation, in this case based on a judgment of the UK Supreme Court.

Based on the hope that this might be so, the *Senedd* document supports a proposal of the Constitution Reform Group that a new Act of Union bill should make clear that 'the peoples of (the constituent nations and parts of the UK) have chosen... to continue to pool their sovereignty for specific purposes.'[12] The pooling of sovereignty, which was effectively rejected when the UK voted to leave the European Union, would return via the effort to maintain a British Union against a growing desire of some of its constituent parts to leave.

---

10   See p. 3 of the document 'Reforming Our Union' 2nd edition, June 2021 https://www.g ov.wales/sites/default/files/publications/2021-06/reforming-our-union-shared-gover nance-in-the-uk-june-2021-0.pdf

11   See Bogdanor, *Beyond Brexit*, pp. 72–73.

12   https://www.constitutionreformgroup.co.uk/the-herald-new-act-of-union-bill-publi shed/

Joining the EU meant that the UK was required to implement EU Law in the areas to which it applied. This gave a crucial role to the courts in determining whether EU Law had been infringed. The European Court of Justice in Luxemburg issued binding regulations and directives, but national courts also had a crucial role in determining whether directives had been correctly transposed into national legislation and were being adhered to. That role is lost if the UK is to revert after Brexit to the principle that 'what the King enacts in Parliament is law', for there will be nothing left for the courts to determine. However, if the post-Brexit devolution settlement were to follow the guidelines given by the Welsh proposals, it will require the involvement of the courts. Where they once determined whether European Law required that an Act of Parliament should be disapplied, they will now have to determine whether an act of the UK Parliament should be disapplied, for instance if it infringes upon the powers of the devolved governments.

What the *Senedd* report proposes may lead to protests that the courts are 'interfering' in the political process and putting themselves against the people. But 'interference is a loaded description. What is being argued is that there should be a sharing (or separation) of powers at the institutional level, where the courts are given a role that is not unusual in other countries such as the United States of America. Such 'interference' is perfectly acceptable in countries where the judicial review of primary legislation is a part of the constitution. Hence it was possible for the Supreme Court in the USA to determine whether aspects of the so-called 'Obamacare' health reforms were unconstitutional. But since the UK had no history of the judicial review of primary legislation outside the period when it was part of the EEC/EU, such an approach is seen as something threatening and unusual.

It should be clear that the Welsh proposals could not take effect without the involvement of a judicial body like the Supreme Court. It needs to be remembered that when the devolved bodies were first created, it was recognised that there might be disputes on whether the devolved bodies were acting within their competences. These would be referred to the Judicial Committee of the Privy Council, and then from 2009 to the new Supreme Court of the United Kingdom. Though 'bringing in the judges' is a system often presented as 'foreign' to the UK's constitutional arrangements, it is difficult to see how it can be avoided in the context of devolution.

But it is also clear that the courts would merely be acquiring once more the sort of powers which they had when the UK was a member of the EU. In the past they determined whether European Law had been properly applied in a member state, a responsibility which might require them to demand an Act of Parliament be disapplied. In a similar manner, under a Constitution of the UK, the courts should have the power to determine whether an act of the UK Parliament should be disapplied, for instance if it infringes upon the powers of the devolved governments. The judicial review of primary legislation could therefore be introduced into the UK.

Would this compromise the nature of the UK as a democracy? That depends on whether people would find it more acceptable for elected politicians to decide whether their rights were under threat than for judges to do so. Bogdanor recalls Lord Hailsham's description of the UK system, in his Dimbleby lecture of 1976, as an 'elected dictatorship'.[13] Yes, parliament was elected, but once elected it appeared to wield supreme power – and there was no other body which could threaten its supremacy – not the courts abroad, like the European Court of Justice, and not the courts at home, even the Supreme Court. Bogdanor noted how unusual it was, after the UK withdrew from the European Union and therefore also from the Charter of Fundamental Rights, for a country to move away from a system where the courts were able to judge whether human rights had been infringed to one where Parliament alone could decide. Under the present First Past the Post system a party can win an absolute majority in Parliament with as little as 35% of the vote. Why is it more democratic to say that 326 people, representing little more than a third of the votes in an election, must be treated as if all their decisions are binding and any legal ruling about what they have decided is 'interference'? If a party with extreme views wins power, there is nothing to stop it enacting whatever it likes. There will be no court with the power to disapply legislation that might be passed by that body. It is not reassuring that this was the route by which Hitler rose to power in Germany.

The emphasis in the *Senedd* report is upon the fact that the Supreme Court should have in its membership individuals identified with every part of the UK.[14] It is right to insist that the nations are all represented in the Court, but the more important point concerns what the Supreme Court will do. It should be made clear that the Court will have a crucial role in resolving disputes between the member nations and providing a legal framework within which they must work.

---

13   Bogdanor, *Beyond Brexit*, pp. 260–261.

14   See proposition 19 of the document 'Reforming Our Union', on p. 25.

Nearly a decade ago a commission under Sir William McKay reported to the Liberal Democrat-Conservative Coalition government in 2013 on the consequences of devolution for the House of Commons. Part of his report was devoted to explaining why a 'federal' system for the UK wouldn't work. One may note the Commission's comment that:

> Any federal system requires a delineation of competences, which are usually arbitrated by a supreme court that would be able to overrule the UK parliament, as well as binding the devolved institutions. This would be a radical departure from UK constitutional practice.[15]

The McKay report was right in the first sentence above. If there are to be several parliaments in England, Wales, Scotland and Northern Ireland, as well as a 'federal' Parliament in Westminster, then a judicial body which can determine whether decisions by any one of these is *ultra vires* would be unavoidable. As McKay puts it, there must be a body to determine the 'delineation of competences.' Otherwise, we return to the situation outlined earlier, where the Westminster Parliament decided arbitrarily in passing the Internal Market Act that the situation was not 'normal' enough for the agreed form of devolution to apply. But the second sentence, describing the use of a supreme court as 'a radical departure from UK constitutional practice,' is certainly open to question. It shows that the authors of the report were oblivious to the fact that membership of the EU was just such a radical departure because it involved the willingness to be bound by decisions of the European Court of Justice. It would not be a radical departure from UK constitutional practice at all if the power of the courts, surrendered when the UK left the EU, should now be reintroduced in order to provide the cornerstone of the UK Union.

The House of Lords

An obvious part of any constitutional settlement would be a reform of the House of Lords. The *Senedd* document suggests:

> A reformed Upper House of Parliament should be constituted, with a membership which takes proper account of the multi-national character of the

---

15   It can be downloaded and read from the House of Commons Library at https://researc
hbriefings.files.parliament.uk/documents/SN06821/SN06821.pdf

Union, rather than (as the House of Commons is) being based very largely on population. This Upper House should have explicit responsibility for ensuring that the constitutional position of the devolved institutions is properly taken into account in UK parliamentary legislation.[16]

There is a precedent for this. The German Basic Law confers on the *Bundesrat* (its second chamber or Upper House) distinctive responsibilities and powers in respect of Bills impacting on the constitutional position of the *Länder* (the German regions).[17]

The *Senedd* document points out that this would chime in with the particular responsibility which the House of Lords has claimed for itself in respect of UK constitutional issues. It suggests that...

> This tradition could be built upon if a reformed Upper House was given explicit responsibility for ensuring that the interests of the devolved territories and their institutions are protected and properly respected in UK parliamentary legislation.

It is noteworthy how difficult it has been to find a role for the House of Lords in recent decades, despite the fact that as an unelected body it is obviously in need of reform and remains a constant reminder of the democratic deficit at the heart of the UK political system. The problem has been that were it to receive added legitimacy it would threaten the powers of the House of Commons. For this reason, efforts to reform it have often produced an unholy alliance of right-wing and left-wing MPs determined to prevent any change. The right-wingers have a traditionalist preference for the status quo; the left-wingers fear that the lower house would find it necessary to share power with a reformed upper house.[18] The *Senedd* proposals, making the Upper House the protector of the

---

16   See proposition 7 of the document on p. 14.

17   See https://www.bundesrat.de/EN/funktionen-en/aufgaben-en/aufgaben-en-node.h tml for an account (in English) of the powers of the *Bundesrat*. Section 3, 'Decisions on Consent Bills', outlines policy areas where the *Bundesrat* has veto power over bills. These include bills affecting the budgetary revenue and administrative responsibilities of the regions. Clearly the Constitutional Court will have a key role in deciding whether a particular bill can be vetoed or not.

18   It is difficult to disagree with Gavin Esler's comment that the House of Lords, still unelected despite all the attempts to 'modernise' it, is 'symbolic of the constipation of British governance'. See *How Britain Ends*, p. 293 and the whole chapter 'Muddle England', pp. 261–307.

rights of the devolved territories, would provide a way of giving it a valid role in government without appearing to duplicate the role of the House of Commons.

The subsidiarity principle

The document speaks in favour of the principle of subsidiarity. It says that...

> The subsidiarity principle requires that legislative and governmental responsibilities should be allocated to the most local level at which they can be performed efficiently and effectively.

This is the principle of subsidiarity that was argued for so strongly by the UK while it was in the EU, insisting that certain things decided in Brussels could more efficiently be decided by the individual member states. First outlined in the Treaty of Maastricht in 1993, it was strengthened by the Treaty of Lisbon, which emphasised that member states could examine proposed EU legislation in their own national parliaments and determine whether it was something best decided upon at the national rather than European level. With the usual EU fondness for complexity there was talk of holding up a 'yellow' and even (if enough supported it) an 'orange' card to proposed legislation (though not a red one).[19] But subsidiarity, championed at the EU level by the UK, can also be made to apply at the national level when championed by Wales or Scotland or any of the other devolved bodies. This is unsurprising, since the question is one of multi-level governance, or the appropriate level for making decisions, will apply whether at the European or the national level. Is the UK willing to see the principle it supported so strongly within the European Union apply within a UK Union? Irrespective of the weight of various yellow, orange or red cards, there is the question of who acts as referee. Once again, it is clearly impossible to make the system work without bringing in the courts.

---

19   See the useful glossary to Cini, ed., *European Union Politics*, 5th edition, p. 413 (orange card) and 419 (yellow card). More instructive, perhaps, would be to reflect on the psychological implications of the Commission's determination to wrap complex measures in a veil of 'popular' language. Compare the idea of a 'six-pack' to describe measures to manage eurozone countries in debt.

Other proposals: Council of Ministers and Constitutional Convention

The Welsh proposals call for 'a decision-making UK Council of Ministers' with an independent secretariat, 'with arrangements analogous to those from which the British Irish Council benefits.' The British/Irish Council, as we have seen, was created under the Belfast Agreement to promote 'the harmonious and mutually beneficial development of the totality of relationships among the people of these islands.'[20] The Welsh proposals show that the power-sharing agreements developed in Ireland, both in the North and (potentially) on both sides of the border, can serve as the springboard for a wider settlement in the Isles as a whole..

Finally, the proposals note that 'citizens across the UK should also have an organised ability to contribute' and call for a constitutional convention. This is a proposal that has come from several quarters, for instance in an address by former Prime Minister Gordon Brown to the Fabian Society in 2016 on constitutional reform.[21] Similar calls for a citizens' convention are made within the EU, which has been holding a *Conference on the Future of Europe*.[22] They raise the question of alternatives to the familiar forms of representative democracy through citizens' assemblies and 'deliberative mini-publics'. A later chapter considers a form of direct democracy within the EU that could also apply within the UK.

Reception

As we have seen from mentioning the McKay Commission, others have a very different idea of the constitutional issues flowing from devolution to those of the Welsh *Senedd*. In November 2019, Lord Dunlop produced a 'Review into UK Government Union Capability',[23] an odd title possibly reflecting the author's uncertainty about what language he should use in order to describe a UK Union. Its 'we're the best' opening declaration that 'Our Union – the United

---

20   This is a quotation from the original 2019 version of the document. It does not seem to have made it into the second edition in 2021.

21   https://gordonandsarahbrown.com/2016/11/gordon-brown-proposes-uk-peoples-con stitutional-convention/

22   https://futureu.europa.eu/?locale=en This is the official EU website for the Conference on the Future of Europe, available in all the official languages of the EU.

23   https://assets.publishing.service.gov.uk/government/uploads/system/uploads/attac hment_data/file/972987/Lord_Dunlop_s_review_into_UK_Government_Union_Capa bility.pdf

Kingdom – is the most successful multinational state in the world' did not in-
spire confidence in its ability to recognise the severity of the issues at stake. The
Dunlop review proposed in the time-honoured manner that problems could be
solved by a committee, in this case by the formation of a UK Intergovernmental Council (UKIC, presumably to be clearly distinguished from UKIP) with
various sub-committees. There was a lot of talk of 'a forum seeking to make
co-decisions by consensus' (the internal market sub-committee) and a 'multi-
layered approach' which would 'provide devolved administrations a substantive platform to be involved in the UK government's approach to trade negotiations, while respecting that trade negotiations are ultimately a reserved matter'. Such language promised involvement without the power of veto, consultation without control and fell short of the sovereignty-sharing which is called
for in the Welsh document.

Despite the suggestions of the Welsh Labour Party, the Scottish Labour
Party appears much less willing to think in terms of sovereignty-sharing. Instead, like the Dunlop report, it talks only of greater cooperation and all sorts
of bodies which can supposedly make it work. Scottish Labour Party leader
Anas Sarwar had a similar view to the *Senedd* document where the reform of
the House of Lords was concerned but did not respond to the proposals for
a sharing of sovereignty. Instead, in July 2022, he called for a new 'legal duty
of cooperation' between governments in Westminster and Holyrood and 'joint
governance councils,' but spoke of them as providing 'fresh models of inter-
governmental working'.[24] Beneath the rhetoric, it is difficult to see this as more
than intergovernmentalism in another form, with a Council of the UK playing
a role similar to the Council of Europe. Sovereignty-sharing which was a step
too far for so many people when considering whether to join the EEC, as the
first part of this book tried to show, again threatens to be a step too far where
the reform of the UK is concerned.

The 2nd edition of the Welsh report noted a proposal for a Bill of Union
produced in April 2021 by the Constitution Reform Group.[25] Headed up by the
Marquess of Salisbury, this body describes itself as 'a group of politicians and
officials from all parties and none' which has been working on constitutional
reform for some years. The proposed Bill of Union would...

---

24   https://www.scotsman.com/news/politics/anas-sarwar-calls-for-legal-duty-to-make-
      uk-and-scottish-governments-cooperate-3754969

25   Its Act of Union Bill 2021 can be downloaded from its website at https://www.constitu
      tionreformgroup.co.uk/publications-2/

Provide a renewed constitutional form for the peoples of England, Scotland, Wales and Northern Ireland to continue to join together to form the United Kingdom.

In particular, it would...

affirm that those peoples have chosen, subject to and in accordance with the provisions of this Act, to continue to pool their sovereignty for specified purposes.

The 'pooling of sovereignty for specified purposes' is precisely what happens within the European Union, where some policy areas are national competences and others community competences. Within a British Union the distinction would apply to a different set of policy areas. For instance, matters like defence and foreign policy would be determined at the UK level, whereas in the EU these are very much national competences. Nevertheless, the system itself, based on pooling sovereignty in some areas and not others, replicates the EU system. On the other hand, given that Section 29, parts 5 and 6 of the Constitution Reform Group's proposed Act of Union Bill declare that 'the UK Parliament continues to exercise the authority of the Sovereign Parliament of the United Kingdom' and 'Nothing in this Act diminishes or otherwise affects the extent of that Sovereignty,' one suspects that radical proposals are being bolted onto a system of parliamentary sovereignty with which they are fundamentally incompatible.

Finally, it should be mentioned that some proposals for constitutional reform are emerging from the Labour Party in advance of the expected general election in 2024. At present, however, they are rather sketchy. It comes as no great surprise to learn that House of Commons Speaker Sir Lindsay Hoyle is opposed to Labour's plan to replace the House of Lords with an elected chamber, offering the familiar refrain that it would undermine the authority of the House of Commons. We have already seen that if it had a specific role as the protector of the rights of the devolved territories, this threat to duplicate the role of the Commons could be avoided. But once you introduce the concept of a 'British *Bundesrat*' in which regions and devolved nations are fully represented, you are bound to have to consider the wider issue of a separation of powers and the role of the courts in ensuring that they are adhered to.

At the time of writing, it is not clear whether the Labour Party is really prepared to embrace the implications of this. Keir Starmer's recent adoption of the Brexiteers' slogan 'Take back control' strengthens the suspicion that Labour's reforms may not amount to the radical changes that are needed.[26] It is all very well to imagine the benefit of having less decided at the centre and more decided by local councils, regional authorities, and the devolved nations. It may well be right to do this. But as this book has constantly tried to make clear the real issue, where the future of the United Kingdom is concerned, it not how to give power away but how to share it. Whether or not the Labour Party is prepared to embrace this notion remains open to doubt. The danger is that a few more powers given away will be bolted onto the same old principle of parliamentary sovereignty that lies at the root of the problem.

Conclusion

This chapter examined proposals for constitutional reform coming from Wales and looked in some detail at a document produced by the Welsh Parliament in 2019. As Keating points out, referring to the repatriation of powers after the UK's withdrawal from the EU:

> The Welsh government saw an opportunity to transfer ideas from how the EU works into the UK context, consistent with its vision of union and cooperative federalism.[27]

The report by the Welsh Parliament reminds us that it is not a question of devolving more things but of a different understanding of what devolution really is. The heart of the Welsh proposals lies in their view of how the nations of the UK could *jointly* make decisions rather than simply receive a new division of the spoils of government in terms of who does what – the system that Keating in the quotation above calls 'cooperative federalism.' If we consider the points made in the previous chapter about the history of Wales, we can see how this would make sense. Decisions – even ones that have had favourable results for the country – have for long been made *for* Wales, not *with* Wales. It is in these terms that it was admitted to the industrial revolution which (to borrow the phraseology of the extreme right) meant that it was swamped by English

---

26   At the moment it is difficult to say. See 'Britain's 'Take Back Control' déjà vu', an article published by *Politico* in January 2023. https://www.politico.eu/article/britain-take-bac k-control-deja-vu-brexit-keir-starmer-labour/

27   Keating, *State and Nation*, p. 101.

immigrants with severe consequences for its national identity (think of the effects on the Welsh language). Joint decision-making, on the other hand, means the sharing of sovereignty – precisely the heart of the European Union's institutional system. It might be said that it means trying to maintain the British Union by adopting a 'federal' system, but the concept of 'federalism' has to be treated with care. Indeed, most proposals for a more federal UK find it unnecessary to question the principle of parliamentary sovereignty.[28]

The Welsh report shows that several parliaments can work together only if a legal authority like the Supreme Court is able to make binding judgments concerning whose responsibility a piece of legislation is, demanding if necessary that legislation by one of the parliaments, including the Westminster parliament, be disapplied. Though bringing in the judges is a system often presented as foreign to the UK's constitutional arrangements, it is difficult to see how it can be avoided in the context of devolution.

The *Senedd* proposals go on to suggest that the House of Lords should be given responsibility for ensuring that the constitutional position of the devolved institutions is properly considered in UK parliamentary legislation. Proponents say that this is a good way of giving the upper house a meaningful role – and the democratic legitimacy of elections – without duplicating the role of the lower house and this part of the document has received wide support, not least in proposals from the Labour Party suggested at the end of 2022 for reform of the Upper House.[29]

The proposals also emphasise the principle of subsidiarity, earnestly championed at the EU level by the UK since its introduction by the Treaty of Maastricht. The question is essentially one of multi-level governance. Finding the appropriate level for making decisions is bound to be an issue, whether you are looking at the European Union or the UK Union. But this only reinforces the point that a legal authority is needed to determine the appropriate level at which decisions should be made.

---

28   See Schütze and Tierney (eds.) *The United Kingdom and the Federal Idea*; Torrance, *Britain Rebooted: Scotland in a Federal UK.*

29   See the document 'A New Britain: Renewing our Democracy and Rebuilding our Economy. Report of the Commission on the UK's Future' published by the Labour Party at the end of 2022. See especially pp. 135–143 for Labour's proposals – which may or may not still be there at the time of the next general election – for reform of the House of Lords. See https://labour.org.uk/wp-content/uploads/2022/12/Commission-on-the-UKs-Future.pdf

The Welsh proposals call for 'a decision-making UK Council of Ministers' with an independent secretariat. They talk of 'arrangements analogous to those from which the British/Irish Council benefits.' This raises the possibility even of arriving at a constitution for the Isles. This will be considered in more detail later. It is important to make clear that such a proposal would in no way undermine the integrity of the Irish Republic as a separate nation-state. But that is just the point – the EU could have a constitution without ceasing to be made up of 27 nation-states, and the Isles could have a constitution without ceasing to be two nation-states and four or five nations.

The *Senedd* document notes that 'citizens across the UK should also have an organised ability to contribute' and calls for a constitutional convention. This raises questions about various forms of direct democracy and what form citizens' participation could take in the future. A later chapter looks at this in more detail.

The reception of the *Senedd* document has been mixed. In November 2019, Lord Dunlop produced a report that felt no radical fix was required for the world's 'most successful' multinational state. The Constitution Reform Group, on the other hand, supported 'the pooling of sovereignty for specified purposes.' Yet the Labour Party's proposals at the end of 2022 show that the document's ideas are beginning to enter the political mainstream as the clear policy of a party or parties that might win power in the UK in what will probably be a 2024 election. Nevertheless, elements of the Labour proposals remain vague and where devolution is concerned the emphasis is often upon more cooperation without much consideration of the legal and political framework that might make such cooperation effective.

What is clear is that the *Senedd* proposals have proved controversial partly because they require an alternative structure to one which insists that the sovereignty of the Westminster Parliament is the only foundation for any future constitutional arrangements. It is this insistence upon parliamentary sovereignty that is so hard to dislodge – and yet it must be dislodged if a constitution of the UK or even of the Isles is to have any credence. A later chapter will examine why it is seen as such a crucial part of the UK constitution – insofar as the UK has a constitution at all. But first it would be useful to move across the Severn for a moment in order to consider the rather different perspective from England.

Chapter Thirteen: The Future of the UK and the Problem of Little England

The implicit assumption behind the discussion in recent chapters is that a way needs to be found of providing a constitution that will hold together the United Kingdom. During the discussion it has been suggested that there needs to be a form of devolution whose focus is upon joint decision-making by the four nations, rather than upon which extra powers can be 'given away' to the devolved members. It was also pointed out that this would entail a radical rethinking of the idea that the sovereignty of the Westminster Parliament was the unshakeable foundation of any arrangements that could make devolution work. But it has to be recognised that there is an implicit assumption behind this approach, namely that there is an overwhelming desire to make devolution work, not only in the devolved nations but in England itself. It is not clear that this is so. As pointed out already, whilst about half the Scots want independence, about half the English want it too. The 'Very well, alone!' mentality, once turned upon Europe, can also be turned upon the other members of the United Kingdom outside England. The present chapter therefore considers the problem of what it calls 'Little England.'

The term has a long pedigree. When the UK made its second application to join the European Economic Community in 1966, the Labour Prime Minister, Harold Wilson, declared at the Lord Mayor's banquet in London that 'there is no future for Britain in a Little England philosophy.'[1] One of the dangers of Brexit is that it will encourage 'Little Englanders' not only to disentangle their country from Europe but to disentangle themselves from the rest of the UK. There are some who would welcome this as a sign of England finally discarding its inner empire in the way it has (almost) discarded its outer empire, enabling it

---

1   Preston, Christopher *The Enlargement and Integration of the European Union: Issues and Strategies*, p. 29.

at last to be at ease with itself (as Professor Edgerton put it in a podcast entitled 'Brexit, Ideology and the Decline of the British State' posted in April 2021).[2] But another possibility is that having broken away from its internal union as well as its association with the EU, it will become more introverted and possibly more intolerant. At the very least it will discover that what it has tried to achieve by removing apparently extraneous elements is a chimera. If real homogeneity is what it's looking for, it can't be found anywhere. It is precisely this that so enrages the nationalist, convinced that discarding another layer will enable the true nation to emerge, that prising open the oyster will reveal the pearl, when in fact all that happens is that another part of the onion is stripped away, and nothing ever emerges except a further layer to tear off.

Seeking 'national purity'

The last century has seen a considerable re-drawing of the boundaries of Europe, but it would be wrong to consider the process as akin to tidying up a house, an operation in which things that do not 'really belong' in one room are removed and other things that have been put elsewhere regain their rightful place. The present discussion of the European and British unions takes place within a Europe which has continued to see an increase in the number of nation-states within the continent. The three Baltic states of Estonia, Latvia and Lithuania became independent nation-states (as they once were before between the first and second world wars) in the 1990s and in 2004 joined the European Union. The end of the Soviet Union has meant a number of nation-states emerging in Eastern Europe, whose dependence on Russia is clear but who have a theoretical independence, namely Belarus, Moldova and Ukraine; and of course the recent Russian invasion of Ukraine shows how difficult it is to realize its entitlement to independence. One might also include some of the new states in the Caucasus region, such as Georgia and Armenia, within this list, depending on where Europe is deemed to begin and end (both countries, alongside Azerbaijan, are members of the Council of Europe, as is the Russian Federation itself).

Sometimes separation has been relatively successful and has happened without bloodshed. The 'velvet revolution' which ended communism in

---

2   You can hear the podcast at https://euromovescotland.org.uk/podcast/brexit-ideolog y-and-the-decline-of-the-british-state/

Czechoslovakia in 1989 was followed by a 'velvet divorce' between the Czech Republic and Slovakia in 1993. The two countries then applied separately to become members of the European Union. Other break-ups were less successful. The former Yugoslavia saw five wars in the 1990s, resulting in thousands of deaths and tens of thousands of refugees. The Western Balkans is now host to several states, two of which, Croatia (since 2013) and Slovenia (since 2004), have become part of the EU and four of which, North Macedonia, Montenegro, Serbia and Albania, are candidate countries to join it. About other parts of the Western Balkans – Kosovo and Bosnia – there are differing opinions on whether they can be considered states at all.[3]

Part of the problem is that linked to the idea of smaller communities as a form of progress is the idea that it is ethnicity or language that defines the nation-state, a principle which has encouraged expulsions and even exterminations as nation-states seek to 'purify' themselves of extraneous elements. The problem (quite apart from the sheer barbarism of such a procedure) was that such 'purity' was as impossible to achieve inside most of the smaller nation-states into which Europe appeared to be resolving itself in the twentieth century as it had been within their larger forbears. The small states were not in fact more 'ethnically' or 'linguistically' pure than the larger states or empires that they had emerged from.[4] More rooms might have been created in the house, but this didn't mean that objects had at last found their 'rightful place'. It was also a view of nationality that made life very difficult for groups that were not linked to any particular nation, like the Roma and the Jews. Instead of enriching the state they lived in, they were seen as foreign elements infecting it. Moreover, the very impossibility of achieving ethnic or linguistic purity encouraged the view that some 'foreign' element was perpetually sabotaging the state and preventing it from achieving its 'natural' condition.

---

3   22 of the 27 EU countries currently recognise Kosovo as an independent state.

4   One of the most disturbing books on the power of small differences to generate mass slaughter is Niall Ferguson's *The War of the World*. Ferguson takes H.G. Wells' classic science-fiction novel of a century ago, *The War of the Worlds*, and suggests that the destructive force Wells imagined coming from outside the world came in reality from within it in the most brutal and violent century we have yet lived through.

Black and Asian English?

We can find evidence of this outlook in more recent times. The preceding section suggested that if you insist on ethnic or religious or linguistic sameness as the essential force holding your nation together, then you are likely to see those whose ethnicity or religious and cultural values are different as something less than true citizens of your nation. Perhaps for that reason a multinational state might be thought to represent a more comfortable home for people from BAME (Black and Minority Ethnic) communities than one which threatens to associate a particular ethnicity with citizenship.

In March 2021, the Labour MP for Tottenham and later Shadow Foreign Secretary, David Lammy, criticised the wording of the English census, observing that there was no option to be Black and English. He noted that the Welsh Census allowed respondents to identify as Black Welsh or Asian Welsh as well as Black British. But Black English or Asian English didn't seem to be an option.

From the perspective of the Office for National Statistics (ONS), most of England's black and minority ethnic population identify as more British than English. On the other hand, a significant minority, like Lammy, identify as English. As Professor John Denham, former MP for Southampton Itchen and later Director of the *Centre for English Identity and Politics* at the University of Southampton pointed out,

> When the state Census denies ethnic minorities the right to declare their identity as English, it simply reinforces the message that 'this identity is not for you'.[5]

A spokesperson for the ONS (Office of National Statistics) explained to *The Times* (August 3rd, 2021) that it had 'reviewed the wording of the high-level categories in the ethnicity question and, after testing different options in England and Wales, we recommended a change in the Welsh questionnaire to include Black Welsh and Asian Welsh, alongside Black British and Asian British.[6] The evidence did not support a change to include Black English in England.' What is not clear is what 'the evidence' amounted to. But we can perhaps guess.

---

5   The comments by Denham can be found at https://www.southampton.ac.uk/ceip/pu blications/ethnic-identity-in-the-census.page

6   See David Sanderson's article in *The Times*, https://www.thetimes.co.uk/article/why-is nt-black-english-a-census-option-asks-david-lammy-qxn00zcg9

In March 2021, Lammy debated the topic with a caller on his LBC radio show who insisted he couldn't be English.[7] She told him: 'You will never be English, you are African-Caribbean.' 'I'm of African descent, African-Caribbean descent, but I am English,' he replied at the time. The caller then went on to insist that it was 'fine' for Lammy to say he was British, but that he was 'not English'.

The conversation might have simply been another illustration of racial prejudice, and yet the willingness of the caller to accept that Lammy was British but not that he was English is striking. It suggests that whereas for some people Britishness is seen as something that can embrace people of any background, Englishness is something else. It is no wonder that many people from minority ethnic backgrounds will tell the census that they prefer to be British rather than English.

In his radio discussion Lammy pointed out:

> Here I am, having grown up in this country, have been born of this country, and actually the truth is it's a myth there's one English ethnicity – there's not... England has always been a country in which Huguenots, Danes, all sorts of people have passed through.

Lammy is quite right to point out the diversity of background and ethnicity implicit in being English. One can understand his hostility to the suggestion, implicitly made by those who were formulating the census, that you somehow have to be white in order to be English. The result is that many Black and Asian people associate being 'English' with the sort of Little Englander mentality displayed by the woman referred to in the phone-in. They therefore prefer to call themselves Black British or Asian British despite the fact that even as a percentage of the population of each nation there are far more BAME people in England than in Scotland and Wales. They see a mark of exclusivity in the term 'English' that does not apply to 'British' or even to 'Scottish', 'Welsh' or 'Irish,' and this is why they prefer to talk about 'Black and Asian British'.

Compare an observation made by Jeremy Paxman in a book published in 1998. Though the book came out a generation ago, it is interesting that Paxman wrote as follows about an earlier black MP for Tottenham, Bernie Grant:

---

7   See Lucy Campbell's report for *The Guardian on 29th March 2021*, which includes a recording of the actual interview. https://www.theguardian.com/world/2021/mar/29/david-lammy-praised-for-response-to-lbc-caller-who-said-he-was-not-english

...it is still noticeable that while you will often meet a person who describes themselves as 'Black British' or 'Bengali British', you rarely come across someone who says they are 'Black English'. Bernie Grant calls himself British, because 'it includes other oppressed peoples, like the Welsh or the Scots. It would stick in my throat to call myself English.'[8]

Whilst it would be welcome to suppose that over a generation 'English' has become a more inclusive and therefore acceptable term, reflecting a greater inclusiveness in English society, it is not clear how far this is so – and if it is so, it may be much more evident in the London represented by these two MPs than in the rest of England. Polls suggest that those with the greatest consciousness of being English as opposed to British were far more enthusiastic about Brexit than those who thought of themselves as British rather than English.[9] It would imply that people with a strong sense of being English find it much more difficult to think of belonging to a wider community, something that the smaller nations – as we have seen in the case of Wales – have had thrust upon them through their association with England within the UK. If the Scots could accept a Union with the English without ceasing to be Scottish, they were unlikely to fear the consequence of becoming part of the European Union. The caller speaking to David Lammy in March 2021 represented a perspective from which Britain can be stormed by 'outsiders' but the inner sanctum, England, cannot be. For her, with what one guesses to be a rather nostalgic view of England's 'green and pleasant land', the English core must remain unsullied. Even though on any definition of ethnic or racial diversity England is more diverse than the other nations within the UK, the perspective of the caller remains a powerful one. She is still convinced that somewhere inside the shell there's a pearl of Englishness waiting to be discovered, cherished and protected.[10]

---

8   Paxman, Jeremy *The English*, p. 74.

9   John Denham's blog for the LSE (London School of Economics) has some useful analysis. He suggests that 'those most open to non-English identities, including European, were most likely to vote Remain.' Note that the blog was written in 2019, after the referendum but before Brexit had finally taken place. See https://blogs.lse.a c.uk/brexit/2019/02/14/is-it-the-english-question-or-the-british-question-the-three-strands-of-britishness/

10   See the insights of Curtice and Montagu in their 2018 study. http://natcen.ac.uk/our-r esearch/research/do-scotland-and-england-wales-have-different-views-about-immi gration/ For analysis, see Kenny, *The Politics of English Nationhood*.

Sitting on the rock

In his *Nations and Nationalism since 1780*, the economic historian Eric Hobsbawm pointed out that in the nineteenth century there were many who believed in a 'threshold principle,' according to which a nation-state had to be of a certain size.[11] For this reason, Mazzini, despite championing Italy as an independent state, did not think that Ireland would achieve statehood. The presumption was that human progress naturally meant expanding into larger units, as families became clans, clans became tribes and tribes became nations. To split larger communities into smaller ones was to go against the tide of progress. There was a clear connection between acquiring broad-mindedness and belonging to a larger community. Hobsbawm quotes a section of Mill's *Utilitarianism*, published in 1861:

> Nobody can suppose that it is not more beneficial for a Breton or a Basque of French Navarre to be... a member of the French nationality, admitted on equal terms to all the privileges of French citizenship... than to sulk on his own rocks, the half-savage relic of past times, revolving in his own little mental orbit, without participation or interest in the general movement of the world. The same remark applies to the Welshman or the Scottish Highlander as members of the British nation.[12]

One imagines that talk of a Scotsman or a Welshwoman 'sulking on a rock' might not go down too well today. Such comments were made at a time when a 'small state mentality' was seen in negative terms. Terms such as 'balkanisation' (as applied to the crumbling Ottoman empire) were used to highlight not an achievement of independence but a retreat into narrow-minded isolation, resisting the march of progress.[13] Yet whatever the limitations of such an approach, I would argue that it recognises something important about the dangers of trying to create nation-states on the basis of an imagined cultural, religious and/or ethnic identity which certainly doesn't exist within the dozens of nation-states making up the European continent.

---

11   Hobsbawm, *Nations and Nationalism since 1780*, p. 31.

12   Mill's *Utilitarianism, Liberty and Representative Government* quoted in Hobsbawm, *Nations and Nationalism since 1780*, p. 34.

13   See Hobsbawm, *Nations and Nationalism since 1780*, p. 31. On the same page he also notes the use of the German word *Kleinstaaterei*, the system of mini-states, as derogatory.

Thirty years on from Hobsbawm's claim that the 'Wilsonian system' (President Woodrow Wilson's attempts after the First World War to make state frontiers coincide with frontiers of language and nationality) 'demonstrated to no great surprise that the nationalism of small nations was just as impatient of minorities as what Lenin called great-nation chauvinism,[14] there is still no reason to dispute his claim. Indeed, it is noteworthy that Professor Vernon Bogdanor, despite a very pungent critique of the structures of the European Union in his recent works, was a self-confessed 'Remainer' in the 2016 referendum precisely because he saw the EU as essentially being a peace project. He believed that conflicts such as those which broke out in the former Yugoslavia in the 1990s could be mitigated if the different groups had what he called 'a roof over their heads', something he compared to the Austro-Hungarian Empire a century earlier.[15]

Can the United Kingdom also be a roof over the heads of different parties in the Isles? Optimists suggest that if England leaves the British Union there will no longer be resentment against its other members. No more complaints about their 'exploiting' the Barnett formula to receive 'subsidies' (though Joel Barnett himself denied that the system which bore his name was a needs-based formula, something that he would have personally preferred), just as there are no longer complaints about the UK 'subsidising' Brussels with its contribution to the EU budget.[16] But one could also take a more pessimistic view, suggesting that those who acquire the habit of resentment never cease to find something or someone to be resentful about. 'I find it instructive,' writes Gavin Esler, 'that the former Yugoslavia could survive Croat, Bosnian, Slovene or Kosovar nationalism, but it could not survive the nationalism of the biggest player, Slobodan Milošević's Serbia. Perhaps a lopsided union becomes especially vulnerable when nationalist passions grow strongly in the most powerful component.'[17] It doesn't sound so different from the typically strident language of Tom Nairn in 1977 when he talked about how England had become 'culturally and politically isolated, imprisoned within her dying imperialism' and therefore 'vulnerable to Enoch Powell's nationalist demagoguery... a mushrooming carica-

---

14   Hobsbawm, *Nations and Nationalism since 1780*, p. 31.

15   See his recent *Britain and Europe in a Troubled World*.

16   Bogdanor gives a good account of the formula in *Beyond Brexit*, pp. 224–228. As he notes, English complaints about England supposedly not receiving its fair share tend to come from poorer regions of the North and Midlands.

17   Esler, Gavin. *How Britain Ends*, p. 64.

ture of patriotic destiny."[18] Nearly half a century on, one might consider this exaggerated, but both these somewhat pessimistic analyses need to be taken seriously in their concern about how a dangerous English nationalism could emerge. At least we might note the measured tone of Professor Keating's remarks:

> The threat to unions has, indeed, often come not from complaints from the smaller components but from a growing reluctance of the larger one so to subsume its identity into the whole to accommodate the smaller ones.[19]

The principle of self-determination associated with Woodrow Wilson's approach to the post-war settlement at the time of the Versailles treaty in 1919 was not a case of allowing people who shared the same values, beliefs and language to be together at last in the way they wanted, as if families were at last being re-united after a long separation. To some extent it was a question of establishing buffer states to keep the new Soviet Union with its Bolshevik government at bay. Nationalist feeling could be a means of insulating countries against communism.[20] But ignoring the geopolitical considerations, it wasn't and isn't possible to 'sort out' Europe's differences by simply redrawing a few lines.

It might be tempting to conclude from a consideration of the break-up of the Ottoman and Austro-Hungarian empires, not to mention the collapse of the Soviet Union, that the end of the British Union would simply represent a further illustration of a trend which is visible elsewhere in Europe. Such a position is further encouraged by the 'thin end of the wedge' view of devolution which concludes that it is bound to lead eventually to independence. But whatever the fissiparous tendencies of former empires, there has been no consistent pattern of states breaking up. Sometimes, indeed, movement has gone the other way. There have been strong movements for separatism that have even-

---

18   Nairn, Tom *The Break-up of Britain*, p. 277.

19   Keating, *State and Nation in the United Kingdom*, p. 19.

20   See Hobsbawm, *Nations and Nationalism since 1780*, pp. 132–134. Hobsbawm points out (p. 134) that 'the nationalism of small nations was just as impatient of minorities as what Lenin called "great-nation chauvinism."' See Hobsbawm's *Age of Extremes*, pp. 31–34 for an account of the motives behind the Treaty of Versailles. He suggests that the best way of dealing with Bolshevism's triumph in 1917 was seen as being the creation of what he calls a '*cordon sanitaire*' of anti-communist states around it (see *Age of Extremes* p. 32).

tually been resolved by former separatists consenting to be part of a greater whole that affords them a high degree of autonomy. Hobsbawm comments:

> Even in regions where the classic aspiration for separate nation-states might be expected to be strong, effective devolution or regionalisation has pre-empted it, or even reversed it. State separatism in the Americas, at any rate south of Canada, has declined since the American Civil War. And it is significant that the states defeated in World War II, on which a high degree of devolution was imposed – presumably in reaction against fascist centralisation – lack most of the separatist movements of the rest of western Europe, though on paper Bavaria and Sicily are at least as obvious breeding-grounds for such movements as Scotland and the francophone parts of the Bernese Jura.[21]

Hobsbawm believes that the high measure of autonomy given to the fifty states in the USA, or to the Länder in Germany whose autonomy is protected by its powerful second chamber the *Bundesrat*, or the regional autonomy legislation passed in Italy in 1946, has helped to offset the sort of separatist pressure which is likely to be seen in more centralised states like (despite devolution) the UK and France. In other words, he believes that devolution can work and is not destined to lead to nations or regions, having once tasted a measure of autonomy, wanting more and more until eventually they achieve full independence.

The Churn and the Cathedral

As the comments of the lady in the phone-in with David Lammy make clear, it is easy to have a distorted vision of how the nations we live in came into being. We can recall Lammy's comment that 'England has always been a country in which Huguenots, Danes, all sorts of people have passed through.' We can also bear in mind Norman Davies' comment about the Isles, namely that we all like to believe that we 'possessed' our lands since time immemorial. In reality, he goes on, 'wherever one looks on the map of Europe, except perhaps Iceland, one sees layer upon layer of settlement, statehood and occupation.'[22] Rather in the way that a cathedral turns out to have been constructed and reconstructed

---

21   Hobsbawm, Eric, *Nations and Nationalism since 1780*, p. 187.
22   Davies, *The Isles*, p. 35.

over centuries, through adaptations reflecting new styles or theological developments, and in some cases rebuilt entirely because of fire or destruction in war, so countries (and continents) that like to parade their continuity with a distant past turn out to be amalgams born of migrations, invasions and conquests.

In his classic text *Imagined Communities*, Benedict Anderson calls a nation an 'imagined political community'. It is a community because it is thought of in terms of 'a deep, horizontal comradeship,'[23] whatever divisions and inequalities may lie within it. It is 'imagined,' a word loaded with the idea of falsity, as in 'you're just imagining things,' but intended to mean that people will only ever encounter a small percentage of their fellow nationals and can only presume a common bond with them. Many motives might encourage people to seek such a bond. It may be the idea that their nation lives on after they die (it sometimes doesn't, as Davies' *Vanished Kingdoms* makes clear). They may be drawn by common religious commitment, a common dynastic heritage or a common language. They may sense that nations, like individuals and families, develop through linear time, their public spaces filling with clocks and calendars, with newspapers bought and sold for particular days and then immediately obsolescent as 'yesterday's news'. And they will develop a bond through myths and rituals, preferably ones that go right back to their misty origins.

'Imagined' might, as Anderson carefully points out, be something closer to 'consider oneself as', a phrase he takes from Seton-Watson's *Nations and States*, than 'invented'.[24] At the same time, there surely *is* a degree of invention in the way recently formed traditions are presented as ancient. As with the cathedral whose grandeur makes one all too easily think of a particular architect and a particular time of construction, there is a tendency to think of a nation arriving at a particular point with its columns and buttresses, in the form of its language, values and culture, already in position. But the Gothic pile that towers above the landscape may turn out to be a 'neo-Gothic' construction that emerged in Victorian times. The nation's ancient traditions may turn out to be much more recent than they are commonly believed to be. Indeed, the same can be said of communities and institutions within the nation. Hobsbawm's

---

23   Anderson, *Imagined Communities*, p. 7.

24   See Anderson, *Imagined Communities*, p. 6. He quotes Seton-Watson remarking in *Nations and States*, p. 5 that 'All that I can find to say is that a nation exists when a significant number of people in a community considers themselves to form a community or behave as if they formed one.'

remarkable autobiography *Interesting Times* describes his years as a student at Cambridge University and refers in the following terms to the experience that, he explains, later inspired *The Invention of Tradition*:

> Everything was designed to make us into pillars of a tradition reaching back to the 13th century, though some of the most apparently ancient expressions of it, such as the Festival of Lessons and Carols on Christmas Eve in King's College Chapel, had in fact been invented only a few years before I arrived in the college. Undergraduates wore their short black gowns to go to lectures and supervisions, into the obligatory collective dinner in college halls and (with caps) whenever out in the streets after dark, policed by more amply gowned and capped Proctors, assisted by their 'bulldogs.' Dons entered lecture rooms with their long gowns billowing and the squares planted with precision on their heads.... The Cambridge past, like the ceremonial fancy-dress past of British public life, was not, of course, a chronological succession of time, but a synchronic jumble of its surviving relics.[25]

Just as one likes to think of the cathedral springing up fully formed as an expression of one person's grand idea, so the beginnings of nations often have 'founders' whose activities are surrounded by myths and legends. In reality, a hotchpotch of traditions and customs will have emerged over time, some of them pointing back to a distant past that never existed. The chinks in their complicated development will be ironed out and they may even be treated as if nations somehow emerged without any outside influences at all. England, as Lammy pointed out, has been built up through waves of immigration. He mentions the Huguenots, Protestants fleeing waves of persecution in France in the sixteenth and seventeenth centuries, in many cases ending up in England. He also mentions the Danes, perhaps going back to the Viking invasions of the ninth and tenth centuries. This was not an instance of one fully formed nation invading another, but was part of a constant churn as various groups formed and re-formed, pushing each other aside or amalgamating in the process. He uses the term 'passing through', which some obviously did, while others stayed. But his main point is to stress the churn, the complexity of movement in and out even after borders become relatively secure, as waves of migration continued across the continent and the Isles.

Yet recognising the haphazard and even artificial manner in which nations have emerged does not take away the common bond engendered by patriotic

---

25   Hobsbawm, *Interesting Times*, p. 103.

feeling. Change is not the enemy of identity. In the case of cathedrals, there is nothing in the discovery that they have been damaged or razed to the ground, then to be patched up or even rebuilt by new architects, which alters the sense of encountering a single building. Even a change in the nature of the religion in whose name they were built (one thinks of the effects of the Reformation upon England's cathedrals and the way some of them lost their statues and their saints) need not mean that they lose their identity.

The same can easily be said of nations. In this instance too, it is easy to forget the way in which they have been 'damaged' and 'rebuilt' over time. Some of their traditions seek to create a fictitious past in order to strengthen an identity which tries to base itself upon rituals and customs going back centuries. *The Invention of Tradition* (originally written some forty years ago but reprinted as recently as 2012) contains essays on the highland tradition in Scotland, the 'hunt for the Welsh past in the Romantic period' and 'the British monarchy and the invention of tradition', in each case showing that what is presented as a tradition going back centuries is in fact something much more recent. The kilt is an eighteenth-century invention (by an Englishman), Welsh national costume is a nineteenth-century invention to boost tourist revenues from eisteddfods and the trappings of the British monarchy emerged only when monarchs had lost enough power to make their glorification through ceremonial acceptable, again in the nineteenth century.[26]

The Invention of Tradition applies the process of invention to Scotland and Wales as much as to England, as well as to the monarchy which tries to unite all three. But none of this needs to undermine their distinctive identity or the attachment their citizens feel. The 'horizontal comradeship' spoken of by Anderson is still able to develop across the nation.

The question is how far the haphazard and even artificial manner in which nations have emerged affects the question of whether the 'four nations' of the UK can reasonably continue to be part of a single nation-state. No definitive answer can be given, but the very complexity of the amalgam surely confirms the view made earlier that for the English to peel off the Scots and Welsh and

---

26   See Hugh Trevor-Roper's chapter 'The Invention of Tradition: The Highland Tradition of Scotland' for the kilt, Prys Morgan's 'From a Death to a View: The hunt for a Welsh Past in the Romantic Period' for Welsh costume and the eisteddfod, and David Cannadine's chapter 'The Context, Performance and Meaning of Ritual: The British Monarchy and the "Invention of Tradition," c1820-1977' for the monarchy. They are all chapters of *The Invention of Tradition*, edited by Hobsbawm and Ranger.

arrive at some kind of pure kernel that can be regarded as the 'true nation' is a chimera.

For this reason, we might be a little less confident than people like Professor Edgerton are about a future England at last being 'comfortable in itself', as if it had just successfully come through an operation on conjoined twins (or triplets). It might well simply find that the prejudices and resentments have been transposed to a new level – and possibly even intensified. Like David Lammy's interlocutor, it may be that some people 'expect' that once they can be nothing but English they will be able to slough off the sort of multicultural associations that seem to give them trouble and at last reach the sort of inner purity they aspire to. When she says that the MP can be British but not English, it is as if she is willing to let the invader break down the outer wall but never the inner – forgetting that the inner core is just as 'corrupted' – in her terms – as the outer.

A comment on immigration

Professor Vernon Bogdanor, in a lecture delivered to the Glasgow Philosophical Society online during COVID-19,[27] was unable to understand why the Scots might find the constraints of being inside the EU less overpowering than those of being part of the UK. He made some perfectly fair points. Inside the British Union, he pointed out, the Scots have 10% of the seats in Parliament; inside the European Parliament they would have far fewer. They would have to allow their economy to be regulated by the rules of the single market. As a country joining after the Treaty of Maastricht, they would be unable to retain their own currency. They would have to accept the free movement of people, one of the four unavoidable principles of the single market and one which effectively meant that they would be unable to control their own immigration policy. If the Scots really wanted independence, he continued, surely it made more sense for them to become an independent nation-state outside the Union like Switzerland or Norway (although he failed to make clear that these countries too were bound by many of the rules of the single market, including the free movement of people).

---

27   'The EU without Britain: Never Closer Union?' – a lecture and discussion given to the Royal Philosophical Society of Glasgow. See https://www.youtube.com/watch?v=LO5o IYIEzBw

What Bogdanor misses is the extent to which the other nations inside the British Union feel a pressure from England that England does not feel from them. Immigration from elsewhere in the European Union was undoubtedly a factor in the UK vote to leave the European Union. But Scotland and (in particular) Wales have a very good reason for not being too disturbed by immigration. As an earlier chapter tried to illustrate, Wales has had to endure waves of immigration from the English and has had to maintain its identity despite being part of a union which the English have effectively controlled.

Nothing that immigration from the EU could throw at the UK in the twenty-first century could possibly approach the effect of the 'Ulster plantations' upon one of Ireland's provinces. Nothing in the 'wave' of young Polish workers in search of jobs in the UK after their country joined the EU in 2004 could match the effect of thousands of English workers moving to the coalfields of South Wales in the first decade of the twentieth century. It is quite natural that someone from Scotland, Wales or Northern Ireland could welcome EU membership as a way of lessening their dependence upon England. In an analogy which is questionable on many fronts, Professor Bogdanor suggested that a divorce between England and Scotland would make little sense if one of the divorcees (presumably the man) then went off with 27 mistresses. But from the perspective of the non-English nations inside the UK, it is more a case of seeking some sort of social life outside a marriage which has become intolerably oppressive. Indeed, what seems to be lacking in Bogdanor's approach (and is particularly evident in his address to the Glasgow Philosophical Society in 2021) is his lack of awareness of how European people in Scotland feel, something that has been observed by a number of writers and which obviously has roots in the history of a nation reaching out for alliances 'auld' and new against England.[28]

Conclusion

For the English, following Simms' description, the association with Scotland, Wales and Ireland was more a case of running to close the back door while

---

28 Bogdanor's address (and some discussion of it) can be found on https://www.youtube .com/watch?v=LO5olYlEzBw. For observations on a strong sense of European identity among Scots (not necessarily, it should be stressed, favouring independence) see McCrone, 'What Makes a European in Scotland?'

facing dangerous threats at the front of the house. They weren't enriching themselves by association; they were grabbing additional baggage from 'outside' with which to fortify their own house against their enemies. This makes it easier for them to slide into a view that new 'enemies' in the form of waves of immigration are threatening to storm the fortress in their turn.

No one denies that there are distinctive characteristics of England as of the other nations of the UK or the other states of Europe. But this 'imagined' community with many of its 'invented' traditions is being constantly re-fashioned from outside. To suppose that someone like David Lammy is not part of the remaking of England but someone interfering with it from beyond is not just a racist attitude but one with no sense of how England has always been made and re-made through the centuries.

The other nations inside the UK have more of a sense of being made from outside because of the influence of England on their making. But the narrative myth of England's survival, with its emphasis upon the island fortress seeing off waves of invaders, lays all the emphasis upon being *threatened* from beyond and thereby loses the sense that it has been *made* from beyond as well. It may be that the 'Little England' mentality can be cast aside by a nation once again 'comfortable with itself' as Professor Edgerton suggests, but this chapter has tried to show that it might produce a combination of introversion and resentment as the promised return to its 'pure core' proves illusory.

Chapter Fourteen: The strange romance of the sovereignty of parliament

An earlier chapter discussed the *Senedd* proposals for constitutional reform and noted that while some of them seem to have been widely accepted – such as reform of the House of Lords – others have not. In particular, there is resistance on all sides of the political spectrum to any form of governance that does not preserve the sovereignty of the Westminster Parliament as the only foundation for any future constitutional arrangements. It is this insistence upon parliamentary sovereignty that is so hard to dislodge – and yet it must be dislodged if a constitution of the UK or even of the Isles is to have any credence. The Welsh proposals, we remember, declared that...

> Parliamentary sovereignty as traditionally understood no longer provides a sound foundation for this evolving constitution.

Why is that so hard to accept? For in one sense, it should be perfectly acceptable to argue that the principle of parliamentary sovereignty as traditionally understood is inappropriate for a new constitution of the UK or the Isles. This would not only be because it was undermined by the UK's membership of the European Union, and the willingness to submit to binding European Law. It would also be because the sovereignty of Parliament was undermined by the very referendum which produced a decision by the UK to leave the EU.

The referendum vote showed that a majority of voters wished to leave the EU, while a majority of MPs wished to remain in it. This was doubly important because the earlier referendum in 1975, where people were asked whether they wished to stay inside the European Economic Community, forerunner of the EU, showed an alignment between the will of the people expressed in the referendum (in that case a 2:1 majority in favour of staying) and the opinion of a majority of MPs. Similarly, the referendum in 2010 on whether to introduce the Alternative Vote (AV) as a replacement for First Past the Post, which was rejected by the electorate, was also rejected by a majority of MPs, since AV was opposed by the Conservatives, the Democratic Unionist Party and some Labour MPs. The European Union Act of 2011 interestingly declared that any changes in EU treaties extending the competences of the EU should not be approved unless supported by both Parliament and a referendum of the people, perhaps assuming that these two would in practice coincide as they had in the past.[1] The problem with the 2016 referendum was not – or not only – the narrowness of the vote in favour of withdrawal, but the fact that it had produced a clear division between the opinion of the electorate in a referendum and the opinion of the majority of MPs in Parliament, since there were far more 'Remainers' on the Conservative side than there were Leavers on the Labour side, while most of those belonging to other parties supported Remain.

This division between the 'will of the people' and the 'will of the politicians' was played out (though not quite in those terms) over the next four years. Technically, the sovereignty of Parliament meant that the referendum could only be consultative; politically, Parliament found that it could not stand in the way of the 'will of the people' (leaving aside arguments about the narrowness of the vote, the rules about who could or could not vote and so on). By insisting (in effect) that the members of the House of Commons accept the vote in the referendum, popular sovereignty asserted itself over parliamentary sovereignty, even though one of the arguments for leaving the EU was the protection of parliamentary sovereignty.

Since it would appear that the limitations of Parliamentary sovereignty had been revealed in the way the United Kingdom was taken out of the EU despite the wishes of a majority of its MPs, the Welsh *Senedd* was entitled to feel that those limitations might be accepted in the context of strengthening the UK

---

1   Bogdanor, *Beyond Brexit*, p. 90 gives the result of the 1975 referendum and analyses its consequences. He discusses the Alternative Vote referendum on p. 107 and the European Union Act, of which he says that 'it is doubtful if a more absurd piece of legislation has ever been enacted at Westminster,' on pp. 82–83. But the important point is the root of this absurdity, which is that you cannot at one and the same time pledge to be bound by the result of a popular referendum and declare that the sovereignty of parliament remains paramount. After 2016 Parliament had to consider whether to agree to the outcome of a referendum, with whose result a majority of them disagreed, in order supposedly to restore their own sovereign powers. It is hardly surprising that it took them four years to solve this conundrum, or perhaps to find the best way of living with it.

Union through new constitutional arrangements. But the principle of parliamentary sovereignty, even if arguably something more honoured in the breach than the observance, remains an object of romantic attachment on both sides of the political spectrum, not least the Left side. Part of the Left recalls the campaigns to extend the franchise over the last two hundred years and sees a process whereby parliamentary and popular sovereignty effectively became one. It is this that has given so many on the left of the Labour party a romantic attachment to the House of Commons as if it was the only possible source of reform and as if 'popular' sovereignty and 'parliamentary' sovereignty must always be one. One only has to think of Tony Benn putting up (illegally) a plaque in a broom cupboard in the Chapel of St Mary Undercroft to commemorate the suffragette Emily Davidson, or Michael Foot's unholy alliance with Enoch Powell to prevent reform of the House of Lords, or Dennis Skinner's constant presence on the green benches and his annual quip when Black Rod was barred from entering the Commons.[2] Of course, they did use the Commons to promote important reforms, while their oratory has been wonderfully preserved through their presence in Parliament, but one feels there is something more, the powerful romantic appeal of an institution that fought against monarch, Lords and the 'upper class' to make the people 'masters now' (as Labour famously had it after their surprise victory in 1945). Judges, on the other hand, are seen as representatives of an establishment which fought over the centuries to preserve the status quo, and this inclines the Left to support those who want to maintain the sovereignty of Parliament over 'legal interference'. The idea that Parliament itself might come to be a barrier to the sovereignty of the people is understandably hard for them to accept.

---

2   Foot and Powell had already campaigned together in order to support a 'No' vote in the 1975 referendum on whether to stay inside the EEC. See Stephens, *Britain Alone*, p. 183. What is interesting is the way in which Foot's opposition to the EEC in the 1975 referendum campaign was similar to his opposition to a reformed House of Lords – it would necessarily undermine the sovereignty of the Commons. Hence he was hostile to proposals for an elected European Parliament just as he was hostile to an elected House of Lords. Democracy was only permissible, it seemed, for the House of Commons. See the fascinating debate between Michael Foot and Edward Heath, the Prime Minister who took the UK into the EEC, from 1975 preserved on YouTube: https://www.youtube.com/watch?v=CuZrzwm6CJs

Back to the 70s?

Tom Nairn recognised, when a devolution bill was introduced in the House of Commons in 1976, that the question would become one 'of building up a new, fairer, more federal British order, not the dingy, fearful compromise of 'devolution' but a modern, European, multi-national state'.[3] But he also saw that such a multi-national state was very unlikely to arise given the outlook of the Westminster government. He understood the nub of the problem fifty years ago, when the prospect of devolution in the 1970s and at the same time British entry to the EEC raised important constitutional issues during the same decade. In *The Break-Up of Britain* (first published, it should be remembered, in 1977) Nairn argued that 'though modern constitutions typically locate the source of sovereignty in "the people", in Britain it is the Crown in Parliament that is sovereign.'[4] It is this that makes UK citizens technically 'subjects' rather than 'citizens.' It also runs risks of an elected dictatorship. It is still unnerving to read the standard authority on such matters, A.V.Dicey's *Introduction to the Study of the Constitution*, which affirms that

> The principle of parliamentary sovereignty means neither more nor less than this, namely that Parliament thus defined has, under the English constitution, the right to make or unmake any law whatever; and, further, that no person or body is recognised by the law of England as having a right to override or set aside the legislation of Parliament.[5]

Quite apart from the fact that Dicey talks about the 'English' constitution and the 'law of England', thereby opening up all sorts of questions about whether this principle should apply to the rest of the UK, it is unnerving because it suggests that a Parliament of rogues would have carte blanche to pass whatever laws it wished.

When Nairn wrote his book, some half a century ago, there was still a degree of complacency about the constitutional status of the United Kingdom. A Royal Commission on the Constitution under Lord Kilbrandon had deliberated between 1969 and 1973. The Kilbrandon Report was a typical celebration of the status quo. Nairn quotes its extraordinary remarks about the Isle of Man and the Channel Islands, two crown dependencies that it calls 'unique miniature

---

3   Nairn, Tom *The Break-up of Britain*, p. 81.
4   Nairn, Tom *The Break-up of Britain*, p. 30.
5   Dicey, *Introduction to the Study of the Law of the Constitution*, p. 39.

states with wide powers of self-government.' So full of 'anomalies, peculiarities and anachronisms' are they, that they are 'not capable of description by any of the usual categories of political science'. More 'logical and orderly races' would have swept them away long ago. Yet since they are perfectly happy with the status quo, they have been left in peace. They understand the point of the argument that was later used to defend the continuing existence of the House of Lords in its present form – 'if it ain't broke, don't fix it.' The implication would seem to be that if only the Welsh and the Scots could be equally content with their lot, however apparently 'anomalous and anachronistic', they could be as happy as the Channel Islanders. Such mystification was hardly an approach which demonstrated a serious attempt by Lord Kilbrandon to get to grips with the constitutional issues raised by the United Kingdom.[6]

Such an approach coincided with the first stirrings of devolution to Scotland and Wales, the collapse of the Sunningdale agreement in Northern Ireland and the devolution of decision-making power to the people in referenda (the first referendum, on whether to stay inside the European Economic Community or EEC, took place in 1975). Yet significant though these moves were, they were rarely seen as challenging the fundamental belief in parliamentary sovereignty, even though all three represented precisely such a challenge. The introduction of referenda into the UK political system opened up the possibility of a clash such as we have just described between the will of the people and the will of their politicians. Entry into the EEC meant agreeing to be bound by European Law and disapplying legislation that conflicted with it – this also has been illustrated in earlier chapters. And the introduction of devolution, which was eventually delayed until the end of the 1990s, meant that there was bound to be a question of how parliamentary sovereignty could be reconciled with the devolved powers of Cardiff, Edinburgh and Belfast.

Nairn noted that when the devolution debate took place in Parliament in 1976, Michael Foot, Leader of the House of Commons, emphasised it would 'strengthen and sustain the unity of the United Kingdom.' But he could only maintain this view by suggesting that whatever powers were afforded to the proposed Welsh and Scottish assemblies would not, in his words, 'mean that

---

6   For a more charitable view of the Kilbrandon Report, see Daintith, Kenneth, 'Kilbrandon: The Ship That Launched a Thousand Faces?' *The Modern Law Review* Vol. 37, No. 5 (September 1974), pp. 544–555.

the House of Commons need not retain its full power to deal with these matters in the future.'[7]

It is difficult to see what this means. What Nairn called Foot's belief in the 'mystic unity' of the UK essentially involved a conviction that parliamentary sovereignty need not be shared in the context of devolution. The belief seemed to be that somehow one could hand down power to the devolved nations without infringing the sovereignty of the Westminster parliament. Ironically a year earlier, when the first referendum on UK membership of the EEC took place, Foot had consistently argued that parliamentary sovereignty could not be maintained in the context of joining the European Community and was one of those who voted against it. He was consistently opposed to any sharing of sovereignty, whether inside the EEC or within the UK. The same outlook also informed his consistent opposition to trying to reform the House of Lords, in which he allied himself (as he did on the issue of remaining inside the EEC) with the Right in the form of Enoch Powell. He was afraid that a reformed House of Lords might end up entitled to a share of power with the House of Commons.

God and the British Constitution

Writing in *The Scotsman* in 1977, Neal Ascherson commented at a Rowntree Trust conference on 'The Future of Parliament' in the following terms:

> The English doctrine of the absolute, arbitrary, illimitable sovereignty of Parliament, born in the 17th Century carried into the new Parliament of the Union and reaching its full, preposterous stature in the Victorian age, still holds.[8]

Back in 1977 Ascherson insisted that 'imagining a House of Commons which was limited, which could be defied...was as impossible... as imagining the world the morning after one's own death.'[9] It is as if some logical inconsistency was involved – as if by speaking of limiting parliamentary sovereignty you were revealing the fact that you didn't understand what the term meant. There cer-

---

7   Nairn, Tom *The Break-up of Britain*, p. 54.

8   See Nairn, *The Break-up of Britain*, p. 292.

9   See Nairn, *The Break-Up of Britain*, pp. 292–293. Ascherson's comment is from an article entitled 'Divine Right of Parliaments' in *The Scotsman* published on February 18th, 1977.

tainly are lawyers who have claimed that Parliament's sovereignty is supreme and by definition cannot be shared. This was the argument used at the time of the European Communities Act by Lord Hailsham, the Lord Chancellor and Sir Geoffrey Howe, the Solicitor-General. Yet as Bogdanor points out, it was not the argument of Dicey himself, the one who first codified the theory of parliamentary sovereignty in his classic *Introduction to the Study of the Law of the Constitution*.[10] Dicey wrote:

> The impossibility of placing a limit on the exercise of sovereignty does not in any way prohibit, either logically or in matter of fact, the abdication of sovereignty.[11]

Dicey points out that an autocratic Czar may relinquish supreme power by choosing to abdicate, and so may a sovereign Parliament. It is a fascinating example of how what might be called the political establishment chooses to bypass the question of whether a limitation of parliamentary sovereignty is a good or bad thing by simply claiming that it is logically impossible.

Bogdanor compares their argument to those theologians who claim that it is impossible for God to be unaware of the future because this would compromise Her omnipotence.[12] They claim that even a self-limitation of God's power chosen by God Herself is something She cannot do – because it would contradict Her own nature. The theological answer to this is that an omnipotent God can choose to limit Her powers if She wants to, and one must beware claiming to know the nature of God better than God does. As the great theologian Karl Barth put it, God cannot be made the prisoner of Her own power.

Theological tangents, fascinating though they are, should perhaps be avoided, but there is a parallel with the argument about the sovereignty of Parliament. One side points out that if 'what the King enacts in Parliament is law', that does not prevent Parliament from choosing to limit its own powers if it wishes to do so. The other side insists that this would be akin to a contradiction – Parliament doing what it is by definition unable to do. If one followed the proposals outlined by the Welsh *Senedd* in the last chapter by saying something like: 'what the King enacts in Parliament is law, so long as it does not override the powers of the devolved nations as laid out in the Constitution of the Isles,'

---

10   See Bogdanor, *Beyond Brexit*, p. 64.

11   Bogdanor, *Beyond Brexit*, p. 64.

12   Bogdanor, *Beyond Brexit*, p. 67.

the accusation would be that one had somehow failed to understand what the very idea of 'Parliamentary sovereignty' entailed.[13]

There is nothing quite so difficult to challenge as a lawyer confident about the meaning of a legal term, unless it is a theologian confident in a doctrine. Nevertheless, this book would follow Bogdanor's reasoning in saying that just as an all-powerful God may voluntarily choose to limit Her powers (as the so-called kenotic theologians attest) so it is within the powers of a sovereign Parliament to limit its powers too. Otherwise, both God and Parliament would effectively be subject to a higher authority laying down what they might do, and that might be a little much to claim even for the late Lord Hailsham.

However, there is an important distinction to be made, which connects with the discussion of constitutional reforms proposed by the Welsh government and discussed above. The real problem is not that sovereignty cannot be given away by Westminster; it is that it cannot be shared – precisely the principle underlying the European Union. For Westminster clearly has given sovereignty away in practice – for instance to the self-governing dominions in the Statute of Westminster in 1931. In principle, one could say that the UK government was willing to give it away in the event of a referendum on Scottish independence producing a 'Yes' vote. This might have happened in 2014 and (assuming that those who say that referenda can only be once-in-a-generation events should be taken literally), it might happen in 2039. It is difficult to see how David Cameron could have refused surrendering sovereignty over Scotland in 2014 had the vote produced a majority favouring independence. It is the sharing of sovereignty that Westminster governments find so difficult to accept and that is why they feel driven to interpret devolution as a process of giving away powers rather than a way of sharing them. One can argue with the devolved nations over 'who does what' but bringing them together in a mechanism for the joint exercise of power in decision-making that affects them all has received very little attention.

---

13   Hence Howe's language in 1977 suggesting that 'the ultimate supremacy of Parliament will not be affected, and it will not be affected because it cannot be affected.' It is as if any other suggestion was akin to trying to defy the law of gravity. See Bogdanor, *Beyond Brexit*, chapter 2: 'Europe and the Sovereignty of Parliament', pp. 51–86, esp. pp. 64–72. Howe's comment is discussed on p. 64.

Another narrative arc

Chapter Two of this book called for an appreciation of the 'narrative arc' which demonstrates how firmly what has become the United Kingdom has been tied to the rest of the European continent. But there is another narrative arc where the history of England and later the United Kingdom is concerned, one which portrays ancient rights preserved through the centuries by a Parliament which certainly had limited powers in earlier times, but which became the means by which the powers of the sovereign were held in check.

Eight hundred years ago Magna Carta declared that the King had no right to tax his subjects arbitrarily. The date of the agreement in 1215 between King John and the barons at Runnymede, June 15th, was proposed as a public holiday in 2006. It hardly spelt out precisely how curbs upon royal power could be managed, but it seemed logical to suppose that some kind of Parliament was the only means of doing so (in fact both sides soon broke the agreement).

In later centuries it was King John's agreement with the barons at Runnymede that was seen as the first step in a long process of curbing the arbitrary exercise of divine power.[14] When the writer Rudyard Kipling wrote his famous poem *The Reeds of Runnymede* in 1922, the barons are presented as those who first challenge the so-called Divine Right of Kings, the idea that the institution and powers of the monarchy were a direct expression of God's will:

> When through our ranks the Barons came,
> With little thought of praise or blame,
> But resolute to play the game,
> They lumbered up to Runnymede;
> And there they launched in solid time
> The first attack on Right Divine--
> The curt, uncompromising 'Sign!'
> That settled John at Runnymede.[15]

These days, when the monarchy seems well established as a symbol of national unity, it should not be forgotten that in the seventeenth century a king was executed (in 1649) and the country became a republic for eleven years, over a century before the same thing happened in France, at that time ruled by a king with absolute powers. The belief in a divine right of kings insisted that God

---

14   See Starkey, David *Magna Carta: The True Story behind the Charter.*
15   See Rudyard Kipling, *Collected Poems.*

willed kings as God had once willed the patriarchs and the kings of Israel. It was for those who rejected this view in the seventeenth century to show that they were not dangerous revolutionaries but were somehow reaching back to an earlier tradition, including the Anglo-Saxon principles enshrined in Magna Carta.

Hence Charles I was accused by his opponents of subverting the ancient laws and liberties of the nation – it was the King, not his ministers, who was the 'subversive radical', seeking to restore arbitrary government. For this reason, Edward Coke's *Petition of Right*, approved by both houses of parliament in 1628, was received with bonfires and the ringing of church bells. For the rights and liberties which it proclaimed, including freedom from taxation without parliamentary approval, were seen as going back four hundred years to the agreement at Runnymede. Those who found themselves opposing the king were therefore able to present themselves as the traditionalists.[16]

After the interregnum what happened in 1660 has become known as a 'restoration', restoring what might be seen as the proper balance between the monarch and his or her ministers. Then just 28 years later James II was forced to abdicate (alongside his infant son) because he had supposedly upset this balance. Out of his forced abdication came the Bill of Rights in 1689, which laid down limits on the powers of the monarch and set out parliamentary rights, including the requirement for regular parliaments, elections, and freedom of speech in Parliament.

Magna Carta became the white noise of seventeenth century political discourse. It was the standard under which Parliament fought the Civil War, and it can be argued that it remained the standard in later centuries. In the 1840s the Chartist movement took its name from the People's Charter, which petitioned for parliamentary reform in six areas, including the need for secret ballots, the payment of MPs, and the right for all adult males to have the vote. At the time they were unsuccessful, but apart from annual elections all their demands were eventually met. Their choice of the word 'Charter' was significant and drew consciously on the powerful symbolism of Magna Carta, the 'Great Charter' being the foundation of English liberties which the People's Charter would secure for working men (they were not yet calling for women to have the vote). But as agitation for women's rights grew at the end of the nineteenth century, Magna

16   See John Witte, *The Blessings of Liberty*, Chapter 2: Magna Carta Old and New: Rights and Liberties in the Anglo-American Common Law', pp. 45–76, especially 51–55 discussing Coke and the *Petition of Right*.

Carta was cited once more. It was invoked by suffragettes and a 1911 issue of their official newspaper *Votes for Women* depicted the barons presenting Magna Carta to King John. An accompanying article defended the direct action of the suffragettes as a modern equivalent of the direct action of the barons in compelling King John to sign.[17]

Thus, one can observe a long tradition during which over some seven centuries Magna Carta was seen as the lynchpin of the slow and ultimately successful fight for democracy in what was to become the UK. Moreover, insofar as that long campaign was focussed on the powers of parliament, initially to curb the arbitrary behaviour of monarchs but later in order to ensure that all the people were represented within its walls, the long campaign for the sovereignty of the people could easily be identified with a long campaign for the rights of Parliament and the rights of all adults to have the vote. It has even become embedded in the national consciousness that the House of Commons is the great defender of our liberties. The ritual of Black Rod knocking three times at the door of the Commons, which accompanies the annual state opening of Parliament, is based on the moment where in 1642 King Charles I sought to arrest five members. The attempt to protect the rights of Parliament against arbitrary divine rule is turned into an event to dramatise the protectors of liberty resisting any challenge to their authority. It is an interesting aspect of the British attraction to monarchy that it is associated with a successful campaign to limit its powers, something that links with the point that having lost real power it has come to play a crucial symbolic role in maintaining the unity of the Kingdom.

What Nairn criticised as Foot's belief in the 'mystic unity' of the UK was earthed in a belief in the incontestable sovereignty of the House of Commons. Such a belief on the Left is often based on a reading of history which sees the House of Commons fending off those who would challenge its powers as if it was a case of the 'workers' parliament' being threatened by upper-class peers, foreigners from Brussels and in earlier centuries by the overweening powers of the monarchy. They are prepared to talk in terms of the sovereignty of Parliament – or at least of the Commons – rather than of the people because they simply identify the two. It is, after all, the 'commons', the parliament of the 'common' people. It therefore becomes very difficult for sections of the Labour Party – one might call them the Little Englanders of the Left – to view the 'sharing of sovereignty' as anything other than an invitation to compromise with the

---

17   Votes for Woman, Vol IV No. 151, produced on Friday, January 27th, 1911. See https://im
      agesonline.bl.uk/asset/157581/

privileged classes. Even a radical like Dennis Skinner often seemed to be glued to the green benches during his long career as an MP. He became known above all for preparing an annual quip for when Black Rod arrived at the doors of the Commons, a habit which put him in danger of being adopted as a 'national treasure' for his devotion to the central institution of state.[18]

The limitations of parliamentary sovereignty

The trouble with this view of Parliament, as pointed out earlier, is that it assumes that a body of (now) around 650 men and women, elected under a system which can give a single party a majority of seats in the lower house on the basis of support from only 35% of the voters, will always be the champion of liberties that the tradition outlined above has tried to make it. A closer study of history reveals that there are limitations to the view that Parliament (or even the elected House of Commons alone) is the guarantor of liberty.

The complexities of the fascinating period during which the English beheaded their King before 'restoring' his son make that clear enough. A number of movements emerged during the Civil War period, not all of them convinced that Parliament, whatever its difficulties with the King, was always the protector of their liberties. One of the most notable among them was the Levellers, a group of whom produced a manifesto in July 1646 called *Remonstrance of Many Thousand Citizens*. Addressed to the House of Commons, it argued that the very parliamentarians who were attacking the King for arbitrary practices did the same once they were in power[19]. After all, the so-called Long Parliament, origi-

---

18   This is inevitably an impression, but a good way to consider how justified it is would be to read the excellent trilogy of diaries by Chris Mullin, who was Labour MP for Sunderland South between 1997 and 2010, and who was a close friend but not uncritical supporter of Tony Benn. See (among other things) the presentation of a brass plaque to Tony Benn in a broom cupboard in the Crypt beneath Parliament (*A Walk-On Part*, p. 79), enthusiasm for an appointed rather than elected House of Lords (*A View from the Foothills*, pp. 343–344), and later the admission that 'fogies such as me were against ('democratising' the Lords) on the grounds that an elected upper house will only undermine the authority of the Commons' (*Decline and Fall*, p. 156). A fourth set of diaries on the period after he left the Commons is due to be published in June 2023.

19   Article IV of the *Remonstrance* declared that 'Seeing divers Parliament-men, Committees, Sequestrators, Excize-men, and others, have enriched themselves these times of trouble; If any two honest men can testifie upon Oath what every such Parliament-man, Committee-man, Excize-man, or Sequestrator, &c. was worth in Personal Estate

nally elected in 1640, had given no clear indication of when it would cease to sit. Meanwhile, two of the Levellers' own leaders, John Lilburne and Richard Overton, had been imprisoned and had received no help by appealing to the House of Commons. The only recourse was to appeal over the heads of parliament to the people.

There was a certain ambiguity to the Levellers' approach. Sometimes they petitioned Parliament for the radical reforms they wished to see, presumably convinced that Parliament might legislate to achieve them. But at other times, as in the final version of their *Agreement of the People*, a written document published in May 1649, they appeared to be going beyond an appeal to the Parliament. It is notable that Gary S De Krey refers to the Levellers in the following terms:

> their pre-1649 efforts can be tied to popular opposition to the Cromwellian Protectorate, to popular support for the revived Commonwealth of 1659, to sectarian hostility to the re-establishment of religious coercion in the reign of Charles II (1660–1685) and even to approval of a fundamental law in the reign of James II (1685–1688) that would have established religious toleration and placed it beyond parliamentary repeal.[20]

The idea of being able to put a measure of toleration 'beyond parliamentary repeal' reminds us both of the way in which the forced abdication of James was not necessarily a victory for toleration and of the fact that the role of parliament might be to hinder radical measures rather than to promote them.

There was a similar ambiguity in the way the Levellers read the past. The 'narrative arc' linking *Magna Carta* to the *Petition of Right* had begun after the Norman Conquest. But some of the Levellers chose to look further back to a period before 1066, when Saxon laws had supposedly not yet been superseded by what they called the 'Norman yoke'. The *Remonstrance* had dubbed Magna Carta a 'beggarly thing' and tried to look beyond it, though this was more the

---

at the beginning of this Parliament, or how much he stood indebted at such time as this Parliament began, he shall enjoy only that Estate he then had, and no more: and if indebted, the Debts he hath paid since, [as well as the Estate he hath since got] shall be liable to make Satisfaction to all and every Free Commoner that hath been any wayes damnified either by *KING* or PARLIAMENT, since the beginning of these un-natural troubles'. The Levellers recognised, then as now, that Parliament might be an avenue for personal enrichment and corruption and was not the inevitable agent of radical change.

20   De Krey, Gary S. *Following the Levellers*, p. 2.

view of William Walwyn, one of the movement's leaders, than John Lilburne. Levellers like Walwyn idealised supposedly Saxon laws and institutions and in October 1645 he published *England's Lamentable Slaverie*, his famous rebuke to John Lilburne, calling Magna Carta 'a small set of concessions wrestled out of the pawes of (Norman) conquerors.'[21]

Less radical voices than the Levellers were prepared to extend the narrative arc even further. Rather than seeing Saxon rights swamped by the Norman invasion, they believed that there was continuity between Saxon times and life after the Norman Conquest. Proponents of the theory of continuity, represented best by Sir Edward Coke, and later by the parliamentarians during the Civil War, argued that whatever happened in 1066 it wasn't a 'conquest'. William had claimed the throne by ancient right, they argued, and English laws and customs remained inviolate. It was the same desire for continuity evidenced by those who insisted that 1660 was a 'restoration'. This was the basis of Coke's emphasis upon 'common law', whose defining characteristic was that it was based upon precedent. A common law court would look to decisions of the relevant courts in the past and apply them to present facts. It was Coke who first attempted a comprehensive compilation of centuries of common law in his *Institutes of the Lawes of England*.[22]

Continuity was therefore established in the legal system, the monarchy (lost for a decade but then 'restored') and Parliament. Parliament itself was believed to have had Saxon origins and then continued to develop under the Normans. The sovereignty of Parliament, rather than being a Norman 'invention' established through Magna Carta, was extended backwards to the misty origins of England itself.

Yet Walwyn's objection that Parliament might be a usurper rather than a defender of human rights had not been answered. He observed that many believed Parliament to be above *Magna Carta*, whatever the deficiencies of the

---

21   For a discussion of seventeenth century attitudes to Magna Carta, see Foxley, Rachel 'More Precious in Your Esteem than It Deserveth'?: Magna Carta and Seventeenth-Century Politics' pp. 61–78 or *Magna Carta: History, Context and Influence*, edited by Lawrence Goldman.

22   See Davies, Norman *The Isles*, p. 328. Coke, he writes, 'formulated the ultraconservative and quite unsustainable theory that England possessed a body of immemorial law of Anglo-Saxon vintage which had been regularly 'reaffirmed', most prominently by Magna Carta.' Unsustainable it may have been, but as Davies goes on to say 'Coke's ideology was adopted by the victorious parliamentary cause, and it became the basis of a lasting national tradition.' (p. 329).

latter, that it remained unbounded by its own laws, and could dispose of lives and properties at its own pleasure, simply because it was chosen by the people and allegedly entrusted with their safety.[23] Moreover, there were no courts or judges who could enforce the liberties of the people against the tyranny of Parliament. His justification for making this claim might have been a questionable one, namely that all the legal authorities in England were the offspring of the Norman Conquest, but his general argument was worth consideration. It was the point that the sovereignty of Parliament gives no weight to the possibility that parliamentarians may themselves act against the liberties of the people. There were – and after Brexit there are – no legal constraints upon its activities – those that the Supreme Court in the USA, for instance, can exercise to reign in the executive and the legislature.

What the seventeenth-century debates brought out was that there was something more to the narrative arc than a conflict between an increasingly constrained King and an increasingly empowered Parliament. There was a conflict between what Lilburne called the law of Equity and those who would threaten it, whether Kings or Parliaments. For the law of Equity could save people from the tyranny of parliaments as well as the tyranny of kings. Moreover, such a view would have been a natural conclusion for many of those who lived through the tumultuous two decades leading up to the 'restoration'.

During these years parliaments had come and gone, able to do little to check the exercise of arbitrary power. The Long Parliament continued from 1640 until it was eviscerated by the army in 1648 in Pride's Purge (Colonel Thomas Pride reduced its numbers by more than half, removing all those who favoured a deal with the King). The following year the King was executed. In 1653 the so-called Rump Parliament created by Pride's Purge was dissolved and a nominated assembly of religious zealots replaced it which became known as Barebone's Parliament (one of its members was called Praise-God Barebone). Barebone's Parliament came and went in a single year.[24]

This was followed by Oliver Cromwell assuming the position of Lord Protector, during which time (1653–1658) two protectorate parliaments met and

---

23   See the article by Eunice Ostrensky, 'The Levellers' conception of Legitimate Authority,' *Araucaria*, 20 (39) pp. 157–186. Ostrensky argues that for the Levellers it was the people as a 'collective agent' rather than parliamentary representation which would improve the life of citizens.

24   Still useful as an account of events is Godfrey Davies' *The Early Stuarts: 1603–1660*, part of the Oxford History of England Series.

an attempt at a codified constitution was made, the *Instrument of Government*. The Lord Protector would be assisted by a Council of about 20 members and a Parliament. It would be unfair to describe the *Instrument of Government* as a dictator's charter and indeed some American constitutionalists saw it as anticipating their own separation of powers, but its life was in any case short, to be followed by another attempt at a codified constitution, the *Humble Petition and Advice* (at this time Cromwell was offered and refused the title of monarch).[25]

When Cromwell died, his son Richard became Lord Protector but was forced to dissolve Parliament by the army, which restored the Rump Parliament. Richard then resigned as Lord Protector and an army under General Monck marched south from Scotland to London, restored the Long Parliament with the members who had been excluded by Pride's Purge, and prepared the way for Charles II to return.

Such a summary as this is woefully inadequate in relation to the nuances of two extraordinary decades, but it does illustrate that in the explosive environment of England's temporary life as a republic more was in play than a simple contest between the power of kings and that of parliaments. The 'purging' of parliament by military force, the attempts to arrive at a codified constitution, the continuing demands of radical voices that ancient liberties be respected, all pointed to issues that went beyond that contest. There were also the issues that lead people now to talk about the need for a written constitution and, linked to that, the need for the legislature to be bound by the rule of law rather than simply prescribe what that law is. Finally, there is the irony of the fact that this 'civil war', often now referred to as the 'war of three kingdoms' to point out the importance of what was happening in Ireland and Scotland at the time, not only shows the limitations of parliamentary sovereignty but also the fact that it was not the Westminster parliament alone that was involved in the events of these years. Studying the so-called Civil War period not only helps to illustrate what constitutional arrangements are necessary to prevent what Lord Hailsham called an 'elective dictatorship', but also helps us to recognise the 'war of three kingdoms' as part of the formation of the multinational state that has emerged from the struggles of earlier centuries.

---

25   For a perspective more focused on the radical movements emerging at the time, see Christopher Hill's *The World Turned Upside Down*.

Human rights and parliamentary sovereignty

One of the most famous passages of Magna Carta runs as follows:

> No free man shall be seized or imprisoned, or stripped of his rights or pos-
> sessions, or outlawed or exiled, or deprived of his standing in any other way,
> nor will we proceed with force against him, or send others to do so, except
> by the lawful judgement of his equals or by the law of the land...

Should we see 'the lawful judgment of his equals' or 'the law of the land' in terms
of a judgment by parliament or the judgment of a jury in a court?

In 1997, shortly after the election of the first Labour government in the UK
in eighteen years, a bill went to Parliament entitled *Rights Brought Home: The Human Rights Bill*.[26] Three years later, in 2000, the Human Rights Act was passed
and introduced into UK law rights contained in the European Convention. The
purpose of the bill was to allow people to go to British courts rather than have
to go to Strasbourg in order to enforce their rights under the European Convention on Human Rights. Yet whereas the Convention was incorporated into
devolved law by the devolution statutes, so that devolved legislation could actually be struck down by the courts if it conflicted with the Convention, the
courts could not strike down Westminster laws. They could make a statement
of incompatibility between the Convention and Westminster law, but it was for
Parliament to have the last word on what to do.

The role of the court became an issue again in 2022, when the UK gov-
ernment sought to avoid a ruling by the European Court of Human Rights
concerning its plan to deport certain asylum-seekers crossing the Channel
to Rwanda. At the start of 2023, it remains unclear what form the proposed
Human Rights Act will take. However, it is unlikely that the rights given by the
Westminster Parliament will match those enshrined either in the Charter of
Fundamental Rights, now disapplied, or the European Convention on Human
Rights, likely to be partially dismantled. As was pointed out in the chapter
of Northern Ireland, this is another way in which Brexit causes problems for
the future of Ireland, since there will be different rights for people North and
South of the border and the rights of Irish citizens North of the border will not
be those which apply to other members of the EU.

---

26   It can be read at https://assets.publishing.service.gov.uk/government/uploads/system
     /uploads/attachment_data/file/263526/rights.pdf

Though the actions of the Blair government could be considered progressive, the position it took on the sovereignty of Parliament was not. The Human Rights Bill presented to Parliament in October 1997 considered 'whether it would be right ... to go further and give to courts in the United Kingdom the power to set aside an Act of Parliament which they believe is incompatible with the Convention rights.' The 1997 bill insisted that there is 'an essential difference between European Community law and the European Convention on Human Rights, because it is a *requirement* of membership of the European Union that member States give priority to directly effective EC law in their own legal systems. There is no such requirement in the Convention.'[27] This is perfectly true, but there was nothing to stop the Labour government from permitting the courts to disapply acts of parliament that were believed to be incompatible with Convention rights. Instead, the bill merely allowed the courts to make a 'declaration of incompatibility' between the two, leaving it to Parliament itself to decide whether it would take any action to remedy the incompatibility. It is worth quoting one section of the bill in full (section 2.12):

> The Government has reached the conclusion that courts should not have the power to set aside primary legislation, past or future, on the ground of incompatibility with the Convention. This conclusion arises from the importance which the Government attaches to Parliamentary sovereignty. In this context, Parliamentary sovereignty means that Parliament is competent to make any law on any matter of its choosing and no court may question the validity of any Act that it passes. In enacting legislation, Parliament is making decisions about important matters of public policy. The authority to make those decisions derives from a democratic mandate. Members of Parliament in the House of Commons possess such a mandate because they are elected, accountable and representative. To make provision in the Bill for the courts to set aside Acts of Parliament would confer on the judiciary a general power over the decisions of Parliament which under our present constitutional arrangements they do not possess and would be likely on occasions to draw the judiciary into serious conflict with Parliament. There is no evidence to suggest that they desire this power, nor that the public wish them to have it. Certainly, this Government has no mandate for any such change.[28]

---

27   See paragraphs 2:12 and 2:13 of the Bill.

28   This is discussed in Bogdanor, *Beyond Brexit*, pp. 143–6, where he makes clear what the Human Rights Act did and did not manage to do.

It is very odd to see the bill claiming that 'Parliament is competent to make any law on any matter of its choosing and no court may question the validity of any Act that it passes.' This was not true – as the Bill itself elsewhere admits – because of the European Communities Act. However, it could be true post-Brexit. On the other hand, if there is to be an adequate constitutional settlement for what is called preserving the Union (British, not European), it is the argument of this book that it will be necessary to consider precisely the 'conferring on the judiciary of a general power over the decisions of Parliament' that we see here condemned in 1997 as something neither desired by the courts nor the public. It is precisely parliamentary sovereignty, which we see Labour governments committed to as strongly as Conservative governments, that will have to go if the sort of constitutional settlement proposed by the Welsh *Senedd* is to have any hope of succeeding.

Keating concludes a discussion of what he calls 'the sovereignty conundrum' with a remark that:

> What we are left with is a tantalising series of suggestions that devolution may have changed the way that sovereignty and parliamentary supremacy work, but reluctance on the part of the judges to take the matter beyond speculation.[29]

This would appear to be a fair comment. Judges will use an expression to try to give special status to the devolution settlement, such as 'constitutional law', but however grand the expression is it always falls at the last hurdle when confronted by parliamentary sovereignty. Lord Justice Laws in 2002 (*Thoburn v Sunderland City Council*) considered an issue concerning a greengrocer's right to advertise his products in imperial rather than metric measures. The issue blew up as the 'metric martyrs' took their concerns to higher courts. Eventually it went to the high court where Lord Justice Laws declared that the European Communities Act was a 'constitutional law', but he also claimed that Parliament could amend or repeal such a law if it wanted to, something that was difficult to square with the primacy of EU Law which he also affirmed.[30] This issue died down with later common-sense provisions concerning the possibility of displaying both measures but illustrated how easily 'little issues' could provoke a storm of 'us-against-them' feelings that might have been avoided in the first

---

29   Keating *State and Nation*, p. 67.
30   See Bogdanor, *Beyond Brexit*, pp. 80–81.

place. Sunderland was to vote overwhelmingly for Brexit in the 2016 referendum.

Lord Hope, ten years after the 'metric martyrs' ruling, declared that the Scotland Act was also a 'constitutional' act, but once again accepted that Parliament could amend or repeal it. It simply had to be an 'express' rather than 'implied' repeal – but the power for Westminster to repeal was still there.[31] One might also cite Douglas-Scott's argument that when the UK ignored the refusal on the part of the devolved nations of legislative consent to the EU Withdrawal Act it was acting in a way that was not 'constitutional' but was 'legal'.[32] The real impact of these terminological niceties is the absence of reason at the heart of them, as so many people scurry around trying to square the circle. They are desperate to find a form of words which can allow one to preserve the absolute sovereignty of the Westminster Parliament and its supposed role in history as the defender of all our liberties, while at the same time appearing to make the maximum possible concessions to the devolved bodies. In the end it is always made clear that the sovereignty of the Westminster parliament trumps the judiciary and the devolved parliaments, while Brexit makes the ambiguity of its position when the UK was part of the European Union irrelevant.

Conclusion

The book mentioned 'the invention of tradition,' and among those traditions was one surrounding the monarch, who once effectively without power in the realm was reinvented as a glamorous symbol of imperial and later national unity. Alongside this tradition runs another of the steady emergence of parliament as the vehicle of human liberty. The arc extends from the barons who (in Kipling's presentation) ordered King John to sign up to Magna Carta at Runnymede through the seventeenth century debates on royal power, reaching their climax in the execution of Charles and the 'restoration' of his tamed son as successor, before moving on to nineteenth-century demands for a widened franchise in the 'People's Charter' and finally the taming of the House

---

31   Keating, *State and Nation*, p. 67. See pp. 71–74 for an account of how courts tried to introduce distinctions to muddy the waters rather than to enlighten.

32   Douglas-Scott, Sionaidh. 'The Constitutional Implications of the EU (Withdrawal) Act 2018: A Critical Appraisal'.

of Lords and the emergence of a House of Commons elected by all adults and empowered to protect the liberties of the people.

The romance of parliamentary sovereignty presents a narrative arc in which an ancient constitution is preserved through the ages to become the foundation of English (and presumably later British) liberties. It is not a written constitution, but lies embedded in a set of precedents and practices, the principle underlying the development of the common law. It enables a degree of continuity to be claimed, through Saxon origins and the time of the 'Norman yoke.' Words like 'precedent' and 'convention' describe the mystical continuity that weaves its way through the ages, surviving regime change and the lack of written form. It is the basis for Burke's magnificent *Reflections on the French Revolution*, with its emphasis upon the power of tradition, a contrast between a country that has had sixteen constitutions since 1789 (Bogdanor recalls how someone asked in a French bookshop for a copy of the French constitution and was told that they didn't stock periodicals) and one that has not repeatedly tried to tear up the past and start afresh with everything changed including even (in the case of the 1789 Revolution) the calendar.[33] The emphasis is on terms like 'adaptation' and 'evolution' rather than root-and-branch renewal.

Yet there is an element of complacency in this view, an absence of any sense that a universal franchise can lead to tyranny, as it arguably did in Germany in 1933. What is lacking in a narrative such as this is the need for an independent judiciary with the right to hold the government in check and ensure that it has respect for human rights. Yet as the Human Rights Bill of 1997 shows, the courts are not allowed the power to disapply acts of Parliament that conflict with the European Convention on Human Rights. Parliamentary sovereignty trumps the power of the judiciary. Perhaps for this reason the ideas of the Levellers, who certainly saw how parliament could act against them as much as it could be their champion, had more influence in the USA than the UK. When Walwyn complained that Parliament 'when they might have made a newer and better Charter, have falne (fallen) to patching the old', he was calling on them not simply to legitimate their demands in terms of an ancient constitution and even the principles of *Magna Carta*, but to embrace a new constitution based on reason, rather than custom and precedent, an approach more suggestive of the

---

33   See Bogdanor, 'Europe, subsidiarity and the British Constitution' *RSA Journal* Vol. 142, No. 5448, April 1994, pp. 41–54.

French and American Revolutions a century later.[34] New wine does not belong in old wineskins. (Mark 2:18-22)

As an ex-imperial power, the UK is used to giving power away, and might even be willing to do so to parts of the UK that vote for independence. It is the sharing of power that UK governments find it so difficult to accept. They interpret devolution as a process of giving away powers rather than a way of sharing them in a joint management of the 'four nations.' By doing this, they risk giving up what would be an essential condition of continuing with a United Kingdom. As we move through the 2020s, that risk has certainly not gone away.

---

34   'From his work in 1645, Englands Lamentable Slaverie', to be found in J. R. McMichael and B. Taft (eds.), *The Writings of William Walwyn*, pp. 147–148.

Chapter Fifteen: Elites and Populists: Upending the top-down approach

As 'a tale of two unions' this book argues that some of the forms of government which the UK became part of when it joined the European Economic Community, and which it later sought to escape, may have to return if it is to succeed in maintaining its own four-nation (or conceivably three-nation) union. The book will later offer suggestions about such a union. But before it does so, we need to consider various movements that are too easily ignored when books attempt to get down to the constitutional nitty-gritty, namely movements 'from below' representing various forms of direct democracy, and which are obviously encouraged by the existence of social media.

This is not a book considering the complicated issues around the rise of 'populism' and the extent to which it is dangerous or encouraging (or both). Nevertheless, it is important to take seriously the rise of movements which are dubbed 'populist'. Are they simply seeking a more effective way of making public opinion known than that afforded by representative democracy? This is important, since any 'Constitution of the UK' with a hope of succeeding must have the sort of popular backing that was so clearly lacking in the case of the reforms pushed through by Jean Monnet. The same can be said about structural reforms of the EU that might overcome its own 'democratic deficit'. This book will argue that some form of direct democracy needs to be built into whatever constitutional arrangements are likely to succeed.

Jean Rey, a Belgian, succeeded Walter Hallstein in 1967 to become the second President of the European Commission from 1967 to 1970. He then continued to be active in politics at national level and was elected to the European Parliament in 1979, the first year in which there were direct elections to that body. In 1974 he learned of the UK's decision to hold a referendum on whether to stay inside the European Economic Community. He remarked as follows during a visit to London:

> A referendum on this matter consists of consulting people who don't know the problems instead of consulting people who know them. I would deplore a situation in which the policy of this great country should be left to housewives. It should be decided instead by trained and informed people.[1]

Half a century later such a comment appears to come from another age. Apart from the suggestion that 'housewives' were the last people one would leave decisions to (Belgium was one of the last European countries to give full voting rights to women – in 1948 – but Rey had had a generation to get used to this) the notion that consultation should only be with those who 'knew the problem' and who were 'trained and informed' (rather than consulting the people – as in a referendum) suggests the sort of elitist mentality that infuriates so many people today.

It is difficult to avoid feeling that anyone who even fifty years ago could make such a comment after being President of the Commission and then an elected member of the European Parliament shows that there is something wrong with the institutional arrangements in the EU and the mentality of some of those working in them. This chapter will try to be more precise about what that means.

Change from above to below

The great merit of the EU system lies in the way that a sovereignty-sharing system brings nations together, as a diplomat once remarked of France and Germany's involvement in the Coal and Steel Community, in an embrace so close that neither could draw back far enough to hit the other.[2]

This image is a powerful one. It is arguably the genius of Jean Monnet, born of long experience with other systems that failed, to have insisted upon the need for nations jointly to create bodies whose decisions they would regard as binding, thereby voluntarily making themselves bound to comply with European Law.

---

1   See Bogdanor, Vernon. *Beyond Brexit: Towards a British Constitution*, p. 92.
2   See the second of Vernon Bogdanor's six lectures on Britain and Europe given to Gresham College in 2014, 'From the European Coal and Steel community to the common Market' which can be heard on YouTube at https://www.youtube.com/watch?v=cETz_eOYBjo

But this was a system that came 'from above' rather than as an expression of popular demands 'from below'. Monnet took this weakness in the system he proposed with insufficient seriousness, as did Robert Schuman, the French foreign minister who adopted the plan. The result of this, often discussed in terms of a so-called 'democratic deficit,' is that there has always been a question about how far the gradual evolution from European Economic Community through Economic Community to European Union, from many currencies to (for 20 countries from January 2023) one, through seven different treaties and through the creation (and re-creation) of several different EU institutions has really represented the will of the people or simply a degree of jockeying for power and divvying up of benefits on the part of Europe's elite.

Yanis Varoufakis was the Greek finance minister during the fraught negotiations between the so-called Troika (International Monetary Fund, European Commission and European Central Bank) and the left-wing Syriza government in Greece over the country's debt crisis in 2015. He eventually resigned rather than comply with what he saw as an effective capitulation to the Troika's demands over the terms of a loan. He has written many books linked to the financial crisis and the eurozone debt crisis. He is not opposed to the European Union in principle and campaigned for the UK to remain a member of it in 2016. However, as a founder of DIEM25 (Democracy in Europe Movement 2025) he remains a consistent critic, not of the EU itself, but of what he considers to be its present, essentially undemocratic, make-up.

This is not a minor criticism. It changes the whole way in which the European project is perceived. Thus, Varoufakis is able to present the first example of sovereignty-sharing, the European Coal and Steel Community, which Schuman rightly recognised as being a ground-breaking development, in a very different light to that offered by its supporters. They had celebrated the way in which the industries which fuelled war between European nations a few years earlier were now becoming the instruments of peaceful cooperation, as if swords were finally being beaten into ploughshares. But Varoufakis has a different take upon what was happening:

> ...the European Union began life as a cartel of coal and steel producers which, openly and legally, controlled prices and output by means of a multinational

bureaucracy vested with legal and political powers superseding national parliaments and democratic processes.[3]

This is the picture Varoufakis paints of the unique sovereignty-sharing body
created by the Treaty of Paris in 1951. And in his view, this is essentially how it
remains. The 'multinational bureaucracy', initially a High Authority and then
later the European Commission, becomes the instrument of serving an elite,
initially a cartel of rich industrialists and later a wider range of beneficiaries
from the single market. As he argued in *Adults in the Room*, sub-titled *My Battle
with Europe's Deep Establishment*, this 'deep establishment' puts a question mark
against the claims of the European Union to express the will of the people.[4]

It might be argued that Varoufakis represents a particular political viewpoint. But it is a position echoed on the other side of the political spectrum
to his own. There are distinct similarities to the kind of Eurosceptic approach
that tends to come from a right-wing perspective. *The Great European Rip-off*, a
book written as the debate about MPs expenses was raging in the UK a decade
ago, turned its attention to MEPs' (Members of the European Parliament) expenses and the costs of maintaining a European Parliament which met in two
different places. Section headings and chapter titles like 'la dolce vita', 'drown-
ing in money', 'time for a jolly' and 'sharing the trough' make the point clearly
enough, while various perks are stressed, including special European schools
which enable 'the children of eurocrats to spend their childhood almost completely isolated from the uncouth progeny of the country where their parents
work.'[5] No mention was made of the fact that the last UK Prime Minister, Boris
Johnson, attended one of these schools (as well as Eton, which also might be
thought a somewhat insular institution).

The Great European Rip-off is hardly more than a continued rant rather than
the sustained argument offered by Varoufakis. But it's an argument in a similar
vein. Craig and Elliott talk about 'a self-perpetuating elite that becomes ever
more remote from – and uninterested in – the lives of those whose taxes so

---

3   Varoufakis, Yanis *And the Weak suffer what they must? Europe, Austerity and the Threat to
     Global Stability* p. 59.

4   Despite his experiences during the eurozone crisis, Varoufakis was a supporter of the
     Remain vote in the UK referendum. He helped to inaugurate the DiEM25 (Democracy
     in Europe) movement whose purpose, he writes, is 'constructive disobedience within
     the EU, of being both in and against this illiberal and anti-democratic Europe.' See Varo-
     ufakis, *Adults in the Room*, p. 485.

5   Craig and Elliott, *The Great European Rip-off*, p. 38.

philanthropically support it.'[6] Varoufakis compares the members of this elite to medieval lords who exchanged pleasantries together while their feudal levies did the fighting on their behalf. In both cases the fact that people from twenty-seven different countries are working together without enmity in order to try to find European solutions to problems that cut across their national boundaries is reduced to the self-protecting bubble of a pampered elite who protect nothing but their own interests.

This is not to suggest that either Varoufakis or Craig and Elliott provide a fair assessment. But it seems clear that there is a reason why tirades against the 'Brussels bubble' carry more weight than criticisms of the 'Westminster bubble,' even when written during the expenses scandal. Even sharp critics of 'time for a jolly' in Westminster have a sense that MPs can be brought to account by the people. An MP, after all, has clear accountability to an electorate. They have to work in their constituencies. They travel every week between their constituencies and the Commons. They attend meetings and hold 'surgeries' (a word suggesting doctors giving time to their patients) every weekend in the places they represent. Many of them take risks because of the exposure that comes from being a public figure. One of them, Jo Cox, was stabbed and shot to death by a right-wing nationalist shouting 'Britain First' five years ago, outside a library where she was due to hold a surgery. The only person with her was a 77-year-old man who received multiple stab wounds for his efforts to save her. Another MP, a Conservative this time, was killed holding a surgery in 2021, the police arriving just in time to (very questionably) prevent the local parish priest from administering the last rites to him. Most people in the UK recognise that their MPs, whatever the bad behaviour of some, put in a lot of time and run a lot of risks representing their constituents. Under the 'first past the post system,' whatever its faults, each MP has his or her 'patch' whose interests they seek to uphold. Even those in safe seats know they must stay in touch with the electors. MPs do, of course, have to spend time considering government legislation at the national level. But with the exception of cabinet ministers (and perhaps not even in their case), they also spend time working with councillors in their communities, visiting schools and hospitals, trying to improve local transport facilities and so on. They remain grounded in the concerns of their localities.

This does not apply to officials who work for the Commission, whose jobs make them effectively civil servants with a job for life, together with some of the perks accorded to diplomats who work away from their country of origin.

---

6   Craig and Elliott, *The Great European Rip-off,* p. 38.

It is even doubtful whether it is true in quite the same way of MEPs, elected members of the European Parliament. The argument is therefore not that MPs are less corrupt than MEPs or those who work for the other institutions of the European Union. It is that there is a clear form of accountability for MPs – the people put them in and the people can throw them out. Such accountability is not so evident in the case of the European Union, even in the case of its directly elected Parliament. Euro-constituencies tend to be huge, and it's very doubtful whether most people even know the name of their MEP. At the same time, most of the MEPs are chosen under a list system, which means that national parties effectively decide who is most likely to be elected. In the case of MPs, the idea that they've been 'getting away with murder' is tempered by the sense that they can be held to account. In the case of the EU the same idea is made much stronger by the feeling that there's no way of stopping them continuing to get away with behaving improperly.

The principle of nations agreeing to create a body empowered to make decisions that are accepted as binding upon them is the essence of sovereignty-sharing. The main argument of this book is that sovereignty-sharing was the principle on which what became the EU was held together and that something similar might be able to hold a UK Union together outside the EU. Yet if such a development represents a decision made by political and administrative leaders alone and is in no sense an expression of the popular will, it will not win respect. Sovereignty-sharing will be seen as a programme for the few rather than the many. It will be viewed as leading only to a transnational elite gathering, whether in Brussels or in London, and enjoying the privileges that go with the job.

Selling Europe to Europeans

How can the EU (or the UK) be turned from a decision made by political leaders into an expression of the popular will? Earlier chapters recounted a famous saying attributed to Massimo d'Azeglio, a pioneer of Italian unification, that 'we have made Italy; now we must make Italians.' D'Azeglio's remark came less than 15 years after Metternich had dismissed Italy as a 'geographical expression'.[7] The same dismissive remark has been made about Europe – and as with Italy, there have been and are many arguments about what the exact geographical contours of Europe are. As we saw in the chapter on Europe's narrative arc, there is a question about what sort of Europe is being considered. The conclusion of that chapter was that to turn a 'geographical expression' into a real source of identity, it was necessary to strengthen the structural reforms which have produced a unique form of governance inside what has become the European Union. That strengthening involves finding a way in which these reforms can be seen as an expression of the popular will rather than a clever idea on the part of an official (Monnet) which was then smuggled into existence by a politician (Schuman) who felt himself to be cornered (by the need to allow for German economic revival). But how exactly can Europe be 'sold' to Europeans?

One way of doing so fails to move away from the top-down approach described in the last section. It is to employ the techniques of advertising and sell Europe like soap powder. One example of this can be seen from the de Clercq report. Willie de Clercq was a Belgian MEP who was invited by the European Commission in 1993 to produce a report on how to rescue the EU's flagging image (it had flagged to the point where France came within a whisker of rejecting the Maastricht Treaty). Working with a team of communications 'experts' and Commission staff, (the group was called the *Comité des sages* – Committee of The Wise) the report recognised the problem – that Europe was 'a concept based far more on the will of statesmen than on the will of the people'. But its proposed solution was that Europe needed to be 'engrained on people's minds' and to do so it turned to communications experts who had recently moved from 'manufacturing consent' in the commercial sphere (by selling cars and soap powder) to manufacturing consent in the political sphere (by publicising the sort of 'Third Way' politics represented by Bill Clinton and Tony Blair in the 1990s). They would therefore find a way of manufacturing consent to Europe, an exercise which, among other things, included producing birth certificates granting 'European citizenship,' a European 'order of merit' which would outrank all national honours, a European library and museum, a European dimension to school syllabi and a series of television appeals by the Commission President to the 'women and youth of Europe'[8] It was a case of forget explaining complex

---

7   See Hobsbawm, *The Age of Capital*, p. 110. He agrees with Metternich, saying that 'there was no historical precedent later than Ancient Rome for a single administration of the entire area from the Alps to Sicily.'

8   Shore, Cris *Building Europe: The Cultural Politics of European Integration* p. 55.

treaties and start selling the EU product in direct and simple terms as if it was soap powder.

The EU became a wonderful new product which the punters didn't yet want to buy, but which with deft rebranding could be made popular in the way so many other things that people took for granted in their lives had been made popular – televisions, mobile phones, computers, cars. What the de Clercq approach did not appreciate in the early 1990s was that popularising the European Union was not a question of finding a better way of 'selling' it to the people, presented as passive consumers waiting for the right form of manipulation to make them love the EU. It failed to grasp that it should be the people themselves selling the European Union.

Working for the top-downers

For a decade between 2010 and 2020 I was part of a team of freelance 'conférenciers' or visiting speakers employed by the European Commission to speak to groups of visitors at its headquarters in Brussels – students, civil society representatives, diplomats and others – about the nature and role of the Commission as the 'executive' of the European Union. Many of these visitors filed into the Charlemagne and Berlaymont Buildings during the years of the eurozone crisis.

As freelancers we were kept under a tight leash, presented with fixed powerpoint slides which we had to explain and provided with briefings on the issue from officials. Such was the atmosphere of deference among EU officials to their heads of units and (further up) directors that it was clear on the inside that the whole organisation was a form of managerial totalitarianism. The outside world might marvel at the imitation of 'business practices' like team building and awaydays bonding in country houses. The inside world revealed that this is light years away from the sort of encouragement given to thinking outside the box by staff in the most successful companies. The Commission on the outside might be all about collaborative working. On the inside it is more like an army on the march, its commanders unsure of where exactly they are going.

We could tell that our presence was not something the officials themselves liked. In the end, three years into a four-year contract, they got rid of us (we were effectively in the situation of those on zero-hours contracts, to be used when and if the Commission wanted to use us) and replaced us with volunteers from their own ranks, many of whom rather relished the prospect of talking about what they did rather than doing it. Ironically (I was invited to sit in on some of their presentations) the officials themselves were far freer with their criticisms of the Commission than we had ever been. The 'volunteers' tended to come from the ranks of the disaffected, who welcomed the opportunity to sound off.

A powerpoint presentation on social media prepared for us in early 2018 had only one overall approach – to emphasise that social media provided new opportunities for the Commission to get its message across. *We are living in the era of the digital citizen...And there is no turning back*, declared the notes added to the first slide. *What's different—and compelling—about digital citizens is how they can initiate and dictate the dynamics of the citizen-to-institution relationship like never before.* So far, so good. The Commission appeared to be waking up to a groundswell of grassroots initiatives. *The central question for us then becomes: How must we change to better relate to digital citizens?*

The next slides began to explain what changes the Commission had in mind. 'Different platforms, different audiences', one of them began. All at once the language had changed. The digital citizens with the capacity to initiate had turned into 'audiences.' Hadn't they become rather passive all of a sudden? Another slide was entitled 'planning and management' – and by now we understood that it was all about how to get the Commission's 'message' across in a better way. It's not 'we want to hear from you'; it's 'we want to make sure that you hear from us.' 'Not all channels are relevant for all your target audiences', ran a further slide. Not even an audience now, but a 'target audience'. People to get through to, not people to hear from.

There followed a list of clichés it is hardly necessary to repeat, but once again they were all about getting 'our message' through to 'them'. Optimise your communication – understand your impact – be an influencer, a 'brand ambassador', a 'multiplicator'. 'Prepare early for points of criticism or engagement opportunities' – in other words get your defensive positions ready to ward off attacks – but don't think about how some of what 'they' say to 'you' might be something which changes your own policy positions. Though there is a mention of 'feedback', one suspects that it can only be about how effectively you got your ideas through to them – not about how they might get their ideas through to you.

The 'top-down' approach is, of course, related to the Commission's own hierarchy. But that only reflects the fact that the Commission's relationship to the world outside is similar to the relations between the higher and lower levels of the Commission. The leadership has a line to give and the various departments (or directorates and units) of each department or DG (Directorate-General) receive it. The policies trickle down from top to bottom and then they trickle down again, like water falling over the edge of a step, to the people outside. But nothing ever flows in the other direction. Gravity wouldn't allow it.

The EU defends itself against this view by talking about extensive consultations with civil society organisations, but Youngs (in a book called *Europe Reset*) argues that these tend to be 'insider' organisations:

> EU institutions today roll out many initiatives that ostensibly consult civil society about reforming integration, but they still engage overwhelmingly with insider groups that are part of what outsiders believe is a self-serving network.[9]

Hence the EU is not talking to 'outsiders', even when it is supposedly consulting civil society. Instead, civil society organisations (some of them receiving grants from the EU) are made to take part in 'very focused consultations', presumably meaning that they are limited as to what they can discuss. It is reminiscent of the practices that used to be familiar to democratic centralism in the former communist states of Eastern Europe and the Soviet Union. Were there elections in which the people voted? Of course. You never had an election without an opposition candidate, but it was never a 'real' opposition candidate since those wouldn't have been allowed to stand. But the puppets that remained in the field to 'challenge' the President were important because they allowed the country to offer the image of a democracy. Under the communist system there was never any shortage of emphasis upon the people – what could be a better rallying-cry for the grassroots empowerment championed by Youngs and others than the call: 'All power to the soviets', essentially the village councils that ignited the communist revolution of 1917? Yet it did not take long for this principle to be buried in the power of the party as the vanguard of the proletariat.[10]

---

9   Youngs, *Europe Reset*, p. 108.

10   One can see the difficulties this created by reading comments by the future Czech President Václav Havel in the months during which the fateful Prague Spring sought to introduce democracy without provoking an invasion by the Warsaw Pact (which happened in 1968). Havel understands that 'internal democratisation of the Communist Party' would not 'provide a sufficient guarantee of democracy', but he is also unsure about reviving the existing non-communist parties which he believes have compromised themselves too much over the years. Democracy requires 'two comparable alternatives', but an effective alternative to the Communist Party simply wasn't there.

The question is how far this model might be applied to the European Union hierarchy, its Commission officials a well-rewarded *nomenklatura* and the huge banner draped from the Berlaymont building in Brussels during the last presidency proclaiming 'Team Juncker,' as if a new politburo was setting out its five-year plan for the next Commission. Many officials from former Communist countries who joined the Commission after the enlargement of 2004 were struck by attitudes that they had last encountered before the revolutions in their own countries.

Youngs' conclusion in this part of *Europe Reset* was that:

> Existing participative consultations are about communicating formal EU narratives downwards to citizens more than conveying popular demands upwards to decision-makers.[11]

He has recently developed his arguments in *Rebuilding European Democracy: Resistance and Renewal in an Illiberal Age*. The key point being made is that although there are numerous initiatives to consult with/involve/empower/listen to the voice of the citizens at grassroots level, these are all organised and even orchestrated 'from above'. What actually happens at the grassroots level is ignored altogether, or else it is seen as an enemy attempting to stoke the forces of populism. 'Attend events like the Global forum on Modern Direct Democracy', writes Youngs, and one finds that EU experts 'are completely absent from these forums.' The argument is that 'intense civic empowerment at the local level' gets 'no look in when leaders gather to discuss "the future of the EU"'. What should be aimed at instead is for 'nascent local-led initiatives' to be 'harnessed to cascade upwards into a revitalised debate about the EU's future.'[12] Gravity, in other words, needs to be defied.

Deliberative Democracy

On 25 February 2019, the parliament of the German-speaking community of Belgium, a relatively small population of about 77,000 people, adopted a Citizens' Council made up of 25 randomly selected citizens who were to decide

---

This was a problem right up to – and perhaps after – the moment that communism fell in 1989. See Fowkes, *Eastern Europe 1945–1969*, pp. 122–123.

11   Youngs, *Europe Reset*, p. 112.

12   Youngs, *Europe Reset*, p. 94.

on topics for consideration by separate citizens assemblies. There would be between one to three assemblies per year, each consisting of between 25–50 people, meeting across several days on a single topic proposed by the Council. Recommendations from the Assembly would then be considered by the elected Parliament.

Later, the Brussels Region of Belgium, a larger community of over one million inhabitants, decided to follow suit in establishing a permanent procedure to engage randomly selected citizens in policymaking alongside parliamentarians. Recommendations from the Citizens' Assemblies were not binding upon the Parliament. They were to be presented and debated in an open committee session and then the relevant parliamentary committee and minister would prepare a response.[13] At the federal level in Belgium, some have called for a similar transformation of the upper chamber, the Senate, into a chamber for citizen participation.

Similar proposals have been made in other countries, including the idea of turning one of the chambers in bi-cameral constitutions – for instance the House of Lords in the UK or the Senate in the USA – into a chamber whose membership is determined by what is sometimes called 'sortition', essentially the random selection of citizens such as that which produces juries in many countries. In his 2017 presidential election platform, the left-wing French politician Jean-Luc Mélenchon proposed a constitution for a projected sixth republic in France, whose upper house would be made up of randomly selected citizens.[14]

Some of the most interesting developments have taken place in Ireland. For the last decade Citizens' Assemblies have been formed to consider a range of issues. It is true that they did not themselves choose the issues, but it is not unreasonable to suppose that many of the topics reflected the core interests of the citizens and would have been chosen by them anyway. One, for instance, concerned how to make Ireland a leader in tackling climate change. Another concerned how to respond to the challenges of an ageing population. The one

---

13   See https://www.bertelsmann-stiftung.de/en/our-projects/democracy-and-participa tion-in-europe/shortcut-archive/shortcut-9-deliberative-committees-a-new-approac h-to-deliberation-between-citizens-and-politicians-in-brussels

14   In 2022 there was similar pressure for a Sixth Republic, with Mélenchon promising to convene a constituent assembly whose members would be either elected or drawn by lots. Their draft constitution would then be submitted to the people via referendum.

that drew most attention was on the issue of abortion, where the Citizens' Assembly recommended liberalisation, and changes were later confirmed by a referendum. The latest report by the assembly was on gender equality, its findings delivered to the Houses of the Oireachtas, the parliament of the Republic of Ireland, in June 2021.[15]

Thus, although it could be argued that the Irish Citizens' Assembly is organised to consider one-off issues (it is described as having 'a mandate to look at a number of key issues over an extended time period') rather than having a permanent character and a right to determine its own agenda, the fact that it has considered controversial and wide-ranging topics suggests that it would not be difficult to make it a permanent feature of the constitution. Indeed, most recently there have been calls from prominent politicians for a new citizens' assembly on the topic of a possible border poll on a united Ireland.[16] One can hardly accuse those who set the agenda of the Citizens' Assemblies of shying away from controversial issues!

Citizens' Assemblies (sometimes referred to as DMPs or 'deliberative mini-publics') are increasing in importance but they have limited powers. One limitation is that they do not always have the power to set the agenda. Another is that they may be only temporary, convened for a matter of months or years to consider a particular issue. A third is that whilst they may be able to make recommendations, their recommendations are not binding, so that even when, as in the Brussels parliamentary committee, parliamentarians and citizens sit together, they take separate votes and even vote in different ways, with that of the citizens being a secret ballot.

Will these limitations be overcome – and should they be? It needs to be borne in mind that Citizens' Assemblies are not themselves without criticism. There is a question of how enthusiastic people will be to engage in politics when they are randomly selected. It is for this reason that there is usually an initial invitation based on random selection to allow people who aren't interested to refuse. Unlike jury service, it cannot be construed as a public duty to attend.

---

15   See https://citizensassembly.ie/overview-previous-assemblies/ for an account of previous citizens' assemblies. There is one ongoing in 2023 on drug use.

16   Though in reality it is up to the government what the citizens get to discuss. The Irish Foreign Minister, Simon Coveney was quick to say in May 2022, after Sinn Fein came out top in elections to the Northern Ireland Assembly, that convening a citizens' assembly on having a border poll was not even 'on the radar,' reported the *Irish Examiner*. https://www.irishexaminer.com/news/politics/arid-40868039.html

Secondly, a fair representation of the public has not only to consider matters of age, race, class, gender, location and so on, but make sure that those who are less well-off are not simply unable to afford the time to participate. It needs to be made clear that no one will be put out of pocket by participating.

A third and more difficult point worthy of consideration is that elected representatives receive feedback, are voted in and can be voted out. The Citizens' Assembly sounds like an eminently democratic arrangement, but the chosen few (by lottery) do not have to account for themselves to an electorate. People who try to make a career out of politics have to persuade people in order to stand for a parliament and in order to be elected to it and to stay in power. The image that supporters of direct democracy have is of 'ordinary' people, too modest to put themselves forward but nevertheless founts of wisdom and brimming with common sense, who are given the opportunity to make their voice heard. But another view would be that this gives an assortment of randomly chosen people the chance to sound off in a completely unaccountable manner. To be fair, that is not at all the experience of those who have organised such Citizens' Assemblies, but it is obviously a possible criticism (even though 'sounding off in a completely unaccountable manner' might be a fair description of many an elected politician!)

The case for making Citizens' Assemblies an established part of the constitution rather than, like referenda, a one-off response to a particular issue, appears compelling. It also seems reasonable to insist that no one is made poorer by participating – this may be less an issue of financial compensation than an acceptance on the part of employers that taking part in a Citizens' Assembly, like jury service or maternity leave, must be accepted as a valid reason for missing work. More than that, since the work of the assembly will probably involve considering reports by an expert advisory group of some kind, participating will not only involve attending meetings but also reading and considering reports. It will take time. There is also a case for citizens having the right to set the agenda and not simply respond to one that has been handed down to them.

A key issue is one of size. Direct democracy is appealing in smaller communities – clubs, schools, localities. The great cry of the Bolshevik Revolution, 'All power to the soviets', essentially referred to village councils. The Athenian democracy in which 'everyone had the vote' (excepting slaves) might have led to the participation of a few thousand people at a meeting. The relatively small size of the German speaking region in Belgium (at 77,000, hardly more than the population of a town) meant that the judgements of the Citizens' Council and Assemblies would be widely disseminated, making any refusal to implement recommendations difficult. People would encounter each other in the community, strengthening the sense of accountability.

But it is not clear that the same thing applies in larger communities. The Irish form of direct democracy means an assembly of 100 citizens meeting to discuss a particular issue – but that is about 1 person in every 50,000. Much may be made of its representative nature, and it's perfectly true that you can get a fairly accurate view of political opinion by taking a carefully adjusted representative sample just as a polling organisation does. But this still represents a very limited degree of involvement, unlike the village councils in the USSR or the meetings in ancient Athens, where almost everyone could participate. It is essentially representative democracy rather than participatory, with people 'represented' not by those whom they elect but by whoever is identified as coming from their region, belonging to their class, or having their gender. This could even feel rather disempowering for people. Instead of being able to listen to someone's views and support those they liked, they would simply have to hope that the hundred people chosen by lottery with quotas for particular groups would be able to reflect their views.

No one who examines in detail the Citizens' Assembly in Ireland called to examine climate change, for instance, whether it be the individual submissions, the presentations or the eventual proposals on which a vote was taken could fail to be impressed.[17] But it was impressive in the way a conference might be impressive, both for those who took part and those who were able to read the minutes later. That implies some limitations. Everything was packed into two weekends – four days of presentations and discussions – though there was an opportunity to work on the issue outside meetings. The Assembly on climate change was focused on the issue: 'how the state can make Ireland a leader in tackling climate change', which rather steered the subject away from what individuals might do.

The Assembly announced that *'an Expert Advisory Group will be established to assist the work of the Assembly in terms of preparing information and advice.'* This raises another important point, since selecting the specialists from various organisations and advocacy groups who were to appear before each assembly would affect the nature of the discussion. Several high-ranking members or former members of the European Commission delivered keynote presentations, including Connie Hedegaard, a former Danish Minister for Climate

---

17   https://2016-2018.citizensassembly.ie/en/How-the-State-can-make-Ireland-a-leader
      -in-tackling-climate-change/

and Energy and European Commissioner for Climate Action. But people with a more critical attitude towards the EU's actions to counter climate change might also have been selected as 'keynote speakers.'

There is no doubt that the findings of the Citizens' Assembly on climate change in Ireland did lead to a government response. A special parliamentary committee was established to take forward the assembly's recommendations. Its report shaped to a significant degree Ireland's Climate Action Plan which was published in the following year (2019) and included measures for phasing out coal and peat-fired power generation and making car and van sales 100% electric by 2030.[18] Yet there remains more to be done in order to manage Youngs' 'upward cascade.'[19] A permanent forum in which a Citizens Assembly can develop new initiatives of its own would be a more effective expression of grassroots involvement.

Conclusion

The first part of this chapter reiterated the basic principle of sovereignty-sharing, namely that nations agree to create a body empowered to make decisions that are accepted as binding upon them. This is the principle on which what became the EU was held together and something similar might be able to hold a UK Union together outside the EU. Yet this will only be the case if those who work for both are clearly held to account. If the structures that emerge are vehicles for enhancing the careers of political and administrative leaders and are not expression of the popular will, the institutions will not win respect. Sovereignty-sharing will be seen as a programme for the few rather than the many. It will be viewed as leading only to a transnational elite gathering, whether in Brussels or in London, and enjoying the privileges that go with the job.

The chapter therefore examined ways in which citizens might have more influence upon government policies, focusing on the EU in particular. It was critical of initiatives that merely regard citizens as a target audience to whom

---

18   See the Irish Government website which also includes an update for 2023. https://ww
      w.gov.ie/en/publication/ccb2e0-the-climate-action-plan-2019/#

19   His favourite phrase, but a useful one. See for instance pp. 96–97 of *Europe Reset*:
      'Nascent local initiatives must be harnessed to cascade upwards into a revitalised de-
      bate about the EU's future.'

everything organised at the top has to be explained, rather than examining how initiatives might proceed from below and then, in Youngs' words, 'cascade upwards'. From the examination of various attempts to provide effective bottom-up initiatives in this chapter, three conclusions can be drawn.

Firstly, Citizens' Assemblies should be established as permanent entities rather than simply hired and fired to consider particular issues. A Citizens' Assembly should be part of the constitution rather than something summoned occasionally for particular purposes.

Secondly, whilst it is reasonable to say that Citizens' Assemblies should not be forced to abide by a prearranged agenda as if they were nothing more than focus groups, it is perfectly reasonable to say that legislation should only be passed by elected bodies, so that the role of Citizens' Assemblies should be to propose rather than pass laws. A group of citizens elected by lottery, however representative they may be of different social categories, does not have the authority of those who have put their ideas forward in public debate and have received endorsement from voters. They should have a right of initiative in precisely the way that the European Commission has a right of initiative in the EU.

Thirdly, Citizens' Assemblies are much more effective than a simple attempt to throw out additional participation channels. It sounds desirable to talk of providing citizens with a 'European public space,' but there are dangers involved. Such fora can be hijacked by governments which use private citizens and NGOs to push through their own agendas, an exercise in laundering policy priorities. The fora become colonised from above by governments and other organisations with their own agendas. These organisations are happy to be presented with a way of repackaging their agendas as a bottom-up initiative from the grassroots. Once again top-down policies are enabled to masquerade as bottom-up ones. Citizens' Assemblies, on the other hand, are made up of people who are randomly selected. They therefore cannot be hijacked in this way. Though the chapter has pointed to a certain disadvantage in that members of such assemblies don't have to appeal for support and justify their political position, this does at least prevent them from being a conduit for powerful interest groups seeking to present their policies as the outcome of grassroots initiatives.

How, then, might institutional arrangements both at the EU and the UK level develop in a way that does justice to this bottom-up approach and facilitates a true 'upwards cascade' of policy ideas?

Chapter Sixteen: On embedding the upward cascade

The next two chapters will explore what can be done to reform the two unions which have been the subject of this book. The first will consider the European Union, picking up the argument made in the last chapter that a permanent forum in which a Citizens Assembly can develop new initiatives of its own would be a more effective expression of grassroots involvement than one-off or occasional events like a 'forum' or 'convention' for the future of Europe.

The difficulty in determining a different approach lies in knowing what Youngs' 'upward cascade' means. There is much talk of Citizens' Assemblies, of consultations with the people through conventions and conferences, but the right to participate is not the right to decide. There is a lot of talk about being able to 'mainstream substantive new policy ideas', but 'mainstreaming' requires institutional support. Citizens' Assemblies will do little as a voice to be heard unless they become part of the decision-making process.

To be fair to Youngs, this is something he himself recognizes in *Europe Reset* and elsewhere. He writes as follows:

> In some sense, participation across Europe can sometimes feel curiously depoliticized. Citizens' initiatives individualize citizen engagement—they are predicated on citizens participating as individuals. This risks deflecting attention away from the ways citizens still need collective organizations, like parties, unions, and associations. Without these, democracy is left devoid of its necessary collective transmission belts between the individual and the state.[11]

The phrase 'collective transmission belts' expresses very well the need to channel the cascade upwards. To some extent the explosion of citizens' groups,

---

1   See Chapter Four of Youngs' *Europe Reset*, 'Europe as a Citizens' Project', pp. 83–105.

lobby organisations, NGOs and social media groups is in danger of producing noise without substance. Doubtless this is a difficult point to make, in that it sounds like saying the anti-elitist groundswell of support needs some elitist management! 'All power to the soviets' threatens to turn into the vanguard of the proletariat and a new democratic centralism. But channelling does not have to mean controlling.

What it does mean is that 'citizens' participation mechanisms' have to be more than question and answer dialogues or one-off conferences. There are plenty of suggestions about how European citizens could have an impact on EU decisions – influencing the annual work programme of the Commission, shaping the EU budget and so on. But none of this is likely to be effective if it simply boils down to a vague promise to 'listen to the people' when making decisions on spending or deciding priorities. A 'permanent participatory mechanism' means that however impressive the citizens' involvement sounds, *it has to be an ongoing part of the EU structure.*

A resolution from the European Parliament on 'Citizens' Dialogues and Citizens' Participation in EU decision-making', published in June 2021, spoke of a 'transnational European citizens agora, which could be concluded on Europe Day.'[2] The use of an ancient Greek word for a public meeting-place conjured up ideas of citizens filling up the open spaces with ideas and proposals. But this is more likely to be spray than flow. 'Participatory mechanisms' have to be a permanent part of EU decision-making, or else they amount to little more than display.

Piecemeal measures are relatively easy to take. They could be presented in terms of citizens (perhaps randomly chosen) and members of parliament working together on specific issues in a single forum or deciding on a particular budget line (or tapping into 'pilot projects' where small amounts of money for pet projects are agreed). But a 'permanent participatory mechanism' would mean more than this. It would mean that citizens themselves have a 'right of initiative' in determining what issues are to be discussed. The whole structural mechanism under which the EU institutions operate would have to be radically changed. It is this that could make promoting citizens' participation effective if it is taken seriously.

The focus has to be on the Commission, since this is the body with the right of initiative at present. Even when it deliberately seeks to invite outsiders' input, for instance through its European Citizens' Initiative, it tends to be 'insid-

---

2   https://www.europarl.europa.eu/doceo/document/TA-9-2021-0345_EN.html

ers' (well-known NGOs, often part-funded by the EU) who organise the peti-
tions (a million signatures from several different member-states within a year
is a demanding ask, after all). Those outsiders who have heard of it don't think
of it as a vehicle for real change. When one initiative found the requisite million votes (and the vast majority fail to do so) to challenge one of the Juncker
Commission's ten priorities, the planned trade deal with the USA (TTIP – or
the Transatlantic Trade and Investment Partnership), the Commission simply
refused to accept it.[3]

To manage an effective upward cascade, the 'permanent participatory
mechanism' can only be introduced through major institutional reform. Introducing it would certainly represent an attempt to deal with some of the
'democratic deficit' often spoken about in the context of the European Union
and the way it emerged more from a decision by its leaders than through
popular pressure. It would also be appropriate to the British Union or even a
future Union of the Isles. However, 'cascading upwards' is not always an easy
thing to arrange or even very popular. The next section will try to consider this
further.

Permanent participatory mechanisms

The European Union conducted a 'Conference on the Future of Europe', which
it described as a 'citizens-focused, bottom-up exercise' for Europeans to have
their say on what they expect from the European Union.[4] Mindful of problems
with an earlier Convention on the Future of Europe some two decades ago,
which prepared the ill-fated Treaty on a Constitution for Europe that was rejected in national referenda, this time there was meant to be a much greater
opportunity for citizens to become directly involved. The aim was that citizens
should be able to shape the agenda and not simply respond to pre-packaged
recommendations. The Commission produced a preliminary analysis of proposals stemming from the conference in June 2022,[5] and more proposals were

---

3   See Cambien, Kochenov and Muir, editors, *European Citizenship under Stress*, Chapter
     15 'The European Citizens' Initiative in Times of Brexit' by Natassa Athanasiadou,
     pp. 387–410.
4   See https://commission.europa.eu/strategy-and-policy/priorities-2019-2024/new-pus
     h-european-democracy/conference-future-europe_en
5   https://ec.europa.eu/commission/presscorner/detail/en/IP_22_3750

to be outlined in the President's State of the Union address in September 2022, though events in the East meant that Ukraine took centre stage.[6]

Yet this process too had the character of a 'one-off'. Moreover, as with European Citizens' Initiatives, there is uncertainty concerning how far the proposals coming from the Conference will be taken seriously. It remains the case that people are being asked to give their views without any commitment being made to follow up on what they say. Indeed, twelve member states made clear that the conference should create no legal obligations and should not interfere with 'the established legal processes.'[7]

The best way of ensuring that citizens should be able to shape the agenda and not simply respond to pre-packaged recommendations would be to provide for a Citizens' Assembly that could work with members of the Commission in framing legislation. In this way the surfeit of 'dialogues', 'conventions' and 'conferences on the future of Europe' would be replaced by a powerful body which is able to overlook whatever the Commission proposes and is able to make proposals itself. The 'movers and shakers' to whom Monnet went in his day in order to introduce new policies would be unable to move and shake without the consent of the people.

The Economic and Social Committee and the Committee of the Regions are a permanent feature of the EU institutional structure and have to be consulted in many areas where the Commission proposes new legislation, though their powers fall short of co-decision. They are in a similar position to the European Parliament in the earlier years of its existence, when it was merely consulted by the European Council and had no power of co-decision as a legislative authority. It might be possible to link the Citizens' Assemblies with these two bodies that are designed to reflect the interests of the different regions, localities and social groupings in society.

---

6   For the text of the address, see https://ec.europa.eu/commission/presscorner/detail/en/speech_22_5493.

7   Interestingly, the Commission declared that from mid-December 2022 to the end of April 2023, three Citizens' Panels – each with around 150 participants – would have the opportunity to develop concrete recommendations on some of the key initiatives of the 2023 Commission Work Programme. This is the annual work programme which is decided by the Commission – essentially the topics it intends to focus on in the coming year as part of its agenda-setting role within the EU. But as I go on to suggest, input from citizens has to have more bite if it is to be effective. For the Citizens' Panels, see https://citizens.ec.europa.eu/index_en

The power of co-decision in proposing new legislation is the only effective way of managing Youngs' cascade upwards. It must be a permanent mechanism, a reverse flow rather than mere spray. The Citizens' Assembly would have the power to propose legislation, as would the Commission, and since each would have the power to veto the proposals of the other, both Commission officials and citizens' representatives would have to work together in framing legislation. But like the Commission itself, the Citizens' Assembly could not decide what happened to its proposals, even if they were not vetoed by the Commission. Passing them into legislation would remain the business of the Parliament and the Council, who each have the power of co-decision when it comes to passing legislation. A Citizens' Assembly would be a means of introducing the power of co-decision into the right of initiative, while leaving elected bodies to pass legislation.

Ursula von der Leyen promised the following in her candidate's speech when agreeing to be put forward as President of the Commission:

> I want citizens to have their say at a Conference on the Future of Europe... bring together citizens, including a significant role for young people, civil society, and European institutions as equal partners...[8]

'Having their say' is not enough; being 'equal partners' is more appropriate, and it can only work by taking permanent form in the EU structure. The idea of citizens' assemblies, designed perhaps to 'tame' elected politicians, is perfectly suited for 'taming' appointed officials. The descendants of Monnet's 'Commissariat' need to work hand in hand with the people themselves in order to propose new legislation.

The Commission receives reports from groups of experts. There is always an issue about the nature of the expert advice which is being given. No one who studies the history of the EU institutions fails to encounter a lot of arguments about lobbyists (or 'interest groups'). Do they really represent a full range of opinion? How effective is the Transparency Register? Some of the NGOs, including some 'radical' ones, that give their advice to the Commission are also part-funded by it – is that not a problem? The Commission, whatever some of the media have suggested, is a small body of perhaps 30,000 officials, about

---

8   It was repeated in her joint declaration launching the Conference on the Future of Europe with the other EU presidents. See https://futureu.europa.eu/uploads/decidim /attachment/file/6/EN_-_JOINT_DECLARATION_ON_THE_CONFERENCE_ON_THE_ FUTURE_OF_EUROPE.pdf

the same number as those who manage a large city. They could not manage the administration of substantial parts of the affairs of 27 states without relying on outside information.

Yet what is noticeable about the Citizens' Assemblies that have met in the UK or in Ireland, for instance, is that they have received submissions from similar groups of experts – indeed very often, as the example of the Climate Change Citizens' Assembly in Ireland shows, from members of the Commission themselves. It would not be difficult for them to receive, analyse and form their own opinions about the same sets of experts that report to Commission officials. It may be that some of the briefings which officials receive come from sources whose objectivity might be questioned. It may be that the expert groups who advise the Commission, often on an annual basis, may have a clear economic interest in the areas they are giving advice on, even if it is less overt than that of the lobbyists. But this is not the only point. When the problem of lobbying is debated, the focus is usually upon widening the range of groups who are asked to give advice. But it may be that one should also widen the groups to whom the reports are made. The Citizens' Assemblies could be brought together with Commission officials to consider reports from experts.

Like the officials, they will need expert briefings in order to avoid being taken in by the lobbyists who beat their way to their door. But there is no reason to suppose that the ordinary citizen is any less capable than those who have been successful in civil service examinations in understanding how to exercise independence of judgment. If the lobbyists really have Brussels in their clutches, as the title of a recent book by Peter Teffer[9] suggests, a cross-section of citizens will be as effective as any other grouping in releasing their grip.

Radical blinkers

This chapter has proposed to give 'deliberative mini-publics' a permanent place in the institutional mechanism of the European Union. This might help to remove the blinkers from many who claim to stand in a tradition of radical thought in the Anglo-Saxon world, but whose attitude towards the European Union is one of sustained hostility.

---

9   Teffer, Peter *Het lijkt Washington wel: hoe lobbyisten Brussel in hun greep hebben*. See also his article in *EU Observer* 9th May 2020.

One can see this clearly from the publications of Verso books, with its claims to be the leading publisher of 'radical' books on both sides of the Atlantic. In his recent work published by Verso, Roberto Mangabeira Unger discusses the world crises we are all familiar with and suggests fairly obviously that international cooperation is needed but claims that we must foster that cooperation in a world in which sovereign states remain in command. What a conservative basis on which to erect a supposedly radical analysis![10] There is no sense of the opportunity provided by sovereignty-sharing to find a way past the obstacles created by the 'Westphalian' system, unlike many others who would claim to have a more practical approach to fostering international cooperation.[11] Part of the reason for this is the unshakeable conviction on the part of the radical Left that the EU is an elitist organisation in which the people have little or no purchase on their representatives, a theme that runs throughout Perry Anderson's densely packed indictment of one EU institution after another in *Ever-Closer Union? Europe in the West*.[12]

Enough has been said in this book to make clear that there are failings in the European Union where democratic accountability is concerned, failings which go back to Monnet himself. However, the only effective way in which to challenge the continuing criticism from Right and Left of the unique sovereignty-sharing system which is the foundation of the European Union's institutional structure is to place citizens clearly at the centre of that structure. And this can be done not through much-publicised one-off conferences on the future of Europe, but through placing European citizens at the heart of that institutional structure.

Other proposals for reform of the EU

Because so many proposals for reforming the EU fail to recognise its unique character as a supranational system, they try to change it into the only model they think appropriate, that of the nation-state. It must therefore either change itself into 27 nation-states who are in a much looser relationship than applies at present under a sovereignty-sharing system, or they must become

10   See Unger, Roberto Mangabeira *Governing the World without World Government*.
11   See Mc McClintock, John *The Uniting of Nations: An Essay on Global Governance*; Corner, Mark *The Binding of Nations: From European Union to World Union*.
12   See Anderson, Perry *Ever-Closer Union? Europe in the West*.

one nation-state with 27 different regions, the 'superstate' option. Proposals oscillate between the two but they both use the template of the nation-state and its workings. They share the same inability to recognise that the EU is neither a nation-state in the making nor a loose association of states agreeing to have regular discussions together.

This is not the place to go into detail about all the different reform proposals, but we can say that generally they take two forms. The less interesting ones plump for a clearly inter-governmental arrangement. Proposals for new laws would come from the Council of Ministers, which would have to secure the agreement of all member states for legislation to be put forward. The Council would make use of a revised Commission as a civil service to prepare the new laws it wished to introduce. The Parliament would essentially maintain its present role.

Unsurprisingly, this is a structure favoured by French Gaullists. It was de Gaulle, who called for a *Europe des patries*, a Europe made up of nation-states for whom sovereignty-sharing was inappropriate. Essentially, it is the institutional form appropriate to an inter-governmental body like the Council of Europe.[13]

More interesting are proposals that call for a federal Europe much closer in structure to that of the United States. This approach takes to heart the occasionally voiced opinion that the European Union has five presidents and should concentrate on having one. It argues that a good way to restore unity and a sense of purpose to the EU would be by directly electing one EU President, for instance as the USA or France has one elected president, and then allowing that president to co-exist with the present institutional structure.[14]

The Commission President would no longer emerge as the so-called 'Spitzenkandidat' in advance of European elections, as happened with Juncker, or emerge from nowhere like Ursula van der Leyen. Instead, the President of the Commission would be directly elected. Clearly having the powerful post of President of the Commission subject to election rather than horse-trading

---

13   See Duff, *Britain and the Puzzle of European Union*, pp. 22–23. Duff points out that in vetoing UK accession de Gaulle 'deprived himself of a natural ally in his war against federalism' (p. 22).

14   Bogdanor's recent *Britain and Europe in a Troubled World* is careful to emphasise that following Brexit there will not only be a problem for Britain without Europe but also for Europe without Britain. See Chapter 4 of Bogdanor's book, 'Never Closer Union: Europe Without Britain,' pp. 115–145.

between national leaders behind the scenes has advantages. However, it would change the nature of the Commission itself. Instead of being an independent body proposing legislation much in the manner of Monnet's *Commissariat du plan*, the Commission would be subject to the EU President who would take on an executive role. The commissioners would be recast as a kind of cabinet around the President of the Commission on the U.S. model.

In one way an American president appears to have a great deal of power and much more authority, for instance, than a British Prime Minister. A prime minister is constrained by a cabinet. If an important member of a cabinet resigns it can effectively force a Prime Minister from office, as Geoffrey Howe arguably did when he resigned from the cabinet in 1990 and precipitated the end of Margaret Thatcher as Prime Minister. An American president has a cabinet, but he or she can replace them without difficulty. Sometimes a president will appoint someone to be secretary of state who is from another party – as Kennedy did when he made Dean Rusk Defence Secretary. They keep their power for as long as the president wants them there. For this reason, when someone argues in the UK that the Prime Minister is assuming too much power and ignoring his or her cabinet colleagues, the response is often that they are becoming 'presidential.'

However, although this is an accurate description of the executive authority of the president, it fails to take into account their lack of control over the legislature. The American system is based upon a separation of powers. Congress, the Senate and the Supreme Court all have an important role to play, and that includes having the power to reject proposals from the president. In the UK, a Prime Minister has to carry the cabinet, but once that it done there is rarely a problem in having a bill put before parliament passed and turned into law. The upper house, the House of Lords, only has a delaying power. The lower house, the House of Commons, usually has a majority of MPs from the Prime Minister's own party, though coalition governments are not unknown (most recently the Liberal Democrat-Conservative coalition of 2010–2015). In the United States, Congress and the Senate may well have a majority from the main opposition party – in fact it is unusual for an American President to have both Congress and the Senate containing a majority from their own party.

Often in American history a President has found himself (there has yet to be a woman President) unable to get agreement from Congress or the Senate for what he has wanted to do. After the First World War, Woodrow Wilson was unable to secure ratification by the Senate of the Versailles Treaty, thereby ensuring that the United States never joined the League of Nations, forerunner of the

United Nations. Franklin Roosevelt was unable to bring the United States into the Second World War until the bombing of Pearl Harbour in December 1941, despite his support for Britain.[15] Domestic policy has also been severely constrained, as it has been recently over President Biden's spending plans (those of Barack Obama after the financial crisis encountered similar resistance). It is Congress, not the President, that has the right to declare war.

The separation of powers also gives a key role to the Supreme Court. It is the Supreme Court which determines whether a particular decision should rightly be made at the federal level or at the state level. It is the Supreme Court that decides when a president has exceeded his powers, as when President Nixon was required to hand over the tapes which eventually led to his impeachment over Watergate. It was the Supreme Court that determined that President Clinton was not allowed to veto parts of a bill rather than the whole bill (the so-called line-item veto) claiming that for the President to be able to amend or repeal parts of statutes passed by Congress was unacceptable.[16] A bill had to be approved or rejected by a president in its entirety.

The point is not to assess the rights and wrongs of this particular decision but simply to show that although presidential powers might look overwhelming when seen in terms of the president's executive authority, that authority is constrained by the other institutions in the USA – Congress, the Senate and the Supreme Court.

Insofar as both involve a separation of powers and firm control over the executive, the institutional arrangements in the United States bear some resemblance to those in the European Union. The European Union also relies on a 'Supreme Court', the European Court of Justice, to make decisions on whether the European institutions are acting in conformity with European Law. The Commission is often called the 'executive' of the European Union. It is more constrained than an ordinary executive since it can only propose legislation in certain policy areas. Nevertheless, like any US President, it knows that its proposals must win the approval of both the other key institutions, in this case the

---

15   Professors Vernon Bogdanor and Christina Rodriquez gave an interesting lecture on the British and American constitutions at Gresham College, London in 2008. It is possible to access the transcript at https://www.gresham.ac.uk/watch-now/british-and-americ an-constitutions

16   See the report of the National Constitution Center. Its blog is entitled 'Looking Back: The Supreme Court decision that ended Nixon's Presidency.' In other words it was the Court which had the ultimate say. https://constitutioncenter.org/blog/anniversary-of-united-states-v-nixon

Council of Ministers and the European Parliament, which under the ordinary legislative procedure must both agree to pass its proposals if they are to become European Law.

There is certainly much about the structure of the European Union and its separation of powers that does bear comparison with the United States, even though it is a Union of twenty-seven nation-states rather than one. Indeed, this should not be surprising. In both cases there was the pressure of an outside power forcing unity upon distinct groupings that were often at loggerheads with one another, the thirteen colonies breaking away from Britain in one case, Western Europe under the threat of communism and the Soviet Union (and now the Russian Federation) on the other. In both cases a difficult but necessary unity provided the basis for further expansion, despite setbacks such as the civil war in America. There are certainly crucial differences, of which the fact that the USA is a single nation-state is fundamental. But there is a shared recognition that external threats made compromise and new forms of association unavoidable. In its own way the growth of the USA was a 'peace project', to cite Bogdanor's phrase, like the European Union. The New World, finding migrants from Europe often settling in particular states, was determined to prevent the differences evident in the old world from reproducing themselves on the other side of the Atlantic. America's involvement in promoting peace in Europe after World War II, forcing cooperation between previous combatants through the Marshall Plan, was vital to European recovery. But America had itself received millions of Europeans in the previous century and had managed to accommodate them without finding itself host to their conflicts. The power of the American constitution as the birth certificate of a new country and even a new order has to be seen in this context.

But does this resemblance between the two mean that the institutional set-up of the EU could be recast in order to become more like that of the USA? It is difficult to see how this could happen in the case of twenty-seven different nation-states. Would the Council of Ministers accept such a diminution of its role if the EU President were to have equivalent powers to an American President? Would President Macron or Chancellor Scholz really accept having the sort of authority in the European Union that even a powerful senator has in the USA?

The same problem arises with another option which would try to recast the role of the European parliament so that it became more like a national parliament. To do that it would have to have parties vying with one another before elections, identifying themselves with manifestos and then implementing them when in power. The victors would need to form a government to implement the manifesto after each election. How would that be done? Once again, the Commission's role would essentially be that of a civil service, implementing the policies of the government chosen by the elected European Parliament rather than the policies of an elected President.

Meanwhile the Council of Ministers would have a role similar to that of *Bundesrat* in Germany, in which the different *Länder* are represented and where special emphasis is put upon regional interests (in the case of the EU it would be the interests of the different member states). In the UK many propose this as a role which the House of Lords could have in a new British Constitution.[17] However, as with the idea of an elected President, it is doubtful whether there is a sufficient degree of unity among the twenty-seven different states for such a system to be workable. Would the Council of Ministers really accept a reformed House of Lords role in this new constitution, protecting the interests of individual member states and perhaps with a power of veto over one or two pieces of legislation thrown at them? Lord Macron sounds as unlikely as Senator Macron.

The radical options oscillate between, on the one hand, treating the EU as a single federal state with a lot of autonomy for its internal regions, like the USA, and on the other hand a treaty arrangement in which states reach an agreement but lack an effective means of enforcing it. A single elected leader or a single European government formed out of parliamentary elections suggest one nation-state; on the other hand, an all-powerful Council of Ministers would end up acting only on the basis of unanimity without any binding European law.

None of these proposals recognises the way in which the EU is a unique system which is constantly being 'reduced' to a single nation-state in the making, or else to 27 nation-states in some sort of loose but non-binding confederation. It is neither of these things. But it is precisely the role of the Commission as a neutral body that represents the key to maintaining the EU's unique character. Turn the Commission into a civil service carrying out the wishes of an elected

---

17   Not least the Labour Party in its recent document which calls for the replacement of the House of Lords with 'a democratic chamber that is permanently closer to the British people because it is more representative of the nations and regions of the United Kingdom.' (p. 9) See https://labour.org.uk/wp-content/uploads/2022/12/Commission-on-t he-UKs-Future.pdf

President or Parliament, or the decisions of an all-powerful Council of Ministers, and you are essentially returning to the form of governance that applies to the nation-state.

It is the independent character of the Commission, as a neutral body that can propose but not pass laws, which is crucial to the EU structure. But how can that be maintained without it being seen as an elitist grouping of unelected officials, living comfortably and behaving unaccountably, as it is seen by both Right and Left in the UK? The argument of this book is that it can only be done by introducing a much more important role for 'deliberative mini-publics' in the formulation of legislation, integrating a citizens' assembly into the institutional structure of the EU rather than making it an optional extra when EU leaders decide that they need to seek the views of EU citizens. That is the proposal being made here. It would maintain the structure of a supranational organisation but overcome the democratic deficit through the power of the citizens' assembly to initiate new legislation and exercise veto power over the proposals of Commission officials. It would seek to deal with the democratic deficit without undermining the unique structure of the European Union.

Conclusion

Andrew Duff, in his *Britain and the Puzzle of European Union*, points out that a number of important reforms have been carried through in the last couple of years as a response to the pandemic crisis.[18] He cites the Recovery and Resilience Facility of 672.5 billion euros which was agreed in February 2021, as a new phase in the development of EU fiscal policy. He also mentions a decision taken in 2020 to create fresh sources of revenue for the EU budget in the form of new taxes. The Russian invasion of Ukraine is bound to create movement towards a common energy policy and more military collaboration. He also has a number of useful suggestions for improving the role of the EU institutions, particularly the Parliament of which he was once an MEP. However, the point of this chapter was not to explore specific proposals for reform but to try to elucidate how the unique nature of the EU might be preserved in the context of making necessary reforms.

---

18   Duff, Andrew *Britain and the Puzzle of European Union* Chapter 10 'The State of Europe.' See pp. 136–137 for the discussion of fiscal policy.

In *The EU: An Introduction*, I suggested that measures to reform the EU rarely show much understanding of its unique character. In his book *Roller-Coaster* Ian Kershaw suggests that the Europe most Europeans identify with is…

> …neither the "Europe of the fatherlands" favoured by Charles de Gaulle (and others) nor the supranational entity that was associated with Jacques Delors; rather, it stands as a unique entity somewhere between.[19]

Yet 'somewhere between' will not do. What makes the history of Europe unique in the years after World War Two is precisely the supranational entity associated with Monnet and Schuman (Delors came later). The 'unique entity' created out of a mass of warring (and still warring) European states is precisely the sovereignty-sharing relationship between nation-states envisaged by the founders of a supranational system. There is no halfway house somewhere between this and de Gaulle's 'L'Europe des Patries.' De Gaulle's idea is simply a continuation of the old inter-governmental system reaching back to the Treaty of Westphalia in 1648 and beyond.

It is remarkable how few of those who write about the European Union understand that we are dealing neither with the traditional forms of cooperation between nation-states nor with the attempt to create one large superstate – a USE to be a powerful bloc on the other side of the Atlantic to match the USA. We return to the point of the EU's uniqueness. It is not an inter-governmental union, because its members have agreed to share sovereignty. Nor is it a federal union in which a single nation-state gives a great deal of autonomy to its constituent parts, as in the case of Belgium. It could perhaps be called 'confederal', depending on how the word was defined. In practice, however, it needs to be recognised that its distinctive character must be reflected in its distinctive institutions. Having one person elected to the presidency of 27 states does not reflect that distinctive character. Asking whether one could imagine President Macron – or any French President – as the leading senator considering legislative proposals from the elected president of the EU may not appear to be a very 'systematic' approach to assessing constitutional proposals, but it surely does point to the likely reception such proposals would receive.

It is for this reason that the book does not propose the sort of radical overhaul to deal with the EU's 'democratic deficit' that would essentially change it into something that fits the nation-state template but not its own unique character. It has proposed instead that the most appropriate institutional reform

---

19   Kershaw, Ian *Roller-Coaster: Europe 1950–2017*, p. 545.

for the European Union would be one in which 'deliberative mini-publics' or citizens' assemblies became a permanent part of the institutional structure of the EU rather than an additional option for consultations on specific issues. This would not be an unimportant change, since so much of the criticism of the EU, from both sides of the political spectrum, stresses its 'democratic deficit' and in particular the fact that the Commission comprises unelected officials who in most policy areas have an exclusive right of initiative. If this is indeed the ghost of Monnet's *Commissariat du plan*, it needs to have representatives of the people with an equal power to propose new legislation and veto that of officials.

This is a proposed reform that would not upset the unique nature of the European Union as a sovereignty-sharing body, whereas other proposals would compromise that uniqueness. They would either send the EU in the direction of becoming an inter-governmental talking shop, in the manner of the Council of Europe, or else in the direction of becoming a single nation-state writ large, with the member states reduced to regions of a European 'superstate'. It cannot be stated too often that these two apparently very different approaches in fact amount to the same thing, a belief in the inviolability of the nation-state unaffected by any binding legal framework such as European Law. Gaullists and some of the federalists want the same thing – the rule of the untrammelled nation-state, with the only difference being that some of the federalists want to create a very big nation-state out of the different members of the European Union. They argue that the EU has helped to curb the excesses of nationalism, but then they talk of the EU as if it ought to become another nation-state writ large. Thus, they manage to bury the very uniqueness of the Union which they are trying to defend.

The de Clercq report which was examined in the last chapter provides an example of this. Like many other attempts to popularise the EU, it seems on the one hand to say that the nation-state is the source of all conflict and then on the other hand that it wants to turn the 27 members of the EU into a big nation-state. The icons that are supposed to mediate the enchantment of the EU to the people – the famous flag, once described as a clock-face without any hands, the anthems, the passports, the trophies and public holidays ('Europe Day', May 9th, is the date of the Schuman Declaration in 1950) – are essentially the trappings of nationhood. A 'rebranding exercise' designed to sell Europe as something different from those national groupings which had spent much of the previous century at war with one another ends up presenting Europe as a bigger version of what was supposed to be causing all the problems. Quite apart from the fact that selling the EU as a commodity is not a way of making it democratically accountable, many of those tasked with selling it don't understand what is unique about the product they are selling.

Hence while the idea of having a power of co-decision (jointly exercised by the Commission and the Citizens' Assembly) in the proposing as well as the passing of European legislation might appear less radical than proposals seeking something more like the American presidential system or the inter-governmental arrangements of the Council of Europe, it is arguably more consistent with the unique character of the European Union as a sovereignty-sharing body. It is this unique character of a sovereignty-sharing body that must be maintained in any proposals for reform.

What, however, about that other union, the one which might hold together the United Kingdom in future years? What sort of structure might that have? The next chapter will consider this.

Chapter Seventeen: The Future of the UK

When in 2019, with Lady Hale sporting her famous spider-shaped brooch, the Supreme Court disallowed the government's advice to the Queen on the prorogation of Parliament, it declared (in paragraph 40 of its ruling) that though the UK did not have a single document setting out the constitution of the UK, it had one 'established over the course of our history by common law, statutes, conventions and practice'.[1] This chapter considers the chances of something more focused emerging in the next few years than a set of conventions and practices garnered through time.

The first point to make is that it is unlikely that significant constitutional reform will happen under the present Conservative government. During the 2019 British general election, Boris Johnson's Conservative government promised to instigate major constitutional reforms. However, this has not happened.[2]

It is undoubtedly the Labour Party which takes the idea of constitutional reform most seriously. It has a clear practical reason for being interested in saving the Union – or at least Great Britain. Its strength – perhaps its survival – in electoral terms is closely associated with the survival of Britain. Before the rise of the Scottish National Party, Labour had the overwhelming majority of seats in Scotland, as it still has in Wales. Its position might be compared to that of the Liberal Party a century ago, which was then heavily dependent on the votes of Irish MPs. In 1910 the Liberal government remained in power because it had the support of 80 Irish MPs, even though the Conservatives had just as many seats as the Liberals. By 1922, when the Irish Free state had been formed whose

---

1   UK Supreme Court 41 (2019), Judgment (on the Application of Miller) (Appellant) v The Prime Minister (Respondent).
2   See Schleiter, P., Fleming, T.G. *Radical departure or opportunity not taken? The Johnson Government's Constitution, Democracy and Rights Commission.* British Politics (2022).

MPs attended the Irish Parliament or *Dail* rather than Westminster, that support had gone. Indeed, the Irish MPs who remained in the Westminster Parliament were Unionists from Northern Ireland who supported the Conservatives.[3] Unless one wants to call the Coalition government of 2010–15 a 'Liberal' government, one can say that the Liberals never formed a government again (though for other reasons besides the loss of Irish support).

There is evidence that the Labour Party might embrace some of the reforms made by the Welsh *Senedd*, whose leader is, after all, also the leader of the Labour Party in Wales. Three years before the *Senedd* proposals, in November 2016, former Labour Prime Minister Gordon Brown made a speech to the Fabian society calling for a 'people's convention' on the constitution and outlining suggestions for constitutional reform. There was also a long report (234 pages) overseen by Labour peer Pauline Bryan, made for Jeremy Corbyn, the leader of the Labour Party in 2016, called *Remaking the British State*.[4] It anticipated the *Senedd* proposals in calling for the Lords to be replaced with a federal senate of the nations and English regions – effectively a UK version of the German *Bundestag* – and proposed various new financial and policy powers for the devolved nations. It is noteworthy that theScottish Labour leader Anas Sarwar has also backed replacing the Lords with an elected 'senate of the nations and regions.' Of all the reform proposals in the *Senedd*report, this is perhaps the one most likely to succeed.

In December 2020, the new Labour leader, Keir Starmer, announced that Labour intended to launch a UK-wide constitutional commission and the former Prime Minister Gordon Brown was appointed to lead it. At the Scottish Labour annual conference of 2022 Starmer assured delegates that it would 'create a new blueprint for a new Britain'. After an earlier suggestion that more details would be available in time for the Labour conference in 2022, it turned out that they would be forthcoming 'in the coming months.' Then at the end of 2022 Labour announced proposed constitutional reforms, although once again further details are yet to be released. However, there was a clear call for the Lords to be replaced by a body representing the nations and regions.[5] This has con-

---

3   See 'The General Election of January 1910 and the bearing of the results on some problems of representation' by S. Rosenbaum in the *Journal of the Royal Statistical Society*, Vol 73, No 5 (May 1910), pp. 473–528.

4   See https://www.scottishlabourleft.co.uk/uploads/6/4/8/1/6481256/remaking_the_british_state_for_the_many_not_the_few_final_report_v2.pdf

5   The document has now been published https://labour.org.uk/wp-content/uploads/2022/12/Commission-on-the-UKs-Future.pdf. There is a short but useful summary of the

sistently been the core of Labour reform proposals. At the same time there are a lot of questions that remain unanswered in Labour's programme, not least whether it recognises that power needs to be shared rather than simply given away under its newly adopted 'take back control' slogan.

The Liberal Democrats have long pressed for constitutional reform because of their concern about the voting system and they have a long history of supporting an elected second chamber and devolution. They would probably back some of the reforms Labour proposes. No one can predict with any confidence what is likely to happen in the next election and beyond, but one can have a glimmer of hope that serious constitutional reform might finally be embraced by a Westminster government. At least there is a possible roadmap for it to happen, most likely through the election of a Labour government or some kind of left-wing coalition which is both determined to maintain the Union and has some conception of what needs to be done to ensure its survival.

Bearing in mind the points made discussing the *Senedd* proposals, we can suggest the basic ingredients of what, whether or not it becomes enshrined in a UK written constitution, we consider necessary in order to strengthen the United Kingdom as a multinational state and its ties to the Republic of Ireland.

The *first* ingredient must be an acceptance that the House of Commons will not have the sort of supremacy in a future UK Union that is claimed for it now under the principle of the sovereignty of Parliament (or of the House of Commons). Since 1975, when the first referendum on Europe took place (and people voted by two to one to remain in the EEC), the principle of parliamentary sovereignty has effectively been undermined, even if the referenda have strictly speaking been consultative. It could be said that by his attempted prorogation in 2019 Johnson was simply reminding Parliament that it had to carry out the will of the people, whatever its own views – and many people interpreted Johnson's actions in this way at the time.[6] Doubtless he also recognised that this was a position that could carry him to power with a healthy majority as the 'people's champion' (which it did at the end of that year). But it also meant that the basis of whatever constitution the UK had began to look more like the

---

proposals and problems associated with them by the *Institute for Government*. See http s://www.instituteforgovernment.org.uk/explainer/labours-constitutional-proposals

6   Two former Conservative Prime Ministers accused him of stifling democratic debate. But he could always claim that he was only stifling the ability of MPs to override the decision of the people – and proceeded to call a General Election in December 2019 which he won. See Stephens, *Britain Alone*, p. 408.

sovereignty of the people than the sovereignty of Parliament. Though there was a great deal in the popular press that represented the issue as one of parliament versus the courts, it should more appropriately have been seen as one of parliament, supported by the courts, versus the people and their 'leader.' It was the sovereignty of elected representatives in Parliament on the one hand, and the sovereignty of the people expressed through a referendum on the other. When in 2019 the Supreme Court declared that the government's advice to the Queen on the prorogation of Parliament should be disallowed, it made clear that it viewed the outcome of the Brexit vote, though not 'legally binding', as 'politically and democratically' binding.[7]

Brexit undermined the sovereignty of Parliament because it was a political decision based on a referendum in which the people voted against the wishes of most MPs, including the leaders of all the major parties. For four years and through changes of government the MPs struggled to accept a verdict that most of them believed to be against the interests of their country. However, in the end they had to go along with it. They decided that you can't first ask the people and then ignore their answer. It is therefore arguable that the absolute sovereignty of Parliament is not even something that Parliament itself feels committed to. By its actions if not its words, the Westminster Parliament has shown that it would be better to begin, like the American constitution, with 'We the people' as the basis of any constitutional arrangements for the UK.

If one begins with 'the people' one is free to move away from parliamentary sovereignty and towards a system which is more like both that of the United States and the European Union, containing checks and balances. The sovereignty of Parliament as traditionally understood would give way to a separation of powers.

How would such a separation of powers appear if it was to be adopted by a UK Constitution? One obvious element, and probably the one which receives the most support, would be the creation of an effective second chamber. The *second* ingredient of a UK constitution is reform of the House of Lords. People generally feel that it needs reform (though some prefer abolition), but there is concern that a reformed House of Lords might be a threat to the supremacy of the Commons. Hence a separation of powers proves an unavoidable element of constitutional reform. While the House of Lords remains a Ruritanian body, its very insignificance means that it does not raise too many difficult questions.

---

7   See paragraph 7 of the judgment cited in note 1.

But give the Upper House a clear role which is distinct from that of the Commons, and you are bound to raise the question of how the relation between the two houses is going to be mediated in the event of disagreement.

While such views are understandable, it is noteworthy that despite a century of reform proposals, none of them has included what might be called a territorial element. This is surely an oversight. The future role of the Upper House lies in what Gordon Brown in his Fabian lecture called 'replacing the Lords with a federal senate of the nations and English regions', in other words something akin to the German *Bundesrat*, similar to the report Pauline Bryan made for Jeremy Corbyn and which seems to have been endorsed in proposals made by Labour at the end of 2022, backed by its leader Keir Starmer. One could also point to the way the U.S. Senate is made up of two senators per state, whatever the population of the state (which varies considerably), and the way Canadian senators, though appointed by the Prime Minister, come from specific provinces. About one quarter of the members of the Spanish senate are chosen by regional legislatures. In all these cases some attempt is made to ensure that a second chamber reflects the importance of regional differences. It is noticeable, moreover, that Brown suggested in his lecture 'significant devolution of policymaking and financial powers to English regions and councils, including borrowing,' and this seems to be maintained in the Labour Party's proposals at the end of 2022. The English regions, rather than the English nation as a whole, are therefore treated as part of a devolution settlement alongside the devolved nations.

Gordon Brown was right to point to the need for additional powers at the local/regional level in England. There can be all sorts of arguments about how 'the regions' should be defined. Would one of these regions be the capital, with its ten million inhabitants as large as all the devolved nations outside England combined? Would there be some sort of division between 'inner London' and 'outer London'? There would certainly be some difficulties in what might be called dividing up England, but two things make the inclusion of regions a good idea. One is the obvious need for more devolution of power to councils in England, which have had their powers steadily eroded since the 1970s, when their budgets were increasingly determined from the centre and their powers limited by reorganisation, for instance through the abolition of the metropolitan county councils in the 1980s by the Conservative government under Margaret Thatcher. The other is the advantage of a grouping of members one of which (England) does not comprise five-sixths of the UK in terms of population. Even a single authority for Greater London would not be anything remotely as dominant.

Hence an Upper Chamber which is made up of what Gordon Brown called a senate of devolved nations and English regions makes sense. Like the *Bundesrat* it could be given the power to veto some legislation. He also suggested that it could have the power to ratify international treaties, including the sort of trade deals which Boris Johnson referred to as facilitated by Brexit but without showing that he wanted the devolved nations to be required to give their consent. It should be noted that Gordon Brown, partly because of his years representing a Scottish constituency, has consistently emphasised the way in which Brexit throws the future of the Union into doubt and even described it, as a BBC News report quoted him saying, as 'sleepwalking into oblivion and nationalism' in a speech given in August 2019.[8]

If there are to be two effective chambers, there has to be an independent arbiter to determine what legislation may come before the Upper House and whether it is a subject on which it should exercise its veto power. Hence the second ingredient of a UK Constitution demands the *third* ingredient, an effective Supreme Court. In Germany the Federal Constitutional Court (*Bundesverfassungsgericht*) is responsible for making sure that all government institutions comply with the constitution. The judges are elected equally by both Houses of Parliament (*Bundestag* and *Bundesrat*). The court has the power to disapply legislation that does not comply with the constitution, and it also decides whether a bill adopted by the *Bundestag* requires the consent of the *Bundesrat* in order to become law (all legislation is passed to the 'upper house', but it may only veto legislation which has particular significance for the regions, a principle which is obviously subject to interpretation). As the website of the German Parliament itself makes clear:

> Disagreements on this issue are not uncommon between the Federal Government and the Bundestag on the one hand and the Bundesrat on the other. The Federal Constitutional Court has had to decide more than once whether a bill requires, or should have required, the consent of the Bundesrat. If the Bundesrat fails to give its consent to a bill of this kind, then the bill becomes null and void.[9]

---

8   https://www.bbc.com/news/uk-politics-49309113
9   https://www.bundestag.de/en/parliament/function/legislation/14legrat-245876

Apart from being required to determine what should properly come before the two houses of parliament, the Supreme Court will have a further role, which is connected to the *fourth* ingredient of a UK constitution, subsidiarity. The principle of subsidiarity, which the UK insisted must be a part of the institutional set-up of the European Union when it was a member, emphasised that measures should be taken at the lowest level of government consistent with efficiency. This is a good principle and is another area where the Supreme Court should be able to make a final ruling. For instance, The Welsh government suggested in 2021 that the devolved institutions should be responsible for policing and the administration of justice in their territories. It pointed out that during the COVID pandemic the Welsh Government created wide-ranging criminal offences that were part of its own response to COVID, differing in several respects from those in England. It was perfectly entitled to do this – the four nations had different policies on handling COVID. However, political responsibility for policing and enforcing these offences remained nominally with the Home Secretary, with no accountability to the democratic institutions of Wales.[10] This made no sense, and it would be justifiable to ask for further devolution in this regard. But it should be for a legal body like the Supreme Court to decide the matter.

The chapter on Wales in this book used the example of funding for the HS2 project to suggest that railway infrastructure should be managed by Wales rather than by England and Wales together. In Scotland, to give another example, Monica Lennon, a member of the Scottish Parliament, has proposed devolving extra powers like drugs policy and social security.[11] Again, in his lecture to the Fabian Society, Gordon Brown suggested that employment law might be devolved in order to preserve the employment protections contained in the social chapter, which the Conservatives had opted out of at the time of the Maastricht treaty and then the Labour government of 1997 opted back into.

---

10   See the Welsh government's programme for reform of the justice system in Wales. https://www.gov.wales/delivering-justice-for-wales-summary-and-work-prog ramme-html

11   As *The Scotsman* reported, she was in favour of 'devo max' rather than independence. Her desire to devolve drugs policy was associated with a desire to decriminalise certain drugs, but the point here is to stress that she wanted more things devolved. See https://www.scotsman.com/news/politics/monica-lennon-insists-scottish-labour -should-not-stand-in-the-way-of-a-second-scottish-independence-referendum-3105 531

The same argument could be used over the powers enjoyed by – or withheld from – the English regions. One can give examples where the English regions could make a case for more control of their affairs, just as one could give examples from the devolved nations. Indeed, that was a point frequently made by the so-called 'metro mayors' during the recent pandemic, when it was argued that local areas should have more autonomy when deciding on measures like lockdown.[12] Subsidiarity when the UK was inside the EU was all about 'not having everything decided by Brussels'. Now it will be about 'not having everything decided by Westminster' – and once again, it is the courts that must arbitrate.

The *fifth* ingredient concerns the method by which the different members of a multinational and multi-regional state work together. It therefore requires an effective Council of Ministers. It has been repeatedly emphasised that what is fundamental to a future UK Union is not only how much is handed downwards (or conceivably taken back up), but how the different members of that Union should be able to decide certain policies together. As Keating puts it, 'while the UK settlement provides for extensive self-rule, shared rule is almost completely absent.'[13]

If it is a question of how power can be *shared* as well as how it can be divided, there need to be intergovernmental mechanisms so that ministers of the different governments inside the UK become used to sitting round a table together. 'Joint Ministerial Committees' of the UK were, indeed, established as part of the devolution settlement, but the only one to meet regularly was the one on Europe, where a common position to be taken at the European Council was discussed. At the invitation of the UK, devolved ministers were allowed to participate in the UK delegation to the Council of the EU. They had to represent the UK as a whole rather than their own interests, but the fact this happened at all shows they were trusted to be able to speak for the UK. Ironically, it was precisely in a European context that joint working between the nations became a reality – a joint working that Brexit has put paid to. Worse still, when Brexit made it clear that there would be a repatriation of powers to the UK, the last thing the UK government was willing to do was share those repatriated competences with the devolved nations to develop a policy of joint working on

---

12   *The Guardian* reported on COVID-19 measures being too 'nationally driven'. See https://www.theguardian.com/world/2020/may/18/covid-19-strategy-too-nationally-driven-warn-uks-regional-mayors

13   Keating, *State and Nation*, p. 75.

matters such as agriculture and fisheries which had previously been EU competences. It insisted that the powers would be brought back to Westminster, though later modifying its position to one of doing so if necessary. In either event, its allergy to teamwork remained firmly in place. In 2018 the Advocate General, Lord Keen declared in the House of Lords in March 2018 that 'if we are to have a single market for the United Kingdom, we require a body to have jurisdiction over that single market...that ultimately has to be the Parliament of the United Kingdom.'[14] In the previous year the Welsh Government had proposed UK-wide frameworks negotiated on the basis of equality among the four nations, but such proposals for teamwork (beyond offers of 'consultation' with the devolved nations) were ignored.

It is therefore vital to determine how the 'four nations' (or if regions are thrown in the dozen or so nations and regions inside the UK) should address issues that *can only be tackled jointly*. This is increasingly an issue in the early 2020s as the Conservative government emphasises post-Brexit trade opportunities and the devolved nations object to the way they are being railroaded into them.[15]

It has already been mentioned that where the EU trade deal with Canada was concerned, Belgium could not ratify it without securing ratification from the regions – and Wallonia took some time to give its consent. There is a good case for saying that the UK cannot devolve to the regions all the powers that used to be held by Brussels when the UK was a member of the European Union and was part of the common commercial policy. It has to be able to reach a trade deal of its own as the United Kingdom. But it may well be that this should involve the nations working together in order to reach a joint position on a trade deal. How would that work? Would each nation be given a veto? Might the UK reaching a trade deal have to wait upon, for instance, Welsh consent in the way that a trade deal between the EU and Canada waited upon Wallonian consent? What is needed, as Mark Drakeford recognised in the *Senedd*'s proposals, is a viable way in which the nations can jointly reach a decision in areas that are of

---

14   It should be added that Lord Keen later resigned as Advocate General over Prime Minister Boris Johnson's plans to breach parts of the Brexit divorce treaty.

15   See the update on the latest deals given in September 2022 by the BBC in one of its useful 'reality checks'. https://www.bbc.com/news/uk-47213842 Note that deals with New Zealand and Australia have provoked concerns among UK farmers about being undercut by cheap imports. This is precisely the argument used by EU farmers to defend the Common External Tariff imposed by the EU under the Common Agricultural Policy.

concern to all of them. The devolved governments certainly have considerable scope in policy matters but are not part of any effective bodies that enable them to participate in the joint management of UK policies. And in the modern era trade deals involve questions of labour standards and environmental rules that take them beyond purely economic considerations. A joint approach therefore becomes even more necessary.

The allocation of resources between the different parts of the United Kingdom is another area in which joint decision-making is woefully lacking and so a consistent system remains unavailable. Everyone accepts the limitations of the so-called Barnett Formula, which has lasted decades (as did its predecessor the Goschen Formula, based on relative levels of probate duties in the different parts of the UK), largely because it is relatively easy to apply.[16] It is not, however, a needs-based system, which would be more appropriate both for the devolved nations and for disadvantaged regions of England. The particular needs of disadvantaged areas are therefore dealt with through bargaining between the centre and a troublesome part of the periphery in order to produce a one-off bespoke deal to lessen tension with that particular part of the UK. If, however, there was really joint management of the allocation of resources, a needs-based system could be developed and applied with a clear explanation of why particular areas received more. A welfare state whose remit runs to all parts of the UK should be managed jointly by those different parts.

Pan-UK welfare measures are now a century old, dating back to the Liberal government of 1906 which brought in unemployment insurance and old age pensions. These were extended by the Labour government of 1945–51.[17] They are not, however, universally applied, even if disagreement is basically 'tinkering at the edges' rather than about fundamental principles. England has toyed with introducing market mechanisms into the health service and has introduced university fees. Scotland has rejected such moves and (like Wales) has abolished prescription charges. Whether one is in favour of such measures or not, the usual approach is to say that these must be devolved matters and if the Scots decide to use their money in this way it's their decision. But even though this must be appropriate for many areas of expenditure, it would be useful to consider for a moment what it would look like if Scotland and Wales sat round a table with English representatives to discuss the workings of the

---

16   See Keating, *State and Nation*, Chapter 9, pp. 153–169 which discusses Goschen and Barnett.

17   See Keating, *State and Nation*, pp. 153–156, 'The Welfare State'.

supposedly 'national' health service, devised by the Welsh politician Aneurin Bevan to be the same everywhere in the UK, and reached a common position on (say) prescription charges, which possibly might entail a veto exercised by Scottish, Welsh, Northern Irish and a number of English regional representatives who could manage a blocking minority in the manner of the system used in the European Union. It is this way of working that has never been properly tried. Everything is based on a hand-out to the Scots who can go and 'make their own mess' if they want. The one thing they can't do is sit at the top table and join in the decision-making process at the highest level – even for what is clearly applicable throughout the UK, like the NHS or the interestingly named 'universal credit,' a fledgling and controversial system of benefit payments which might also be jointly determined by the different parts of the Kingdom to which that universality supposedly belongs. Keating is right to observe that...

> Neither Labour nor Conservative governments have been open to the idea that the devolved bodies should be able to restrain Westminster or bind it to higher standards of universal services.[18]

This is where a Council of Ministers is crucial. It could take decisions on the basis of unanimity or through a form of majority voting, depending on the issue (as happens inside the European Union). When the Council of Ministers from different parts of the UK met a majority vote would be binding upon dissenting members. Given that nine of the dozen members of this Council would be from England, it might be necessary to say that if unanimity wasn't required any two or perhaps three dissenting members would be enough to derail a proposal. Alternatively, there could be a form of weighted voting. There is a European precedent in terms of 'qualified majority voting' (QMV), which means that larger member states can't simply steamroller over the wishes of smaller ones. A form of QMV for the UK could ensure that a proposal needed support from outside England as well as within it.

In the EU some matters are community competences to be determined at the EU level. Other matters are 'national competences' to be determined at the member state level. Similarly, one could say that certain matters within the UK are to be determined at UK level, and certain matters at the national or regional level, for instance by the Welsh *Senedd* or Greater Manchester. In some cases, unanimity would be required for action to be taken and in other cases a qualified majority.

---

18   Keating, *State and Nation*, p. 169.

It is not only the European Union which provides a useful point of comparison for a Council of Ministers. The all-Ireland Council which was part of the Belfast Agreement provides another. The power-sharing which was so essential to the Belfast Agreement could be extended to all the devolved nations in addressing such issues as reaching trade agreements post-Brexit. The imagination shown in helping to bring the 'Troubles' (hopefully) to an end needs to be repeated in seeking to maintain the United Kingdom intact, or even in creating a Union of the Isles, so long as this would in no way affect the status of the Republic of Ireland as an independent nation-state just like other members of the EU such as France or Italy.

The *sixth* ingredient is the involvement of a Citizens' Assembly. The UK's use of Citizens' Assemblies so far has been open to question. Climate Assembly UK produced a report in September 2020 called the *Path to Net Zero*.[19] The assembly was treated rather like a focus group used by advertisers to see what products are acceptable to the public. It was commissioned by cross-party select committees of the House of Commons with an emphasis on the need for a cross-party consensus – i.e., explicitly looking for something that could be supported by as many people as possible. 'Forging consensus is what we do on our cross-party select committees, on the basis of the evidence and what in our judgement is acceptable to the public,' explained the Conservative Committee Chairs, Mel Stride MP and Darren Jones MP.[20] Moreover, even if they accepted the recommendations of the Citizens' Assembly, as select committees they could only advise government, not determine its policy.

When the Conservative government published its 'net zero strategy' in response to the report, it was accompanied by a blueprint from a so-called 'behavioural insights team' which studied how to change public behaviour. Though the blueprint was withdrawn a few hours later, the notion of a so-called 'nudge unit' reminds us once again of the techniques of persuasion developed by advertisers. The report stressed that governments had been prepared to use legislation to change behaviour in the past – such as rules on where people could smoke (and the price of nicotine), rules to make driving as safe as possible (wearing seat belts, not drinking or using mobile phones when driving) or insisting on vaccinations (for instance MMR jabs for children). There would be little difference in 'nudging' people by means of similar methods to eat less

---

19   https://www.climateassembly.uk/report/read/

20   See the Foreword from Committee Chairs, part of the Preface to 'The Path to Net Zero'. https://www.climateassembly.uk/report/read/plain.html

meat or make fewer flights, even though one could expect similar protests about restricting human freedom. But this is not the cascading upwards explored in an earlier chapter. It is trying to make the flow coming down acceptable to those who are about to be drenched.

In other words, the UK's Citizens' Assembly was a testing-ground to determine what policy initiatives from above would be broadly acceptable. It could certainly be argued that this is a case of listening to the people, but it is not a model which invites any new initiatives *from* the people. The people have been turned into passive consumers rather than active policymakers. It is a top-down approach (since the proposals come from the top) masquerading as a bottom-up approach. It is a way of testing public responses to government measures rather than inviting the citizens to take the initiative in producing measures of their own. An effective Citizens' Assembly has to avoid being hijacked in this way. In relation to a reformed EU, it needs to be a permanent part of the constitutional structure, a forum for citizens not simply to react but to initiate legislation. The same must apply to the role of a citizens' assembly within a British Union. It could not pass legislation but it could certainly initiate it.

There is a *seventh* ingredient, namely a declaration of human rights. The Human Rights Act of 2000 was at least willing to introduce into UK law rights contained in the Convention, whereas the present Conservative government plans to adopt a more pick-and-choose approach. Since there is no European Law binding upon member states in the case of the European Court of Human Rights, the UK will remain a member of the Council of Europe while effectively choosing how to interpret the rulings of the European Court.[21] This will not do. The most important requirement is that any Human Rights Act passed by a future government in the UK gives the courts the right to disapply an act of Parliament that conflicts with the Act, a right which they had when the UK was part of the European Union if there was an infringement of the Charter of Fundamental Rights.

It is difficult to avoid the impression that the present system in the UK allows the British government to roam unhindered through the judicial undergrowth treading on whatever it doesn't like, claiming all the while that is merely reflecting a commitment to the sovereignty of Parliament. This only reinforces the point that the sovereignty of Parliament is no basis for guaranteeing human rights. There is no doubt that a supreme court, like a parliament, can act

---

21   See Bogdanor, *Beyond Brexit*, chapter 5, 'Europe and the Rights of the Citizen', pp. 135–167.

in such a way as to challenge human rights rather than to protect them, as the recent debate over abortion rights in the USA shows. But the whole point of a Charter of Fundamental Rights (such as applies inside the European Union) or the weaker European Convention on Human Rights (which applies to all members of the Council of Europe, including the UK) is to provide some kind of template enabling people to see whether their liberties have been undermined – not least by acts of government. That template is undermined if the UK government decides that Parliament is the sole determinant of whether a decision of the European Convention on Human Rights is applicable within the UK. If it does so decide, then 'elective dictatorship' moves a stage nearer. To avoid such a dictatorship, there needs to be a clear statement of human rights to which all governments must be bound – and that only makes sense if the decisions of a Supreme Court, the ultimate arbiter of whether rights have been infringed, are binding upon governments of all political persuasions. As Bogdanor (quoting Lord Bingham) has pointed out,[22] those who react with shock when courts challenge the decisions of parliaments should note that there are plenty of countries in the world where the courts can be relied upon always to echo the views of those in power. Russia is a good example. But would one want to live under such a regime?

Conclusion

The suggestions made in this chapter do not presume that the constitution of a multinational state could simply be a replica of the European Union, but there are lessons to be learned from that union. According to what is proposed, a Council of Ministers drawn from the different nations and regions within the UK will be established to manage tasks which can neither be devolved nor clearly identified as a responsibility of central government alone. These tasks will be shared between central government and the devolved nations and regions. The House of Commons would not have the supremacy in a future UK Union that it currently enjoys. The House of Lords would become a senate of the nations and English regions, akin to the German *Bundesrat*. To oversee the manner in which legislation passes between the two houses of Parliament, an independent arbiter is needed, and the Supreme Court should fulfil this role.

---

22   See the interview with Professor Bogdanor organised by the Constitution Society and hosted by Dr Andrew Blick, https://www.youtube.com/watch?v=8WixxocvUso

It will also determine how tasks are divided between the devolved nations and regions on the one hand and central government on the other. The Supreme Court, acting on the basis of a clearly defined statement of human rights, perhaps enshrined in a written constitution, will determine whether governments of whatever persuasion are protecting human liberties in what they enact. If an act is passed which the Supreme Court judges to be unconstitutional, it will be able to strike the act down. Finally, any citizens' assembly should be made a permanent part of the constitution with the right to initiate legislation.

Such an arrangement may appear to be a far cry from the present form of governance adopted by the UK. Yet that present form looks like a system of devolution which has been bolted on to another system of parliamentary sovereignty with which it is incompatible. There is a chance that a new government may be more imaginative in its attempt to preserve the Union, not least one in which the Labour Party plays a leading role, simply because Labour needs the Union more than the Conservative Party does in order to have a chance of power. Its proposals put forward at the end of 2022 show that it is at least thinking seriously about constitutional reform. Moreover, in relation to Northern Ireland, both major parties have been prepared to show imagination and flexibility with regard to constitutional arrangements. Whether they will feel the same compulsion to be innovative in the case of the UK as a whole is another question, but the possibility of doing so is there.

It might even be possible to think of extending a constitution for the UK to a constitution for the Isles, so long as it is recognised that this would in no way compromise the Republic's status as a separate nation-state. It is interesting that since 1922 Ireland has combined a firm assertion of its complete independence as a nation-state – for instance by refusing to be part of the (British) Commonwealth – with a willingness to accept a close partnership with the UK on many practical issues, most notably the common travel area. If a future constitution of the Isles maintained the autonomy of the two nation-states involved, just as the European Union itself maintains the independence of 27 member-states, then it might be willing to be included in a Council of the Isles, which could in turn help to heal wounds that extend over centuries and remain raw in parts of the western isle.

Chapter Eighteen: Conclusion

In *State and Nation* Professor Michael Keating declares that:

> The UK is not a state, unitary or federal, but a union, and as such does not necessarily need a hard core or sovereignty or purpose.[1]

A Tale of Two Unions does not agree that being a 'union' provides some kind of exemption from establishing a constitution. At the same time, it has not tried to suggest that a future constitution for the UK might simply be a replica of the European Union. It is aware of the fact that a union of 27 different nation-states requires a different structure to that of one multinational state. However, it believes that the institutional structure of the EU provides useful pointers to the future constitution of a multinational state, should the UK be prepared to move in that direction and should it be determined to preserve its own union rather than simply tolerate or even welcome its disintegration. That is what this book hopes for. It is based on my fear that Brexit might prove to be a halfway house towards the final dismantling of the United Kingdom into its constituent parts.

The book began by referring to two narrative arcs. It suggested that the first, which concerned the development of what became the United Kingdom, is not always sufficiently recognised when there is too much focus upon a country going it alone, whether it be England pressing ahead with the break from Rome in the sixteenth century or the UK surviving alone after the fall of France in 1940 until the invasion of the Soviet Union a year later. The second narrative arc, which concerned the development of Europe, highlighted the way in which a continent riven by factions emerged, a continent without fixed borders and without fixed identity, in which Christian fought Christian as well as Muslim and Islam mixed with Christianity in helping to form its character,

---

1   Keating, *State and Nation*, p. 50.

as they do today. Europe might like to see an expression of respect for diversity in the many different states inside its undefined borders, but small states have been as intolerant towards minorities as large ones in this warlike western peninsula of Asia. If it is appropriate to talk of 'European values,' then it will be more a case of institutions building values than reflecting values that are already there.

What, then, are these institutions that may help to form 'European values?' The next part of the book tried to show why sovereignty-sharing was a vital ingredient in creating an enduring peace on the continent. The system which eventually emerged through the European Union was a means of having effective supranational supervision without creating a superstate. From this perspective it is at least possible to appreciate the problem to which the European Union tried to provide an answer, even if the EU continues to have major failings. When the book turned to consider the contribution of Jean Monnet and the origins of what became the European Union, it made clear what his own failings were.

The road to the European Union began with its forbear the Coal and Steel Community. This was something new in the history of nations. It was the creation of an institution to which nation-states voluntarily ceded the power to make decisions that were binding upon them. For Jean Monnet, the most important influence behind this approach to managing relations between states, it was to be promoted in a manner he had always adopted, by going to the great and the good and persuading them of the value of a particular policy initiative. Precisely because he had been used to working for wartime coalitions or unstable post war governments, Monnet did not sufficiently recognise that a popular mandate is not an optional extra where radical political change is concerned. As for the French foreign minister Schuman who implemented Monnet's ideas, he did so under the constraints of necessity rather than conviction. For all his grandiose words in the *Salon d'Horloge*, he smuggled sovereignty-sharing past the people having first smuggled it past the French cabinet.

That was the context in which this book turned to a consideration of British entry into the European Economic Community (which later became the EU). To those aware of the narrative arc, the proposal for a European Economic Community might have been seen as an opportunity for the UK to pursue its traditional alliance-making in Europe. But to those focused upon the 'highlights', the echoes of its single-handed resistance to German might between 1940 and 1941 overrode its search for alliances and encouraged a confidence in its ability to make its own way in the world, in peacetime as in the early years of wartime.

The war had been followed by the first ever Labour government with a working majority, determined to 'win the peace' after winning the war. Any suggestion of sharing power with others, whether at home or abroad, was anathema.

Over the following thirty years the UK tried to change the Coal and Steel Community and then the European Economic Community from without, seeking to make them more like organisations it was prepared to belong to. When this was no longer possible, it sought to join the EEC and then change it into something 'acceptable' from within. However, accession took two vetoes and fourteen years and at the end of that period the Community was too well-established to be moulded into a different form.

If you genuinely believe that a sovereignty-sharing body is less a close relationship between states than an artifice to create a new and more powerful state out of several smaller ones, then you are bound to perceive it as another behemoth upsetting the balance of power on the continent, as Harold Macmillan perceived it when the Treaty of Rome was signed. You insist that there is no halfway house between the system of nation-states acting independently and the creation of a superstate in which existing countries are turned into little more than regions. Most politicians in the UK, whichever party they belonged to, appeared to take this view. They did not try to articulate what sovereignty-sharing meant. Perhaps few of them really understood what it meant.

Hence the Conservative government which finally took the UK into the European Economic Community presented the EEC as if it wasn't a sovereignty-sharing body. Like its Labour predecessor, it ignored the fact that the veto which could apply to any new legislation did not apply to what had already been agreed. It also ignored the method by which such legislation was implemented, namely European Law which was binding upon member states, and which overrode national law in the areas to which it applied. That system still stood in 1973. Moreover, if the Community resolved to abandon the principles of the Luxembourg Compromise in times to come, then the system of European law was in place to make future decisions binding upon member states too. This is precisely what happened – ironically under Margaret Thatcher's premiership, when the Single European Act was passed in 1986.

It was during her premiership that what was to become the EU began to work as an effective supranational body. Jacques Delors was a powerful Commission President, but at the same time the Parliament received new powers to oversee and in some areas veto Commission proposals (alongside the Council of Ministers). There was a period during the 1990s when the Left in the UK began to appreciate that the European Union was not simply a capitalist club.

Poorer nations like Spain, Greece and Portugal had joined in the 1980s and appeared to benefit. Social legislation had been made a part of European Law and ensured that the single market protected the rights of workers. This, after all, had been precisely what Margaret Thatcher had complained about in her Bruges speech, claiming that the frontiers of socialism, rolled back in Britain, were being reimposed by Brussels. A ruling of the Law Lords (on 3rd March 1994) during John Major's premiership established that procedures over redundancy pay and unfair dismissal were discriminatory and breached European law. The 16-hour-per-week threshold for employment protection legislation had to be abandoned. At the same time, important environmental legislation was being introduced and enforced. It would have been the right time to make clear what the EU system of sovereignty-sharing was and how it could be to the benefit of member-states. Instead, the UK made it a decade of bickering over Maastricht and on the Left strict avoidance of anything perceived as too controversial.

For so-called europhiles, the high point was reached at the turn of the century when the Conservatives failed completely to motivate the country to 'save the pound' by voting for William Hague in the 2001 election, and Labour was rewarded with a second landslide. Thereafter, things started to go wrong. The new century saw old ghosts come rushing back through the EU's mishandling of the eurozone crisis. Daily television pictures of Greeks forced by the Troika to lose their pensions or Cypriots queuing to get money from the bank reinstated the myth of the capitalist club. The immigration debate was made to feed into this perception, with those arriving from Central and Eastern Europe seen on the Left as cheap service fodder for wealthy Western clients looking for someone to install their fridge freezers or look after their children.

The referendum in 2016 produced the narrowest of majorities for withdrawal and did so by excluding significant parts of the population, such as the 16 and 17-year-olds who had just voted in the Scottish referendum, who would be affected all their lives by the vote, and many of the expatriates whose lives would be upended by a 'No' vote over which they had no say. Unlike in the 1970s when the Scots were deemed not to have voted 'Yes' to devolution in sufficient numbers, there was no required minimum turnout or majority for this vote to count. But all of that is beside the point. The candle burned just enough at both ends, and the nationalist Right joined with the anti-capitalist Left just as the Gaullists and the Communists in France had combined half a century earlier to destroy the European Defence Community.

The book then moved from considering the UK's experience of being in a supranational union to its own development as a multinational state. To the extent that it might be seen in terms of the expansion of England, it was an expansion determined by fear of external enemies. Wales was effectively annexed in 1536, shortly after the English Reformation and at a time when it was known that many people in both England and Wales were opposed to the reforms. The Union with Scotland came out of fears of the power of Louis XIV and the possibility of a 'War of the Stuart Succession' as Scotland supported the Stuart line and England the Hanoverian. The Union with Ireland came once more in the context of the threat from France, this time from Napoleon.

Yet each stage of the expansion was different. In the case of Wales, earlier invasions had effectively removed anything for the English to unite with. The Welsh Act was passed by England alone, without any members from Wales. The Act of 1536 made no use of Offa's Dyke, an eighth-century earth embankment designed to mark off the border with Mercia, much of which is still visible today. A boundary was created to serve the purposes of England, much as boundaries were created by seven European powers in order to create over fifty countries in Africa without regard to the various ethnic groups who were affected. Though Wales was certainly to benefit from the economic expansion that came with the industrial revolution, it was always on terms dictated by England. Railways were built to take the English to the coast rather than to unite the different parts of Wales. The coal mines were flooded with English (and English-speaking) incomers who caused an immigration crisis and had a severe effect on the Welsh language. The Welsh certainly understood how they benefited from that expansion, but they also understood that they were not part of deciding how it should take place. That surely affects the Welsh approach to devolution today. A joint approach to tackling problems that affect both countries is at least as important as deciding which responsibilities can be handed over to the Welsh. But sharing power, as opposed to giving it away, is the aspect of devolution that always gets left out.

In the case of Scotland, it was more a matter of receiving or at least retaining powers that Wales didn't have. Scotland was collaborator as well as victim, the junior partner in a project of imperial expansion. It was an Act of Union between England and Scotland rather than an annexation, allowing Scotland to keep its own legal, educational and religious system. This was de facto devolution from the start and caused problems for anyone who tried to claim that the Westminster parliament was sovereign and could legislate as it wished. How was this compatible with the agreement to give Scotland the right to its own presbyterian church, legal processes and educational system? A reasonable conclusion to draw from this would be that accepting a degree of sovereignty-sharing can not only help to strengthen a British Union post-Brexit but can help to formalise the Act of Union through which England and Wales first joined with Scotland to form Great Britain.

Ireland, on the other hand, was not a partner in the imperial project but more a colony itself, controlled by what was effectively a viceroy in Dublin Castle. An early example of this approach was the so-called 'plantation of Ulster.' At the start of the seventeenth century Ulster was the most Gaelic, Catholic and traditional province in Ireland. Its nature was radically changed by 'plantations.' It became an equivalent to Massachusetts which was created for a similar reason, to maintain a 'purer' religion than that which was practised in the home country. Looking at how these 'plantations' were perceived, it was similar to the way settlers and indigenous inhabitants were perceived in African colonies. If one tries to imagine how, in 1922, the UK was able to accept the loss of one-third of its territory – more than Germany was forced to lose after its defeat in the First World War – the reason lies in the fact that what became the Irish Free State was viewed more as another colony or dominion demanding independence than as a part of the UK precipitating a civil war.

The mention of colonies is important, because imperial expansion beyond the Isles meant that there was later a question of how the colonies and dominions would relate to the so-called 'mother-country'. They had their reservations about 'Empire Free Trade', which seemed to condemn them to supplying raw materials to Britain on favourable terms while receiving British manufactures in return. However lucrative this might be in the short term, they wanted to industrialise themselves. They also disliked the way in which they had simply been 'summoned to war' in 1914 on the basis of an imperial edict issued by George V. They played a huge part in that war. Australians at Gallipoli and Canadians at Vimy Ridge have long been recognised. Less recognised has been the large number of Indians, their numbers in hundreds of thousands, who lost their lives in the trench warfare of the Western front. As the movement towards self-determination gathered pace after the First World War, it was clear that a new arrangement would be needed and that it would mean full independence for the dominions – after all, this was the principle of self-determination which had ended the Austro-Hungarian Empire in 1918. If Yugoslavia and Czechoslovakia were the consequence of that principle, how could anything other than full independent statehood be granted to Canada, New Zealand, Australia and indeed Ireland? And how long before Egypt and India followed?

Hence the earliest thoughts of Home Rule within the Isles were inseparable from the future of the Empire. Home Rule All Round could represent Home

Rule all Round the UK or Home Rule All Round the Empire, with Westminster retained as an Imperial Parliament. In the end, however, Home Rule All Round proved impossible for either the 'internal' or 'external' empire. It failed to prevent the dissolution of the British Empire. It also failed to prevent the formation of the Irish Free State in 1922. Ironically, Home Rule ended up as Home Rule in One Place Only, Northern Ireland, which resulted in protests and later violence for thirty years in the second half of the century. Unsurprisingly, many concluded that the nation state was the only kid on the block, and further attempts at some form of home rule received little attention between the 1920s and the 1970s. At the time of the Scottish Covenant in the 1940s the Labour government under Clement Attlee was increasingly aware of the fact that nothing short of independence could follow the Empire. British India had just collapsed into different independent nations (more were to follow), with over a million dead. Solutions in terms of increased autonomy, however defined, were easily seen as a useless halfway house between regional status and full independence. The Scottish Covenant was largely ignored at Westminster.

The disillusionment with early attempts at devolution affected the UK's opposition to sovereignty-sharing in the run-up to membership of the EU. The failure of Home Rule encouraged a view that there was no alternative to the so-called Westphalian system. The only option for the future was the jostling pack of independent nation-states, the Hobbesian 'state of nature' transposed to the international realm. There was no possibility of going above the level of the nation-state in order to solve the problems of the nation-state. The 'Monnet system' not only appeared to limit the UK's powers but was in any case seen as unworkable.

It also awoke the demons of an Empire gone by. The pioneer of the so-called 'four nations' approach to the future of the UK was a New Zealander, J.G.A Pocock, whose 'British History: A Plea for a New Subject', was first published in 1975, the year that the UK finally voted to stay in the EEC. Far from seeing the four-nations approach as something worthy of comparison with the six-nation approach of the EEC, the latter was simply condemned as a way of discriminating against Commonwealth producers. The ghost of imperial preference was roused back to life by the impact of the Common Agricultural Policy, which supported farmers through a guaranteed floor price together with a common external tariff to prevent that price floor being undercut by cheap imports. Joining the EEC would be making the UK buy more expensive food from Europe rather than cheaper food from the Commonwealth. It was a letting down of 'kith and kin.'

This background had some impact on the way devolution was presented when it finally happened at the end of the twentieth century, both in the Belfast Agreement of 1998 on the future of Northern Ireland and the successful referenda to support the creation of a Scottish Parliament and a Welsh Assembly. Little was done to connect these agreements to the UK's participation in the European Union. Yet once the various agreements are examined, it is clear that there are many important connections between what this book has called two unions.

It is from Wales that the most developed proposals for constitutional reform of the United Kingdom have come. Because Wales voted narrowly in favour of Brexit and is not dominated by a nationalist party in the way Scotland is, it has been able to concentrate more on how to foster Welsh interests inside the British Union than on how to leave that Union. The heart of the Welsh proposals for effective devolution is an understanding of how the nations of the UK could *jointly* make decisions rather than simply receive a new division of the spoils of government in terms of who does what. The chapter on the history of Wales sought to show how this approach would make sense. Wales has been a beneficiary of the economic expansion that came with the industrial revolution and its aftermath, but on terms dictated by England. Decisions have too often been made *for* Wales, not *with* Wales, as the examination of its railway system, for instance, sought to illustrate.

The Welsh proposals make their position clear where they say:

Wales is committed to this association, which must be based on the recognition of popular sovereignty in each part of the UK; Parliamentary sovereignty as traditionally understood no longer provides a sound foundation for this evolving constitution.

The traditional doctrine of the sovereignty of Parliament no longer provides a firm foundation for the constitution of the UK. It needs to be adjusted to take account of the realities of devolution, just as it was adjusted to take account of the UK's membership of the European Union.[2]

---

2   See Proposition 1 of the General Principles outlined by the document. The first sentence comes from the statement off the principle and the second sentence comes from the 'Narrative' associated with it. See 'Reforming our Union: shared governance in the UK', published in 2019. https://www.gov.wales/reforming-our-union-shared-governance-in-the-uk-html

The key sentence is the one which affirms that 'the traditional doctrine of the sovereignty of Parliament no longer provides a firm foundation for the constitution of the UK.' The question is whether the UK will be prepared to accept this. The idea of parliamentary sovereignty embedded in the mists of time as the keystone of the UK's development as a democracy is a very powerful one, offering a narrative arc linking the barons forcing John to sign Magna Carta at Runnymede to the execution of the King in the seventeenth century, the 'People's Charter' put forward by the Chartists in the nineteenth century and the campaign of the suffragettes a century ago. The implication is that the development of democracy is inextricably linked to the development of the powers of Parliament, despite the fact that there have been many radical thinkers who have echoed Walwyn in suggesting that Parliament can as much inhibit democratic change as promote it.

There is an element of complacency in this story of progress through the centuries, reminiscent of the arguments some half century ago about the so-called 'Whig interpretation of history.' Even on the Left, the image of the 'workers' parliament' threatened by upper-class peers, foreigners from Brussels and in earlier centuries by the overweening powers of the monarchy makes it easy to talk in terms of the sovereignty of Parliament – or at least of the Commons – as if the two can be identified. It forgets that parliament could be a vehicle of dictatorship as much as democracy, as it proved to be in Germany in 1933. Dictators can ride into power on the basis of a popular mandate, their support coming from no more than a large minority of voters, especially under the electoral system used for Westminster elections which has produced parties with absolute majorities in Parliament on the basis of little more than one-third of the vote and one-fifth of the electorate.

It may be that such a view is overly pessimistic. Yet such a development is not avoided simply by breaking the United Kingdom up, leaving the system of parliamentary sovereignty to apply to England alone. As we have seen, the nationalism of small nations can be just as impatient of minorities as that of large ones, particularly when they find that by downsizing they haven't somehow arrived at a homogeneous core. They may adopt the sort of attitude discussed in terms of David Lammy's radio conversation with a listener who was prepared to allow him to be 'British' but never to penetrate the inner sanctum of Englishness.

The proposals outlined in this book largely follow those of the Welsh *Senedd* first laid out in 2019. Some of the proposals have come from elsewhere too – for instance the recent suggestions of the Labour Party for a reformed second chamber. Unsurprisingly, criticism of the proposals has come from the Commons Speaker (though himself a Labour MP) Douglas Hoyle, who makes the familiar point that such a reform would threaten the supremacy of the Commons. This is perfectly true – and reiterates the point that the UK cannot be effectively reformed unless it is prepared to give up precisely this supremacy of the Commons. The House of Lords would become a Senate of the nations and English regions, akin to the German *Bundesrat*, but even if that solves the problem of giving it a separate role to that of the Commons and not simply duplicating the work of the lower house, there will still be the problem of arbitrating between the different responsibilities of the two houses. There will have to be a way of dealing with the question of which house should deal with what or whether the upper house would have a veto over a particular law – the sort of issues which come before the German constitutional Court under the bicameral system in Germany. A separation of powers is the only way in which the reformed House of Lords can be managed successfully, without either abolishing it or giving it some menial task like 'tidying up bills', as Douglas Hoyle described its present role. A powerful second chamber alongside the House of Commons requires an arbiter between the two.

Hence, the most difficult aspect is not the reform of the House of Lords, but what must result from a bicameral system. The House of Commons would not have the supremacy in a future UK Union that it currently enjoys. To oversee the manner in which legislation passes between the two houses of Parliament, an independent arbiter will be needed, and the Supreme Court must surely fill this role. It will determine how tasks are divided between the devolved nations and regions on the one hand and central government on the other. It will therefore keep an eye on subsidiarity, another very important principle of both unions, the British and the European, but one which requires a body which can determine what is the lowest level of management compatible with efficiency.

Mention the important role of the judiciary, and such an approach is often presented as 'foreign' to the UK's constitutional arrangements, but it was the system that applied while the UK was a member of the European Union, when UK legislation incompatible with European Law was disapplied. This system often seemed to go under the radar even when the UK was part of the European Union, despite the concerns of many on the Left and the Right with preserving parliamentary sovereignty intact. It is noteworthy that even cases like *Factortame*, where it was clearly demonstrated that Westminster legislation, whatever the arguments about the supremacy of Parliament, would be disapplied if they contravened European Law, aroused relatively little interest. The indispensable role of national courts in determining whether UK legislation was compatible with European Law, and if not disapplying it, received hardly any attention, even among those calling for sovereignty to be 'restored' to Parliament.

Because that role of the courts was underplayed during UK membership of the EU, the idea of a role of the courts in any post-Brexit arrangement is seen as a complete break with tradition. Earlier we looked at the McKay report of 2013 which reported to the Liberal Democrat-Conservative Coalition government on the consequences of devolution for the House of Commons. We quoted it saying that:

> Any federal system requires a delineation of competences, which are usually arbitrated by a supreme court that would be able to overrule the UK parliament, as well as binding the devolved institutions. This would be a radical departure from UK constitutional practice.[3]

McKay was right to determine that there must be a body which is able to determine the 'delineation of competences.' Otherwise, we return to the situation where the Westminster Parliament decided arbitrarily in passing the Internal Market Act that the situation was not 'normal' enough for the agreed form of devolution to apply. It would make no sense for Westminster to be able to determine whether, under a bicameral system, the new upper house had acted in a manner that went beyond its authority. But the use instead of a supreme court would not be 'a radical departure from UK constitutional practice' at all. The authors of the report were simply oblivious to the fact that membership of the EU was just such a radical departure because it involved the willingness to be bound by decisions of the European Court of Justice.

It is not, however, the reform of the House of Lords alone that requires an active judiciary, but the whole process of devolution. This has not been recognised sufficiently because throughout the process of devolution, beginning from the end of the last century, parliamentary sovereignty has been the unspoken anchor which supposedly keeps the giving away of powers under

---

3   See paragraph 71 of the report, which can be read in full at webarchive.nationalarchiv es.gov.uk/20130403030652/http:/tmc.independent.gov.uk/wp-content/uploads/2013 /03/The-McKay-Commission_Main-Report_25-March-20131.pdf

some sort of control.[4] The limitations of the idea of parliamentary sovereignty have been pushed to one side and devolution has been bolted onto a system of parliamentary sovereignty with which it is fundamentally incompatible. 'Further devolution' or 'devo max' is seen as giving away even more powers to the devolved nations or to the regions. What is neglected is all those matters where the question is not whose responsibility a particular issue is but how it can be managed jointly by the nations working together. This is where a Council of Ministers will be necessary to manage tasks which can neither be devolved nor clearly identified as a responsibility of central government alone. These tasks will need to be shared between central government and the devolved nations and regions. It could even be argued that devolution is in danger of giving too many powers away, creating piecemeal arrangements for what is meant to be universal provision, precisely because the sharing of power, in a manner that might be compared to the way decisions are made inside the European Union, is seen to be anathema.

It is arguably the one part of the UK in which devolution was introduced from the very beginning, namely Northern Ireland, which suggests a way in which it could be made to work. Both the Irish Republic and the UK were prepared to show imagination and flexibility with regard to the constitutional arrangements underpinning the Belfast agreement of 1998, where both sides of the border were given a veto over constitutional changes which altered the status of Northern Ireland. The veto power provided in the Belfast Agreement could be extended to an arrangement incorporating the 'four nations' of the United Kingdom. Had the 'four nations' inside the British Union possessed veto power, the fact that two of them wished to be outside the EU and two of them didn't so wish would have been unable to produce a binding decision in favour of withdrawal. In 2017 the UK Supreme Court unanimously held that the consent of Northern Ireland voters had not been required to leave the European Union. Yet the continuation of Northern Ireland as part of the United Kingdom is a matter in which Northern Ireland *is* effectively allowed a veto on its future. The logic of the Good Friday agreement is that decisions on the future of this 'nation' should be subject to the agreement of both the Irish Republic and Northern Ireland. In other words, both could exercise a veto on the agreement. It would have made sense to apply the power of veto to other decisions

---

4   See Rose, *Understanding the United Kingdom*, written some forty years ago after the first efforts at devolution in the 1970s had been rejected and the successful proposals of the 1990s had not yet been formulated.

which have had profound implications for Northern Ireland, such as member-ship of the EU. Veto powers for the devolved bodies could be part of any future constitutional changes. Such powers would be controversial, but they would make more sense than the present movement towards giving more and more powers away while trying to reserve the rest for Westminster with the deter-mination of a dog protecting its bone. The best approach to devolution would be to give less away while being prepared to share more. Certainly if 'sharing' means accepting that a binding decision must be based upon a majority vote (possibly a 'qualified' majority vote requiring an overwhelming vote in favour) or even cannot be made at all because of a veto, it may seem to produce the sort of roadblock that has been encountered for long periods in Northern Ireland. But by encouraging joint working it might be able to advance cooperation be-tween the different nations and regions far more effectively than working out what crumbs – or even slices – from the rich man's table will keep them quiet.

Final thoughts on sovereignty, constitutions – and the chance of reform

It is interesting how far the Republic of Ireland has gone in finding common ground with the UK on a number of issues like the common travel area, while remaining absolutely committed to its own sovereignty – staying out of the Commonwealth, not being tied up in any way with the royal family, pursuing an independent foreign policy and yet remaining perfectly prepared effectively to share sovereignty with the UK in areas where it makes sense. If there is one example which more than any other shows up the nonsense of the UK's belief that by sharing sovereignty in certain areas it was in danger of losing its inde-pendence, that example is the Irish Republic. Independence for the Republic was won at the cost of much bitterness and blood; the country was ruthless in asserting that independence, whether by staying out of World War Two or staying out of NATO after it. Yet this determination to maintain its indepen-dence and its identity has not ruled out arrangements with the United King-dom which involve a pooling of sovereignty in certain areas, either when both countries were inside the EU together or when they work out how to maintain their relationship after Brexit.

The example of the Republic of Ireland shows that even nation-states de-termined to preserve their independence are willing to share sovereignty in particular areas. It is this that the UK has always failed to see, whether in the early years after the war when it was thinking of whether to apply to join the European Coal and Steel Community and later the European Economic Community, or in the later years when it eventually decided upon withdrawal. Yet ironically it has been willing to practise what it doesn't preach in terms of its relationship with the Republic of Ireland itself, formerly itself part of the United Kingdom. Here it has not tried to raise the drawbridge against the free movement of people and may even be willing to develop a shared commitment to human rights.

The hostility of the English in particular to joint working may have something to do with the narrative arc of the United Kingdom's emergence. As England, Wales, Scotland and Ireland grew into the United Kingdom, the English did not see the process as a means of enriching themselves by association; they were grabbing additional baggage from 'outside' with which to fortify their own house against their enemies. Now they are in danger of battening down the hatches inside their own Kingdom. The other nations in the United Kingdom have a sense of being made from outside because of the influence of England on their making. But in the case of England, the narrative myth with its emphasis upon the island fortress seeing off waves of invaders lays all the emphasis upon being threatened from beyond and thereby loses the sense that it has been *made from beyond* as well. In an odd way the English seem to combine a longing to discover their true identity with a determination to carve an identity out of having none at all.[5] A United Kingdom in which each nation recognised that it had become what it was through the influence of the others would understand that joint working – and even the sharing of sovereignty – was a natural reflection of the way the nations' affairs are interrelated and less like an unwelcome imposition from outside upon the affairs of each nation.

When the European Union decided to establish a constitution some two decades ago, it was presented by the former French President Valéry Giscard d'Estaing, who declared that it was something any schoolchild could understand, despite running to 200 pages. The American Constitution, by way of contrast, can be absorbed in a few minutes and is frequently quoted. Constitutions need to be brief and effective, summarising the salient points. A Constitution for the UK would have to be similarly brief. The constitution which the European Union tried and failed to reach agreement on was anything but.

The Treaty Establishing a Constitution for Europe, which was drafted largely by politicians at both national and European level, was signed in 2004

---

5   Roberts, R.H. *Religion, Theology and the Human Sciences*, p. 221.

and then rejected in referenda by the Netherlands and France. D'Estaing then sought to have the main parts of the Treaty incorporated in a subsequent Treaty, the Treaty of Lisbon, which contained much the same reforms but with, as he put it, the 'constitutional vocabulary removed.'[6] This was a revealing comment. It suggested that what had particularly generated opposition was not the detailed reforms to the powers of various institutions, but the idea they added up to something called a 'constitution', which was seen as something more appropriate to a nation-state. The British foreign secretary, Jack Straw, tried to defuse this argument by pointing out that golf clubs had constitutions too, but this did little to remove the suspicion that referring to a proposed European 'Constitution' meant envisaging a European super-state.

In the *Nicomachean Ethics* Aristotle describes the constitution (*politeia*) as the formal cause of the city-state (or *polis* – from which we get our term 'politics'). It was a way of ordering the inhabitants of the city-state, a community of a few thousand people. Aristotle compares it to what gives life to an organism, the animating principle or 'soul' of the nation. We come closest to this, perhaps, when we describe someone as having a 'good constitution', which means that they are hardy and resilient. It is this meaning that arguably made the Treaty on a Constitution for Europe unpalatable to many people – not the different institutions and their roles within the European Union, but what having a 'constitution' meant for the idea of Europe not as a collective but as akin to an individual whose 'strong constitution' would refer to their ability to function as a living, breathing whole. They feared that if the EU was trying to devise a 'constitution' it was seeking something that properly belonged to nation-states and therefore must be trying to become a nation-state itself.

The outline proposed here in terms of a supreme court, a bicameral parliamentary system of two houses, a principle of subsidiarity and an active council of ministers which can promote joint working is being applied to a single nation-state, and therefore the idea of developing a written constitution would hardly be controversial. However, though it is not advocating the sort of institutional structure seen in the European Union, it certainly does bear similarities with that structure. It calls for a separation of powers, but that is not only characteristic of the European Union. It is also characteristic of the United States of America, and no one is suggesting that the USA, despite its problems

---

6   He declared in October 2007 that the aim was to get the provisions of the earlier treaty accepted without having recourse to referenda. See https://euobserver.com/eu-politi cal/25052

a century and a half ago, is currently in danger of ceasing to be a single nation-state.

We have seen that there is a problem of a 'democratic deficit' in the European Union. The top-down approach that is embedded in the structure of the Commission must be changed. Sovereignty-sharing has to be an expression of the popular will rather than simply being an opportunity for a transnational elite to gather in Brussels and enjoy the privileges that go with the job. It is not a question of being able to find a better way of 'selling Europe' to consumers, but of finding more effective ways in which the views of Europeans can make themselves known to those with power in the institutions. Having discussed the pros and cons of 'deliberative mini-publics' and having given some examples of citizens' assemblies, the book has suggested that they should become a permanent part of the EU structure. Endless talk of dialogues, conventions and conferences on the future of Europe must be channelled into a powerful body which is able to overlook whatever the Commission proposes and is able to make proposals itself. The 'movers and shakers' to whom Monnet went in his day to introduce new policies would be unable to move and shake without the consent of the people. The descendants of Monnet's 'Commissariat' need to work hand in hand with the people themselves to propose new legislation.

This must also be the case where a constitution of the UK is concerned. Citizens' assemblies are not focus groups designed to be a testing bed for government to try out new policies. They must be a means by which the people have a chance to propose their own legislation and not just respond to initiatives from the government. This provides a further route through which a reformed House of Lords might acquire a distinctive character. Some of its members could be decided through sortition, in the way jurors are. It would be another way of representing the nations and regions of the UK in all its diversity than that which concentrates on geographical location alone.

All of these are matters open to discussion and doubtless there will be many different proposals for reforming the House of Lords over the months before the next election, as there indeed have been in the past. But the fundamental barrier which has to be overcome remains the issue of parliamentary sovereignty. Unless the House of Commons is prepared to share it, then no meaningful reform of the House of Lords is possible. Nor can there be any meaningful devolution without such a sharing of sovereignty.

It is Michael Keating who above all has been able to understand the way in which rather than 'muddling through' the UK has been lagging behind:

The devolution reforms at the end of the 20th century were an opportunity to break decisively with the model of the unitary state imposed on a plurinational union, but instead tried to bolt devolution onto that unitary state. Statecraft is once again behind the times.[7]

Devolution cannot, as Keating puts it, be bolted onto a unitary state. The state has to change its form, accept a separation of powers and allow the courts to oversee the workings of a bicameral parliament, including a right to determine whose responsibility a particular issue may be. The courts should also have the right to disapply legislation which is incompatible with an effective Human Rights Act (which could be based on the EU's Charter of Fundamental Rights, a more up-to-date version of the European Convention.) That will mean allowing courts to 'interfere' with decisions of parliament, but it is worth asking why this is perceived to be such a problem. Do politicians want a system where the courts always agree with the decisions of elected representatives? Is Russia a good model for the future of democracy in the UK? Above all, a Council of Ministers should embed joint working among the nations and regions where appropriate. As this book goes to press, a row is brewing over trans rights between Scotland and Westminster. Yet the debate is entirely about who has responsibility for what. Nowhere is there a suggestion of working together to find a solution that might be acceptable to the UK as a whole. It is like the piecemeal reforms to the health service that threaten, for instance, to overthrow Aneurin Bevan's conception of a nationwide service and replace it with one in which prescriptions are free in one part of the UK but not in another. What is needed for the nations and regions is a seat at the top table where they can hammer out solutions together, even if it means agreeing that a proposal from England could be blocked by the others. Whatever was jointly agreed would then become law and would be binding upon all the members of the UK. In other words, it would be similar to the way things work inside the European Union.

By pursuing Brexit Boris Johnson made constitutional change much easier. The sovereignty of the people would be a much better basis for establishing a constitution for the UK than the sovereignty of Parliament. The paradox is that, though himself a Unionist, Johnson has undermined the very principle that would seek to maintain that Union in the traditional manner. Once you begin from a sovereign people rather than a sovereign Parliament, you have to build institutions out of a commitment to liberty, rather than build a commitment to

---

7   Keating, *State and Nation*, p. 201.

liberty out of institutions. The proposals of the Welsh *Senedd* look like a mature response to this challenge; re-iterating the sovereignty of a Parliament whose authority Johnson effectively undermined does not.

Despite being behind the times, it is still possible that British statecraft could put the pieces in place both for the future of an integrated United Kingdom and for a continued close relationship between not only the UK and the Republic but conceivably between Britain and a United (or Re-united) Ireland. If one could look beyond the presumption of insurmountable barriers between nation-states, one might develop a constitution of the Isles that respected the integrity of four nations and two nation-states. Such ideas are already being discussed in the Republic, where people understand that a united Ireland, if it is possible at all, must make provision for a considerable degree of autonomy North of the border.

At the beginning of 2023 it is difficult to be optimistic, although it is a good sign that constitutional reform is an issue which the Labour Party is prepared to embrace. What is not clear is whether it will embrace to deceive. In the meantime, the UK is marked by a consistent failure to devise a successful constitutional arrangement whereby the people of the two islands could maintain their separate cultures and traditions within a single nation-state. There is still a danger that history will repeat itself with the same British insouciance failing to take measures that might prevent further layers being torn off the onion of UK statehood. Powers repatriated to the UK after Brexit have been seized by Westminster and measures like the Internal Market Bill forced through against the wishes of the devolved authorities. Meanwhile Westminster has flexed its muscles with lots of dinky little deals that are supposed to mark up the presence of the UK in all its constituent parts – a city deal here, a partnership there, what Michael Keating calls 'flying the unionist flag.' Behind such nonchalance is the conviction that it doesn't matter if a little more of the UK is shaved off, the great Westminster tradition will carry on, the 'mother of parliaments' will continue to spread its moral authority wherever it goes and whether it's left-wing heroes like Dennis Skinner glued to his green bench or Tony Benn rummaging around in the cellars of Westminster putting up plaques, or right-wing figures like Enoch Powell celebrating the English alternative to a lost Empire, the parliamentary myth will continue to drive out real constitutional reform. Even the 'reformists' and most of the 'federalists' end up bowing to the great mother whose sovereignty must remain intact. It may be that the Labour Party's proposals will go the same way.

The outcome of this tale of two unions is that where belonging to the European Union is concerned, the United Kingdom may have come and gone, but it has to maintain its own integrity beyond Brexit, not only with the rest of Europe but also with the rest of the Isles. There is a chance over the next five years of realising the principle of 'unity in diversity' in practical terms on two islands which have spent so much of their history in inner conflict as well as facing external aggressors. The United Kingdom has spent countless decades maintaining constitutional absurdities like the House of Lords. It has spent four decades refusing to recognise that it was part of a system of shared sovereignty, and two decades trying to avoid such a system at home. Since 1998 it has been steadily *giving* power to those with whom it always refuses to *share* power. The dynastic conglomerate that is the United Kingdom tries desperately to unite itself around the deaths and coronations of monarchs, not to mention the lifestyle of a dysfunctional royal family. It seems determined to prefer Ruritania to reform. It is time to get real.

Bibliography

Anderson, Benedict *Imagined Communities: Reflections on the Origin and Spread of Nationalism* (London: Verso, 1983).

Anderson, Perry *Ever-Closer Union? Europe in the West* (London: Verso, 2021).

Armstrong, Kenneth *Brexit Time. Leaving the EU. Why, How and When?* (Cambridge: Cambridge University Press, 2017).

Ashcroft, Lord 'England and the Union', Lord Ashcroft Polls https://lordashcro ftpolls.com/2019/10/england-and-the-union/

Bainton, Roland *Penguin History of Christianity* (Harmondsworth: Penguin, 1964).

Bartolini, Stefano *Restructuring Europe: Centre Formation, System Building and Political Structuring between the Nation State and the European Union* (Oxford: Oxford University Press, 2005).

Bill, James A. *George Ball: Behind the Scenes of U.S. Foreign Policy* (New Haven: Yale University Press, 2008).

Blair, Alasdair *The European Union since 1945* (Harlow: Pearson, 2010).

Bogdanor, Vernon *Beyond Brexit: Towards a British Constitution* (London: I. B. Tauris, 2019).

────── *Britain and Europe in a Troubled World* (New Haven: Yale University Press, 2020).

────── 'The EU without Britain: Never Closer Union?' – a lecture and discussion given to the Royal Philosophical Society of Glasgow. See https://www.yout ube.com/watch?v=LO5olYIEzBw

Bradley, John 'The History of Economic Development in Ireland, North and South', *Proceedings of the British Academy* 88 pp. 25–68.

Brand, Jack *The National Movement in Scotland* (London: Routledge, 2021).

Broad, Roger and Preston, Virginia (eds.), *Moored to the Continent? Britain and European Integration* (London: Institute of Historical Research, 2001).

Bryant, Christopher *The Nations of Britain* (Oxford: Oxford University Press, 2006).

Burke, Edmund *Reflections on the Revolution in France* (Oxford: Oxford University Press, 2009).

Cambien, Nathan, Kochenov Dimitry and Muir, Elise (eds.), *European Citizenship under Stress: Social Justice, Brexit and Other Challenges* (Leiden: Brill, 2020).

Carpenter, David *Penguin History of Britain, The Struggle for Mastery. Britain 1066–1284* (London: Penguin, 2004).

Chesterton, G.K. *What's Wrong with the World* (San Francisco: Ignatius Press, 1994). The book was originally published in 1910.

Churchill, Winston *The Second World War: Volume 1. The Gathering Storm* (London: Penguin, 2005).

Cini, Michelle and Borragán, Nieves Pérez-Solórzano *European Union Politics*. 5th Edition (Oxford: Oxford University Press, 2015).

Clarke, H.D., Goodwin, M and Whitely, P. *Brexit: Why Britain Voted to Leave the European Union* (Cambridge: Cambridge University Press, 2017).

Colls, Robert *Identity of England* (Oxford: Oxford University Press, 2002).

Conrad, Joseph *Heart of Darkness* (London: Penguin Classics, 2007).

Cooper, Robert *The Breaking of Nations* (New York: Atlantic Monthly Press, 2003).

Corner, Mark *The Binding of Nations: From European Union to World Union* (London: Palgrave Macmillan, 2010).

——— *The EU: An Introduction* (London: I. B. Tauris, 2014).

Craig, David and Elliott, Matthew *The Great European Rip-off* (Maryland: Arrow, 2009).

Cross, Leslie and Livingstone, Elizabeth A. *Oxford Dictionary of the Christian Church*. 3rd Edition (Oxford: Oxford University Press, 2005).

Daintith, Kenneth, 'Kilbrandon: The Ship That Launched a Thousand Faces?' *The Modern Law Review* Vol. 37, No. 5 (1974), pp. 544–555.

Davies, Godfrey *The Early Stuarts: 1603–1660* (Oxford: Oxford University Press, 1959).

Davies, John *A History of Wales*. Revised edition (London: Penguin, 2007).

Davies, Norman *Europe: A History* (Oxford: Oxford University Press, 1996).

——— *The Isles* (London: Macmillan, 1999).

——— *Vanished Kingdoms: The History of Half-Forgotten Europe* (London: Penguin, 2011).

Dawson, Christopher *Understanding Europe* (London: Sheed and Ward, 1952).

de Gaulle, Charles *Memoirs of Hope*. Translated by Terence Kilmartin (London, Weidenfeld and Nicolson, 1971).

De Krey, Gary S. *Following the Levellers Volume 2: English Religious and Political Radicals from the Commonwealth to the Glorious Revolution 1649–1688* (London: Palgrave Macmillan, 2018).

Deniau, Jean- François *L'Europe Interdite* (Paris: Seuil, 1977).

Dicey, A.V. *Introduction to the Study of the Law of the Constitution*. Introduction by E.C.S.Wade (Basingstoke: Macmillan, 1959).

Dinan, Desmond *Europe Recast: A History of European Union* (London: Palgrave Macmillan, 2004).

Douglas-Scott, Sionaidh 'The constitutional Implications of the EU (Withdrawal) Act 2018: A Critical Appraisal'. *Queen Mary School of Law Legal Studies Research Paper* No. 299/2019.

Duchêne, François *Jean Monnet: First Statesman of Interdependence* (New York: W. M. Norton & Co., 1994).

Duff, Andrew *Britain and the Puzzle of European Union* (Abingdon: Routledge, 2022).

—————— *On Governing Europe: A Federal Experiment* (CreateSpace Independent Publishing Platform, 2018).

Duroselle, Jean-Baptiste *Europe: A History of its Peoples*. Translated by Richard Mayne (London: Viking, 1990).

Eden, Anthony *Memoirs: Full Circle* (London: Cassell, 1960).

Edgerton, David *The Rise and Fall of the British Nation: A Twentieth-Century History* (London: Allen Lane, 2018).

—————— Podcast entitled 'Disunited Kingdom', 28/1/2020. https://shows.acast.com/opinionhasit/episodes/60dc5b861f5e91001249f664

Elias, Norbert *The Civilising Process* (Oxford: Blackwell, 2000).

Esler, Gavin *How Britain Ends: English Nationalism and the rebirth of four nations* (London: Apollo, 2021).

Ferguson, Niall 'Too much Hitler and the Henrys'. *Financial Times* April 9th 2010.

—————— *The War of the World* (London: Penguin, 2007).

Finer, S.E., Bogdanor, Vernon and Rudden, Bernard *Comparing Constitutions* (Oxford: Clarendon Press, 1995).

Fimister, A.C. *Neo Scholastic Humanism and the Reunification of Europe* (Brussels: Peter Lang, 2008).

Foley, Michael *The Silence of Constitutions. Gaps, 'Abeyances' and Political Temperament in the Maintenance of Government* (London: Routledge, 2012).

Fowkes, Ben *Eastern Europe 1945–1969: From Stalinism to Stagnation* (Harlow: Longman, 2000).

Foxley, Rachel 'More Precious in Your Esteem than It Deserveth?: Magna Carta and Seventeenth-Century Politics.' In Goldman, Lawrence (ed.) *Magna Carta: History, Context and Influence* (London: University of London Press, 2018).

———— *The Levellers and the English Constitution in the English Civil War* (Publications de la Sorbonne), ID : 10.4000/books.psorbonne.54403.

Gillingham, John R. *The EU an Obituary* (New York: Verso, 2016).

Girvin, Brian *From Union to Union. Nationalism, Democracy and Religion in Ireland – Act of Union to EU* (Dublin: Gill and MacMillan, 2002).

Glover, Daniel and Kenny, Michael 'Answering the West Lothian question? A Critical Assessment of English Votes for English Laws in the UK Parliament' *Parliamentary Affairs* 71/4, pp. 760–782.

Goldman, Lawrence (ed.) *Magna Carta: History, Context and Influence* (London: University of London Press, 2018).

Gordon, Michael *Parliamentary Sovereignty in the UK Constitution: Process, Politics and Democracy* (Oxford: Bloomsbury Hart Publishing, 2015).

Grotius, Hugo *On the Law of War and Peace*. Edited and annotated by Stephen Neff (Cambridge: Cambridge University Press, 2012).

Habermas, Jürgen 'The Postnational Constellation and the Future of Democracy' Chapter 4, in: *The Postnational Constellation: Political Essays*. Translated by Max Pensky (Cambridge, Massachusetts: MIT Press 2001), pp. 58–112.

Hargreaves, David and O'Keeffe, Margaret-Louise *As We Were* (Croydon: Whitefox, 2021).

Hattersley, Roy *David Lloyd George: The Great Outsider* (London: Abacus, 2010).

Hechter, Michael *Internal Colonialism. The Celtic Fringe in British National Development 1536–1966* (London: Routledge, 1975).

Hewitt, Gavin *The Lost Continent* (London: Hodder and Stoughton, 2013).

Hill, Christopher *The World Turned Upside Down: Radical Ideas during the English Revolution* (London: Penguin 1991).

Hobbes, Thomas *Leviathan*. Edited by A. P. Metternich & Brian Battiste (London: Broadview Press, 2011).

Hobsbawm, Eric & Ranger, T (eds.) *The Invention of Tradition* (Cambridge: Cambridge University Press, 1992).

Hobsbawm, Eric *Age of Capital* (London: Abacus, 1997).

———— *Age of Extremes: The Short Twentieth Century 1914–1991* (London: Abacus, 1995).

———— *Interesting Times: A Twentieth-Century Life* (London: Abacus, 2003).

———— *Nations and Nationalism since 1780* (Cambridge: Cambridge University Press, 1990).

Howe, Stephen *Ireland and Empire: Colonial Legacies in Irish History and Culture* (Oxford: Oxford University Press, 2000).

Jackson, Robert *Sovereignty: Evolution of an Idea* (Cambridge: Polity Press, 2007).

Jenkins, Roy *A Life at the Centre* (London: Macmillan, 1991).

Johnes, Martin *Wales: England's Colony?* (Parthian, Cardigan: Parthian Press, 2019).

Jones, Carwyn 'Our Future Union-A Perspective from Wales' (2014) https://www.instituteforgovernment.org.uk/events/keynote-speech-rt-hon-carwyn-jones-am-minister-wales-our-future-union---perspective-wales/

Jones, Edward, Jones, Beryl and Hayhoe, Michael *Roman Britain* (London: Routledge, 1972).

Judt, Tony *Postwar: A History of Europe since 1945* (London: Pimlico, 2007).

Keating, Michael *The Independence of Scotland: Self-Government and the Shifting Politics of Union* (Oxford: Oxford University Press, 2009).

———— *State and Nation in the United Kingdom: The Fractured Union* (Oxford: Oxford University Press, 2021).

Kenny, Michael *The Politics of English Nationhood* (Oxford: Oxford University Press, 2014).

Kershaw, Ian *Roller-Coaster: Europe 1950–2017* (London: Allen Lane, 2018).

Kipling, Rudyard *Collected Poems* (London: Wordsworth Editions, 1994).

Kitromilides, Paschalis 'Review of Jean-Baptiste Duroselle's Europe: A History of its Peoples'. *European History Quarterly*, vol. 24, issue 1, pp. 123–127.

Krasner, Stephen D. (ed.), *International Regimes* (Ithaca, New York: Cornell University Press, 1983).

Kumar, Krishan *The Making of English National Identity* (Cambridge: Cambridge University Press, 2003).

Kundera, Milan 'The Tragedy of Central Europe'. *New York Review of Books*, vol. 31, n. 7. April 26, 1984.

Laffan, Brigid, O'Donnell, Rory and Smith, Michael *Europe's Experimental Union: Rethinking Integration* (London: Routledge, 2000).

Lloyd-Jones Naomi & Scull, Margaret M *Four Nations: Approaches to Modern British History: A (Dis)united Kingdom?* (London: Palgrave Macmillan, 2018).

Lukacs, John *Five Days in London: May 1940* (New Haven: Yale University Press, 1999).

MacCormick, Neil *Questioning Sovereignty: Law, State and Nation in the European Commmonwealth* (Oxford: Oxford University Press, 1999).

Macmillan, Harold *At the End of the Day* (London: Macmillan, 1973).

MacShane, Denis *Brexit, No Exit* (London: I.B. Tauris, 2017).

Mangold, Peter *The Almost Impossible Ally: Harold Macmillan and Charles de Gaulle* (London: I.B. Tauris, 2006).

Marshall, Henrietta Elizabeth *Our Island Story: A Child's History of England* (London: T.C. and E.C. Jack, 1905).

May, Alex *Britain and Europe since 1945* (Harlow: Longman, 1999).

McClintock, John *The Uniting of Nations: An Essay on Global Governance* (Brussels: Peter Lang, 2010).

McCormick, John *Understanding the European Union.* 5th Edition (London: Palgrave Macmillan, 2011).

McCrone, David, Stephen Kendrick and Pat Shaw (eds.) *The Making of Scotland: Nature, Culture and Social Change* (Edinburgh: Edinburgh University Press/ British Sociological Association, 1989).

McCrone, David *Understanding Scotland: The Sociology of a Stateless Nation* (London: Routledge, 1992).

——— 'What makes a European in Scotland?' *Scottish Affairs* 28/2 (2019), pp. 228–243.

McMichael J.R. and Taft, B (eds.), *The Writings of William Walwyn* (Athens, Georgia: University of Georgia Press, 1989).

Milward, Alan *The European Rescue of the Nation-State* (Oxford: Oxford University Press, 1992).

Monnet, Jean *Memoirs* (New York: Doubleday, 1978).

Morgan, Kenneth *Wales, Rebirth of a Nation* (Oxford: Oxford University Press, 1981).

Mullin, Chris *A Walk-On Part: Diaries 1994–9* (London: Profile Books, 2012).

——— *A View from the Foothills. Diaries 1999–2005* (London: Profile Books, 2010).

——— *Decline and Fall. Diaries 2005–2010* (London: Profile Books, 2011).

Nairn, Tom *The Break-up of Britain.* 3rd edition (London: Verso, 2021).

O'Grada, Cormac 'The population of Ireland 1700–1900: a survey'. *Annales de Démographie Historique* 1979, pp. 281–299.

O'Leary, Brendan *A Treatise on Northern Ireland.* 3 volumes (Oxford: Oxford University Press, 2019).

Osborne, John *Luther* (London: Faber and Faber, 1961).

Ostrensky, Eunice 'The Levellers' Conception of Legitimate Authority.' *Araucaria* 20/39 (2018), pp. 157–186.

Pagden, Anthony (ed.) *The Idea of Europe: From Antiquity to the European Union* (Cambridge: Cambridge University Press, 2002).

Paley, William *Natural Theology; or Evidences of the Existence and Attributes of the Deity, collected from the appearances of nature* (London, 1802).

Pánek, Jaroslav et al (eds.) *A History of the Czech Lands* (Prague: Charles University Press, 2009).

Paxman, Jeremy *The English* (London: Penguin, 2009).

Pocock, J.G.A. 'What do we mean by Europe?' *The Wilson Quarterly*, vol. 21 no. 1 (Winter 1997), pp. 12–29.

Preston, Christopher *The Enlargement and Integration of the European Union: Issues and Strategies* (London: Routledge, 2003).

Rawlings, Richard *Delineating Wales: Constitutional, Legal and Administrative Aspects of National Devolution* (Cardiff: University of Wales Press, 2003).

Roberts, J.M. *A History of Europe* (Oxford: Helicon, 1996).

Roberts, R.H. *Religion, Theology and the Human Sciences* (Cambridge: Cambridge University Press, 2002).

Rose, Richard *Understanding the United Kingdom: The Territorial Dimension in Government* (London: Longman, 1982).

Rosenbaum, S 'The General Election of January 1910 and the Bearing of the Results on some Problems of Representation.' *Journal of the Royal Statistical Society*, vol .73, no. 5 (May 1910), pp. 473–528.

Royle, Trevor *The British Civil War: The Wars of the Three Kingdoms 1638–1660* (London: Palgrave Macmillan, 2014).

Salway, Peter *A History of Roman Britain* (Oxford: Oxford University Press, 1993).

Sawyer, P.H. *From Roman Britain to Norman England* (London: Routledge, 1998).

Scarisbrick, J.J. *Henry VIII.* (Berkeley: University of California Press, 1968).

Schleiter, P. & Fleming, T.G. 'Radical departure or opportunity not taken? The Johnson Government's Constitution, Democracy and Rights Commission.' *British Politics* (2022). https://doi.org/10.1057/s41293-022-00206-x

Schütze, Robert and Tierney, Stephen (eds.) *The United Kingdom and the Federal Idea* (Oxford: Hart Press, 2018).

Seeley, J.R. *The Expansion of England* (London: Macmillan, 1883).

Seton-Watson, Hugh *Nations and States: An Enquiry into the Origins of Nations and the Politics of Nationalism* (Boulder, Colorado: Westview Press, 1977).

Shore, Cris *Building Europe: The Cultural Politics of European Integration* (London: Routledge, 2000).

Simms, Brendan *Britain's Europe: A Thousand Years of Conflict and Cooperation* (Milton Keynes: Allen Lane, 2016).

Skidelsky, Robert *Britain since 1900: A Success Story?* (London: Vintage, 2014).

Starkey, David *Magna Carta: The True Story behind the Charter* (London: Hodder and Stoughton, 2015).

Stephens, Philip *Britain Alone: The Path from Suez to Brexit* (London: Faber and Faber, 2021).

Stubbs, Alexander and Nelsen, Brent *The European Union: Readings on the Theory and Practice of European Integration* (Boulder, Colorado: Lynne Reiner, 1994).

Suganami, Hidemi *The Domestic Analogy and World Order* (Cambridge: Cambridge University Press, 1989).

Szele, Bálint. 'The European Lobby: The Action Committee for a United States of Europe'. *European Integration Studies*, vol. 4 no. 2 (2005), pp. 109–119.

Taylor, A.J.P. *English History 1914–1945* (Oxford: Oxford University Press, 1992).

Teffer, Peter *Het lijkt Washington wel: hoe lobbyisten Brussel in hun greep hebben* (Amsterdam: Volt, 2020).

Thatcher, Margaret *The Downing Street Years* (New York: HarperCollins, 1993).

Thomson, David *England in the Nineteenth Century* (London: Penguin, 1991).

Torrance, David *Britain Rebooted: Scotland in a Federal UK* (Edinburgh: Luath Press, 2014).

Trevelyan, George Macaulay *History of England* (London: Longmans, 1926).

Unger, Roberto Mangabeira *Governing the World without World Government* (London: Verso, 2022).

Varoufakis, Yanis *And the weak suffer what they must? Europe, Austerity and the threat to Global Stability* (London: Vintage, 2016).

———— *Adults in the Room, My Battle with Europe's Deep Establishment* (London: Random House, 2017).

Wagner, Ines *Workers without Borders: Posted Work and Precarity in the EU* (Ithaca: Cornell University Press, 2018).

Weber, Eugen *Peasants into Frenchmen: The Modernisation of Rural France 1870–1914* (Redwood City, California: Stanford University Press, 1976).

Wells, Sherrill Brown *Jean Monnet: Unconventional Statesman* (Boulder, Colorado: Lynne Rienner Publishers, 2011).

Welsh government. 'Brexit and Devolution' (2017), https://gov.wales/sites/default/files/2017-06/170615-brexit%20and%20devolution%20(en).pdf

Whitehead, Philip *The Writing on the Wall: Britain in the Seventies* (London: Michael Joseph Ltd, 1985).

Wiener, Antje, Börzel, Tanja A. & Risse, Thomas (eds.) *European Integration Theory*. 3rd Edition (Oxford: Oxford University Press, 2019).

Wilson, Kevin and van der Dussen, Jan (eds.) *The History of the Idea of Europe* (London: Routledge, 1993).

Witte, John Jr *The Blessings of Liberty: Human Rights and Religious Freedom in the Western Legal Tradition* (Cambridge: Cambridge University Press, 2021).

Wyn Jones, R and Scully, R. *Wales says Yes. Devolution and the 2011 Welsh Referendum* (Cardiff: University of Wales Press, 2012).

Young, Arthur *A Tour in Ireland 1776–1779* (London: T. Cadell and J. Dodsley, 1780).

Youngs, Richard *Europe Reset: New Directions for the EU* (London: I.B. Tauris, 2018).

——— *Rebuilding European Democracy: Resistance and Renewal in an Illiberal Age* (London: Bloomsbury, 2021).

Zielonka, Jan *Europe as Empire: The Nature of the Enlarged European Union* (Oxford: Oxford University Press, 2006).

Mark Corner has taught in universities in England, the Czech Republic and Belgium. He was also a Labour politician in local government from 1988-1992. For ten years he was a speaker in Brussels introducing the European Commission to groups of visitors. During his life he has become increasingly aware of the "EU system" as a unique set of institutions that more than any other can help to curb the destructive effects of nationalism.

GPSR Authorized Representative: Easy Access System Europe, Mustamäe tee
50, 10621 Tallinn, Estonia, gpsr.requests@easproject.com

www.ingramcontent.com/pod-product-compliance
Lightning Source LLC
Chambersburg PA
CBHW070054030426
42335CB00016B/1881